THE NEW WAY TO
COOK LIGHT

ISBN-13: 978-0-8487-3468-8
ISBN-10: 0-8487-3468-8
Printed in China
First printing 2012

Be sure to check with your health-care provider before making
any changes in your diet.

Oxmoor House

VP, Publishing Director: Jim Childs
Editorial Director: Leah McLaughlin
Creative Director: Felicity Keane
Brand Manager: Michelle Turner Aycock
Senior Editor: Heather Averett
Managing Editor: Rebecca Benton

Cooking Light® The New Way to Cook Light

Editor: Rachel Quinlivan West, RD
Project Editors: Sarah H. Doss and Holly D. Smith
Assistant Designer: Allison Sperando Potter
Senior Production Manager: Greg A. Amason

Contributors

Editor: Krista Ackerbloom Montgomery, MS
Project Editor: Allyson Angle
Designers: Luke Hayman & Regan Johnson, Pentagram
Wine & Beer Writer: Gretchen Roberts
Copy Editors: Kate Johnson, Tara Trenary
Proofreaders: Jasmine Hodges, Dolores Hydock
Indexer: Mary Ann Laurens
Interns: Erin Bishop; Mackenzie Cogle; Jessica Cox, RD;
    Laura Hoxworth; Alison Loughman; Ashley White
Photographer: John Autry
Photo Stylist: Mary Clayton Carl
Food Stylists: Charlotte Autry, Ana Price Kelly
On-Set Director: Karin Fittante

Time Home Entertainment Inc.

Publisher: Richard Fraiman
Vice President, Strategy & Business Development:
    Steven Sandonato
Executive Director, Marketing Services: Carol Pittard
Executive Director, Retail & Special Sales: Tom Mifsud
Director, Bookazine Development & Marketing: Laura Adam
Executive Publishing Director: Joy Butts
Finance Director: Glenn Buonocore
Associate General Counsel: Helen Wan

Cooking Light®

Editor: Scott Mowbray
Creative Director: Carla Frank
Executive Managing Editor: Phillip Rhodes
Executive Editor, Food: Ann Taylor Pittman
Special Publications Editor: Mary Simpson Creel, MS, RD
Senior Food Editors: Timothy Q. Cebula, Julianna Grimes
Senior Editor: Cindy Hatcher
Assistant Editor, Nutrition: Sidney Fry, MS, RD
Assistant Editors: Kimberly Holland, Phoebe Wu
Test Kitchen Director: Vanessa T. Pruett
Assistant Test Kitchen Director: Tiffany Vickers Davis
Recipe Testers and Developers: Robin Bashinsky,
    Adam Hickman, Deb Wise
Art Directors: Fernande Bondarenko, Shawna Kalish
Associate Art Director: Rachel Cardina Lasserre
Designers: Hagen Stegall, Dréa Zacharenko
Assistant Designer: Nicole Gerrity
Photo Director: Kristen Schaefer
Assistant Photo Editor: Amy Delaune
Senior Photographer: Randy Mayor
Senior Photo Stylist: Cindy Barr
Chief Food Stylist: Kellie Gerber Kelley
Food Styling Assistant: Blakeslee Wright
Production Director: Liz Rhoades
Production Editor: Hazel R. Eddins
Assistant Production Editor: Josh Rutledge
Copy Chief: Maria Parker Hopkins
Assistant Copy Chief: Susan Roberts
Research Editor: Michelle Gibson Daniels
Administrative Coordinator: Carol D. Johnson
CookingLight.com Editor: Allison Long Lowery
Nutrition Editor: Holley Johnson Grainger, MS, RD
Associate Editor/Producer: Mallory Daugherty Brasseale

Thanks to our many contributors, including these, whose recipes
    have frequently appeared in the magazine: Lidia Bastianich;
    Mark Bittman; David Bonom; Maureen Callahan, MS, RD;
    Lorrie Corvin; Ruth Cousineau; Cheryl and Bill Jamison;
    Jeanne Kelley; Susan Hermann Loomis; Ivy Manning;
    Jackie Mills, MS, RD; Krista Ackerbloom Montgomery, MS;
    Joan Nathan; Steven Raichlen; Mark Scarbrough; Barton Seaver;
    Bruce Weinstein; Joanne Weir

To order additional publications, call 1-800-765-6400 or
    1-800-491-0551.
For more books to enrich your life, visit oxmoorhouse.com
To search, savor, and share thousands of recipes, visit myrecipes.com

THE NEW WAY TO COOK LIGHT

Fresh Food & Bold Flavors for Today's Home Cook

By Scott Mowbray & Ann Taylor Pittman

Contents

Vegetarian   Whole-Grain Choice

Arctic Char with Blistered
Cherry Tomatoes, page 104

Bucatini with Green Peas
and Pancetta, page 260

Welcome

You hold in your hands a different sort of cookbook. It's confidently built on 25 years of Test Kitchen success and experimentation at *Cooking Light* magazine, but it's not a birthday book, and it certainly isn't a look back. Rather, it's a collection of recipes, tips, and techniques that represent the new way to cook light—the best route to fresh, light, fully delicious food.

Fully delicious is what interests us: food that proves that a desire to eat healthfully need not sideline you from what I call the revolution in American eating. Millions of Americans are now excited about food that is local, global, authentic, fresh, slow, organic, heirloom, heritage, artisanal: real food. Our nation's fantastic stew of cultures has put more and more global ingredients onto store shelves, and more global dishes onto restaurant menus. An army of food artisans has risen up to ask why an American cheese or sausage has to taste less sublime than its old-world counterpart. (Short answer: It doesn't.) As farmers' markets flourish, farmers rush in with exciting fruit and vegetable varieties saved from the brink, and American chefs have burst out of their kitchens to become high-wattage international celebrities.

Meanwhile, on the nutrition front, the advice has been translated back into English and made radically simple: more plants, more whole foods, less saturated fat, sensible portions. And certainly, have some wine—or beer, or cocktails—in moderation.

At the center of all this fun and ferment stands you, the home cook, who wants to turn out great food for the people you care the most about.

You may ask: If healthy eating is really just a way of participating in the whole, wide food world, isn't light cooking pretty much the same as "regular" cooking? Why does there have to be a book about the new way to cook light?

There is a distinct way to cook for better health, and it requires reliable, tested recipes. These recipes, taken together, are the answers to common questions: If we are to eat more and different vegetables, how do we cook them? How do we eat more whole grains? How do we build a satisfying dish or meal around smaller portions of meat, different species of fish, and lighter sauces?

And when it comes to the tricky matter of reducing saturated fat, particularly in baking but also in sauces and comfort foods, the fact is that someone needs to test and retest recipes, trying new techniques and ingredients, failing and failing again before succeeding. And it might as well not be you, since our Test Kitchen cooks do it for a living.

Hence this book. We believe food should be soul-satisfying, deeply flavored, and real—and should help you step more lightly and joyfully through the world. That's what *The New Way to Cook Light* is all about.

—Scott Mowbray
Cooking Light Editor

Chapter
Cooking

1: Light

The Golden Age of Healthy Cooking

It may surprise some that we call this the golden age of healthy cooking in America. After all, obesity is described as a national and, increasingly, global crisis. There are problems with the food supply, especially affecting the poor. And sustainability is emerging as one of the most vexing food issues of the 21st century. But when locally harvested field peas turn up in an Alabama Piggly Wiggly; when there is sustainable wild-caught salmon at the Superior, Colorado, Whole Foods Market; when dry-farmed tomatoes sweeter than apricots tumble into a San Francisco farmers' market every year; and when young people from Portland, Maine, to Portland, Oregon, think it is as cool to brine pickles or cure meats as it is to work for social media, well, something good is afoot. The battle between convenience and taste now favors taste.

Good cooks are adept at two things: preserving inherent flavors and, through their kitchen alchemy, producing new flavors. This is their gift to the people they feed. Their joy in cooking is rooted also in an understanding that the kitchen is the heart of a healthy home and family. Our recipes derive from this love of flavors and cooking, rather than an interest in nutrition per se. We do hew to firm standards, and you'll find evidence of that in the nutrition analysis at the end of each recipe (see also our basic nutrition guidelines on page 496). But the endgame for us is a good dish resulting from an honest cooking experience. In place of gimmicky ingredient swaps and dubious techniques, *The New Way to Cook Light* employs classic cooking methods that extract maximum flavor from every food you enjoy—and that includes butter, cream, chocolate, and bacon, as well as smoked paprika, Asian chile pastes, peppery olive oils, garden-fragrant basil, and fresh, sweet, milky corn. Our recipes are written with great care concerning steps, timing, and the appearance of food.

At the magazine, we are not just weekend cooks, strolling the markets for hours with our recycled produce bags (though we do that). We have kids. We are madly busy. We shop most often in supermarkets and buy shortcut foods when they make sense. Our recipes are built from these experiences. We know, from being inspired and challenged by our readers, that getting healthy food on the table every day is the goal. The more you cook, the better you eat, the better you feel. This can be *your* golden age of healthy cooking.

Inspired by what's fresh: Superb ingredients require the least fuss. Here, healthy veggies need nothing more than a dab of easy dressing, like the Creamy Buttermilk-Chive Dressing on page 61, and a few wisps of top-notch bacon.

The Nine Simple Principles of *The New Way to Cook Light*

Embrace the new variety.

Eating many different foods is the best way to enjoy a healthy diet. The global pantry and the local farmers' market are open, expanding, and inspiring. Supermarkets and food companies are slowly wising up to our appetite for authentic flavors.

Cook more often.

All the talk about Americans being too busy to cook obscures a truth about millions of them. Our readers report that cooking is a stress-reliever, a bit of "me time" in a frantic world. Every meal cooked is a bit of control regained. Like any habit, cooking begets more of itself.

Eat more whole foods.

The fewer foods in your kitchen that come with long lists of processed ingredients, the better. Whole foods—including whole grains in their many baked and uncooked forms—contain the widest array of nutrients and fiber. This is not a ban on packaged foods but a judicious pruning of those that offer the false convenience of excessive processing.

Favor the healthy fats.

Generally that means more plant oils, more servings of certain oily fish, and less saturated fat from meat and dairy. The good news is that the percentage of fat in your diet is less significant than the source of those fats.

Eat less meat, more plants.

Push vegetables, fruits, and whole grains to the center of your plate, and push meat—beautifully cooked and flavored meat, mind you—to the side, in smaller quantities. Our recipes provide clear guidance on portions, and there's more information on page 494 in Chapter 14.

Cook seasonally and, when possible, locally.

This means enjoying the natural peak of peas and asparagus in spring, tomatoes in summer, apples in fall, root vegetables in winter—and taking advantage of imported foods that actually hold their flavor, like citrus. Out of season, visit the frozen-foods aisle for many vegetables, such as peas and corn, that retain not only their nutrients but also much of their sweet nature.

Learn new cooking techniques.

Kitchen proficiency is its own joy, but it's essential for the daily cook. Confidence comes with practice. Attention to method will break old habits. There are technique and shortcut tips throughout this book, and in Chapter 14, starting on page 480.

Buy the best ingredients you can afford.

Not necessarily the most expensive ingredients, but the best and most flavorful. Shopping in most cities is a great adventure. Find that perfect olive oil, that most intense aged cheddar.

Cook and eat mindfully and responsibly.

Healthy eating is about savoring every bite, being mindful of where food comes from (there are lots of sustainability notes in our fish chapter), preparing it with care, and then sharing it joyfully with friends and family. It's hard not to feel reverence for a farmer's perfect tomato or a baker's perfect *boule*, and then pleasure sharing it with people who also care.

The Challenges of Everyday Healthy Cooking

Applying the principles can be vexing for the busy cook, who generally does not live next door to a California farmers' market and may not be able to convince the kids to move parsnips to the center of their plates. Here are a few practical strategies.

Shopping strategies

At the magazine, we see—and live—our shopping lives as some version of a Venn diagram in which the farmers' market, the supermarket, and a network of favorite specialty stores (Asian, Mexican) overlap to allow us to stock the pantry as well as we can, partake of fresh when fresh is good, and take advantage of the best the big stores have to offer. The notion that a well-stocked fridge and pantry should cut shopping to a once-a-week proposition is dubious, though: For fresh seafood and produce, we like to drop by the store on the way home two or three times during the workweek (many vegetables lose a surprising amount of their nutrients languishing in the fridge). What a good pantry does, however, is speed up that daily shop—you can cruise the periphery of the supermarket, where the fresh stuff is, and zip through a check-out line. Another tactic, if you have a good specialty store on your route, is to drop by, say, an Italian shop and buy everything for the night's dinner.

Local versus imported

On this controversial question, we let taste be our guide: The local tomato wins while the pale, tasteless import is bypassed or, at the very least, oven-roasted until sweet (see recipe, page 316). Out of season, we turn to preserved or canned tomatoes. Local is usually best during the growing season, but there are no local pineapples where we come from, nor any local cloves, coconut milk, chocolate, oranges, or many of the other foods that make the modern diet so pleasurable. We live in a global world, and American demand for responsibly harvested coffee seems to be doing farmers in poor countries some measure of good. That said, with the American food scene now so full of promise and surprise, we buy far fewer imports of European meats and even cheeses. Is there a rule? Local when possible and imported when it makes sense, always paying attention to sustainability.

The cost of healthy eating

There's a taste-price correlation with many foods: higher prices for more flavor. Handcrafting, small-batch brewing, humane raising, and careful harvesting cost more. Still, the $5 farmers' market tomato can be a bit of a shock, and we've had bad $5 tomatoes—sincerity not being the only qualification for being a farmer. The main weapons against cost are: learning to cook less-costly meats, buying foods (such as grains and spices) in bulk, and using high-flavor foods such as cheese in reduced amounts. Also, eating more plants and less meat should bring costs down. More savings come when you cut back on processed foods.

The need to read labels

It's a somewhat irritating job. Though label laws have mandated a lot of data on packaged foods, they have not kept packages free of dubious health claims, often touting the absence of substances that would not, in fact, naturally occur in the food (such as cholesterol).

Packages that appear to contain a single serving may be revealed to contain two or three. The quantity of whole grains in a food—versus their mere presence—requires a near-Talmudic reading of the label. Of course, the fewer foods you eat that have such labels in the first place, the less label reading you need to do. But it's unavoidable. The first question usually is: How much of the thing you want to eat is actually in the food? If there's a lot, it should be near the top of the brief list of ingredients. The second question is: Are the sodium and saturated-fat quantities in line with general nutrition guidelines (listed on page 496)?

The way to attack a healthy recipe

As with any recipe, read it all the way through, looking for steps, tools (parchment paper, grill pan), or techniques that might present a challenge in the moment. You do not want to miss the bit about moving the phyllo dough from freezer to fridge the night before cooking; there is no practical way to rush that thaw. If you're searing scallops, make sure you have a sufficiently large pan to accommodate them, or plan to cook in batches. Also, take total cooking time into account, as rushing a dish can greatly affect its quality. Finally, consider whether you might want to double a recipe,

either for immediate leftovers or to freeze for easy eating later in the month.

Mise en place

The top-drawer restaurant chef, who runs something akin to a military operation every night, is maniacal about getting all the ingredients for a dish ready before preparing the dish—a practice known as *mise en place*. This orderly approach works well at home, too. Stock up on little bowls in which you can put chopped garlic and onion, herbs, and other ingredients, and get everything in order before the serious cooking begins.

Chapter

Appetize

Snacks &

Beverage

2:
rs,
s

Agua Fresca de Pepino, page 44

The importance of the artful appetizer should never be underestimated, nor the satisfaction of the well-chosen snack. Our priorities are taste, surprise, and balance. Great ingredients such as real sherry vinegar make all the difference in flavor depth. We love to see the old classics, such as Green Goddess dressing, reborn. Phyllo, baked, makes a new-wave samosa wrapper—but all those fragrant spices are still there. Sometimes, a flight of whimsy: Peanut butter takes caramel corn out for a delightful makeover. And, of course, a long day ends with a good-for-you drink: Sparkling, fruit-packed sangria, anyone?

Orange and Avocado Salsa 🍃

Healthy fats from silky avocado plus plenty of zing from three citrus fruits.

Serve with spicy tortilla chips, sautéed chicken breast, pork, or fish. Omit the cilantro and avocado if you want to make ahead, and stir them in just before serving. Acid from the citrus slows the browning. For a color boost, use blood oranges, if available. Hands-on time: 15 min. Total time: 15 min.

3 cups orange sections (about 4), chopped

2½ cups pink grapefruit sections (about 2 large grapefruit), chopped

¼ cup minced red onion

2 tablespoons chopped fresh cilantro

1 tablespoon minced jalapeño pepper

2 teaspoons fresh lime juice

½ teaspoon kosher salt

1 diced peeled avocado

1. Combine all ingredients in a bowl; toss gently. Serve immediately.

Serves 10 (serving size: ¼ cup).

CALORIES 86; FAT 3g (sat 0.4g, mono 2g, poly 0.4g); PROTEIN 1.3g; CARB 14.7g; FIBER 3.5g; CHOL 0mg; IRON 0.1mg; SODIUM 98mg; CALC 44mg

TECHNIQUE

Sectioning Citrus: To make a stable cutting surface, cut the top and bottom off of the round fruit. Place fruit flat on cutting board, and use a paring knife to slice down to remove the rind and white pith. Then, while holding the fruit in your hand, gently cut through the natural sections of the fruit to get wedges.

Zesty Green Goddess Dip
This creamy, herb-flecked classic gets a makeover with canola mayonnaise and fat-free Greek yogurt.

Classic versions may have as much as 22 grams of fat and 211 calories in a comparable amount. Hands-on time: 12 min. Total time: 8 hr. 12 min.

- 2 cups trimmed watercress (about 2 bunches)
- ½ cup fresh basil leaves
- ⅓ cup canola mayonnaise
- ¼ cup fresh flat-leaf parsley leaves
- ¼ cup chopped green onions
- ¼ cup plain fat-free Greek yogurt
- 2 tablespoons extra-virgin olive oil
- 1 tablespoon white wine vinegar
- 1 teaspoon anchovy paste
- ½ teaspoon freshly ground black pepper
- ¼ teaspoon kosher salt
- ¼ teaspoon ground red pepper

1. Place all ingredients in a food processor or blender; pulse 8 to 10 times or just until combined. Scrape mixture into a bowl or serving dish. Cover and chill 8 hours or overnight.

Serves 6 (serving size: 3 tablespoons).

CALORIES 92; FAT 8.7g (sat 0.7g, mono 5.5g, poly 1.8g); PROTEIN 1.5g; CARB 1.2g; FIBER 0.4g; CHOL 3mg; IRON 0.4mg; SODIUM 223mg; CALC 33mg

CHOICE INGREDIENT
Greek Yogurt: The time-consuming and messy project of draining yogurt to thicken it is eliminated by using Greek yogurt, which is a thicker product similar in consistency to sour cream.

Roasted Tomato and Green Chile Salsa 🌿

Offers the soul-satisfying pleasure of mashing garlic and peppers into a paste with a Mexican lava-rock mortar and pestle.

A *molcajete* is a Mexican version of a mortar usually made of volcanic rock that needs to be seasoned to remove sand and grit. To season it, grind uncooked white rice using the *tejolote* (pestle) until the rice turns into powder. If the rice powder is gray, repeat the grinding process until the powder is white. Mind you, a food processor will do a nice job with this salsa: Finely process the garlic and chile, then add the tomatoes and pulse the mixture until you have a coarse puree. Hands-on time: 13 min. Total time: 34 min.

6 plum tomatoes (about 1 pound)

3 garlic cloves, unpeeled

2 jalapeño peppers

⅓ cup chopped fresh cilantro

¼ cup finely chopped onion

1 teaspoon fresh lime juice

¼ teaspoon salt

1. Preheat broiler.
2. Place tomatoes, garlic, and jalapeños on a foil-lined baking sheet. Broil 16 minutes, turning after 8 minutes. Cool and peel tomatoes and garlic. Combine garlic and peppers in a molcajete, mortar, or bowl; pound with a pestle or the back of a spoon to form a paste. Add tomatoes, and coarsely crush using the pestle or spoon. Combine tomato mixture, cilantro, and remaining ingredients in a small bowl.

Serves 6 (serving size: ¼ cup).

CALORIES 23; FAT 0.3g (sat 0g, mono 0.1g, poly 0.1g); PROTEIN 0.9g; CARB 5g; FIBER 1.2g; CHOL 0mg; IRON 0.5mg; SODIUM 106mg; CALC 10mg

Black Bean Hummus 🌿

A detour from the Middle East to the Southwest swaps black beans for chickpeas and moves on from there.

What makes this a hummus, instead of a black bean dip, is the tahini (sesame seed paste). Canned no-salt-added or organic beans are convenient without containing silly amounts of sodium. Serve with assorted crudités. Hands-on time: 20 min. Total time: 20 min.

½ cup chopped fresh cilantro, divided
2 tablespoons tahini (roasted sesame seed paste)
2 tablespoons water
2 tablespoons fresh lime juice
1 tablespoon extra-virgin olive oil
¾ teaspoon ground cumin
¼ teaspoon salt

1 (15-ounce) can no-salt-added black beans, rinsed and drained
1 garlic clove, peeled
½ small jalapeño pepper, seeded

1. Place ¼ cup cilantro, tahini, and next 8 ingredients (through jalapeño) in a food processor or blender; process until smooth.

Spoon into a bowl; sprinkle with remaining ¼ cup cilantro.

Serves 8 (serving size: 3½ tablespoons).

CALORIES 67; FAT 4g (sat 0.5g, mono 2g, poly 1.1g); PROTEIN 2.5g; CARB 6.2g; FIBER 2.1g; CHOL 0mg; IRON 0.7mg; SODIUM 78mg; CALC 26mg

Artichoke, Spinach, and White Bean Dip 🌿

Healthy canned white beans, pureed until smooth, do a most amazing job of mimicking cream cheese in this warm, cheesy dip (with 70% less fat).

Perish the thought of the old heavy spinach-artichoke-Parmesan treatment. If you can't find baby artichoke hearts, just chop quartered artichoke hearts. Squeeze thawed spinach with your hands, or wrap it in cheesecloth to eliminate the unwanted, tannic green water. Hands-on time: 15 min. Total time: 35 min.

¼ cup (1 ounce) grated fresh pecorino Romano cheese
¼ cup canola mayonnaise
1 teaspoon fresh lemon juice
¼ teaspoon salt
¼ teaspoon freshly ground black pepper
⅛ teaspoon ground red pepper
2 garlic cloves, minced
1 (15-ounce) can organic cannellini or other white beans, rinsed and drained

1 (14-ounce) can baby artichoke hearts, drained and quartered
1 (9-ounce) package frozen chopped spinach, thawed, drained, and squeezed dry
Cooking spray
½ cup (2 ounces) shredded part-skim mozzarella cheese

1. Preheat oven to 350°.
2. Place first 8 ingredients in a food processor or blender; process until smooth. Spoon bean mixture into a medium bowl. Stir in artichokes and spinach. Spoon mixture into a 1-quart glass or ceramic baking dish coated with cooking spray. Sprinkle with mozzarella. Bake at 350° for 20 minutes or until bubbly and browned.

Serves 12 (serving size: ¼ cup).

CALORIES 87; FAT 5.4g (sat 1.4g, mono 2.3g, poly 1g); PROTEIN 3.7g; CARB 4.9g; FIBER 1g; CHOL 6mg; IRON 0.7mg; SODIUM 232mg; CALC 91mg

Diverse Dippers

Basic Crostini

Little Italian toasts to be topped with meats, cheeses, or vegetables. Better bread yields better crostini.

Preheat oven to 400°. Arrange 20 (¼-inch-thick) slices baguette on a baking sheet. Coat slices with cooking spray. Bake at 400° for 10 minutes or until golden brown and toasted. Cool completely on a wire rack.

Serves 5 (serving size: 4 crostini).

CALORIES 90; FAT 1.7g (sat 0.2g, mono 1g, poly 0.2g); PROTEIN 2.5g; CARB 16.9g; FIBER 0.5g; CHOL 0mg; IRON 0.9mg; SODIUM 184mg; CALC 0mg

Grilled Bread

For an easy garlic-bread variation, halve 2 garlic cloves, and rub them over the hot, crisp bread when it comes off the grill.

Preheat grill or grill pan to medium-high heat. Place 1 tablespoon olive oil in a small bowl; brush both sides of 16 (½-ounce) slices diagonally cut French bread baguette with oil. Place bread slices on grill rack or grill pan coated with cooking spray; grill 2 minutes on each side or until lightly browned.

Serves 8 (serving size: 2 bread slices).

CALORIES 76; FAT 1.7g (sat 0.2g, mono 1.2g, poly 0.2g); PROTEIN 2.4g; CARB 13.5g; FIBER 0.5g; CHOL 0mg; IRON 0.8mg; SODIUM 166mg; CALC 0mg

Pita Chips

For a cumin variation, add 1 teaspoon ground cumin and 1 teaspoon dried oregano with the salt before baking. For a rosemary variation, sprinkle with ½ teaspoon dried rosemary, ¼ teaspoon garlic powder, and ⅛ teaspoon freshly ground black pepper in addition to the salt.

Preheat oven to 375°. Split each of 3 (6-inch) pitas in half horizontally. Coat rough side of pita halves with cooking spray; sprinkle evenly with ¼ teaspoon kosher salt. Cut each pita half into 8 wedges. Arrange in a single layer on 2 baking sheets. Bake at 375° for 12 minutes or until golden brown, rotating baking sheets after 6 minutes.

Serves 8 (serving size: 6 pita chips).

CALORIES 62; FAT 0.2g (sat 0g, mono 0g, poly 0g); PROTEIN 2.6g; CARB 12.4g; FIBER 0.4g; CHOL 0mg; IRON 1mg; SODIUM 120mg; CALC 15mg

Spicy Tortilla Strips

For kid-friendly tortilla strips, omit ground red pepper—unless your kid likes it, which many do.

Preheat oven to 400°. Cut 6 (8-inch) flour tortillas in half; cut each half into 5 strips to form 60 strips. Divide the tortilla strips evenly among 2 baking sheets lined with parchment paper and coated with cooking spray. Place 1½ tablespoons canola oil in a small bowl; brush strips evenly with oil. Sprinkle ⅜ teaspoon cumin and ⅛ teaspoon ground red pepper evenly over strips. Bake at 400° for 10 minutes or until browned, rotating baking sheets after 5 minutes.

Serves 10 (serving size: 6 chips).

CALORIES 106; FAT 4.3g (sat 0.7g, mono 2.4g, poly 1g); PROTEIN 2.3g; CARB 14.2g; FIBER 0.9g; CHOL 0mg; IRON 1mg; SODIUM 176mg; CALC 36mg

Corn Tortilla Chips

Yes, supermarket shelves are bursting with chips—including multigrain and baked—but when you make your own, you get chips of uncommon flavor and sturdiness.

Preheat oven to 400°. Place 1 tablespoon canola oil in a small bowl. Brush 1 side of each of 6 (6-inch) corn tortillas with oil; cut each tortilla into 8 wedges. Place wedges on a large baking sheet; sprinkle evenly with ¼ teaspoon kosher salt. Bake at 400° for 6 minutes or until lightly browned.

Serves 8 (serving size: 6 chips).

CALORIES 46; FAT 2.1g (sat 0.1g, mono 1.1g, poly 0.7g); PROTEIN 0.8g; CARB 6.8g; FIBER 0.8g; CHOL 0mg; IRON 0mg; SODIUM 64mg; CALC 8mg

Crudité Tray

To blanch or not to blanch? Both. Some vegetables greatly benefit from a quick, hot, salty dip to brighten their color and improve their flavor and texture. Others, such as cherry tomatoes, bell peppers, celery, and carrots, are fine with a proper chop.

For the blanchers, have ready a bowl of ice water, a colander, paper towels, and a pot of boiling water with 1 tablespoon kosher salt. Drop vegetables in boiling water for the times listed below. Blanch each type of vegetable separately so colors don't bleed. Remove using a slotted spoon, or gently pour into a colander. Plunge drained vegetables into ice water for a couple of minutes to stop the cooking process; drain again, and pat dry with paper towels.

Blanching time varies depending on the vegetable: **Asparagus:** Snap off tough ends before blanching for 20–30 seconds. **Broccoli:** Cut into bite-sized florets; blanch for 1 minute. **Cauliflower:** Cut into bite-sized florets; blanch for 1 minute. **Green beans:** Trim ends; blanch for 20 seconds. **Sugar snap peas:** Remove ends and strings; blanch for about 15 seconds.

Salsa Verde

Broiling poblanos delivers a smokiness that takes this green salsa beyond what jars deliver—and you control the sodium.

The husks surrounding the tomatillos need to be removed prior to preparation. After they are removed, wash the tomatillos to remove the filmy substance left behind. Serve with purchased tortilla chips (look for chips with less than 200mg of sodium per 1-ounce serving), or make your own (see page 23). Hands-on time: 11 min. Total time: 41 min.

2	poblano peppers
½	cup fat-free, lower-sodium chicken broth
1	pound tomatillos, peeled
2	tablespoons fresh lime juice
2	garlic cloves
⅔	cup chopped onion
⅓	cup chopped fresh cilantro
½	teaspoon kosher salt
1	fresh serrano chile, finely chopped

1. Preheat broiler.

2. Broil poblanos 5 minutes per side or until blackened. Place in a small paper bag; fold to close slightly. Let stand 10 minutes; peel and chop.

3. Combine broth and tomatillos in a medium saucepan; bring to a boil. Cover and simmer 8 minutes. Remove from heat; let stand 20 minutes. Pour into a blender; add juice and garlic, and process until smooth. Pour into a bowl; stir in poblanos, onion, cilantro, salt, and serrano. Chill.

Serves 8 (serving size: ¼ cup).

CALORIES 34; FAT 0.7g (sat 0.1g, mono 0.1g, poly 0.3g); PROTEIN 1.3g; CARB 7g; FIBER 1.7g; CHOL 0mg; IRON 0.4mg; SODIUM 146mg; CALC 10mg

TECHNIQUE

Caring for Fresh Herbs: Place herbs in a glass, as you would a flower arrangement, and fill with water. Put a plastic bag over the leaves, and store in the refrigerator. Change the water every other day. You can also wrap the stems in damp paper towels and store in a zip-top plastic bag.

Marinated Peppers and Mozzarella 🌿
Unimpeachable simplicity.

Use a beautiful olive oil here. With peppers at the base, the hint of lemon, heat, and salt develops into a complex, satisfying appetizer. Reserve excess oil from the marinade, then toss it with pasta and grape tomatoes or sautéed shrimp. The best fresh mozza, made with whole milk, is fantastically creamy and slightly sweet. Hands-on time: 5 min. Total time: 13 hr. 50 min.

4	cups baby sweet peppers
½	cup extra-virgin olive oil
1	teaspoon grated lemon rind
½	teaspoon crushed red pepper
½	teaspoon salt
3	ounces fresh baby mozzarella balls
3	garlic cloves, crushed
¼	cup small fresh basil leaves
1	teaspoon fresh lemon juice

1. Preheat broiler.
2. Arrange sweet peppers in a single layer on a foil-lined jelly-roll pan; broil peppers 4 minutes on each side or until blackened and tender. Cool.
3. Place peppers, oil, and next 5 ingredients (through garlic) in a medium bowl; toss gently to combine. Cover and refrigerate overnight, tossing occasionally. Let stand at room temperature 30 minutes. Stir in basil and juice before serving. Serve with a slotted spoon.

Serves 6 (serving size: about ¼ cup).

CALORIES 83; FAT 7.7g (sat 1.8g, mono 4.3g, poly 0.7g); PROTEIN 1.5g; CARB 2.1g; FIBER 0.6g; CHOL 6mg; IRON 0.2mg; SODIUM 104mg; CALC 5mg

Chickpeas and Spinach with Smoky Paprika 🌿

Do not make this until you've located real sherry vinegar (nutty and complex) and Spanish smoked paprika (almost bacon-y).

Serve on Grilled Bread (page 23). Hands-on time: 10 min. Total time: 40 min.

1 tablespoon olive oil

4 cups thinly sliced onion

5 garlic cloves, thinly sliced

1 teaspoon Spanish smoked paprika

½ cup dry white wine

¼ cup organic vegetable broth

1 (14.5-ounce) can fire-roasted diced tomatoes, undrained

1 (15-ounce) can chickpeas (garbanzo beans), rinsed and drained

1 (9-ounce) package fresh spinach

2 tablespoons chopped fresh flat-leaf parsley

2 teaspoons sherry vinegar

1. Heat a large Dutch oven over medium heat. Add oil to pan; swirl to coat. Add onion and garlic to pan; cover and cook 8 minutes or until tender, stirring occasionally. Stir in paprika; cook 1 minute, stirring constantly. Add wine, broth, and tomatoes; bring to a boil. Add chickpeas; reduce heat, and simmer until sauce thickens slightly (about 15 minutes), stirring occasionally. Add spinach; cover and cook 2 minutes or until spinach wilts. Stir in parsley and sherry vinegar.

Serves 10 (serving size: about ⅔ cup).

CALORIES 86; FAT 1.9g (sat 0.2g, mono 1g, poly 0.2g); PROTEIN 3.1g; CARB 14.6g; FIBER 3.5g; CHOL 0mg; IRON 1.8mg; SODIUM 168mg; CALC 64mg

Wine Pairing

Dry fino sherry is a classic accompaniment to tapas, or Spanish appetizers. The sherry's light, almost salty acidity complements the smoked paprika.

CHOICE INGREDIENT

Smoked Paprika: Smoked paprika is key to the flavor profile of this Spanish tapa. If you don't have the spice made from dried, smoked pimiento peppers, substitute 1 teaspoon sweet paprika and ¼ teaspoon ground red pepper.

Tomato and Arugula Salad–Topped Eggplant Crostini ✿
An homage to farmers' market treasures.

Salad, on top of tangy-smoky eggplant spread, on top of crunchy bread. Grab brightly colored heirloom tomatoes, baby lettuces, or microgreens for the salad. Although this recipe calls for a regular globe eggplant, if you see baby eggplants or other fresh seasonal varieties, they will work just as well.
Hands-on time: 14 min. Total time: 30 min.

1	(1-pound) eggplant
¼	cup extra-virgin olive oil, divided
	Cooking spray
16	(½-ounce) slices 100% whole-grain multigrain baguette
¼	cup plain whole-milk Greek yogurt
2½	tablespoons fresh lemon juice, divided
½	teaspoon freshly ground black pepper, divided
¼	teaspoon salt, divided
1	garlic clove, minced
1	cup arugula
1	cup red, orange, yellow, and green cherry tomatoes, quartered
2	tablespoons fresh mint leaves, torn
1	ounce shaved Parmigiano-Reggiano cheese

1. Preheat grill to medium-high heat.
2. Slice eggplant into 1-inch-thick slices; brush both sides evenly with 1 tablespoon oil. Place eggplant in a single layer on grill rack coated with cooking spray; grill 6 minutes on each side or until eggplant is tender. Brush both sides of bread slices evenly with 2 tablespoons oil. Place bread slices in a single layer on grill rack coated with cooking spray; grill 1 minute on each side or until toasted.
3. Place eggplant, yogurt, 1 tablespoon juice, ¼ teaspoon pepper, ⅛ teaspoon salt, and garlic in a food processor; pulse until coarsely chopped. Spoon about 1 heaping tablespoon eggplant mixture on each bread slice.

4. Combine arugula, tomatoes, mint, and remaining ¼ teaspoon pepper in a bowl. Drizzle with remaining 1½ tablespoons juice and remaining 1 tablespoon oil. Sprinkle with remaining ⅛ teaspoon salt; toss to coat. Divide salad mixture evenly among bread slices; top evenly with cheese.

Serves 8 (serving size: 2 crostini).

CALORIES 175; FAT 10g (sat 2.1g, mono 5.2g, poly 0.8g); PROTEIN 6.2g; CARB 17.5g; FIBER 5.9g; CHOL 4mg; IRON 1.1mg; SODIUM 256mg; CALC 196mg

Wine Pairing
Serve with a bright sauvignon blanc from Chile or New Zealand—a refreshing foil to the earthy eggplant and peppery arugula.

TEST KITCHEN SECRET
Juicing Lemons: Room-temperature lemons yield more juice, so if your fruit is cold, microwave for 10 to 20 seconds.

Phyllo Samosas with Mint Chutney

Changing the wrapper lets you bake these potato-filled Indian apps instead of frying—still crunchy, still spice-fragrant.

Use leftover mashed potatoes, or grab a container from the grocery store. Remember to thaw phyllo dough overnight in the fridge. Prepare all the other ingredients before opening the dough, and cover any dough you aren't using with wax paper and a damp towel to keep it moist. Hands-on time: 42 min. Total time: 1 hr. 13 min.

Chutney:

- 1 cup fresh mint leaves
- 1 cup fresh cilantro leaves
- 1 tablespoon fresh lime juice
- 1 tablespoon water
- 1 teaspoon finely chopped seeded jalapeño pepper
- 1 teaspoon chopped garlic
- ½ teaspoon minced peeled fresh ginger

Dash of salt

Samosas:

- 2 tablespoons olive oil, divided
- ¼ cup finely chopped onion
- ⅔ cup shredded carrot
- ⅔ cup frozen green peas, thawed
- 2 teaspoons mustard seeds
- 1½ teaspoons garam masala
- ½ teaspoon salt
- 1 cup leftover mashed potatoes or packaged mashed potatoes
- 8 (14 x 9-inch) sheets frozen phyllo dough, thawed

Cooking spray

1. Preheat oven to 350°.

2. To prepare chutney, place first 8 ingredients in a food processor or blender; process 1 minute or until smooth. Spoon mixture into a bowl; cover and refrigerate.

3. To prepare samosas, heat a large nonstick skillet over medium heat. Add 1 tablespoon oil to pan; swirl to coat. Add onion to pan, and cook 2 minutes, stirring occasionally. Add carrot, and cook 2 minutes, stirring occasionally. Add peas, mustard seeds, garam masala, and salt; cover and cook 2 minutes. Stir in potatoes; remove from heat.

4. Working with 1 phyllo sheet at a time, cut each sheet lengthwise into 3 (3 x 14-inch) strips, and coat with cooking spray. (Cover remaining phyllo dough to prevent drying.) Spoon 1 tablespoon potato mixture onto 1 end of each strip. Fold 1 corner of phyllo dough over mixture, forming a triangle; keep folding back and forth into a triangle to end of strip. Place triangles, seam sides down, on a baking sheet. Brush triangles with remaining 1 tablespoon oil. Bake at 350° for 23 minutes or until lightly browned. Serve warm or at room temperature with chutney.

Serves 12 (serving size: 2 samosas and 1½ teaspoons chutney).

CALORIES 89; FAT 3.6g (sat 0.7g, mono 2.3g, poly 0.5g); PROTEIN 2.2g; CARB 13g; FIBER 1.6g; CHOL 1mg; IRON 0.9mg; SODIUM 193mg; CALC 21mg

TECHNIQUE

Shaping Samosas:
Traditionally, these pastries are folded from a round piece of dough, but we used phyllo to encase the filling. Here's how to fold with success:

1. Spoon filling onto bottom end of rectangle, leaving a 1-inch border.

2. Fold bottom corner over mixture, forming a triangle.

3. Fold back and forth to end of phyllo strip to form a triangular packet.

Broiled Oysters with
Garlic-Buttered Breadcrumbs

Broiled Oysters with Garlic-Buttered Breadcrumbs

Buttery crunch gives way to soft, whiff-of-the-ocean morsels.

A generous serving has only 90 calories but 22% of your daily iron needs. Hands-on time: 15 min.
Total time: 20 min.

1 tablespoon unsalted butter

2 teaspoons extra-virgin olive oil

2 garlic cloves, minced

1 teaspoon fresh lemon juice

1 (2-ounce) slice French bread baguette

⅛ teaspoon salt

⅛ teaspoon freshly ground black pepper

24 shucked oysters
Cooking spray

1 tablespoon chopped fresh flat-leaf parsley

1. Preheat broiler.
2. Melt butter in a skillet over medium heat. Add oil and garlic; cook 1 minute, stirring occasionally. Remove from heat; stir in juice.
3. Place bread in a food processor; pulse 10 times or until coarse crumbs measure 1 cup. Combine breadcrumbs, butter mixture, salt, and pepper; mix well.

4. Arrange oysters on a broiler pan coated with cooking spray; top oysters with breadcrumb mixture. Broil 3 minutes or until breadcrumbs are golden. Sprinkle with parsley.

Serves 6 (serving size: 4 oysters).

CALORIES 90; FAT 5.1g (sat 1.9g, mono 1.8g, poly 0.9g); PROTEIN 4.6g; CARB 6.4g; FIBER 0.2g; CHOL 35mg; IRON 4mg; SODIUM 218mg; CALC 39mg

Grilled Stuffed Jalapeños

These bacon-and-cheese poppers are chargrilled rather than breaded and deep-fried.

The rich and creamy combination of bacon, cream cheese, and cheddar is a nice foil for the muted spice of grilled peppers. If making these for a party, you can stuff the peppers, cover, and chill. Then grill just before your guests arrive. Avoid tumbling peppers by using a vegetable grill pan on the grill.
Hands-on time: 30 min. Total time: 40 min.

2 center-cut bacon slices

½ cup (4 ounces) block-style cream cheese, softened

½ cup (4 ounces) block-style fat-free cream cheese, softened

¼ cup (1 ounce) shredded extra-sharp cheddar cheese

¼ cup minced green onions

1 teaspoon fresh lime juice

¼ teaspoon kosher salt

1 small garlic clove, minced

14 jalapeño peppers, halved lengthwise and seeded
Cooking spray

2 tablespoons chopped fresh cilantro

2 tablespoons chopped seeded tomato

1. Preheat grill to medium-high heat.
2. Cook bacon in a skillet over medium heat until crisp. Remove bacon from pan, and drain on paper towels. Crumble bacon. Combine crumbled bacon, cheeses, and next 4 ingredients (through garlic) in a bowl. Divide cheese mixture evenly among pepper halves. Place peppers,

cheese sides up, on grill rack or grill grate coated with cooking spray. Cover and grill 8 minutes or until bottoms of peppers are charred and cheese mixture is lightly browned. Place peppers on a serving platter. Sprinkle with cilantro and tomato.

Serves 14 (serving size: 2 pepper halves).

CALORIES 56; FAT 4.1g (sat 2.2g, mono 1.1g, poly 0.2g); PROTEIN 2.9g; CARB 2.1g; FIBER 0.5g; CHOL 13mg; IRON 0.2mg; SODIUM 157mg; CALC 55mg

Pan-Fried Egg Rolls

This Chinese menu staple gets a makeover with a cooking method that yields crispy egg rolls without the fuss, fat, and mess of full-on deep-frying.

You'll find sweet chili sauce, made from sun-ripened chile peppers and garlic, in the Asian foods section of most supermarkets. Hands-on time: 25 min. Total time: 39 min.

¼ cup sweet chili sauce, divided

12 ounces fresh bean sprouts, chopped

12 (8-inch) egg roll wrappers

12 cooked jumbo shrimp, peeled, deveined, and split in half lengthwise (about 13 ounces)

6 tablespoons chopped fresh cilantro

¼ cup peanut oil

1 tablespoon rice vinegar

2 teaspoons lower-sodium soy sauce

¼ teaspoon grated peeled fresh ginger

⅛ teaspoon freshly ground black pepper

1. Combine 3 tablespoons chili sauce and bean sprouts, tossing well to coat.

2. Working with 1 egg roll wrapper at a time (cover remaining wrappers to prevent drying), place wrapper onto work surface with 1 corner pointing toward you (wrapper should look like a diamond). Spoon about 2 heaping tablespoons bean sprout mixture into center of wrapper; top with 2 shrimp halves and 1½ teaspoons cilantro. Fold lower corner of wrapper over filling; fold in side corners. Moisten top corner of wrapper with water; roll up, jelly-roll fashion. Place egg roll, seam side down, on a baking sheet. Repeat procedure with remaining wrappers, bean sprout mixture, shrimp, and cilantro.

3. Heat a large nonstick skillet over medium-high heat. Add 2 tablespoons oil; swirl to coat. Add 6 egg rolls, seam sides down; cook 7 minutes or until golden, turning occasionally. Place on a wire rack. Repeat procedure with remaining 2 tablespoons oil and 6 egg rolls.

4. Combine remaining 1 tablespoon chili sauce, vinegar, and next 3 ingredients (through black pepper). Serve sauce with egg rolls.

Serves 12 (serving size: 1 egg roll and 1½ teaspoons sauce).

CALORIES 103; FAT 4g (sat 0.7g, mono 1.7g, poly 1.3g); PROTEIN 7.9g; CARB 8.7g; FIBER 0.7g; CHOL 48mg; IRON 1.3mg; SODIUM 207mg; CALC 23mg

TECHNIQUE

Grating Ginger: Peel the papery brown skin using a vegetable peeler or by scraping with the edge of a spoon. Rub a piece of peeled ginger on a Microplane to get grated ginger.

Skillet-Cooked Shrimp with Romesco Sauce

Romesco, one of the world's great sauces—garlicky, creamy, rich in healthy fats—is a blessing on shrimp. Also use it over fish, toss with pasta, or spread on bread.

We like the flavor and texture of shrimp cooked in its shell. If you're unable to find jumbo shrimp, large will work just fine. Hands-on time: 21 min. Total time: 59 min.

1 large red bell pepper

2 tablespoons chopped fresh flat-leaf parsley

2 tablespoons olive oil, divided

1 tablespoon fresh lemon juice

⅛ teaspoon crushed red pepper

16 unpeeled jumbo shrimp (about 1⅓ pounds)

1½ tablespoons blanched slivered almonds

1 (¼-ounce) slice white bread, torn into pieces

1 garlic clove, sliced

1¾ cups chopped tomato

1 tablespoon sherry vinegar or red wine vinegar

¼ teaspoon salt

1. Preheat broiler.

2. Cut bell pepper in half lengthwise; discard seeds and membranes. Place pepper halves, skin sides up, on a foil-lined baking sheet; flatten with hand. Broil 8 minutes or until blackened. Place in a paper bag; fold to close tightly. Let stand 10 minutes. Peel and discard charred skin; coarsely chop.

3. Combine parsley, 1 tablespoon oil, juice, crushed red pepper, and shrimp in a bowl; let stand 15 minutes.

4. Heat a large skillet over medium-high heat. Add remaining 1 table-spoon oil to pan; swirl to coat. Add almonds and bread to pan; sauté 2 minutes or until nuts are golden, stirring frequently. Add garlic; sauté 1 minute, stirring constantly. Add tomato and roasted bell pepper, and sauté 4 minutes or until tomato begins to break down. Place tomato mixture in a blender or food processor; process until smooth. Add vinegar and salt to tomato mixture; pulse until combined. Cool to room temperature.

5. Heat a nonstick skillet over medium-high heat. Add half of shrimp mixture to pan; cook 2 minutes on each side or until shrimp are done. Remove from pan. Repeat procedure with remaining shrimp mixture. Serve with sauce.

Serves 8 (serving size: 2 shrimp and about 2 tablespoons sauce).

CALORIES 133; FAT 5.5g (sat 0.8g, mono 3.1g, poly 1.1g); PROTEIN 16.2g; CARB 4.2g; FIBER 1g; CHOL 115mg; IRON 2.2mg; SODIUM 195mg; CALC 51mg

TECHNIQUE

Roasting Bell Peppers: Roasting peppers softens the texture and adds smokiness. Cut each pepper in half lengthwise, and discard the seeds and membranes.

1. Place pepper halves on a baking sheet lined with foil. Flatten the halves so they'll char evenly.

2. Broil until charred and blackened. Using tongs, place peppers in a clean paper bag; roll up bag, and let steam 10 minutes.

3. After steaming, the blackened skin will easily peel off.

Sweet Chipotle Snack Mix 🌿

A sweet-spicy-crunchy satisfying snack with heart-healthy oils.

Ground chipotle chile pepper and chili spices combine with sugar to coat this three-part combo of pepitas (pumpkinseed kernels), almonds, and cashews. Tossing the nuts in a foamy egg white before baking gives this mix a crisp shell and light texture. Hands-on time: 8 min. Total time: 49 min.

¼	cup sugar
1	teaspoon salt
1	teaspoon ground chipotle chile pepper
½	teaspoon ground cumin
½	teaspoon dried oregano
½	teaspoon chili powder
1	large egg white
1	cup slivered almonds
1	cup unsalted cashews
1	cup unsalted pumpkinseed kernels

1. Preheat oven to 325°.
2. Combine first 6 ingredients in a small bowl, stirring with a whisk.
3. Place egg white in a bowl; stir with a whisk until foamy. Add almonds, cashews, and pumpkinseed kernels; toss well to coat. Sprinkle with spice mixture; toss well to coat. Spread nuts in an even layer on a baking sheet lined with parchment paper. Bake at 325° for 15 minutes, stirring once. Turn oven off. Remove pan from oven; stir snack mix. Immediately return pan to oven for an additional 15 minutes (leave oven off). Remove pan from oven, and place on a wire rack; cool completely. Store snack mix in an airtight container for up to 2 weeks.

Serves 19 (serving size: 3 tablespoons).

CALORIES 130; FAT 9.7g (sat 1.4g, mono 5.8g, poly 2g); PROTEIN 4.5g; CARB 7.3g; FIBER 1.1g; CHOL 0mg; IRON 1.1mg; SODIUM 175mg; CALC 23mg

Toasted Barley and Berry Granola 🌿 🌾

Rolled barley flakes add another note to your whole-grain hymnbook.

They look nearly identical to rolled oats and can be found in whole-food shops or supermarket bulk bins. Eat this granola for a snack, or serve over plain low-fat yogurt for breakfast. Dried blueberries and cranberries can be replaced with other dried fruits, such as dates, raisins, strawberries, apples, or apricots. Hands-on time: 7 min. Total time: 55 min.

¼	cup unsalted pumpkinseed kernels
¼	cup unsalted sunflower seed kernels
⅓	cup maple syrup
2	tablespoons brown sugar
2	tablespoons canola oil
1	teaspoon ground cinnamon
1½	teaspoons vanilla extract
¼	teaspoon salt
⅛	teaspoon ground cardamom
2	cups rolled barley flakes
¼	cup toasted wheat germ
⅓	cup dried blueberries
⅓	cup sweetened dried cranberries

1. Preheat oven to 325°.
2. Place pumpkinseed kernels and sunflower seed kernels on a baking sheet lined with parchment paper. Bake at 325° for 5 minutes. Cool seeds in pan on a wire rack.
3. Combine syrup and next 6 ingredients (through cardamom) in a medium bowl. Stir in toasted kernels, barley, and wheat germ.
4. Spread barley mixture in a single layer on a baking sheet lined with parchment paper. Bake at 325° for 25 minutes or until lightly browned, stirring every 10 minutes.
5. Remove from oven; cool granola in pan on a wire rack. Stir in dried blueberries and cranberries. Store in an airtight container.

Serves 12 (serving size: ⅓ cup).

CALORIES 181; FAT 6.5g (sat 0.7g, mono 2.3g, poly 2.8g); PROTEIN 4.5g; CARB 27.4g; FIBER 3.7g; CHOL 1mg; IRON 1.4mg; SODIUM 59mg; CALC 13mg

Peanut Butter Caramel Corn

Just enough butter for caramel goodness. Peanut butter for heart-healthy richness.

Baking the candy-coated popcorn on low heat in the oven helps it stay crisp, never sticky or soggy.
Hands-on time: 30 min. Total time: 1 hr. 30 min.

Cooking spray

2 tablespoons canola oil

½ cup unpopped popcorn kernels

½ cup sliced almonds

⅔ cup packed brown sugar

⅔ cup light-colored corn syrup

2½ tablespoons butter

½ teaspoon salt

½ cup creamy peanut butter

1 teaspoon vanilla extract

1. Preheat oven to 250°.
2. Line a jelly-roll pan with parchment paper; coat paper with cooking spray.
3. Heat oil in a large Dutch oven over medium-high heat. Add popcorn; cover and cook 4 minutes, shaking pan frequently. When popping slows, remove pan from heat. Let stand until popping stops. Uncover; add almonds.
4. Combine sugar, syrup, butter, and salt in a medium saucepan; bring to a boil. Cook 3 minutes, stirring occasionally. Remove from heat. Add peanut butter and vanilla, and stir until smooth. Drizzle over popcorn; toss well. Spread mixture into prepared pan. Bake at 250° for 1 hour, stirring every 15 minutes. Cool completely.

Serves 20 (serving size: about ¾ cup).

CALORIES 155; FAT 7.4g (sat 1.8g, mono 3.5g, poly 1.6g); PROTEIN 2.6g; CARB 21.3g; FIBER 1.4g; CHOL 4mg; IRON 0.4mg; SODIUM 108mg; CALC 17mg

Citrus, Fennel, and Rosemary Olives 🌿
A lemony, licorice-y, earthy postcard from the Mediterranean.

A mix of fruity and meaty olives works well in this snack that's ideal for cocktail platters, antipasti, or as a gift when placed in a decorative jar. Hands-on time: 5 min. Total time: 48 hr. 5 min.

22 ounces (about 4 cups) assorted olives (such as niçoise, arbequina, kalamata, and picholine)

2 cups extra-virgin olive oil

1 cup finely chopped fennel bulb

1 tablespoon chopped fresh flat-leaf parsley

1½ teaspoons chopped fresh rosemary

1 teaspoon grated lemon rind

¾ teaspoon crushed red pepper

3 garlic cloves, minced

1. Combine all ingredients in a large bowl, stirring well. Cover and refrigerate 48 hours. Serve at room temperature.

Serves 40 (serving size: 2 tablespoons).

NOTE: Refrigerate up to a month.

CALORIES 45; FAT 4.4g (sat 0.6g, mono 3.3g, poly 0.5g); PROTEIN 0.3g; CARB 1.4g; FIBER 0.2g; CHOL 0mg; IRON 0.1mg; SODIUM 200mg; CALC 6mg

CHOICE INGREDIENT

Kalamata olives are a Greek variety that is deep purplish to black, salty, very flavorful, and easy to pit.

Niçoise olives are small French olives that are purple to dark brown. They have a distinct sour taste and a large pit that is difficult to remove.

Picholine olives are light green French olives that are long and pointy, with a slight sweet and salty flavor.

Arbequina olives are small and reddish-brown and have a bit of a smoky flavor. These Spanish olives have less flesh than most olives and are difficult to pit.

Caramelized Onion Spread 🌿

Our nostalgic nod to onion soup mix dip, but the buttery sweetness of caramelized onions is a whole new ball game.

Serve with crostini or melba toast. For a fancier treatment, thinly slice the onions, and caramelize as directed. Then combine cream cheese, mayonnaise, black pepper, and salt. Spread the cream cheese mixture over crostini, and top with caramelized onions and chives. Hands-on time: 15 min. Total time: 57 min.

1	tablespoon olive oil
3	cups chopped yellow onion
4	garlic cloves, minced
½	cup (4 ounces) block-style ⅓-less-fat cream cheese
½	cup canola mayonnaise
2	tablespoons finely chopped fresh chives
½	teaspoon freshly ground black pepper
¼	teaspoon kosher salt

1. Heat a large skillet over medium-high heat. Add oil to pan; swirl to coat. Add onion and garlic to pan, and sauté 5 minutes, stirring frequently. Reduce heat to medium-low, and cook 35 minutes or until very tender and caramelized, stirring occasionally. Add cream cheese to pan, and stir to combine. Remove from heat; stir in mayonnaise and remaining ingredients. Serve at room temperature or chilled.

Serves 10 (serving size: about 2½ tablespoons).

CALORIES 98; FAT 7.6g (sat 1.7g, mono 3.7g, poly 1.5g); PROTEIN 1.7g; CARB 5.4g; FIBER 0.9g; CHOL 8mg; IRON 0.2mg; SODIUM 160mg; CALC 28mg

TECHNIQUE

Chopping Onions: For even cooking, you need pieces that are the same size. Start with a sharp knife, and follow this technique for safe and efficient chopping. Having a flat surface keeps the onion from rolling around on the cutting board.

1. Trim stem end of onion, leaving root portion intact. Remove papery outer layer.

2. Place onion on cutting board with cut side down; slice onion in half through root.

3. Lay one half of onion cut side down. Place tip of knife about ½ inch from root to keep the onion intact, and slice through onion.

4. Place knife parallel to onion root and cutting board; slice through middle of onion, stopping within ½ inch of root.

5. Starting at stem end of onion (portion cut off), make downward slices, moving toward root end. Discard root portion.

Peach Lemonade 🌿

Buy fruit at its peak for perfect peachiness in a glass.

When a peach smells like a peach, you know it's ripe. Add light rum or vodka for the grown-ups.
Hands-on time: 12 min. Total time: 3 hr. 42 min.

4 cups water
2 cups coarsely chopped peeled peaches
¾ cup sugar
1 cup fresh lemon juice
4 cups ice
1 peach, pitted and cut into 8 wedges

1. Combine first 3 ingredients in a medium saucepan over medium-high heat. Bring to a boil; reduce heat, and simmer 3 minutes. Place peach mixture in a blender; let stand 20 minutes. Remove center piece of blender lid (to allow steam to escape); secure blender lid on blender. Place a clean towel over opening in blender lid (to avoid splatters). Blend until smooth. Pour into a large bowl. Refrigerate at least 3 hours.

2. Press peach mixture through a sieve over a bowl, reserving liquid; discard solids. Stir in lemon juice. Place ½ cup ice in each of 8 glasses. Pour about ⅔ cup lemonade into each glass; garnish each with 1 peach wedge.

Serves 8 (serving size: ⅔ cup).

CALORIES 98; FAT 0.1g (sat 0g, mono 0g, poly 0g); PROTEIN 0.5g; CARB 25.9g; FIBER 0.8g; CHOL 0mg; IRON 0.1mg; SODIUM 0mg; CALC 4mg

Blackberry Margaritas 🌿

Fresh blackberry juice boosts this refresher, and your taste buds, to a new orbit.

Making the simple syrup in the microwave speeds things up and eliminates a dirty saucepan.
Hands-on time: 30 min. Total time: 30 min.

1½ tablespoons sugar
½ teaspoon kosher salt
1 lime
1¼ cups water
½ cup sugar
1 cup 100% agave blanco tequila
⅔ cup fresh lime juice
½ cup Grand Marnier (orange-flavored liqueur)
12 ounces fresh blackberries

1. Combine 1½ tablespoons sugar and salt in a dish. Cut lime into 9 wedges; rub rims of 8 glasses with 1 lime wedge. Dip rims of glasses in salt mixture.
2. Combine 1¼ cups water and ½ cup sugar in a microwave-safe glass measuring cup. Microwave at HIGH 2½ minutes, stirring to dissolve sugar; cool. Place syrup, tequila, lime juice, Grand Marnier, and blackberries in a blender; process until smooth. Strain mixture through a cheesecloth-lined sieve over a pitcher; discard solids. Serve over ice. Garnish with remaining lime wedges.

Serves 8 (serving size: about ½ cup and 1 lime wedge).

CALORIES 179; FAT 0.2g (sat 0g, mono 0g, poly 0.1g); PROTEIN 0.5g; CARB 23.1g; FIBER 1.6g; CHOL 0mg; IRON 0.2mg; SODIUM 121mg; CALC 11mg

Peach Lemonade

Agua Fresca de Pepino

A lime-and-cuke Oaxacan cooler, lovely with spicy food.

The small amount of serrano provides a hint of heat. Use the rest of the pepper in your favorite salsa, or toss it into a lime-based salad dressing with cilantro. Hands-on time: 7 min. Total time: 12 hr. 7 min.

3 cups chopped seeded peeled cucumber (about 2 medium)
¼ cup sugar
3 tablespoons fresh lime juice
¼ serrano chile, seeded
3 cups water
Cucumber slices (optional)

1. Place first 4 ingredients in a blender; process until smooth. Stir in 3 cups water; cover and refrigerate overnight.
2. Strain cucumber mixture through a fine sieve over a pitcher; discard solids. Serve over ice; garnish with lime or cucumber slices, if desired.

Serves 4 (serving size: about 1 cup).

CALORIES 59; FAT 0.1g (sat 0g, mono 0g, poly 0g); PROTEIN 0.4g; CARB 15g; FIBER 0.5g; CHOL 0mg; IRON 0.2mg; SODIUM 2mg; CALC 11mg

Fresh Pear Cocktail 🌿

The flavors of fall: floral pear and hard apple cider, puckered up with pomegranate.

Agave nectar dissolves quickly, so it is an ideal sweetener for cold beverages. Hands-on time: 6 min. Total time: 6 min.

1	Bosc pear
2	tablespoons citrus-infused vodka
1	tablespoon pomegranate juice
1	tablespoon fresh lime juice
1	tablespoon agave syrup (or sugar syrup)
3	tablespoons hard apple cider or cidre doux, divided
2	pear slices

1. Shred pear; place pulp on several layers of cheesecloth. Gather edges of cheesecloth together; squeeze over a glass measuring cup to yield ⅓ cup juice. Discard solids.
2. Combine pear juice, vodka, pomegranate juice, lime juice, and agave syrup in a martini shaker with ice; shake. Strain about 3 tablespoons vodka mixture into each of 2 martini glasses. Top each serving with 1½ tablespoons hard apple cider. Garnish with pear slices.

Serves 2.

CALORIES 105; FAT 0g; PROTEIN 0.1g; CARB 17.2g; FIBER 0.3g; CHOL 0mg; IRON 0.1mg; SODIUM 3mg; CALC 4mg

....

Rosé Sangria 🌿

A fizzy, fruity, summery quencher.

Use a sparkling rosé from California, France, or Spain. Combine all the ingredients except the wine up to a day in advance; stir in wine just before serving so the sangria doesn't lose its fizz.
Hands-on time: 7 min. Total time: 1 hr. 7 min.

1	large orange
1	cup quartered fresh strawberries (about 10)
1	cup fresh raspberries
½	cup Cointreau or Triple Sec (orange-flavored liqueur)
½	cup fresh orange juice (about 2 large oranges)
1	tablespoon sugar
1	(750-milliliter) bottle sparkling rosé wine, chilled
8	cups ice cubes

1. Cut orange into thin slices; cut each slice into quarters. Combine orange, strawberries, and next 4 ingredients (through sugar) in a large pitcher; stir gently until sugar dissolves. Cover and chill at least 1 hour. Stir in wine. Place 1 cup ice into each of 8 tall glasses; pour about ¾ cup sangria over each serving. Serve immediately.

Serves 8.

CALORIES 155; FAT 0.3g (sat 0g, mono 0g, poly 0.1g); PROTEIN 0.8g; CARB 16.9g; FIBER 2g; CHOL 0mg; IRON 0.6mg; SODIUM 6mg; CALC 26mg

Eggnog 🌿

After one sip, heavy-cream eggnog is just too much to bear. This lighter take is delicious to the last drop.

You can make this a day ahead. Hands-on time: 13 min. Total time: 4 hr. 13 min.

3½ cups 1% low-fat milk

½ cup fat-free sweetened condensed milk

1 tablespoon all-purpose flour

¼ teaspoon grated whole nutmeg

⅛ teaspoon salt

2 large egg yolks

¼ cup bourbon

2 tablespoons brandy

1 teaspoon vanilla extract

Grated whole nutmeg (optional)

1. Combine first 5 ingredients in a medium saucepan. Bring to a boil over medium heat, stirring constantly with a whisk. Place egg yolks in a medium bowl. Gradually whisk one-third of hot milk mixture into egg yolks. Add yolk mixture to remaining hot milk mixture, stirring with a whisk. Cook over medium heat 1 minute or until slightly thick. Pour into a pitcher; stir in bourbon, brandy, and vanilla.

2. Cover surface of eggnog with wax paper; refrigerate at least 4 hours or overnight. Garnish with additional nutmeg, if desired.

Serves 8 (serving size: ½ cup).

CALORIES 147; FAT 2.3g (sat 1.1g, mono 0.8g, poly 0.2g); PROTEIN 5.8g; CARB 18.1g; FIBER 0g; CHOL 58mg; IRON 0.2mg; SODIUM 113mg; CALC 187mg

Wasabi Bloody Marys

We like a Bloody Mary to be a real wake-up call. Wasabi does the job.

Garnish with pickled asparagus, green beans, or okra. Hands-on time: 6 min. Total time: 1 hr. 6 min.

½ cup fresh lime juice

4½ teaspoons wasabi paste

6 cups low-sodium vegetable juice

3 tablespoons Worcestershire sauce

1¼ teaspoons hot pepper sauce

⅜ teaspoon salt

1½ cups vodka

1. Combine lime juice and wasabi in a small bowl, stirring with a whisk until wasabi dissolves.
2. Combine wasabi mixture, vegetable juice, Worcestershire sauce, pepper sauce, and salt in a pitcher. Chill thoroughly.

3. Stir in vodka. Serve over ice.

Serves 8 (serving size: about 1 cup).

CALORIES 175; FAT 0.3g (sat 0g, mono 0g, poly 0.1g); PROTEIN 1.6g; CARB 11.6g; FIBER 1.5g; CHOL 0mg; IRON 0.7mg; SODIUM 337mg; CALC 24mg

Eggnog

Carrot, Apple, and Ginger Refresher ⬙
How to drink 1½ servings of fruit and veg—deliciously.

Vanilla yogurt smooths out the texture. Hands-on time: 4 min. Total time: 4 min.

½ cup 100% carrot juice, chilled

½ cup unsweetened applesauce

½ cup organic vanilla fat-free yogurt

1 teaspoon fresh lemon juice

½ teaspoon grated peeled fresh ginger

1 frozen sliced ripe banana

5 ice cubes (about 2 ounces)

1. Place all ingredients in a blender; process 2 minutes or until smooth. Serve immediately.

Serves 2 (serving size: about 1¼ cups).

CALORIES 138; FAT 0.1g (sat 0g, mono 0g, poly 0.1g); PROTEIN 4.3g; CARB 32.7g; FIBER 2.3g; CHOL 2mg; IRON 0.3mg; SODIUM 79mg; CALC 126mg

Applejack-Spiked Hot Cider ⬙
America's traditional apple brandy, fragrant with spice and citrus.

Calvados, the French version of apple brandy, would also work in this drink. Hands-on time: 9 min. Total time: 24 min.

2 tablespoons butter

2 tablespoons dark brown sugar

10 black peppercorns

8 whole allspice berries

5 whole cloves

2 (3-inch) cinnamon sticks

6 cups apple cider

1 tablespoon honey

½ teaspoon vanilla extract

2 (2-inch) orange rind strips

2 (2-inch) lemon rind strips

¾ cup applejack brandy

1. Melt butter in a large saucepan over medium heat. Stir in sugar and next 4 ingredients (through cinnamon sticks), and cook 1 minute. Add cider and next 4 ingredients (through lemon rind), and bring to a simmer. Reduce heat to medium-low; simmer 15 minutes. Remove from heat; stir in brandy. Strain; discard solids. Serve immediately.

Serves 8 (serving size: about ⅔ cup).

CALORIES 189; FAT 2.8g (sat 1.8g, mono 0.7g, poly 0.1g); PROTEIN 0g; CARB 28.1g; FIBER 0g; CHOL 8mg; IRON 1mg; SODIUM 41mg; CALC 4mg

Barcelona Hot Chocolate 🌿

Cocoa and espresso together: not as sweet, deeply flavorful.

If you don't have an espresso maker, brew strong coffee by using the normal amount of beans and half the water. Hands-on time: 12 min. Total time: 15 min.

⅔ cup boiling water

2 ounces good-quality dark or bittersweet (60 to 70 percent cocoa) chocolate, finely chopped

1⅓ cups low-fat milk

1 cup brewed espresso or strong coffee

¼ cup unsweetened cocoa

¼ cup packed brown sugar

1 (2-inch) orange rind strip

¼ cup frozen fat-free whipped topping, thawed

Cocoa (optional)

1. Combine ⅔ cup boiling water and chopped chocolate in a medium saucepan, stirring until chocolate melts. Add milk and next 4 ingredients (through rind); cook over medium-low heat, stirring with a whisk. Heat 5 minutes or until tiny bubbles form around edge of pan, stirring frequently (do not boil). Discard rind. Pour 1 cup mixture into each of 4 mugs. Spoon 1 tablespoon whipped topping over each serving. Dust with cocoa, if desired.

Serves 4.

CALORIES 177; FAT 5.4g (sat 3.1g, mono 1.7g, poly 0.1g); PROTEIN 4.4g; CARB 32g; FIBER 1.9g; CHOL 3mg; IRON 1.4mg; SODIUM 62mg; CALC 126mg

Chapter
Salads

These are great days for the salad, with more glorious ingredients available than ever: beets, radishes, and tomatoes in variegated splendor; summer squashes that can be cut into satiny ribbons; greens that range from velvety to wispy-feathery to crunchy. The goal is to work some fresh magic with color, crunch, and contrast. Snip fresh herbs for woodsy, lemony, or even licorice notes. Layer in whole grains for nutty, chewy satisfaction. We add cheese or bacon for nuggets of flavor and richness here and there, in small amounts, and we don't worry about the fat in healthy olive and nut oils, which are good for you.

Bell Pepper, Tomato, Cucumber, and Grilled Bread Salad ✐
Bread salads put day-old loaves to brilliant use.

The crunchy bread (it needs to be good, chewy bread) sops up the dressing, softens, and makes a counterpoint to the vegetables. Toss in grilled shrimp or chicken. Hands-on time: 16 min. Total time: 37 min.

4   (1-ounce) slices day-old country-style bread

4   cups coarsely chopped tomatoes (about 1½ pounds)

1   cup finely chopped onion

¾   cup chopped yellow bell pepper

¾   cup chopped orange bell pepper

½   cup torn fresh basil leaves

1   English cucumber, peeled and coarsely chopped

¼   cup red wine vinegar

½   teaspoon black pepper

¼   teaspoon salt

2   garlic cloves, minced

¼   cup extra-virgin olive oil

1. Preheat grill to medium-high heat.

2. Place bread slices on grill rack; grill 1 minute on each side or until golden brown with grill marks. Remove from grill; tear bread into 1-inch pieces.

3. Combine tomatoes, onion, bell peppers, basil, and cucumber in a large bowl. Add bread, and toss gently.

4. Combine vinegar, black pepper, salt, and garlic in a small bowl, stirring with a whisk. Gradually add oil, stirring constantly with a whisk. Drizzle dressing over salad, and toss gently to coat. Cover and chill 20 minutes before serving.

Serves 6 (serving size: 1⅔ cups).

CALORIES 180; FAT 9.7g (sat 1.3g, mono 6.6g, poly 1g); PROTEIN 3.6g; CARB 19.5g; FIBER 3g; CHOL 0mg; IRON 1.6mg; SODIUM 237mg; CALC 44mg

CHOICE INGREDIENT

Extra-Virgin Olive Oil: It's one of life's sweeter pleasures that olive oil is a healthy fat. You'll want a workhorse oil for cooking—no point putting an expensive, cold-pressed oil into a hot pan. Save the fancy stuff for salads, drizzling on grains or pasta or seafood, and a thousand other things. But *taste* before buying; oils vary tremendously between acidic ones that almost burn the throat (in a nice way) to delicate, fragrant, floral versions. Don't get bamboozled: There is no absolute link between quality and price.

Heirloom Tomato and Avocado Stack 🌿
The great American tomato revival makes this a spectacular dish. Get thee to a farmers' market.

For glorious presentation, choose a variety of heirlooms: purple, orange, green, and red. For an added kick, sprinkle with coarsely ground black pepper. Hands-on time: 16 min. Total time: 16 min.

4   heirloom tomatoes (about 2 pounds)

⅛   teaspoon salt

¼   cup very thinly vertically sliced red onion

1   cup sliced peeled avocado (about 1 small)

Buttermilk-Cilantro Dressing

Grated lime rind (optional)

Cliantro leaves (optional)

1. Slice each tomato crosswise into 4 equal slices (about ½ inch thick), and sprinkle slices evenly with ⅛ teaspoon salt. Place 1 tomato slice on each of 4 plates. Top each serving with a few onion pieces and about 1 tablespoon avocado. Repeat layers 3 times, ending with avocado. Drizzle Buttermilk-Cilantro Dressing evenly over stacks. Garnish with lime rind and cilantro, if desired.

Serves 4.

(Totals include Buttermilk-Cilantro Dressing) CALORIES 131; FAT 9.6g (sat 1.8g, mono 5.5g, poly 1.6g); PROTEIN 2.9g; CARB 10.4g; FIBER 4g; CHOL 5mg; IRON 0.7mg; SODIUM 209mg; CALC 52mg

BUTTERMILK-CILANTRO DRESSING 🌿

Cilantro gives this creamy dressing great fragrance and a light-green tint. If cilantro curls your tongue (some people are genetically unable to countenance it), use basil, instead, and swap lemon rind for lime rind. It keeps a couple of days in the refrigerator, so double the recipe to have extra for another meal.

⅓   cup low-fat buttermilk

¼   cup chopped fresh cilantro

2   tablespoons reduced-fat sour cream

1   tablespoon canola mayonnaise

½   teaspoon grated lime rind

¼   teaspoon minced fresh garlic

⅛   teaspoon salt

⅛   teaspoon ground cumin

Dash of ground red pepper

1. Place all ingredients in a small food processor or blender; process 30 seconds or until smooth, scraping sides of bowl occasionally. Cover and chill.

Serves 4 (serving size: about 2 tablespoons).

CALORIES 45; FAT 3.9g (sat 0.9g, mono 1.8g, poly 0.8g); PROTEIN 0.9g; CARB 1.4g; FIBER 0.1g; CHOL 5mg; IRON 0mg; SODIUM 124mg; CALC 32mg

Grilled Vegetable Salad

Mix and match vegetables according to what's market fresh.

Red, yellow, or orange bell peppers all work; multicolored summer squash can replace one or both of the zucchini and yellow squash, and any color onion is fine. Thin asparagus spears may need to cook only four minutes. Hands-on time: 12 min. Total time: 30 min.

8 ounces asparagus, trimmed

2 (4-inch) portobello mushroom caps (about 6 ounces)

1 zucchini, cut lengthwise into ¼-inch-thick slices

1 yellow squash, cut lengthwise into ¼-inch-thick slices

1 small red onion, cut into ¼-inch-thick slices

1 red bell pepper, halved and seeded

Cooking spray

Sherry Vinaigrette

2 tablespoons chopped fresh basil

1 tablespoon chopped fresh chives

1 tablespoon chopped fresh flat-leaf parsley

6 tablespoons (1½ ounces) crumbled queso fresco

1. Prepare grill to medium-high heat.

2. Coat asparagus, mushrooms, zucchini, squash, onion, and bell pepper with cooking spray. Place vegetables on grill rack; grill 4 minutes on each side or until slightly blackened. Remove vegetables from grill; cool slightly. Cut vegetables into 1-inch pieces.

3. Pour Sherry Vinaigrette into a large bowl. Add vegetables, basil, chives, and parsley to Sherry Vinaigrette; toss gently to coat. Sprinkle with cheese.

Serves 6 (serving size: about ¾ cup salad and 1 tablespoon cheese).

(Totals include Sherry Vinaigrette)
CALORIES 77; FAT 3.1g (sat 0.7g, mono 1.8g, poly 0.4g); PROTEIN 3.6g; CARB 9.7g; FIBER 2.6g; CHOL 2mg; IRON 1.4mg; SODIUM 184mg; CALC 48mg

SHERRY VINAIGRETTE

Once you taste the real thing—it has a haunting, sun-cooked quality—you'll put sherry vinegar into rotation with your other vinegars.

2 tablespoons sherry vinegar

1 tablespoon extra-virgin olive oil

½ teaspoon kosher salt

1½ teaspoons honey

½ teaspoon Dijon mustard

¼ teaspoon freshly ground black pepper

1. Combine all ingredients in a bowl, stirring with a whisk.

Serves 6 (serving size: about 2 tablespoons).

CALORIES 29; FAT 2.3g (sat 0.3g, mono 1.8g, poly 0.2g); PROTEIN 0g; CARB 1.6g; FIBER 0g; CHOL 0mg; IRON 0mg; SODIUM 170mg; CALC 0mg

Fennel Salad with Meyer Lemon and Goat Cheese

A Meyer lemon is not your average lemon. It's sweeter and less acidic and has a floral essence.

It also has a brief season. Grab a good one (usually plump, bright, and thin-skinned—not hard) when you see one. If you can't find Meyers, use tangerines or oranges, maybe with a spritz of lemon juice.
Hands-on time: 25 min. Total time: 1 hr. 25 min.

¼ cup coarsely chopped fresh flat-leaf parsley

2 fennel bulbs, trimmed, halved, and cut into thin vertical slices

1 shallot, halved and cut into thin vertical slices

2 tablespoons extra-virgin olive oil

1 teaspoon sugar

½ teaspoon kosher salt

¼ teaspoon freshly ground black pepper

⅔ cup Meyer lemon sections (about 3)

2 ounces goat cheese, cut into 6 slices

1. Combine first 3 ingredients in a bowl. Drizzle mixture with oil; sprinkle with sugar, salt, and pepper. Toss to coat. Add lemon sections; toss gently to combine. Cover and chill 1 hour. Top with cheese.

Serves 6 (serving size: 1 cup salad and 1 slice cheese).

CALORIES 107; FAT 6.9g (sat 2.1g, mono 3.8g, poly 0.8g); PROTEIN 3.3g; CARB 10.5g; FIBER 3.3g; CHOL 4mg; IRON 1.2mg; SODIUM 238mg; CALC 65mg

TEST KITCHEN SECRET

Slicing a Log of Goat Cheese: This is like a disposable version of the old cheese-cutting wire trick: Wrap a piece of dental floss around both index fingers. Pull the floss tight. Slice downward through the cheese log—no cheese buildup on a knife, and no utensil to wash.

Celery and Parsley
Salad with Golden Raisins

Celery and Parsley Salad with Golden Raisins

Here's one to perk up the palate between courses—the sweet-tangy raisins and balsamic do the rumba with the celery-parsley crunch.

Balsamic plumps the raisins and gives them extra punch before they're whisked into the vinaigrette.
Hands-on time: 12 min. Total time: 14 min.

¼ cup golden raisins

2½ tablespoons white balsamic vinegar

2⅓ cups thinly diagonally sliced celery (including leaves)

1⅓ cups loosely packed fresh flat-leaf parsley leaves

¼ teaspoon kosher salt

¼ teaspoon black pepper

¼ cup extra-virgin olive oil

1. Combine raisins and vinegar in a small microwave-safe bowl; microwave at HIGH 1 minute and 15 seconds or until raisins are plump. Drain raisins in a sieve over a medium bowl, reserving 1 tablespoon vinegar; discard remaining vinegar.
2. Combine raisins, celery, and parsley in a large bowl.
3. Add salt and pepper to reserved vinegar, stirring with a whisk.

Gradually add oil, stirring constantly with a whisk. Drizzle dressing over salad; toss gently to coat.

Serves 4 (serving size: about ⅔ cup).

CALORIES 87; FAT 5g (sat 0.7g, mono 3.4g, poly 0.8g); PROTEIN 1.4g; CARB 11g; FIBER 2g; CHOL 0mg; IRON 1.5mg; SODIUM 191mg; CALC 60mg

....

Cabbage Slaw

Take basic slaw, and add the zing of mint, ground red pepper, and lemon juice.

It's a fantastic topping for fish tacos or sandwiches. To giddy things up, use packaged shredded cabbage.
Hands-on time: 15 min. Total time: 15 min.

4 cups shredded cabbage

1½ cups thinly sliced radishes

½ cup diagonally cut green onions

3 tablespoons olive oil

2 tablespoons fresh lemon juice

⅓ cup chopped fresh mint

½ teaspoon salt

¼ teaspoon ground red pepper

1. Combine first 5 ingredients in a large bowl. Sprinkle with mint, salt, and pepper; toss to combine.

Serves 6 (serving size: ½ cup).

CALORIES 81; FAT 6.9g (sat 1g, mono 4.9g, poly 0.8g); PROTEIN 1g; CARB 5g; FIBER 2g; CHOL 0mg; IRON 0.6mg; SODIUM 218mg; CALC 36mg

Shaved Summer Squash Salad with Prosciutto Crisps

Ribbons of squash have a cool, delicate quality that only a sushi master could achieve with a knife.

So we use a vegetable peeler or a mandoline. A sprinkling of salt brings out the flavor and helps put a fine curl on the squash. Ricotta salata is an Italian sheep's milk cheese: At its best, it's dense, crumbly, earthy, and milky. Hands-on time: 20 min. Total time: 20 min.

2 yellow squash

1 zucchini

⅛ teaspoon salt

2 tablespoons thinly sliced fresh mint

1 tablespoon extra-virgin olive oil

½ teaspoon grated lemon rind

1 teaspoon fresh lemon juice

¼ teaspoon freshly ground black pepper

3 thin slices prosciutto (about 1 ounce), chopped

¼ cup (1 ounce) crumbled ricotta salata or feta cheese

1. Shave squash and zucchini into thin strips using a vegetable peeler. Discard seeds. Place squash and zucchini in a bowl; toss with salt.

2. Combine mint and next 4 ingredients (through pepper) in a small bowl, stirring with a whisk. Pour over squash and zucchini; toss to coat.

3. Heat a small nonstick skillet over medium heat. Add prosciutto; sauté 2 minutes or until crisp, stirring occasionally.

4. Divide salad evenly among 4 plates. Top each serving with 1 tablespoon cheese; sprinkle evenly with prosciutto.

Serves 4.

CALORIES 68; FAT 4.9g (sat 1.1g, mono 3g, poly 0.7g); PROTEIN 3.5g; CARB 3.6g; FIBER 1.1g; CHOL 6mg; IRON 0.5mg; SODIUM 250mg; CALC 36mg

GLOBAL FLAVORS
....

Prosciutto: Prosciutto, cured ham from northern Italy, has many imitators, and some American artisans are having great success mimicking the delicate texture and sweet flavor. But reserve some funds for real Prosciutto di Parma, made from pigs that eat a diet that includes whey from locally made Parmigiano-Reggiano cheese.

Seashell Salad with Creamy Buttermilk-Chive Dressing

This is a cooling version of the classic peas-and-pasta combination, spiked with pan-crunchy prosciutto.

Frozen peas, picked and snap-frozen immediately, are nutritionally sound and—this is the key—when lightly cooked have a great deal of the quality of summer-fresh peas. Add to pasta during the last couple of minutes. Other pastas that would hold onto peas, such as orecchiette or campanelle, would be good substitutes. Hands-on time: 12 min. Total time: 27 min.

8   ounces uncooked seashell pasta

1   cup frozen green peas

Creamy Buttermilk-Chive Dressing

2   cups loosely packed baby arugula

1   teaspoon olive oil

2   ounces finely chopped prosciutto (about ½ cup)

1. Cook pasta according to package directions. Add peas to pasta during last 2 minutes of cooking. Drain and rinse with cold water; drain well.

2. Place Creamy Buttermilk-Chive Dressing in a large bowl. Add pasta mixture and arugula to dressing; toss to coat.

3. Heat a small skillet over medium-high heat. Add oil to pan; swirl to coat. Add prosciutto; sauté 2 minutes. Drain on paper towels. Sprinkle prosciutto over salad.

Serves 4 (serving size: about 1¼ cups salad and 1 tablespoon prosciutto).

(Totals include Creamy Buttermilk-Chive Dressing) CALORIES 373; FAT 14.9g (sat 1.4g, mono 4.4g, poly 7.5g); PROTEIN 13.6g; CARB 45.7g; FIBER 3.6g; CHOL 18mg; IRON 2.8mg; SODIUM 677mg; CALC 50mg

CREAMY BUTTERMILK-CHIVE DRESSING

Try this with a potato or shrimp salad.

¼   cup canola mayonnaise

¼   cup nonfat buttermilk

1   tablespoon minced fresh chives

1   teaspoon chopped fresh thyme

½   teaspoon salt

½   teaspoon black pepper

2   garlic cloves, minced

1. Combine all ingredients in a bowl, stirring with a whisk.

Serves 4 (serving size: about 2½ tablespoons).

CALORIES 109; FAT 11g (sat 0.5g, mono 3.5g, poly 7g); PROTEIN 0.7g; CARB 1.6g; FIBER 0.2g; CHOL 5mg; IRON 0.2mg; SODIUM 400mg; CALC 24mg

Pinto, Black, and Red Bean Salad with Grilled Corn and Avocado

It's a three-bean salad with a reason to be—spicy, creamy, beany.

Convenient no-salt-added canned beans make this side dish high in fiber without adding much sodium. Avocado and olive oil provide satisfying richness. Hands-on time: 18 min. Total time: 37 min.

1 cup halved heirloom grape or cherry tomatoes

1 teaspoon salt, divided

3 ears shucked corn

1 white onion, cut into ¼-inch-thick slices

1 jalapeño pepper

1 tablespoon olive oil

Cooking spray

⅓ cup chopped fresh cilantro

⅓ cup fresh lime juice

1 (15-ounce) can no-salt-added pinto beans, rinsed and drained

1 (15-ounce) can no-salt-added black beans, rinsed and drained

1 (15-ounce) can no-salt-added kidney beans, rinsed and drained

2 diced peeled avocados

1. Preheat grill to medium-high heat.

2. Place tomatoes in a large bowl, and sprinkle with ½ teaspoon salt; let stand 10 minutes.

3. Brush corn, onion slices, and jalapeño evenly with oil. Coat grill rack with cooking spray; place corn, onion, and jalapeño on grill. Grill corn 12 minutes or until lightly charred, turning after 6 minutes. Grill onion slices and jalapeño 8 minutes or until lightly charred, turning after 4 minutes. Let vegetables stand 5 minutes. Cut kernels from cob. Roughly chop onion. Finely chop jalapeño; discard stem. Add corn, onion, and jalapeño to tomato mixture; toss well. Add remaining ½ teaspoon salt, cilantro, and next 4 ingredients (through kidney beans) to corn mixture; toss well. Top with avocado.

Serves 12 (serving size: ⅔ cup).

CALORIES 141; FAT 6.3g (sat 0.9g, mono 4.2g, poly 0.9g); PROTEIN 5g; CARB 18.2g; FIBER 6.8g; CHOL 0mg; IRON 1.2mg; SODIUM 211mg; CALC 38mg

Green Salad with Hazelnut Vinaigrette

This is as simple as salad gets—and as good, if you use perfect ingredients.

Hazelnut oil is rich in monounsaturated fats. It is super-nutty, not subtle. A can will last a long time if stored in the fridge or freezer. Look for artisanal American nut oils. Hands-on time: 8 min. Total time: 8 min.

Hazelnut Vinaigrette

- 4 cups packaged herb salad blend
- ½ shallot, thinly sliced

1. Pour Hazelnut Vinaigrette in a large bowl. Add salad blend and shallots; toss to coat. Serve immediately.

Serves 4 (serving size: about 1 cup).

(Totals include Hazelnut Vinaigrette) CALORIES 59; FAT 5.2g (sat 0.4g, mono 4g, poly 0.6g); PROTEIN 1g; CARB 2.6g; FIBER 1.2g; CHOL 0mg; IRON 0.8mg; SODIUM 94mg; CALC 32mg

HAZELNUT VINAIGRETTE

- 1½ teaspoons red wine vinegar
- ¼ teaspoon Dijon mustard
- ⅛ teaspoon fine sea salt
- ⅛ teaspoon freshly ground black pepper
- 1½ tablespoons toasted hazelnut oil

1. Combine first 4 ingredients in a large bowl, stirring with a whisk. Gradually add oil to vinegar mixture, stirring constantly with a whisk.

Serves 4 (serving size: about 1½ teaspoons).

CALORIES 46; FAT 5.1g (sat 0.4g, mono 4g, poly 0.5g); PROTEIN 0g; CARB 0.1g; FIBER 0g; CHOL 0mg; IRON 0mg; SODIUM 78mg; CALC 0mg

Whole Roasted Endives with Pear, Arugula, and Walnut Salad

Bosc pears have a crisp bite, but a red-skinned pear such as Starkrimson, Red Bartlett, or Red Anjou is gorgeous here, too.

Hands-on time: 35 min. Total time: 50 min.

1 cup apple cider

1 teaspoon sugar

2 whole cloves

1 (2-inch) cinnamon stick

1 small bay leaf

1 teaspoon olive oil

4 heads Belgian endive, halved lengthwise

½ teaspoon freshly ground black pepper, divided

⅜ teaspoon salt, divided

1 tablespoon fresh lemon juice

1 tablespoon toasted walnut oil or olive oil

4 cups arugula

¼ cup chopped walnuts, toasted

1 large ripe Bosc pear, cored and thinly sliced

1. Preheat oven to 450°.

2. Combine first 5 ingredients in a small saucepan; bring to a boil. Cook until reduced to ⅓ cup (about 20 minutes). Strain cider mixture through a sieve into a bowl; discard solids.

3. Brush olive oil on a baking sheet; arrange endive halves, cut sides down, on prepared pan. Brush 2 tablespoons cider mixture over endive; sprinkle with ¼ teaspoon pepper and ⅛ teaspoon salt. Bake at 450° for 10 minutes. Remove from oven; turn endive halves over. Brush cut sides with 2 tablespoons cider mixture.

4. Preheat broiler.

5. Broil endive 4 minutes or until edges begin to brown.

6. Combine remaining ¼ teaspoon salt, remaining ¼ teaspoon pepper, remaining cider mixture, lemon juice, and walnut oil in a large bowl, stirring with a whisk. Add arugula, walnuts, and pear, tossing to coat. Arrange 2 endive halves on each of 4 plates, and top each serving with 1½ cups arugula mixture.

Serves 4.

CALORIES 180; FAT 9.7g (sat 1g, mono 2.3g, poly 5.9g); PROTEIN 3.1g; CARB 23.5g; FIBER 5.8g; CHOL 0mg; IRON 0.9mg; SODIUM 230mg; CALC 66mg

Spinach Salad with Maple-Dijon Vinaigrette

Much less fat than usual—but still with tasty bacon bits!

Bacon fat is the key to the richness of some traditional vinaigrettes, but substituting maple syrup gives the dressing body with a big reduction in saturated fat. Hands-on time: 15 min. Total time: 15 min.

¼ cup maple syrup

3 tablespoons minced shallots (about 1 medium)

2 tablespoons red wine vinegar

1 tablespoon canola oil

1 tablespoon country-style Dijon mustard

¼ teaspoon salt

¼ teaspoon black pepper

1 garlic clove, minced

1 cup sliced mushrooms

½ cup vertically sliced red onion

½ cup chopped Braeburn apple

4 bacon slices, cooked and crumbled

1 (10-ounce) package fresh spinach

1. Combine first 8 ingredients in a large bowl. Add mushrooms and remaining ingredients; toss well.

Serves 8 (serving size: about 1½ cups).

CALORIES 80; FAT 3.3g (sat 0.6g, mono 1.6g, poly 0.7g); PROTEIN 2.6g; CARB 11.1g; FIBER 1.2g; CHOL 3mg; IRON 1.2mg; SODIUM 219mg; CALC 43mg

Whole Roasted Endives with
Pear, Arugula, and Walnut Salad

Grilled Romaine with Creamy Herb Dressing

Don't wait to make this salad when you're grilling your entrée—it's reason enough on its own to fire up the barbie.

The barely wilted romaine picks up smokiness to make a simple salad sublime. Serve with any type of grilled meat, fish, or burgers. Hands-on time: 16 min. Total time: 18 min.

1 large head romaine lettuce, trimmed and halved lengthwise

2 teaspoons olive oil

Cooking spray

⅜ teaspoon salt

¼ teaspoon freshly ground black pepper

Creamy Herb Dressing

1. Preheat grill to medium-high heat.

2. Brush cut sides of lettuce evenly with oil. Place lettuce, cut sides down, on grill rack coated with cooking spray; grill 2 minutes. Remove from heat; cut each lettuce half lengthwise in half again to form 4 quarters. Sprinkle cut sides of lettuce with salt and pepper.

3. Place 1 lettuce quarter on each of 4 plates; drizzle each serving with about 4 teaspoons Creamy Herb Dressing. Serve immediately.

Serves 4.

(Totals include Creamy Herb Dressing)
CALORIES 132; FAT 13.4g (sat 1.3g, mono 7.7g, poly 3.3g); PROTEIN 0.7g; CARB 2.7g; FIBER 1g; CHOL 5mg; IRON 0.5mg; SODIUM 251mg; CALC 19mg

CREAMY HERB DRESSING

1 tablespoon chopped fresh flat-leaf parsley

¼ cup canola mayonnaise

1½ teaspoons chopped fresh dill

2 tablespoons fresh lemon juice

1 tablespoon water

¼ teaspoon freshly ground black pepper

⅛ teaspoon salt

2 garlic cloves, minced

1. Combine all ingredients in a small bowl, stirring well.

Serves 4 (serving size: about 4 teaspoons).

CALORIES 105; FAT 11g (sat 1g, mono 6g, poly 3g); PROTEIN 0.2g; CARB 1.4g; FIBER 0.2g; CHOL 5mg; IRON 0.1mg; SODIUM 175mg; CALC 6mg

Easy Caesar Salad 🌿

This is a lightly cooked dressing, in case raw yolks make you nervous. You'll hail its full-Caesar flavors.

Homemade garlic oil infuses the bread. Make an easy main-dish salad by adding grilled chicken or shrimp. For super-crunchy croutons, we let them sit in the oven while finishing the rest of the salad.
Hands-on time: 15 min. Total time: 34 min.

1   tablespoon olive oil

2   garlic cloves, crushed

3   ounces French bread, cut into ½-inch cubes (about 3½ cups)

1   tablespoon fresh lemon juice

1   tablespoon red wine vinegar

1   tablespoon water

¼   teaspoon Dijon mustard

Dash of salt

3   canned anchovy fillets, patted dry and finely chopped

1   large egg yolk

1   (10-ounce) package chopped romaine lettuce

¼   cup (1 ounce) grated fresh Parmesan cheese

½   teaspoon freshly ground black pepper

1. Heat a small saucepan over medium heat. Add oil to pan; swirl to coat. Stir in garlic. Remove pan from heat; let stand 5 minutes. Remove garlic from oil with a slotted spoon; discard garlic.
2. Preheat broiler.
3. Place bread on a baking sheet. Drizzle bread with 1½ teaspoons oil; toss to coat. Arrange bread in an even layer. Broil 6 inches from heat 2 minutes or until lightly browned, stirring after 1 minute. Turn oven off. Place pan on middle oven rack; close oven door.

4. Add juice and next 6 ingredients (through egg yolk) to remaining oil in pan. Cook over medium heat 30 seconds or until mixture thickens and begins to bubble around edges, stirring constantly. Pour mixture into a small bowl; cool to room temperature.
5. Place lettuce in a large bowl. Add egg mixture, cheese, and pepper; toss gently to coat. Add bread; toss gently to combine. Serve immediately.

Serves 6 (serving size: about 1⅓ cups).

CALORIES 102; FAT 5g (sat 1.5g, mono 2.6g, poly 0.6g); PROTEIN 4.7g; CARB 9.8g; FIBER 1.5g; CHOL 39mg; IRON 1.1mg; SODIUM 281mg; CALC 94mg

Creamy Buttermilk-Herb Potato Salad 🌿

Crème fraîche, buttermilk, and fresh herbs give creamy-style potato salad tang and garden fragrance.

All that, and with 80% less fat than standard potato salad. Since the dressing has dairy, let the potatoes cool to avoid curdling. If you can't find crème fraîche, substitute full-fat sour cream. Hands-on time: 12 min. Total time: 57 min.

3	pounds small red potatoes, quartered
½	cup crème fraîche or sour cream
⅓	cup nonfat buttermilk
¼	cup chopped fresh flat-leaf parsley
2	tablespoons chopped fresh chives
1	tablespoon chopped fresh dill
1¼	teaspoons kosher salt
½	teaspoon freshly ground black pepper
1	large garlic clove, minced

1. Place potatoes in a Dutch oven, and cover with water. Bring to a boil. Reduce heat, and simmer 15 minutes or just until tender; drain. Cool 30 minutes.

2. Combine crème fraîche and next 7 ingredients (through garlic) in a large bowl; stir with a whisk. Add warm potatoes; toss gently to coat. Serve at room temperature or chilled.

Serves 8 (serving size: about 1 cup).

CALORIES 176; FAT 5.5g (sat 3.3g, mono 1.5g, poly 0.3g); PROTEIN 4.1g; CARB 28g; FIBER 3g; CHOL 14mg; IRON 1.4mg; SODIUM 326mg; CALC 34mg

Fingerling Potato Salad with Gremolata Dressing 🌿

We borrowed a punchy, lemony sauce usually served with osso buco. It's superb with the starch of potatoes.

Fingerling potatoes are great for salads because they hold their shape once cooked. Serve with grilled meat or stew. Hands-on time: 10 min. Total time: 1 hr. 7 min.

½	pound white fingerling potatoes
½	pound red fingerling potatoes
2	tablespoons fresh lemon juice
½	teaspoon salt
¼	teaspoon freshly ground black pepper
1	tablespoon extra-virgin olive oil
1	teaspoon grated lemon rind
1	garlic clove, minced
1	tablespoon chopped fresh flat-leaf parsley
1	tablespoon capers, drained

1. Steam potatoes, covered, 12 minutes or until tender. Cover and chill.

2. Combine juice, salt, and pepper in a large bowl; slowly add oil, stirring well with a whisk. Stir in rind and garlic; let stand 10 minutes. Stir in parsley and capers.

3. Cut potatoes into quarters; add potatoes to juice mixture, tossing to coat.

Serves 4 (serving size: ¾ cup).

CALORIES 125; FAT 3.6g (sat 0.5g, mono 2.5g, poly 0.4g); PROTEIN 2.6g; CARB 21.4g; FIBER 2.2g; CHOL 0mg; IRON 1mg; SODIUM 296mg; CALC 16mg

Smoked Potato Salad 🌿

If the same old potato salad has you snoozing, this is a wonderful left turn, courtesy of the grill.

Mesquite wood chips give a strong, distinctive, and slightly bitter flavor that works in this dish, as well as with beef and other meats. Hands-on time: 15 min. Total time: 1 hr. 45 min.

2	cups mesquite wood chips
¼	cup olive oil, divided
½	teaspoon freshly ground black pepper
¼	teaspoon kosher salt
1½	pounds small potatoes
⅓	cup sliced pitted kalamata olives
2	thinly sliced green onions
2	tablespoons chopped fresh flat-leaf parsley
1	tablespoon red wine vinegar
2	teaspoons celery seeds
1	teaspoon Dijon mustard

1. Soak wood chips in water 1 hour; drain.

2. Remove grill rack, and set aside. Prepare grill for indirect grilling, heating one side to medium-high and leaving one side with no heat. Maintain temperature at 400°. Pierce bottom of a disposable aluminum foil pan several times with the tip of a knife. Place pan on heat element on heated side of grill; add 1 cup wood chips to pan. Place grill rack on grill. Combine 1 tablespoon oil, pepper, salt, and potatoes in a medium bowl; toss to coat. Arrange potatoes in a single layer in another disposable foil pan. Place pan over unheated side of grill; close lid. Cook 30 minutes at 400° or until tender, adding remaining 1 cup wood chips after 15 minutes. Remove potatoes from grill. Combine potatoes, olives, and onions in a medium bowl.

3. Combine remaining 3 tablespoons oil, parsley, and next 3 ingredients (through mustard) in a small bowl; stir with a whisk. Drizzle oil mixture over potato mixture; toss well.

Serves 8 (serving size: about ¾ cup).

CALORIES 162; FAT 8.8g (sat 1.2g, mono 6.4g, poly 1g); PROTEIN 2.4g; CARB 19.4g; FIBER 2.2g; CHOL 0mg; IRON 1.4mg; SODIUM 194mg; CALC 29mg

Shrimp Cobb Salad

A very fast riff on the classic, taking a few liberties.

Several shortcuts—packaged lettuce, shredded carrots, and frozen corn—put this on the table in just 20 minutes. Hands-on time: 18 min. Total time: 20 min.

4   center-cut bacon slices

Cooking spray

1   pound large shrimp, peeled and deveined

½   teaspoon paprika

¼   teaspoon freshly ground black pepper

¼   teaspoon salt, divided

2½   tablespoons fresh lemon juice

1½   tablespoons extra-virgin olive oil

½   teaspoon whole-grain Dijon mustard

1   (10-ounce) package romaine salad

2   cups cherry tomatoes, halved

1   cup shredded carrots (about 2 carrots)

1   cup frozen whole-kernel corn, thawed

1   ripe peeled avocado, cut into 8 wedges

1. Cook bacon in a large skillet over medium heat until crisp. Remove bacon from pan; cut in half crosswise. Wipe pan clean with paper towels. Increase heat to medium-high. Coat pan with cooking spray. Sprinkle shrimp with paprika and pepper. Add shrimp to pan; cook 2 minutes on each side or until done. Sprinkle with ⅛ teaspoon salt; toss to coat.

2. Combine remaining ⅛ teaspoon salt, juice, oil, and mustard in a large bowl, stirring with a whisk. Add lettuce; toss to coat.

3. Arrange about 1½ cups lettuce mixture on each of 4 plates. Top each serving with about 6 shrimp, ½ cup tomatoes, ¼ cup carrot, ¼ cup corn, 2 avocado wedges, and 2 bacon pieces.

Serves 4.

CALORIES 332; FAT 15.2g (sat 2.9g, mono 8g, poly 2.6g); PROTEIN 30g; CARB 21.8g; FIBER 7.5g; CHOL 181mg; IRON 4.3mg; SODIUM 551mg; CALC 110mg

Wine Pairing

The tangy Dijon vinaigrette and light shrimp in this twist on the classic salad call for a zingy white wine like sauvignon blanc.

Vietnamese Salad

Grilled pork pairs brilliantly with greens, aromatic herbs, and a sweet-sour dressing.

Substitute flank steak or even chicken, if you like. Hands-on time: 10 min. Total time: 48 min.

1 (1-pound) pork tenderloin, trimmed

1 teaspoon canola oil

Cooking spray

3 tablespoons fresh lime juice

1½ tablespoons fish sauce

1½ tablespoons lower-sodium soy sauce

1½ teaspoons sugar

1½ teaspoons grated peeled fresh ginger

⅛ teaspoon ground red pepper

1 serrano chile, thinly sliced

¾ cup small fresh mint leaves

½ cup thinly sliced red onion

3 thinly diagonally sliced green onions

1 thinly sliced, seeded cucumber, halved

8 cups sliced romaine lettuce

½ cup cilantro leaves

1. Preheat grill to medium-high heat.

2. Brush pork with oil. Place pork on grill rack coated with cooking spray; grill 6 minutes on each side or until a thermometer inserted into thickest portion of pork registers 145°. Remove from grill; let pork stand 5 minutes. Slice pork in half crosswise; slice each half lengthwise into thin strips. Cool.

3. Combine juice and next 6 ingredients (through serrano) in a large bowl. Add pork to juice mixture; toss to coat. Add mint and next 3 ingredients (through cucumber) to bowl; toss. Arrange 2 cups lettuce on each of 4 plates; top each serving with about ⅔ cup pork mixture. Sprinkle with cilantro.

Serves 4 (serving size: 1 salad).

CALORIES 200; FAT 4.3g (sat 1g, mono 1.7g, poly 1g); PROTEIN 27.7g; CARB 13.9g; FIBER 5g; CHOL 74mg; IRON 3.4mg; SODIUM 653mg; CALC 95mg

GLOBAL FLAVORS

Fish Sauce: There's no way around the gobsmacking fishiness of this fermented sauce, but it lends a deep savory flavor to so many Vietnamese and other Southeast Asian dishes and dipping sauces. This stuff is mighty pungent, so use it sparingly. Here are five more ways with fish sauce:

1. Use in place of anchovy for Caesar salad dressing—start with ½ teaspoon and add more, as needed.

2. Add a hint to marinade for chicken to lend richness similar to that of soy sauce.

3. Drizzle a bit into lean ground turkey to "beef" up your turkey burgers.

4. Punch up a basic meat-veggie stir-fry with a splash.

5. Replace a bit of the soy sauce in your standard fried rice recipe with fish sauce.

French Frisée Salad with Bacon and Poached Eggs

Lighter, yes, but we did not deviate from the classic ingredients that define this dish.

Frisée, also known as curly endive, has lacy leaves and a bitterness that marries with the creamy yolk. If you can't find frisée on its own, it's often included in mesclun combinations, along with radicchio—and that's fine. Hands-on time: 16 min. Total time: 1 hr. 2 min.

4   **(1-ounce) slices rye bread, cut into ½-inch cubes**

6   **applewood-smoked bacon slices, cut crosswise into ½-inch-thick pieces**

⅓   **cup white wine vinegar**

1   **tablespoon chopped fresh tarragon**

3   **tablespoons olive oil**

¼   **teaspoon freshly ground black pepper**

⅛   **teaspoon kosher salt**

1   **head frisée, torn (about 8 ounces)**

1   **tablespoon white vinegar**

4   **large eggs**

Cracked black pepper (optional)

1. Preheat oven to 400°.

2. Arrange bread in a single layer on a baking sheet; bake at 400° for 20 minutes or until toasted, turning once. Cool.

3. Cook bacon in a large skillet over medium heat until crisp, stirring occasionally. Remove bacon from pan, reserving 1 tablespoon drippings; set bacon aside. Combine 1 tablespoon drippings, white wine vinegar, and next 4 ingredients (through salt) in a large bowl, stirring with a whisk. Add croutons, bacon, and frisée, tossing to coat. Place 2 cups salad mixture on each of 4 plates.

4. Add water to a large skillet, filling two-thirds full; bring to a boil. Reduce heat; simmer. Add white vinegar. Break eggs into pan; cook 3 minutes or until desired degree of doneness. Carefully remove eggs from pan using a slotted spoon; top each serving with 1 poached egg. Sprinkle with cracked pepper, if desired.

Serves 4.

CALORIES 344; FAT 23.5g (sat 5.6g, mono 12.5g, poly 2.6g); PROTEIN 14.5g; CARB 18g; FIBER 2.3g; CHOL 227mg; IRON 2.4mg; SODIUM 705mg; CALC 101mg

Creamy Chicken Salad

The key here is moist chicken: Poaching yields succulence, and that requires less dressing.

You save 400 calories and 6.2 grams sat fat per serving compared to standard chicken salad. Serve over salad greens, as we did, or in a pita for a sandwich. Hands-on time: 24 min. Total time: 2 hr. 19 min.

2 pounds skinless, boneless chicken breast halves

½ cup light mayonnaise

½ cup plain fat-free Greek yogurt

1 tablespoon fresh lemon juice

1 tablespoon white wine vinegar

1 tablespoon Dijon mustard

1 teaspoon honey

½ teaspoon kosher salt

½ teaspoon freshly ground black pepper

⅓ cup chopped celery

⅓ cup sweetened dried cranberries

7 tablespoons coarsely chopped smoked almonds (about 2 ounces)

6 cups mixed salad greens

1. Fill a Dutch oven two-thirds full of water; bring to a boil.
2. Wrap each chicken breast half completely and tightly in heavy-duty plastic wrap. Add chicken to boiling water. Cover and simmer 20 minutes or until a thermometer registers 165°. Remove from pan; let stand 5 minutes. Unwrap chicken, and shred; refrigerate 30 minutes or until cold.

3. Combine mayonnaise and next 7 ingredients (through black pepper) in a large bowl, stirring with a whisk. Add chicken, celery, cranberries, and almonds; toss well to coat. Cover and refrigerate 1 hour. Serve over salad greens.

Serves 6 (serving size: about 1 cup chicken salad and 1 cup salad greens).

CALORIES 387; FAT 20g (sat 2.1g, mono 10.5g, poly 5.3g); PROTEIN 38.8g; CARB 12.4g; FIBER 2.7g; CHOL 94mg; IRON 1.8mg; SODIUM 484mg; CALC 51mg

TECHNIQUE

Perfectly Poached Chicken: No fat or seasonings are necessary in this cooking process, which retains the natural flavor of the chicken, making it ideal for salads, soups, tacos, and sandwiches. The result is a lower-fat, lower-sodium chicken that is more moist than any heat-lamp-exhausted rotisserie bird.

1. Tightly rolling each breast half in plastic wrap creates a mini steam bath. Twist the ends in opposite directions to ensure a secure cylinder for poaching.

2. Simmer chicken about 20 minutes or until thermometer registers 165°. Turn the chicken at least once for even cooking throughout.

3. To avoid the meat drying out, allow chicken to sit, wrapped, for at least five minutes. Cool in the refrigerator before dressing for proper food safety practice.

Thai Chicken Salad with Peanut Dressing

Peanut butter is one shortcut that turns this Southeast Asian–flavored salad into a fast weeknight treat.

This takes less than 20 minutes. Shrimp or sautéed tofu would also marry well with this dressing. To make your own peanut butter, toss roasted peanuts in a food processor, and pulse. You may need to add canola or peanut oil to get the right consistency. Hands-on time: 12 min. Total time: 17 min.

6	cups torn romaine lettuce
2	cups shredded skinless, boneless rotisserie chicken breast
2	cups fresh bean sprouts
1	cup shredded carrots
¾	cup sliced celery
⅔	cup light coconut milk
1	tablespoon brown sugar
2	tablespoons creamy peanut butter
2	tablespoons lower-sodium soy sauce
1	tablespoon fresh lime juice
⅛	teaspoon ground red pepper
2	tablespoons coarsely chopped unsalted, dry-roasted peanuts
4	lime wedges (optional)

1. Combine first 5 ingredients in a large bowl. Combine coconut milk and next 5 ingredients (through red pepper) in a small saucepan; bring to a boil. Reduce heat, and simmer 5 minutes or until mixture thickens slightly, stirring occasionally. Remove from heat, and cool 2 minutes. Pour warm coconut milk mixture over lettuce mixture. Sprinkle with peanuts, and serve with lime wedges, if desired. Serve immediately.

Serves 4 (serving size: 3 cups salad and 1½ teaspoons peanuts).

CALORIES 262; FAT 11.2g (sat 3.7g, mono 4.5g, poly 2.5g); PROTEIN 27.5g; CARB 17.1g; FIBER 4.4g; CHOL 63mg; IRON 2.3mg; SODIUM 599mg; CALC 67mg

Beer Pairing

Pale ale—a smooth, understated beer—is a refreshing partner to the creamy peanut and coconut milk dressing that's drizzled on this crunchy salad.

NUTRITION MADE EASY

Peanut Butter: Natural peanut butter—made with just peanuts and maybe a bit of salt and sugar—is our choice. There will be a bit of oil separation, but just give it a good stir, and store in the refrigerator. If you're not buying a natural butter, be sure that "partially hydrogenated" isn't listed anywhere in the ingredient list. If it is, the peanut butter contains unhealthy trans fats. Fully hydrogenated oil doesn't contain trans fat.

Ranch Steak Bruschetta Salad

We're not above reaching for a bottle of supermarket ranch dressing, if we can jazz it up with horseradish.

Top the toast slices with the salad mixture, if you like. Ancho chile powder is made from a dried poblano chile; it has mild to medium heat and a slightly sweet fruit flavor, with hints of coffee. Hands-on time: 14 min. Total time: 29 min.

Salad dressing:

6   tablespoons ranch dressing

1½   tablespoons prepared horseradish

Steaks:

2   teaspoons ground coffee

1½   teaspoons ground cumin

1½   teaspoons ancho chile powder

1   teaspoon freshly ground black pepper

4   (4-ounce) beef tenderloin steaks (1 inch thick), trimmed

   Cooking spray

Remaining ingredients:

¼   cup sliced shallots

¼   cup chopped fresh basil

¼   cup chopped bottled roasted red bell peppers

1   tablespoon fresh lemon juice

12   cherry tomatoes, halved

6   cups loosely packed arugula and baby spinach mix

12   (1-ounce) slices French bread, grilled

1. To prepare salad dressing, combine ranch dressing and horseradish in a small bowl; cover and chill.

2. To prepare steaks, combine coffee, cumin, ancho chile powder, and black pepper. Rub both sides of steaks with coffee mixture; let stand 10 minutes.

3. Heat a nonstick grill pan over medium heat. Coat steaks with cooking spray. Add steaks to pan, and cook 3 minutes on each side or until desired degree of doneness. Remove steaks from pan; let stand 7 minutes.

4. Combine shallots, basil, bell peppers, juice, and tomatoes in a small bowl; toss well.

5. Arrange 1 cup greens on each of 6 plates. Cut each steak diagonally across grain into thin slices. Divide steak slices evenly among servings; top each serving with about 2 tablespoons tomato mixture. Drizzle each serving with about 1 tablespoon salad dressing and top with 2 toast slices. Serve immediately.

Serves 6.

CALORIES 384; FAT 13.2g (sat 3g, mono 3.7g, poly 5g); PROTEIN 25.3g; CARB 41.4g; FIBER 3.4g; CHOL 55mg; IRON 4.2mg; SODIUM 565mg; CALC 88mg

Wine Pairing
The incredible spices layered throughout this dish call for a spicy, sweet wine to match. Try a rich, velvety shiraz from Australia.

Tuna and White Bean Salad

The "best ingredients" principle includes top-shelf tuna. Buy it, and this entrée salad is a treat.

Packing tuna in oil adds calories, but the calories are from good fats, and the flavor payoff is huge. Oil-packed tuna is more expensive, but rich, meaty, and satisfying. For the most sustainable choice, look for tuna labeled troll- or pole-caught. There are some good American offerings. For a vegetarian version, add an extra half-can of beans and kalamata olives in place of tuna. Hands-on time: 27 min. Total time: 30 min.

20 asparagus spears, trimmed
1 tablespoon capers, drained
1 tablespoon chopped fresh flat-leaf parsley
2 tablespoons white wine vinegar
2 tablespoons fresh lemon juice
2 tablespoons extra-virgin olive oil
1 tablespoon butter, melted
¼ teaspoon salt
¼ teaspoon freshly ground black pepper
1 cup cherry tomatoes, quartered

1 (15-ounce) can organic white beans, rinsed and drained
4 cups torn butter lettuce (about 1 head)
2 (5-ounce) cans solid white tuna packed in olive oil, drained and broken into chunks

1. Steam asparagus, covered, 3 minutes. Drain and rinse with cold water; drain.
2. Combine capers and next 7 ingredients (through pepper) in a small bowl, stirring well with a whisk.

3. Place ¼ cup juice mixture, tomatoes, and beans in a small bowl; toss gently to combine.
4. Place 1 cup lettuce on each of 4 plates, and top each serving with 5 asparagus spears and about ½ cup white bean mixture. Divide tuna evenly among servings. Drizzle each salad with about 1 tablespoon remaining juice mixture.

Serves 4.

CALORIES 270; FAT 14.6g (sat 3.5g, mono 7.4g, poly 2.5g); PROTEIN 20.2g; CARB 16g; FIBER 5.6g; CHOL 24mg; IRON 2.4mg; SODIUM 467mg; CALC 65mg

Wheat Berry Salad with Goat Cheese 🌿

Tabbouleh fans will love this one.

This salad uses lots of peak-season vegetables, tart lemon juice, and pungent fresh herbs. Serve with toasted pita wedges. Hands-on time: 20 min. Total time: 9 hr. 47 min.

1¼ cups uncooked wheat berries (hard winter wheat)

2½ cups chopped English cucumber

1½ cups loosely packed chopped arugula

⅔ cup thinly sliced green onions

6 tablespoons minced fresh flat-leaf parsley

1 pint grape tomatoes, halved

1 tablespoon grated lemon rind

3 tablespoons fresh lemon juice

1 teaspoon kosher salt

½ teaspoon freshly ground black pepper

½ teaspoon sugar

2 tablespoons extra-virgin olive oil

¾ cup (3 ounces) crumbled goat cheese

1. Place wheat berries in a medium bowl; cover with water to 2 inches above wheat berries. Cover and let stand 8 hours. Drain.

2. Place wheat berries in a medium saucepan; cover with water to 2 inches above wheat berries. Bring to a boil; reduce heat, and cook, uncovered, 1 hour or until tender. Drain and rinse with cold water; drain well. Place wheat berries in a large bowl, and add cucumber and next 4 ingredients (through tomatoes).

3. Combine rind and next 4 ingredients (through sugar) in a bowl; gradually add oil, stirring constantly with a whisk. Drizzle dressing over salad; toss well to coat. Stir in cheese. Let stand at least 30 minutes. Serve at room temperature.

Serves 6 (serving size: about 1⅓ cups).

CALORIES 253; FAT 9.7g (sat 3.7g, mono 4.4g, poly 0.9g); PROTEIN 9.2g; CARB 35.7g; FIBER 6.8g; CHOL 11mg; IRON 1.2mg; SODIUM 401mg; CALC 79mg

CHOICE INGREDIENT

Wheat Berries: Wheat berry kernels are thick, short whole grains that look rather like fat brown rice. The cooked grain is chewy and has a nutty, earthy flavor. White wheat berries are slightly sweeter than the more common red wheat berries.

Cracked Wheat Salad with
Nectarines, Parsley, and Pistachios

Cracked Wheat Salad with Nectarines, Parsley, and Pistachios 🌿

A grain and fruit salad that goes beautifully with grilled chicken, lamb, or salmon.

When nectarines are unavailable, try apricots, peaches, or figs. Hands-on time: 8 min. Total time: 1 hr. 8 min.

1 cup uncooked bulgur

1 cup boiling water

1½ cups thinly sliced nectarines (about 3)

½ cup thinly sliced green onions

¼ cup chopped fresh flat-leaf parsley

1 tablespoon chopped fresh dill

3 tablespoons extra-virgin olive oil

3 tablespoons white balsamic vinegar

¾ teaspoon salt

¼ teaspoon freshly ground black pepper

3 tablespoons chopped pistachios

1. Combine bulgur and 1 cup boiling water in a large bowl. Cover and let stand 1 hour. Stir in nectarines and next 7 ingredients (through black pepper); toss well. Sprinkle with nuts.

Serves 6 (serving size: about ¾ cup).

CALORIES 188; FAT 9g (sat 1.2g, mono 5.9g, poly 1.4g); PROTEIN 4.2g; CARB 24.7g; FIBER 5.7g; CHOL 0mg; IRON 1.2mg; SODIUM 307mg; CALC 29mg

---

Wheat Berry Salad with Dried Fruit 🌿

This is one of our favorite salads for a packed lunch: filling, full of bright flavors, with lots of protein to satisfy.

Make it ahead so the flavors have time to mellow. Hands-on time: 15 min. Total time: 5 hr. 45 min.

3 cups water

1 cup uncooked wheat berries (hard winter wheat)

½ cup minced shallots

¼ cup cranberry juice

3 tablespoons raspberry vinegar

2 tablespoons canola oil

1 tablespoon balsamic vinegar

2 teaspoons Dijon mustard

½ teaspoon salt

½ cup coarsely chopped dried cranberries

½ cup coarsely chopped dried cherries

½ cup (2 ounces) diced Gouda cheese

⅓ cup chopped green onions

⅓ cup slivered almonds, toasted

¼ cup dried currants

¼ teaspoon freshly ground black pepper

1. Combine 3 cups water and wheat berries in a medium saucepan; bring to a boil. Cover, reduce heat, and simmer 1 hour or until tender. Drain and rinse with cold water; drain well.

2. Combine shallots and next 6 ingredients (through salt) in a large bowl. Let stand 30 minutes.

3. Add wheat berries, cranberries, and remaining ingredients to vinaigrette; toss to combine. Chill at least 4 hours or overnight.

Serves 6 (serving size: 1 cup).

CALORIES 357; FAT 11.7g (sat 2.3g, mono 6.4g, poly 2.4g); PROTEIN 9.4g; CARB 55.2g; FIBER 7.8g; CHOL 11mg; IRON 2.1mg; SODIUM 332mg; CALC 118mg

Waldorf Salad with Steel-Cut Oats 🌿🌾

A surprising, delicious, no-mayo update with oats, which are a whole grain and add chewy texture.

The first Waldorf salad, created in New York City in 1893 by the maître d'hôtel of the Waldorf Astoria, consisted only of diced red-skinned apples, celery, and mayonnaise. Later, chopped walnuts were added. Here, Mark Bittman uses steel-cut oats, radicchio, and blue cheese, ramping up the nutrition value and complexity. Rinsing the oats removes excess starch on the outside of the grains, preventing them from becoming too sticky. Hands-on time: 26 min. Total time: 28 min.

1   cup steel-cut oats, rinsed and drained

1   cup water

1   teaspoon kosher salt, divided

⅔   cup coarsely chopped walnuts

1½   teaspoons honey

⅛   teaspoon ground red pepper

3   tablespoons extra-virgin olive oil

2   tablespoons sherry vinegar

½   teaspoon freshly ground black pepper

1½   cups diced Granny Smith apple (about 1 large)

1½   cups torn radicchio

1½   cups seedless red grapes, halved

½   cup (2 ounces) crumbled blue cheese

1. Combine oats, 1 cup water, and ½ teaspoon salt in a medium saucepan; bring to a boil. Reduce heat, and simmer 7 minutes (do not stir) or until liquid almost evaporates. Remove from heat; fluff with a fork. Place oats in a medium bowl; let stand 10 minutes.

2. Combine walnuts, honey, and red pepper in a small nonstick skillet over medium heat; cook 4 minutes or until nuts are fragrant and honey is slightly caramelized, stirring occasionally.

3. Combine oil, vinegar, remaining ½ teaspoon salt, and black pepper in a small bowl, stirring with a whisk. Add dressing, apple, radicchio, and grapes to oats; toss well. Place 1½ cups oat mixture on each of 4 plates; top each serving with about 3 tablespoons walnut mixture and 2 tablespoons cheese.

Serves 4.

CALORIES 410; FAT 26.5g (sat 5.4g, mono 10.5g, poly 9.6g); PROTEIN 9g; CARB 37.9g; FIBER 5.1g; CHOL 11mg; IRON 2mg; SODIUM 683mg; CALC 106mg

Mark Bittman's Chicken Tabbouleh with Tahini Drizzle

Our "Less Meat, More Flavor" columnist turned a minty whole-grain side dish into a satisfying entrée by adding sautéed chicken.

Bulgur is a quick-cooking whole grain. A pot is done when little bubble-holes form on top of the bulgur.
Hands-on time: 26 min. Total time: 37 min.

1¼ cups water

1 cup uncooked bulgur, rinsed and drained

2 tablespoons olive oil, divided

1 teaspoon kosher salt, divided

½ pound skinless, boneless chicken thighs

½ teaspoon freshly ground black pepper

3 cups chopped tomato

1 cup chopped fresh flat-leaf parsley

1 cup chopped fresh mint

1 cup chopped green onions

1 teaspoon minced garlic

¼ cup tahini (roasted sesame seed paste)

¼ cup plain 2% reduced-fat Greek yogurt

3 tablespoons fresh lemon juice

1 tablespoon water

1. Combine 1¼ cups water, bulgur, 1 tablespoon olive oil, and ½ teaspoon salt in a medium saucepan; bring to a boil. Reduce heat; simmer 10 minutes (do not stir) or until liquid almost evaporates. Remove from heat; fluff with a fork. Place bulgur in a medium bowl; let stand 10 minutes.

2. Heat a large nonstick skillet over medium-high heat. Add remaining 1 tablespoon oil to pan; swirl to coat. Add chicken to pan; sprinkle with ¼ teaspoon salt and black pepper. Sauté 4 minutes on each side or until done; shred chicken. Combine bulgur, chicken, tomato, and next 4 ingredients (through garlic) in a large bowl; toss gently.

3. Combine remaining ¼ teaspoon salt, tahini, and next 3 ingredients (through 1 tablespoon water) in a small bowl, stirring with a whisk. Drizzle over salad.

Serves 4 (serving size: about 1½ cups).

CALORIES 395; FAT 18.2g (sat 3g, mono 8.8g, poly 5.1g); PROTEIN 21.5g; CARB 41g; FIBER 10.9g; CHOL 48mg; IRON 4.2mg; SODIUM 573mg; CALC 127mg

Beet, Blood Orange, Kumquat, and Quinoa Salad 🌿 🌾
About 30 minutes: You won't make a healthier meal.

Quinoa, avocado, beets, and citrus: This baby is packed with monounsaturated fat and fiber and is a good source of iron and calcium. When blood oranges and kumquats aren't in season, substitute a combination of oranges, tangerines, and Meyer lemons. Look for precooked beets in the produce section, or wrap each (5-ounce) beet in parchment paper, and microwave 3 to 3½ minutes. Let stand a couple of minutes, then peel and cut. Hands-on time: 30 min. Total time: 32 min.

1 cup uncooked quinoa

1¾ cups water

½ teaspoon salt, divided

1 cup blood orange sections, chopped (about 4 medium)

1 cup diced peeled avocado

6 whole kumquats, seeded and sliced

Citrus-Green Onion Dressing

2 beets, cooked and cut into wedges

1. Place quinoa in a fine sieve, and place sieve in a large bowl. Cover quinoa with water. Using your hands, rub grains together for 30 seconds; rinse and drain. Repeat procedure twice. Drain well.

2. Combine 1¾ cups water, quinoa, and ¼ teaspoon salt in a medium saucepan; bring to a boil. Cover, reduce heat, and simmer 10 minutes or until liquid is absorbed. Remove from heat; fluff with a fork. Combine quinoa, remaining ¼ teaspoon salt, blood orange sections, avocado, and kumquats in a large bowl, tossing gently to combine. Add Citrus-Green Onion Dressing; toss gently to coat. Spoon 1 cup salad onto each of 4 plates; top each serving with about ½ cup beets.

Serves 4.

(Totals include Citrus-Green Onion Dressing) CALORIES 442; FAT 20.7g (sat 2.7g, mono 12.3g, poly 2.1g); PROTEIN 9.1g; CARB 58g; FIBER 10.7g; CHOL 0mg; IRON 3.9mg; SODIUM 486mg; CALC 117mg

CITRUS-GREEN ONION DRESSING 🌿

Use as a marinade for shrimp or chicken.

¼ cup finely chopped green onions

2 teaspoons grated blood orange rind

1 teaspoon grated lemon rind

2 tablespoons blood orange juice

1 tablespoon fresh lemon juice

2 teaspoons finely chopped cilantro

¼ teaspoon salt

¼ teaspoon ground coriander

¼ teaspoon ground cumin

¼ teaspoon paprika

3 tablespoons extra-virgin olive oil

1. Combine first 10 ingredients in a medium bowl, stirring with a whisk. Gradually add oil, stirring constantly with a whisk.

Serves 4 (serving size: 3 tablespoons).

CALORIES 99; FAT 10.2g (sat 1.4g, mono 7.4g, poly 1.1g); PROTEIN 0.1g; CARB 2.1g; FIBER 0.5g; CHOL 0mg; IRON 0.2mg; SODIUM 151mg; CALC 10mg

Yellow Plum Salad 🍃

When it's plum season, this salad is heaven and earthy.

Serve it with grilled chicken, pork, steaks, or seafood. Look for Mirabelle or other golden-fleshed plums.

Hands-on time: 29 min. Total time: 2 hr. 2 min.

2	yellow bell peppers
4	golden beets (about 12 ounces)
2½	tablespoons extra-virgin olive oil
1	tablespoon white wine vinegar
1	tablespoon chopped fresh chives
1	teaspoon chopped fresh thyme
1	teaspoon Dijon mustard
¼	teaspoon salt
⅛	teaspoon freshly ground black pepper
8	yellow-fleshed plums, halved and pitted (about 1 pound)
½	pint yellow pear tomatoes, halved lengthwise
½	cup (2 ounces) crumbled goat cheese

1. Preheat broiler.

2. Cut bell peppers in half lengthwise; discard seeds and membranes. Place pepper halves, skin sides up, on a foil-lined baking sheet; flatten with hand. Broil 13 minutes or until blackened. Place in a paper bag, and fold to close tightly. Let stand 20 minutes. Peel and cut bell peppers into ½-inch-thick strips.

3. Preheat oven to 450°.

4. Leave root and 1-inch stem on beets; scrub with a brush. Place beets in an 11 x 7–inch glass or ceramic baking dish. Add 1 inch of water to dish; cover tightly with foil. Bake at 450° for 1 hour or until tender. Cool; peel and cut into ½-inch-thick slices.

5. Combine oil and next 6 ingredients (through black pepper) in a small bowl, stirring well with a whisk. Place sliced beets in a medium bowl. Drizzle beets with 3 tablespoons vinaigrette; toss gently. Let stand at least 15 minutes. Divide beets evenly among 6 plates, and top each serving evenly with peppers, plums, and tomatoes. Drizzle with remaining vinaigrette. Sprinkle evenly with cheese.

Serves 6.

CALORIES 158; FAT 8g (sat 2.2g, mono 4.6g, poly 0.7g); PROTEIN 4.2g; CARB 20.2g; FIBER 3.5g; CHOL 4mg; IRON 1.4mg; SODIUM 194mg; CALC 35mg

Winter Jeweled Fruit Salad 🌿
A burst of fruit with a wee chile kick.

A popular Mexican street food, *copas de frutas*—fresh fruit sprinkled with lime juice and ground chile—inspired this gorgeous salad. Jicama is one of the crunchiest vegetables on earth, tasting a bit apple-y, a bit potato-y. Look for pomegranate seeds in the produce section, or dig the seeds yourself from the labyrinth of pith, wearing a shirt you don't mind getting splattered. Hands-on time: 20 min. Total time: 20 min.

½   cup pomegranate seeds (about 1 pomegranate)

½   cup julienne-cut peeled jicama

⅓   cup sliced seeded kumquats (about 6 medium)

2   ripe mangoes, peeled and cut into thin slices

2   tangerines or clementines, peeled and sectioned

2   blood oranges, peeled and sectioned

1   pear, thinly sliced

2   tablespoons fresh lime juice

2   tablespoons honey

¼   teaspoon ground red pepper

⅛   teaspoon coarse sea salt

1. Combine first 7 ingredients in a large bowl; toss gently. Combine lime juice, honey, pepper, and salt in a small bowl, stirring well with a whisk. Pour over fruit; toss gently to coat. Serve at room temperature.

Serves 8 (serving size: 1 cup).

CALORIES 118; FAT 0.4g (sat 0.1g, mono 0.1g, poly 0.1g); PROTEIN 1.3g; CARB 30g; FIBER 4.2g; CHOL 0mg; IRON 0.4mg; SODIUM 37mg; CALC 39mg

CHOICE INGREDIENT

Kumquats: These oblong citrus fruits look like miniature oranges. The rind is tangy-sweet, while the inside flesh has an intense tart flavor. Fresh kumquats are in season and most plentiful from December through April. Test them with a gentle squeeze, and buy only firm fruit.

Spring Salad with Grapes and Pistachio-Crusted Goat Cheese ✿

The vintage cheese-ball idea gets updated with goaty tang and pistachio tannins.

Mix it up by substituting crushed pecans or walnuts to coat the cheese, and use strawberries instead of grapes. Hands-on time: 15 min. Total time: 15 min.

¼ cup shelled dry-roasted pistachios, finely chopped

½ cup (4 ounces) goat cheese

¼ cup Easy Herb Vinaigrette

1 (5-ounce) package gourmet salad greens or spring lettuce mix

1 cup seedless red grapes, halved

¼ teaspoon freshly ground black pepper

1. Place pistachios in a shallow dish. Divide cheese into 12 equal portions; shape mixture into 12 balls. Roll each ball in pistachios until well coated. Set pistachio-crusted cheese balls aside.

2. Place Easy Herb Vinaigrette in a large bowl; add greens, and toss gently to coat. Divide greens mixture evenly among 4 plates. Top each serving with ¼ cup grapes and 3 cheese balls. Sprinkle salads evenly with pepper; serve immediately.

Serves 4.

CALORIES 235; FAT 18.4g (sat 5.2g, mono 8.4g, poly 3.9g); PROTEIN 7.8g; CARB 11.8g; FIBER 1.7g; CHOL 13mg; IRON 1.4mg; SODIUM 192mg; CALC 67mg

EASY HERB VINAIGRETTE ✿

Cover and refrigerate for up to five days for quick salad prep. Wildflower honey adds a floral sweetness.

9 tablespoons white wine vinegar

1½ tablespoons wildflower honey

½ teaspoon fine sea salt

1 cup canola oil

3 tablespoons chopped fresh basil

3 tablespoons minced fresh chives

1. Combine first 3 ingredients in a bowl; add oil. Slowly whisk until combined. Stir in basil and chives.

Serves 13 (serving size: 2 tablespoons).

CALORIES 160; FAT 17.2g (sat 1.2g, mono 10.2g, poly 5.1g); PROTEIN 0.1g; CARB 2.1g; FIBER 0.1g; CHOL 0mg; IRON 0mg; SODIUM 89mg; CALC 2mg

Prosciutto and Melon Salad with Cantaloupe Vinaigrette

Rice vinegar and cantaloupe in the dressing completely reset this ham-and-melon classic.

Peppery arugula adds bite. Hands-on time: 10 min. Total time: 10 min.

1   cup (½-inch) cubed cantaloupe
2   tablespoons rice vinegar
1   teaspoon sugar
4   teaspoons canola oil
⅛   teaspoon salt
12 cups arugula leaves
1   honeydew melon, peeled, seeded, and cut into 24 slices

1   cantaloupe, peeled, seeded, and cut into 24 slices
8   very thin slices prosciutto (about 4 ounces)
½   teaspoon freshly ground black pepper

1. Place first 5 ingredients in a food processor; process until smooth.
2. Place 1½ cups arugula on each of 8 plates. Top each serving with

3 honeydew slices, 3 cantaloupe slices, and 1 prosciutto slice. Drizzle each serving with about 1 tablespoon dressing; sprinkle evenly with pepper.

Serves 8.

CALORIES 109; FAT 4.1g (sat 0.7g, mono 2.1g, poly 1.1g); PROTEIN 5g; CARB 14.8g; FIBER 1.8g; CHOL 8mg; IRON 0.9mg; SODIUM 284mg; CALC 61mg

Lemony Cucumber Salad

Crunchy radishes and the deep "green" flavors of flat-leaf parsley are just so summery.

This simple, vibrant salad travels well, making it a must for picnics and potlucks. Buy a bouquet of purple, orange, red, and white radishes, if you can. Hands-on time: 22 min. Total time: 22 min.

1	cup thinly sliced radishes
½	cup finely chopped orange bell pepper
¼	cup chopped fresh flat-leaf parsley
2	English cucumbers, thinly sliced (about 6 cups)
	Lemony Vinaigrette

1. Combine first 4 ingredients in a large bowl. Pour Lemony Vinaigrette over cucumber mixture; toss well to coat. Serve at room temperature or chilled.

Serves 8 (serving size: ⅔ cup).

(Totals include Lemony Vinaigrette)
CALORIES 33; FAT 1.8g (sat 0.3g, mono 1.2g, poly 0.2g); PROTEIN 0.8g; CARB 4.3g; FIBER 0.9g; CHOL 0mg; IRON 0.4mg; SODIUM 156mg; CALC 20mg

LEMONY VINAIGRETTE

Try also with a pasta salad with tomatoes, mozzarella, and arugula.

1	teaspoon finely grated lemon rind
2	tablespoons fresh lemon juice
1	tablespoon extra-virgin olive oil
1½	teaspoons white wine vinegar
½	teaspoon salt
¼	teaspoon freshly ground black pepper

1. Combine all ingredients in a small bowl, stirring with a whisk.

Serves 8 (serving size: about 1½ teaspoons).

CALORIES 16; FAT 1.7g (sat 0.2g, mono 1.2g, poly 0.2g); PROTEIN 0g; CARB 0.4g; FIBER 0.1g; CHOL 0mg; IRON 0mg; SODIUM 148mg; CALC 1mg

A Quartet of Dressings

Classic Vinaigrette

Every cook should be able to make one. Make extra to keep on hand for up to a week in the refrigerator.

3   tablespoons red wine vinegar
2   tablespoons chopped shallots
2   tablespoons Dijon mustard
½   teaspoon salt
¼   teaspoon black pepper
6   tablespoons extra-virgin olive oil

Combine first 5 ingredients. Gradually add oil, stirring well with a whisk.

Serves 12 (serving size: 1 tablespoon).

CALORIES 63; FAT 6.7g (sat 0.9g, mono 4.9g, poly 0.7g); PROTEIN 0.1g; CARB 0.5g; FIBER 0g; CHOL 0mg; IRON 0.1mg; SODIUM 119mg; CALC 1mg

Blue Cheese Salad Dressing

A dressing or dip, with a nice bite and a lot less fat. Canola mayonnaise and fat-free sour cream dramatically reduce the sat fat and calories, allowing for a generous amount of what you really want: blue cheese.

1   cup canola mayonnaise
2   tablespoons cider vinegar
1   tablespoon canola oil
½   teaspoon dried oregano
¼   teaspoon salt

¼   teaspoon black pepper
1   (8-ounce) carton fat-free sour cream
1   garlic clove, crushed
½   cup (2 ounces) crumbled blue cheese

Combine first 8 ingredients, stirring well with a whisk. Stir in cheese. Cover and refrigerate at least 3 hours.

Serves 40 (serving size: 1 tablespoon).

CALORIES 54; FAT 5.2g (sat 0.5g, mono 3.1g, poly 1.5g); PROTEIN 0.6g; CARB 0.9g; FIBER 0g; CHOL 4mg; IRON 0mg; SODIUM 75mg; CALC 16mg

Balsamic Vinaigrette

Even industrial-production supermarket balsamic has a pleasing sweet-tart flavor. But try a syrupy artisanal bottle for astonishing depth. The fancy, expensive stuff, often aged for years, should be drizzled over salads, strawberries, or even Parmesan cheese right before serving. Use this versatile dressing as a marinade for chicken, dressing for salad, or glaze brushed on vegetables before grilling.

2   tablespoons balsamic vinegar
2   tablespoons extra-virgin olive oil
1   tablespoon minced shallots
½   teaspoon Dijon mustard
¼   teaspoon sugar
⅛   teaspoon salt

Combine first 4 ingredients in a bowl, stirring well with a whisk. Stir in sugar and salt.

Serves 6 (serving size: about 1 tablespoon).

CALORIES 47; FAT 4.7g (sat 0.7g, mono 3.3g, poly 0.7g); PROTEIN 0.1g; CARB 1.5g; FIBER 0g; CHOL 0mg; IRON 0.1mg; SODIUM 61mg; CALC 2mg

Poppy Seed Dressing

Walnut oil is the secret to the delicate, toasty flavor of this dressing. Serve over fruit, toss with coleslaw, or create a main-dish salad with grilled chicken, baby greens, strawberries, walnuts, and orange sections.

2   tablespoons cider vinegar
2   tablespoons toasted walnut oil
2   tablespoons reduced-fat sour cream
1½   teaspoons poppy seeds
2   teaspoons honey
½   teaspoon black pepper
¼   teaspoon kosher salt
2   garlic cloves, crushed

Combine all ingredients, stirring well with a whisk.

Serves 12 (serving size: about 2 teaspoons).

CALORIES 31; FAT 2.8g (sat 0.4g, mono 0.6g, poly 1.7g); PROTEIN 0.3g; CARB 1.4g; FIBER 0.1g; CHOL 1mg; IRON 0.1mg; SODIUM 42mg; CALC 11mg

3

SALADS

Chapter
Fish & Sh

4:
ellfish

Most seafood is easy to prepare, and plays well with global ingredients and flavors. When it's lean, it's very lean; when it's rich, the fats are healthy. But demand and pollution threaten the health of the oceans. The conscientious cook patronizes restaurants and stores that transparently promote sustainability. This is tricky: Species responsibly harvested in one area may be decimated elsewhere. Fish farming may be sound, or not. Many American fisheries have made significant progress. Consult lists and apps from organizations such as Monterey Bay Aquarium and the Blue Ocean Institute, and use our sustainability notes for general guidance; the status of species changes.

Grilled Halibut with Peach and Pepper Salsa

Juicy peaches get a heady habanero kick as summer heats up.

We love this salsa on quesadillas, pork chops, and tortilla chips. Hands-on time: 11 min. Total time: 30 min.

1⅓ cups coarsely chopped peeled yellow peaches (about 1 pound)

1 cup chopped red bell pepper (about 1 medium)

⅓ cup thinly sliced green onions

⅓ cup chopped fresh arugula

¼ cup fresh lemon juice

4 teaspoons chopped fresh oregano

⅛ teaspoon salt

1 garlic clove, minced

½ habanero pepper, seeded and minced

4 teaspoons fresh lemon juice

4 teaspoons olive oil

½ teaspoon paprika

1 garlic clove, minced

4 (6-ounce) skinless halibut fillets

⅜ teaspoon salt

⅜ teaspoon freshly ground black pepper

Cooking spray

1. Combine first 9 ingredients; toss gently. Let stand 30 minutes.
2. Preheat grill to medium-high heat.
3. Combine 4 teaspoons juice, oil, paprika, and 1 garlic clove in a large, shallow glass or ceramic baking dish, stirring with a whisk. Add fish to juice mixture; turn to coat. Cover and let stand 15 minutes.
4. Remove fish from marinade; discard marinade. Sprinkle fish evenly with ⅜ teaspoon salt and black pepper. Place fish on grill rack coated with cooking spray; grill 3 minutes on each side or until fish flakes easily when tested with a fork. Serve with salsa.

Serves 4 (serving size: 1 fillet and about ⅔ cup salsa).

CALORIES 267; FAT 8.6g (sat 1.2g, mono 4.6g, poly 1.8g); PROTEIN 35.3g; CARB 11.8g; FIBER 2.3g; CHOL 52mg; IRON 2mg; SODIUM 389mg; CALC 104mg

SUSTAINABILITY NOTE

Halibut: Wild-caught Alaskan halibut is the best option. If not available, opt for other U.S. or Canadian wild-caught Pacific halibut.

NUTRITION MADE EASY

Seafood: The most recent Dietary Guidelines for Americans recommend eating two servings of seafood per week in place of beef, pork, or poultry. Why? Because, simply, seafood is healthier. It's either low in fat (as with tilapia or shrimp) or, even better, rich in healthy fats like omega-3 fatty acids—polyunsaturated fats that have been shown to protect against heart disease and some forms of cancer, reduce blood pressure, and help control inflammation. Good sources of omega-3s include oilier fish like mackerel, salmon, and albacore tuna.

Arctic Char and Vegetables in Parchment Hearts

Parchment might seem a bit twee, but not here:
The package is elegant, and the contents beautifully
steam to a delicate turn.

Think of arctic char as salmon's milder cousin, with a less vibrant hue and subtler flavor. If it's not available from your fishmonger, substitute frozen wild Alaskan salmon. Serve in the parchment paper with Broccolini and mashed potatoes on the side. Hands-on time: 15 min. Total time: 30 min.

1	tablespoon unsalted butter, softened
1	teaspoon grated lemon rind
1	tablespoon fresh lemon juice
1	teaspoon chopped fresh dill
2	(6-ounce) arctic char fillets (about 1 inch thick)
¼	teaspoon kosher salt
⅛	teaspoon freshly ground black pepper
¼	cup julienne-cut leeks
¼	cup julienne-cut red bell pepper
¼	cup julienne-cut carrot
¼	cup julienne-cut snow peas

1. Preheat oven to 450°.

2. Combine first 4 ingredients in a small bowl; stir until blended.

3. Cut 2 (15 x 24–inch) pieces of parchment paper. Fold in half crosswise. Draw a large heart half on each piece, with the fold of the paper along the center of the heart. Cut out the heart, and open. Sprinkle both sides of fillets with salt and black pepper. Place 1 fillet near fold of each parchment heart. Top each fillet with half the vegetables and half the butter mixture. Start at the top of the heart, and fold edges of parchment, sealing edges with narrow folds. Twist the end tip to secure tightly. Place packets on a baking sheet. Bake at 450° for 15 minutes. Place on plates; cut open. Serve immediately.

Serves 2 (serving size: 1 fillet, ½ cup vegetables, and about 1 tablespoon sauce).

CALORIES 361; FAT 20.5g (sat 6.2g, mono 3.5g, poly 8.5g); PROTEIN 37.1g; CARB 5.6g; FIBER 1.4g; CHOL 121mg; IRON 1.4mg; SODIUM 335mg; CALC 32mg

TECHNIQUE

En Papillote: Cooking in parchment paper holds in moisture to steam the food and maintain its flavor and natural nutrients. No fat is needed to cook the fish, so you can add it later, if you like, for a rich finish.

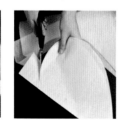

1. To prepare the paper packet, fold parchment paper in half.

2. Draw half of a heart shape on one side of folded paper, and cut along pencil-drawn shape.

3. Arrange fish and vegetables on one side of paper.

4. Make small, tight, overlapping folds down the outside edge to close the packet.

5. To seal, twist the tail end.

Bayou Catfish Fillets

Crispy-crusted catfish without deep-fat frying—brilliant.

Fried catfish is one of the genius dishes of the South. Banish the thought of dull-tasting fish: Today's farmed catfish is sweet and meaty, with a hint of earthiness. Here, the spicy cornmeal breading stays crispy because the fish is baked on a ventilated broiler pan. Hands-on time: 11 min. Total time: 23 min.

2	tablespoons yellow cornmeal
1½	teaspoons seasoned salt
1½	teaspoons dried oregano
1	teaspoon garlic powder
1	teaspoon onion powder
¾	teaspoon ground red pepper
½	teaspoon chili powder
¼	teaspoon ground cumin
¼	teaspoon freshly ground black pepper
6	(6-ounce) catfish fillets
	Cooking spray
6	lemon slices (optional)

1. Preheat broiler.

2. Combine first 9 ingredients in a zip-top plastic bag. Add 1 catfish fillet. Seal bag, and shake well. Remove fillet from bag; place on a broiler pan coated with cooking spray. Repeat procedure with remaining fillets and cornmeal mixture.

3. Broil 6 inches from heat 6 minutes. Carefully turn fillets over; broil 6 minutes or until fish flakes easily when tested with a fork. Serve with lemon slices, if desired.

Serves 6 (serving size: 1 fillet).

CALORIES 247; FAT 13.2g (sat 3.1g, mono 6.1g, poly 2.8g); PROTEIN 27g; CARB 3.8g; FIBER 0.8g; CHOL 80mg; IRON 1.3mg; SODIUM 474mg; CALC 27mg

Grilled Grouper with Basil-Lime Pistou

A zingier, pesto-like sauce with a quick-grilled fish: There's nothing simpler.

If you can't grill the fish outdoors, prepare it in a grill pan, cooking it about four minutes on each side. Double the pistou, and serve the next day over bread, stirred into pasta, or dolloped on vegetable and bean soup. Hands-on time: 12 min. Total time: 20 min.

Pistou:

- 1 cup fresh basil leaves
- ¼ cup (1 ounce) grated fresh Parmesan cheese
- ½ teaspoon grated lime rind
- 2 tablespoons fresh lime juice
- 1½ tablespoons extra-virgin olive oil
- ⅛ teaspoon salt
- 3 garlic cloves, chopped

Grouper:

- 4 (6-ounce) grouper fillets (about ½ inch thick)
- ½ teaspoon salt
- ¼ teaspoon freshly ground black pepper

Cooking spray

1. To prepare pistou, place first 7 ingredients in a food processor; pulse until finely chopped. Let stand 10 minutes.

2. Preheat grill to medium-high heat.

3. To prepare grouper, sprinkle fish evenly with ½ teaspoon salt and pepper. Place fish on grill rack coated with cooking spray; grill 4 minutes on each side or until fish flakes easily when tested with a fork. Serve with pistou.

Serves 4 (serving size: 1 fillet and about 1 tablespoon pistou).

CALORIES 226; FAT 8.2g (sat 2g, mono 4.5g, poly 1.2g); PROTEIN 34.1g; CARB 2.2g; FIBER 0.6g; CHOL 64mg; IRON 1.9mg; SODIUM 514mg; CALC 105mg

SUSTAINABILITY NOTE

Catfish: U.S.-farmed catfish is a sustainability rock star because these freshwater fish are raised in enclosed inland ponds and fed a primarily vegetarian diet. Check the label, which often lists the country where the fish are farmed, to ensure you're not buying imported catfish.

Grouper: Grouper is tricky: Many populations have been overfished, but strict oversight is helping this versatile fish recover. Look for wild red or black grouper, usually from the U.S. Gulf of Mexico, or wild Hawaiian grouper.

Arctic Char with Blistered Cherry Tomatoes

The fish is sautéed to create a beautiful browned crust, then finished in the oven.

Wild arctic char from the northern seas is available only for a few weeks in late summer, when the ice has melted enough for fishermen to reach them. It's a sought-after delicacy, and one that will cost you. If you find fresh, it's worth the splurge. Hands-on time: 15 min. Total time: 15 min.

3 tablespoons extra-virgin olive oil, divided

4 (6-ounce) arctic char fillets

¾ teaspoon coarse salt, divided

½ teaspoon freshly ground black pepper, divided

4 garlic cloves, halved

3 pints multicolored cherry tomatoes

¼ cup thinly sliced fresh basil

2 shallots, thinly sliced

1. Preheat oven to 400°.

2. Heat a large ovenproof skillet over high heat. Add 1 tablespoon oil to pan; swirl to coat. Sprinkle fillets with ½ teaspoon salt and ¼ teaspoon pepper. Add fillets, flesh sides down, to pan, and bake 2 minutes. Place pan in oven; cook at 400° for 3 minutes or until desired degree of doneness.

3. Heat a large cast-iron skillet over medium heat. Add remaining 2 tablespoons oil to pan; swirl to coat. Add garlic, and cook 2 minutes or until lightly browned, stirring occasionally. Increase heat to medium-high. Add tomatoes to pan; sauté 2 minutes or until skins blister, stirring frequently. Remove pan from heat. Sprinkle tomato mixture with remaining ¼ teaspoon salt, remaining ¼ teaspoon pepper, basil, and shallots; toss to combine. Serve with fish.

Serves 4 (serving size: 1 fillet and about ¾ cup tomato mixture).

CALORIES 380; FAT 20.4g (sat 3.8g, mono 11.7g, poly 3.6g); PROTEIN 31.4g; CARB 20g; FIBER 2.9g; CHOL 65mg; IRON 2mg; SODIUM 514mg; CALC 49mg

Wine Pairing

A late-summer fish paired with sun-warmed tomatoes needs a classic summer wine. Rosé is delicate and refreshing, and its crispness rounds off the sweet tomatoes.

SUSTAINABILITY NOTE

Arctic Char: Farmed char is a smart option when fresh wild salmon isn't available. It has a mild flavor and buttery texture. Farmed fish are widely available.

Baked Flounder with Fresh Lemon Pepper

Abandon your commercial lemon pepper in favor of this perfect homemade fish seasoning.

Though generous with the spice, this preparation is perfect for the mild, delicate flavor of flounder. It's also good over pork or tofu. Add asparagus spears to the pan and roast along with the fish.

Hands-on time: 8 min. Total time: 16 min.

2   tablespoons grated lemon rind (about 3 lemons)

1   tablespoon extra-virgin olive oil

1¼   teaspoons black peppercorns, crushed

½   teaspoon salt

2   garlic cloves, minced

4   (6-ounce) flounder fillets

Cooking spray
Lemon wedges (optional)

1. Preheat oven to 425°.
2. Combine first 5 ingredients in a bowl. Place fillets on a jelly-roll pan coated with cooking spray. Rub garlic mixture evenly over fillets. Bake at 425° for 8 minutes or until fish flakes easily when tested with a fork. Serve with lemon wedges, if desired.

Serves 4 (serving size: 1 fillet).

CALORIES 189; FAT 5.4g (sat 0.9g, mono 2.9g, poly 0.9g); PROTEIN 32.2g; CARB 1.2g; FIBER 0.4g; CHOL 82mg; IRON 0.8mg; SODIUM 432mg; CALC 39mg

SUSTAINABILITY NOTE

Flounder: U.S. Pacific-caught flounder is a sustainable option. Common market names for these mild flatfish are sole, sanddab, and hirame. Summer flounder from the Atlantic is also abundant.

Jerk Mackerel with Papaya Salad

One of the healthy oily fishes, mackerel is fishy, yes, but in a totally good way.

It's a fish with character, one that stands up to the heat and depth of jerk flavors. Jicama is super-crunchy and very mild. Papaya and bell peppers add some counterpoint. Hands-on time: 15 min. Total time: 25 min.

Salad:

- 1 cup (2-inch) julienne-cut peeled papaya
- 1 cup (2-inch) julienne-cut peeled jicama
- 1 cup (2-inch) julienne-cut red bell pepper
- 1 tablespoon small cilantro leaves
- 2 tablespoons fresh lime juice
- ⅛ teaspoon salt

Fish:

- ¼ cup Jamaican Jerk Paste
- 4 (6-ounce) mackerel fillets

Cooking spray

1. Preheat broiler.
2. To prepare salad, combine first 4 ingredients; toss. Sprinkle mixture with lime juice and salt; toss gently to coat.

3. To prepare fish, rub 1 tablespoon Jamaican Jerk Paste over each fillet. Place fillets on a broiler pan coated with cooking spray. Broil 10 minutes or until fish flakes easily when tested with a fork. Serve with salad.

Serves 4 (serving size: 1 fillet and ¾ cup salad).

CALORIES 439; FAT 26.3g (sat 6.2g, mono 10.3g, poly 6.4g); PROTEIN 36g; CARB 13.6g; FIBER 3.4g; CHOL 110mg; IRON 3mg; SODIUM 600mg; CALC 52mg

JAMAICAN JERK PASTE

Use gloves when you play with Scotch bonnet pepper or risk getting some serious burning heat on your hands and face if you don't wash thoroughly. Add a tablespoon of olive oil to leftover paste and use the mixture to marinate chicken.

- 1 Scotch bonnet pepper
- ½ cup chopped green onion tops
- ¼ cup finely chopped red onion
- 1 tablespoon brown sugar
- 1½ tablespoons fresh lime juice
- 1 tablespoon water
- 1 teaspoon salt
- 1 teaspoon fresh thyme leaves

- 1 teaspoon minced peeled fresh ginger
- ¼ teaspoon ground allspice
- 2 garlic cloves, chopped

1. Cut pepper into quarters. Remove and discard seeds and membranes from 3 pepper quarters; leave seeds and membrane intact in remaining pepper quarter. Place pepper and remaining ingredients in a mini chopper, and process until a fine paste forms.

Serves 6 (serving size: about 1 tablespoon).

CALORIES 21; FAT 0.1g (sat 0g, mono 0g, poly 0.1g); PROTEIN 0.3g; CARB 5g; FIBER 0.7g; CHOL 0mg; IRON 0.3mg; SODIUM 399mg; CALC 15mg

SUSTAINABILITY NOTE

Mackerel: Canadian Atlantic mackerel and U.S. Spanish and King mackerel are all sustainable choices. These full-flavored fish are easy to prepare because their natural oils keep the fish moist, even if slightly overcooked.

Greek Cod Cakes

Cod and olive oil are divinely married in flavorful patties. Panko drops in from Japan for crunch.

Cooking cod in milk sweetens the fish, making it milder. Measure the parsley, lemon juice, and garlic for both the cakes and the sauce at the same time. Hands-on time: 30 min. Total time: 42 min.

2	cups 2% reduced-fat milk
1	pound cod fillets, cut into 2-inch pieces
½	cup panko (Japanese breadcrumbs), divided
2	tablespoons minced fresh flat-leaf parsley
1	tablespoon grated onion
1¼	teaspoons grated lemon rind
½	teaspoon salt
½	teaspoon freshly ground black pepper
1	large egg, lightly beaten
1	large egg white, lightly beaten
1	garlic clove, minced
2	tablespoons fresh lemon juice, divided
2	tablespoons olive oil, divided
¼	cup canola mayonnaise
1	tablespoon chopped fresh flat-leaf parsley
1	teaspoon chopped fresh dill
1	teaspoon Dijon mustard
1	teaspoon fresh lemon juice
½	teaspoon minced fresh garlic
¼	teaspoon freshly ground black pepper

1. Bring milk to a simmer over medium heat in a medium, heavy saucepan. Add fish; cover and simmer 5 minutes or until fish flakes easily when tested with a fork. Drain well. Combine fish, ¼ cup panko, and next 8 ingredients (through 1 garlic clove); stir in 1 tablespoon juice. Divide fish mixture into 8 equal portions, shaping each into a ½-inch-thick patty. Dredge patties in remaining ¼ cup panko, pressing to coat.

2. Heat a large nonstick skillet over medium-high heat. Add 1 tablespoon oil to pan; swirl to coat. Add 4 patties to pan; cook 4 minutes on each side or until golden. Remove from pan; drain on paper towels. Repeat procedure with remaining oil and patties. Drizzle with remaining 1 tablespoon juice.

3. Combine mayonnaise and remaining ingredients. Serve sauce with cakes.

Serves 4 (serving size: 2 cakes and about 1 tablespoon sauce).

CALORIES 266; FAT 14.4g (sat 1.8g, mono 8.3g, poly 2.8g); PROTEIN 24.3g; CARB 7.7g; FIBER 0.6g; CHOL 122mg; IRON 1mg; SODIUM 531mg; CALC 43mg

Mahimahi with Bacon-Tomato Butter

There's not only bacon and butter, but also garlic and smoked paprika—small amounts to spectacular effect.

Mahimahi has firm flesh with a mild, slightly sweet flavor. Brining the fish pulls in moisture for a more delicate texture. If you grill over charcoal, you'll infuse the dish with even more smoke. Hands-on time: 15 min. Total time: 45 min.

2   cups water
1   tablespoon fine sea salt
2   teaspoons sugar
4   (6-ounce) mahimahi fillets
Cooking spray
⅛   teaspoon table salt
1   center-cut bacon slice, finely chopped
1   garlic clove, thinly sliced
¼   teaspoon hot smoked paprika
2   plum tomatoes, seeded and diced
2   tablespoons butter

1. Combine first 3 ingredients in a shallow dish, stirring until sea salt and sugar dissolve; add fish. Let stand 20 minutes. Drain; pat dry.
2. Prepare charcoal fire in a chimney starter; let coals burn 15 to 20 minutes or until flames die down. Carefully pour hot coals out of starter, and pile them onto one side of the grill. Coat grill rack with cooking spray; put rack in place over coals.
3. Sprinkle ⅛ teaspoon table salt evenly over fish. Lightly coat fish with cooking spray. Place fish, skin side down, over direct heat on grill rack coated with cooking spray; grill 2 minutes or until well marked. Turn fish over and move to indirect heat; grill 12 minutes or until fish flakes easily when tested with a fork.
4. Heat a small skillet over medium heat; add bacon to pan.

Cook 5 minutes or until bacon is almost crisp, stirring occasionally. Add garlic; cook 2 minutes, stirring frequently. Add paprika, and cook 20 seconds, stirring constantly. Add tomatoes, and cook 3 minutes. Stir in butter. Remove from heat. Place 1 fillet on each of 4 plates; top each serving with about 2 tablespoons tomato mixture.

Serves 4.

CALORIES 211; FAT 8g (sat 4.4g, mono 1.7g, poly 0.5g); PROTEIN 31.5; CARB 1.9g; FIBER 0.4g; CHOL 137mg; IRON 2mg; SODIUM 487mg; CALC 31mg

Wine Pairing

Try this with an oaked white wine like semillon from Chile or California; it mimics the sweet and smoky flavors of the bacon and grilled fish.

SUSTAINABILITY NOTE

Cod: Look for wild Atlantic cod from Maine, Iceland, or the northeast Arctic, or U.S. Pacific cod, to ensure a sustainable choice. Avoid cod caught by bottom trawling, which causes harm to the ocean floor.

Mahimahi: The best choice is U.S. Atlantic fish caught by troll or pole-and-line. All domestic mahimahi are a good choice, but avoid imported fish that were caught by longline.

Crispy Salmon with Herb Salad

Because of its high healthy-fat content, salmon crisps up something wonderful.

If you cook salmon until it flakes easily with a fork, it'll likely be overcooked and dry—a shame with such a beautiful catch. Chilling the lettuce and herb mixture before topping with salmon prevents it from wilting quickly. Hands-on time: 12 min. Total time: 17 min.

1½ cups arugula leaves

1½ cup fresh flat-leaf parsley leaves

1 cup fresh cilantro leaves

1 cup small fresh basil leaves

½ cup small fresh mint leaves

2 tablespoons extra-virgin olive oil

1 tablespoon fresh lemon juice

½ teaspoon salt, divided

½ teaspoon freshly ground black pepper, divided

1 garlic clove, minced

Cooking spray

6 (6-ounce) salmon fillets

6 lemon wedges

1. Combine first 5 ingredients in a large bowl. Cover and refrigerate.

2. Combine oil, juice, ¼ teaspoon salt, ¼ teaspoon pepper, and garlic, stirring with a whisk.

3. Heat a large cast-iron skillet over medium-high heat. Coat pan with cooking spray. Sprinkle salmon with remaining ¼ teaspoon salt and remaining ¼ teaspoon pepper. Place fillets, skin sides down, in pan; cook 5 minutes. Turn fillets over; cook 2 minutes or until desired degree of doneness. Combine arugula mixture and juice mixture; toss to coat. Top salad with fillets. Serve with lemon wedges.

Serves 6 (1 fillet, ½ cup herb salad, and 1 lemon wedge).

CALORIES 295; FAT 15.7g (sat 2.4g, mono 7g, poly 5.1g); PROTEIN 34.7g; CARB 2.7g; FIBER 1g; CHOL 94mg; IRON 2.7mg; SODIUM 283mg; CALC 69mg

Brown Sugar–Dill Salmon

Slow roasting yields a silken, melt-in-your-mouth texture.

The cooked fish will have a bright reddish-pink color that is similar to that of gravlax. Hands-on time: 8 min. Total time: 9 hr. 16 min.

½ cup packed light brown sugar

⅓ cup chopped fresh dill

2 tablespoons kosher salt

1 (3-pound) salmon fillet

Cooking spray

½ cup canola mayonnaise

2 tablespoons Dijon mustard

1. Combine first 3 ingredients in a bowl. Place fish, skin side down, in a 13 x 9-inch glass or ceramic baking dish. Rub sugar mixture over fish. Cover and refrigerate 8 hours.

2. Preheat oven to 175°.

3. Wipe off remaining sugar mixture from fish with a paper towel. Coat a jelly-roll pan with cooking spray. Place fish, skin side down, in pan.

4. Bake at 175° for 1 hour and 10 minutes or until desired degree of doneness.

5. Combine mayonnaise and mustard; stir well. Serve mayonnaise mixture with fish.

Serves 8 (serving size: about 5 ounces salmon and about 1 tablespoon mayonnaise mixture).

CALORIES 349; FAT 21.9g (sat 2.2g, mono 10.6g, poly 7.8g); PROTEIN 33.8g; CARB 1.6g; FIBER 0g; CHOL 99mg; IRON 1.4mg; SODIUM 372mg; CALC 22mg

Swordfish Skewers with Cilantro-Mint Pesto

Not many fish are meaty enough for skewering, but good swordfish is.

Beware overcooking: Remove just *before* it seems done, or it will be dry. Orange juice, lime juice, and garlic do double duty in the pesto and the marinade, so prepare at the same time. Hands-on time: 30 min. Total time: 1 hr. 6 min.

Pesto:

- 1 cup fresh cilantro leaves
- ½ cup fresh mint leaves
- 3 tablespoons fresh orange juice
- 2 tablespoons chopped green onions
- 1 tablespoon fresh lime juice
- 2 teaspoons extra-virgin olive oil
- ¼ teaspoon salt
- 1 garlic clove, minced

Skewers:

- 2 teaspoons grated lime rind
- 1 teaspoon grated orange rind
- 2 tablespoons fresh orange juice
- 1 tablespoon fresh lime juice
- 2 teaspoons sugar
- 2 garlic cloves, minced
- 1½ pounds swordfish fillets, cut into (1¼-inch) cubes
- 24 cherry tomatoes
- ¼ teaspoon salt
- ¼ teaspoon freshly ground black pepper

Cooking spray

1. To prepare pesto, place first 8 ingredients in a food processor; process until smooth. Let stand 30 minutes.

2. Preheat grill to medium-high heat.

3. To prepare skewers, combine lime rind and next 5 ingredients (through 2 garlic cloves) in a large zip-top plastic bag. Add fish to bag; seal. Marinate in refrigerator 30 minutes, turning bag once. Remove fish from bag; discard marinade. Thread fish and tomatoes alternately onto each of 8 (8-inch) skewers; sprinkle evenly with ¼ teaspoon salt and pepper.

4. Place skewers on grill rack coated with cooking spray; grill 6 minutes or until fish flakes easily when tested with a fork, turning every 2 minutes. Serve with pesto.

Serves 4 (serving size: 2 skewers and about 2 tablespoons pesto).

CALORIES 206; FAT 7.5g (sat 1.7g, mono 3.6g, poly 1.5g); PROTEIN 25g; CARB 9.5g; FIBER 1.8g; CHOL 47mg; IRON 1.8mg; SODIUM 416mg; CALC 31mg

SUSTAINABILITY NOTE

Salmon: Look for salmon labeled "wild Alaskan salmon." It's plentiful for a few months, usually in late spring and summer. If unavailable, buy frozen Alaskan salmon. Avoid farmed Atlantic salmon. Farming salmon in ocean nets has resulted in pollution and a host of other issues, although U.S. tank-farmed coho, sake, and silver salmon are acceptable choices.

Swordfish: This meaty fish was once overfished, but strict management helped U.S. populations recover. Avoid imported swordfish.

Stuffed Whole Roasted Yellowtail Snapper

Many home cooks avoid the whole-fish routine, thinking it tricky. It's not.

Just as cooking meat on the bone makes for richer flavor and extra succulence, so does cooking fish this way. Scoring the fish helps it keep its shape during cooking. Select whole fish with clear eyes, shiny scales, pink gills, and moist skin. Use this versatile preparation with almost any small, whole fish and your favorite fresh herbs. Garnish with chopped fennel fronds. Hands-on time: 8 min. Total time: 40 min.

2   (1½-pound) whole cleaned yellowtail snappers (heads and tails intact)

2   tablespoons extra-virgin olive oil, divided

¼   cup fresh lemon juice, divided

½   teaspoon salt

¼   teaspoon freshly ground black pepper

Cooking spray

6   tablespoons sliced onion

2   tablespoons sliced fennel bulb

4   rosemary sprigs

4   oregano sprigs

1. Preheat oven to 400°.

2. Score skin of each fish with 3 diagonal cuts. Rub inside flesh of each fish with 2½ teaspoons oil; drizzle each fish with 4½ teaspoons lemon juice. Sprinkle flesh evenly with salt and pepper. Place both fish on a rimmed baking sheet coated with cooking spray. Place 3 tablespoons onion, 1 tablespoon fennel, 2 rosemary sprigs, and 2 oregano sprigs inside each fish. Rub skin of each fish with ½ teaspoon remaining oil, and drizzle each with 1½ teaspoons remaining juice.

3. Roast at 400° for 30 minutes or until fish flakes easily when tested with a fork.

Serves 4 (serving size: about 5 ounces fish and ¼ cup vegetable mixture).

CALORIES 251; FAT 9.2g (sat 1.5g, mono 5.4g, poly 1.6g); PROTEIN 37.5g; CARB 2.7g; FIBER 0.4g; CHOL 67mg; IRON 0.4mg; SODIUM 378mg; CALC 63mg

SUSTAINABILITY NOTE

Yellowtail Snapper: Snapper are prized for their firm, usually white flesh and luscious sweet flavor, but the populations of some varieties, such as red snapper, are in danger. Select U.S. wild-caught yellowtail snapper (also called rainbow snapper).

Sesame Albacore Tuna

This dish is rich with the umami notes of soy and mushroom and the fragrance of sesame.

Fresh albacore (also called tombo) is firm, meaty, and lighter in color than other tuna species. Here, you virtually have a complete meal. But for a healthy starter, try steamed edamame in the shell, sprinkled with sea salt. Hands-on time: 40 min. Total time: 40 min.

2   tablespoons olive oil, divided

4   cups thinly sliced shiitake mushroom caps (about 10 ounces)

¼   cup organic vegetable broth

¼   cup rice vinegar

2   baby bok choy, quartered lengthwise

1   tablespoon sesame oil

2   tablespoons lower-sodium soy sauce

2   teaspoons sesame seeds

2   tablespoons chopped fresh cilantro

4   (6-ounce) fresh or frozen U.S.-caught Pacific albacore tuna fillets, thawed

½   teaspoon salt

¼   teaspoon freshly ground black pepper

2   cups hot cooked long-grain white rice

1. Heat a medium skillet over medium-high heat. Add 1 tablespoon olive oil to pan; swirl to coat. Add mushrooms; sauté 5 minutes or until lightly browned, stirring occasionally. Add broth and vinegar; boil 1 minute or until liquid almost evaporates. Keep warm.

2. Steam bok choy 1 minute. Heat a medium skillet over medium-high heat. Add sesame oil to pan; swirl to coat. Add bok choy, cut sides down; cook 1 minute. Add soy sauce and sesame seeds; cook 1 minute or until thoroughly heated. Add 1 tablespoon bok choy cooking liquid and cilantro to mushroom mixture; stir to combine.

3. Heat a large cast-iron skillet over high heat. Add remaining 1 tablespoon olive oil to pan; swirl to coat. Sprinkle fish evenly with salt and pepper. Add fish to pan; cook 1 minute on each side or until desired degree of doneness. Let stand 1 minute. Cut into ¼-inch-thick slices. To serve, place ½ cup rice on each of 4 plates; top each serving with 2 bok choy quarters. Arrange 1 tuna fillet on each plate; top each serving with ¼ cup mushroom mixture.

Serves 4.

CALORIES 446; FAT 17.7g (sat 2.7g, mono 7.7g, poly 6.1g); PROTEIN 35.4g; CARB 36.2g; FIBER 3.2g; CHOL 47mg; IRON 2.4mg; SODIUM 760mg; CALC 145mg

SUSTAINABILITY NOTE

Albacore Tuna: To make sure you're making a sustainable choice, buy U.S.-caught fresh or frozen Pacific albacore tuna. Fresh albacore is normally available only in the summer months.

Striped Bass with Cilantro-Onion Salad
And we mean an abundance of cilantro and onion: This dish has a wonderful, summery wallop.

Starting the fish skin sides down in the skillet creates crisp skin you'll want to eat. Hands-on time: 10 min. Total time: 20 min.

3	tablespoons fresh lime juice, divided
3	tablespoons plain 2% reduced-fat Greek yogurt
1	tablespoon water
¾	teaspoon salt, divided
1	ripe peeled avocado
3	tablespoons extra-virgin olive oil, divided
4	(6-ounce) wild or farmed striped bass fillets
½	teaspoon freshly ground black pepper
3	cups loosely packed cilantro leaves (about 1 bunch)
2	cups thinly sliced onion
	Chipotle hot pepper sauce (optional)

1. Preheat oven to 400°.

2. Combine 2 tablespoons lime juice, yogurt, 1 tablespoon water, ¼ teaspoon salt, and avocado in a small bowl; mash with a fork until smooth.

3. Heat a large ovenproof skillet over high heat. Add 1½ tablespoons oil to pan; swirl to coat. Sprinkle fish with remaining ½ teaspoon salt and black pepper. Add fish to pan, skin sides down, and cook 2 minutes or until lightly browned. Place pan in oven; cook at 400° for 8 minutes or until fish flakes easily when tested with a fork.

4. Combine remaining 1 tablespoon lime juice and remaining 1½ tablespoons olive oil in a medium bowl, stirring with a whisk. Add cilantro and onion; toss gently to coat. Spoon about 3 tablespoons avocado mixture on each of 4 plates. Top each serving with 1 fillet and ½ cup salad. Serve with hot sauce, if desired.

Serves 4.

CALORIES 372; FAT 21.7g (sat 3.5g, mono 13.4g, poly 3.3g); PROTEIN 32.1g; CARB 13.4g; FIBER 4.9g; CHOL 132mg; IRON 1.9mg; SODIUM 567mg; CALC 63mg

SUSTAINABILITY NOTE

Striped Bass: You have the option of purchasing farmed or wild-caught striped bass: Both are sustainable choices. Wild fish have a more assertive flavor, while farmed fish are milder and more widely available. If cost is a concern, opt for the less expensive of the two. Other common market names for this fish include rockfish and striper.

Grilled Tilapia with Smoked Paprika and Parmesan Polenta

This fish is like the chicken breast of the sea: an American favorite. It's lean, mild, and pleasantly firm.

Creamy polenta complements spice-rubbed fish. Cooking polenta in milk and cheese enriches it with both flavor and calcium. Hands-on time: 15 min. Total time: 30 min.

Polenta:

- 4 cups fat-free milk
- 1 cup quick-cooking polenta
- ¼ teaspoon salt
- ⅓ cup (1½ ounces) grated Parmesan cheese

Fish:

- 1½ tablespoons olive oil
- 1 teaspoon smoked paprika
- ½ teaspoon garlic powder
- ¼ teaspoon salt
- ¼ teaspoon freshly ground black pepper
- 4 (6-ounce) tilapia fillets

Cooking spray

1. To prepare polenta, bring milk to a boil in a medium saucepan; gradually add polenta, stirring constantly with a whisk. Reduce heat, and cook 5 minutes or until thick, stirring constantly; stir in ¼ teaspoon salt. Remove from heat. Stir in cheese; cover and keep warm.

2. To prepare fish, heat a large grill pan over medium-high heat. Combine oil and next 4 ingredients (through black pepper) in a bowl, stirring well. Rub fish evenly with oil mixture. Coat pan with cooking spray. Add fish to pan, and cook 4 minutes on each side or until fish flakes easily when tested with a fork.

Serves 4 (serving size: 1 fillet and 1 cup polenta).

CALORIES 464; FAT 10.5g (sat 3.4g, mono 5.4g, poly 1.3g); PROTEIN 48.4g; CARB 34.1g; FIBER 4.1g; CHOL 95mg; IRON 1.2mg; SODIUM 626mg; CALC 418mg

Wine Pairing

A rich and creamy California chardonnay highlights the cheesy polenta and stands up to the smoky spices without overpowering the mild tilapia.

Blackened Tilapia Baja Tacos

Every cook needs a fish taco in her repertoire; it's one of the world's finest fast foods.

We ditched the fried fish commonly used by those irresistible food trucks and loaded on onion relish to make up some crunch. Shrimp would be a good sub for fish. Hands-on time: 20 min. Total time: 20 min.

¼ cup reduced-fat sour cream

2 tablespoons chopped fresh cilantro

2 tablespoons fresh lime juice

1 jalapeño pepper, seeded and chopped

1 cup thinly sliced white onion

1½ teaspoons paprika

1½ teaspoons brown sugar

1 teaspoon dried oregano

¾ teaspoon garlic powder

½ teaspoon salt

½ teaspoon ground cumin

¼ teaspoon ground red pepper

1 tablespoon canola oil

4 (6-ounce) tilapia fillets

8 (6-inch) corn tortillas

½ ripe peeled avocado, thinly sliced

4 lime wedges

1. Place first 4 ingredients in a food processor; process until smooth. Combine sour cream mixture and onion in a small bowl.

2. Combine paprika and next 6 ingredients (through ground red pepper); sprinkle evenly over fish. Heat a large cast-iron skillet over medium-high heat. Add oil to pan; swirl to coat. Add fish to pan, and cook 3 minutes on each side or until fish flakes easily when tested with a fork.

3. Warm tortillas according to package directions. Divide fish, onion mixture, and avocado evenly among tortillas. Serve with lime wedges.

Serves 4 (serving size: 2 tacos and 1 lime wedge).

CALORIES 362; FAT 13.6g (sat 3.1g, mono 6.4g, poly 2.8g); PROTEIN 37g; CARB 27.1g; FIBER 4.9g; CHOL 79mg; IRON 1.5mg; SODIUM 388mg; CALC 74mg

SUSTAINABILITY NOTE

Tilapia: Avoid fillets from China or Taiwan, which are typically sold frozen. Tilapia is usually farmed, and the practices vary and impact sustainability. Although not abundant, U.S.-farmed tilapia is the best sustainable option. Central and South American fish are the next best alternative.

Pecan-Crusted Trout

Panko is our go-to breading for light crunch. The ground nuts enrich the coating here.

And, of course, pecans and trout are a classic combination. But feel free to try with cod, halibut, or even catfish. Hands-on time: 7 min. Total time: 26 min.

¼ cup pecan halves

¼ cup panko (Japanese breadcrumbs)

1 tablespoon olive oil, divided

4 (6-ounce) rainbow trout fillets, halved

¼ teaspoon salt

¼ teaspoon freshly ground black pepper

1. Place pecans in a mini chopper or food processor; pulse until finely ground. Combine pecans and panko in a shallow dish.
2. Heat a large nonstick skillet over medium-high heat. Add 1½ teaspoons oil to pan; swirl to coat. Sprinkle fish evenly with salt and pepper. Dredge tops of fish in nut mixture, pressing gently to adhere. Place half of fish, breading sides down, in pan; cook 4 minutes or until browned. Turn fish over; cook 4 minutes or until fish flakes easily when tested with a fork. Remove fish from pan; cover and keep warm. Repeat procedure with remaining 1½ teaspoons oil and remaining fish.

Serves 4 (serving size: 2 fillet halves).

CALORIES 267; FAT 15.3g (sat 2.9g, mono 7.2g, poly 4.1g); PROTEIN 27.8g; CARB 3.5g; FIBER 0.8g; CHOL 75mg; IRON 0.6mg; SODIUM 203mg; CALC 91mg

Pan-Fried Trout with Tomato Basil Sauté

Here's one for company: Trout is such an elegant fish. Tomatoes take it into summer-comfort territory, too.

If you don't have pancetta, add prosciutto or bacon. Hands-on time: 10 min. Total time: 22 min.

2 ounces chopped pancetta

2 cups cherry tomatoes, halved

1 teaspoon minced garlic

1 teaspoon freshly ground black pepper, divided

½ teaspoon salt, divided

¼ cup small basil leaves

1 tablespoon canola oil, divided

4 (6-ounce) trout fillets

4 lemon wedges

1. Heat a medium skillet over low heat. Add pancetta to pan; cook 4 minutes or just until pancetta begins to brown. Add tomatoes, garlic, ½ teaspoon pepper, and ⅛ teaspoon salt; cook 3 minutes or until tomatoes begin to soften. Remove from heat, and stir in basil leaves.
2. Heat a large nonstick skillet over medium-high heat. Add 1½ teaspoons oil to pan; swirl to coat. Sprinkle fish evenly with remaining ½ teaspoon pepper and remaining ⅜ teaspoon salt. Add 2 fillets to pan; cook 2 minutes on each side or until fish flakes easily when tested with a fork. Remove fish from pan; keep warm. Repeat procedure with remaining 1½ teaspoons oil and remaining 2 fillets. Top fish with tomato mixture. Serve with lemon wedges.

Serves 4 (serving size: 1 fillet, about ⅓ cup sauce, and 1 lemon wedge).

CALORIES 388; FAT 20.5g (sat 5.9g, mono 7.9g, poly 5.5g); PROTEIN 44.3g; CARB 4.3g; FIBER 1.3g; CHOL 126mg; IRON 1.1mg; SODIUM 604mg; CALC 169mg

Quick Paella-Style Rice

We're not going to offend the purists by claiming this is a full-bore paella, but it's a shockingly quick way to get a good dose of that paella pleasure.

Many convenience items pack on the salt, but here we use no-salt-added tomatoes, frozen edamame, and boil-in-bag rice to keep the sodium low. Hands-on time: 15 min. Total time: 29 min.

1	tablespoon olive oil
6	ounces Spanish chorizo, thinly sliced
2	(3½-ounce) packages boil-in-bag brown rice
½	teaspoon hot smoked paprika
⅜	teaspoon salt
¼	teaspoon freshly ground black pepper
1½	cups water
1	(14.5-ounce) can no-salt-added diced tomatoes, undrained
1½	cups frozen shelled edamame
2	dozen mussels, scrubbed and debearded

1. Heat a Dutch oven over medium-high heat. Add oil to pan; swirl to coat. Add chorizo to pan; sauté 1 minute or until lightly browned, stirring occasionally. Remove rice from bags. Add rice to pan; sauté 1 minute, stirring frequently. Stir in paprika, salt, and pepper; sauté 30 seconds. Add 1½ cups water and tomatoes; bring to a boil. Cover, reduce heat to medium, and simmer 10 minutes or until rice is tender and liquid is almost absorbed.

2. Stir in edamame. Nestle mussels into rice mixture. Cover and cook 4 minutes or until mussels open and liquid is absorbed. Remove from heat. Discard any unopened shells.

Serves 4 (serving size: 2 cups).

CALORIES 542; FAT 21g (sat 5.1g, mono 9g, poly 4.2g); PROTEIN 33.8g; CARB 55.6g; FIBER 8.1g; CHOL 27mg; IRON 4.9mg; SODIUM 562mg; CALC 42mg

Wine Pairing

Like paella itself, rioja, a Spanish red wine, is spicy and complex, highlighting the chorizo and smoky spices. Alternatively, a simple, dry rosado is a classic match.

SUSTAINABILITY NOTE

Trout: Although some purists have concerns over the use of freshwater flow-through systems, U.S.-farmed rainbow trout, a mild freshwater fish, is sustainable. Steelhead trout is another ecofriendly choice of the same species. These pinkish-fleshed fish, similar to salmon, are found in both fresh and salt water.

Mussels: Like many other mollusks, mussels are a good sustainable choice. Most mussels are farmed in an environmentally responsible way, so they have healthy habitats and stocks.

Grilled Maine Lobsters

Lobster—one of the sweetest, richest seafoods—at its simplest.

You'll need someone with a big knife and strong arm to do the one-second mercy killing. The brief time on the grill allows for cooking the lobsters in batches until they are bright red with a few blackened spots. To check for doneness, break a lobster open where the tail and body meet—the meat should be opaque and white, not translucent. If not, return to the grill. Serve with Butter Sauce. Hands-on time: 17 min. Total time: 1 hr. 32 min.

8 (1⅛-pound) whole live lobsters

8 lemon wedges

1. Preheat grill to medium-high heat.

2. Plunge a heavy chef's knife through each lobster head just above the eyes, making sure the knife goes all the way through the head. Pull the knife in a downward motion between the eyes.

3. Place lobsters on grill rack; grill 6 minutes on each side or until done. Serve with lemon wedges.

Serves 8 (serving size: 1 lobster).

CALORIES 122; FAT 0.7g (sat 0.1g, mono 0.2g, poly 0.1g); PROTEIN 25.2g; CARB 2.2g; FIBER 0.2g; CHOL 88mg; IRON 0.5mg; SODIUM 466mg; CALC 77mg

Wine Pairing
Creamy, yeasty hefeweizen beer with a squeeze of lemon is light enough to play second fiddle to the fresh lobster, yet highlights its rich, buttery flavor.

BUTTER SAUCE

Just as oil mixes with vinegar to make vinaigrette, the butter combines with the lemon juice to create a thick, creamy consistency. The indulgent sauce is a perfect pairing with low-fat lobsters. The creamy emulsion stretches further than plain melted butter, so you can get by using less.

1 tablespoon fresh lemon juice

6 tablespoons chilled butter, cut into small pieces

Dash of ground red pepper

1. Heat lemon juice in a small saucepan over low heat. Gradually add pieces of butter, stirring constantly with a whisk until butter is melted and well blended. Stir in red pepper.

Serves 8 (serving size: about 1 tablespoon).

CALORIES 77; FAT 8.6g (sat 5.5g, mono 2.2g, poly 0.3g); PROTEIN 0.1g; CARB 0.2g; FIBER 0g; CHOL 23mg; IRON 0mg; SODIUM 61mg; CALC 3mg

SUSTAINABILITY NOTE

Lobster: Opt for the species called "American lobster"—its population is well managed in Canada and the U.S. in the northeastern Atlantic states.

Curried Coconut Mussels

This Thai-themed dish uses ingredients found in most supermarkets to render it a weeknight treat.

It's a meal that begs for a good sauce-sopping bread. While most mussels are farm-raised and easy to clean, take time to rinse them under cold running water, and be sure to remove any beards (the tough, stringy black fibers). Hands-on time: 20 min. Total time: 25 min.

1 tablespoon olive oil

2 cups chopped onion

1 tablespoon finely chopped peeled fresh ginger

2 garlic cloves, minced

1 jalapeño pepper, chopped

2 teaspoons red curry paste

1 cup light coconut milk

½ cup dry white wine

1 teaspoon dark brown sugar

¼ teaspoon kosher salt

2 pounds small mussels (about 60), scrubbed and debearded

¾ cup small basil leaves, divided

3 tablespoons fresh lime juice

4 lime wedges

1. Heat a large Dutch oven over medium-high heat. Add oil to pan; swirl to coat. Add onion, ginger, garlic, and jalapeño; sauté 3 minutes, stirring frequently. Stir in curry paste; cook 30 seconds, stirring constantly. Add coconut milk and next 3 ingredients (through salt); bring to a boil. Cook 2 minutes. Stir in mussels; cover and cook 5 minutes or until mussels open. Discard any unopened shells. Stir in ½ cup basil and juice. Divide mussels mixture evenly among 4 bowls, and spoon coconut mixture evenly over mussels. Sprinkle each serving with 1 tablespoon remaining basil; serve with lime wedges.

Serves 4 (serving size: about 15 mussels, about ½ cup coconut mixture, 1 tablespoon basil, and 1 lime wedge).

CALORIES 241; FAT 9.9g (sat 4g, mono 3.2g, poly 1.3g); PROTEIN 20g; CARB 19.1g; FIBER 1.7g; CHOL 42mg; IRON 6.8mg; SODIUM 594mg; CALC 80mg

Beer Pairing

A slightly sweet, malty English brown ale helps cut the heat in this dish, but isn't so dark that it overpowers the delicate mussel flavor.

GLOBAL FLAVORS

Red Curry Paste: We use this as a flavor base in many Southeast Asian recipes. It provides heat from dried red chiles, along with numerous spices and aromatics, including lemongrass, ginger, onion, garlic, shrimp paste, and cumin.

Quick Steamed Clams with White Wine and Tomatoes

Deploying the microwave jump-starts the wine-broth process and helps cut cooking time to less than 20 minutes.

Cook clams within 24 hours of purchasing in order to ensure freshness. Be sure to throw out any fresh clams that don't close their shells when tapped; after cooking, toss those whose shells don't open.
Hands-on time: 13 min. Total time: 19 min.

4	(½-inch-thick) slices diagonally cut French bread baguette
1½	cups dry white wine
½	cup fat-free, lower-sodium chicken broth
¼	teaspoon freshly ground black pepper
1	(14.5-ounce) can diced tomatoes, undrained
1	teaspoon olive oil
½	cup prechopped onion
1	teaspoon chopped fresh oregano
1	teaspoon chopped fresh rosemary
1	teaspoon chopped fresh thyme
48	littleneck clams in shells (about 3 pounds), scrubbed
1	tablespoon chopped fresh parsley

1. Preheat broiler.

2. Arrange bread slices on a baking sheet. Broil 5 inches from heat 2 minutes or until toasted.

3. Combine white wine and next 3 ingredients (through tomatoes) in a microwave-safe bowl. Microwave at HIGH 1 minute. Heat a Dutch oven over medium-high heat. Add oil to pan; swirl to coat. Add onion and next 3 ingredients (through thyme); sauté 2 minutes. Add wine mixture to pan; bring to a boil. Stir in clams; cover and cook 5 minutes or until clams open. Discard any unopened shells. Top with parsley, and serve with toasted bread.

Serves 4 (serving size: about ⅓ cup broth, 12 clams, and 1 toast slice).

CALORIES 237; FAT 2.8g (sat 0.4g, mono 1g, poly 0.6g); PROTEIN 17.8g; CARB 27.2g; FIBER 3.1g; CHOL 34mg; IRON 17.2mg; SODIUM 457mg; CALC 98mg

Seared Scallops with Lemony Sweet Pea Relish

The whole trick to the divine caramelized crust on the scallops is giving the shellfish plenty of room in a very hot pan.

For tips on getting the perfect sear on your scallops, see page 128. Hands-on time: 30 min. Total time: 30 min.

1	quart water
1	cup shelled fresh English peas
1½	teaspoons salt, divided
¼	cup extra-virgin olive oil, divided
¼	cup minced shallots
1½	teaspoons grated lemon rind
2	tablespoons fresh lemon juice
1	tablespoon chopped fresh flat-leaf parsley
½	teaspoon freshly ground black pepper, divided
2¼	pounds large sea scallops
1½	cups pea shoots
6	lemon wedges

1. Bring 1 quart water to a boil in a saucepan. Add peas and 1 teaspoon salt; cook 2 minutes. Drain and rinse with cold water; drain. Combine peas, 3 tablespoons oil, shallots, and next 3 ingredients (through parsley). Stir in ¼ teaspoon salt and ¼ teaspoon pepper; toss gently.

2. Heat a large cast-iron skillet over medium-high heat. Add 1½ teaspoons oil to pan; swirl to coat. Sprinkle remaining ¼ teaspoon salt and remaining ¼ teaspoon pepper over scallops. Add half of scallops to pan, and cook 2 minutes on each side or until done. Repeat procedure with remaining 1½ teaspoons oil and remaining scallops. Divide scallops evenly among 6 plates; top each serving with 2½ tablespoons pea mixture and ¼ cup pea shoots. Serve with lemon wedges.

Serves 6.

CALORIES 260; FAT 10.4g (sat 1.4g, mono 6.6g, poly 1.4g); PROTEIN 30.2g; CARB 10.6g; FIBER 1.5g; CHOL 56mg; IRON 1.1mg; SODIUM 513mg; CALC 53mg

SUSTAINABILITY NOTE

Clams: Fresh clams are a sustainable seafood.

Scallops: Diver-caught scallops are considered best of the large variety (because other large scallops are dredged, harming the ocean floor), while most bay scallops, the small kind, are raised by low-impact ocean farming methods and considered a good choice.

Seared Scallops with Cauliflower Puree

We love discovering a new flavor pairing, such as that of the scallop with the gnarly cauliflower: sweet of the sea, sweet of the earth.

See the technique below to get maxiumum crispness on your scallops. Hands-on time: 10 min. Total time: 24 min.

2 cups chopped cauliflower florets

1 cup cubed peeled Yukon gold potato

1 cup water

½ cup fat-free, lower-sodium chicken broth

1 tablespoon canola oil

1½ pounds sea scallops

¾ teaspoon kosher salt, divided

½ teaspoon coarsely ground black pepper

1½ tablespoons unsalted butter

⅛ teaspoon crushed red pepper

1. Place first 4 ingredients in a saucepan; bring to a boil. Cover, reduce heat, and simmer 6 minutes or until potato is tender. Remove from heat. Let stand, uncovered, 10 minutes.

2. Heat a large skillet over high heat. Add oil to pan; swirl to coat. Pat scallops dry with paper towels; sprinkle with ¼ teaspoon salt and black pepper. Add scallops to pan, and cook 3 minutes on each side or until done. Remove scallops from pan.

3. Pour cauliflower mixture into a blender. Add remaining ½ teaspoon salt, butter, and red pepper. Remove center piece of blender lid (to allow steam to escape); secure lid on blender. Place a clean towel over opening in lid (to avoid splatters). Blend until smooth. Serve puree with scallops.

Serves 4 (serving size: about 4 scallops and ½ cup puree).

CALORIES 232; fat 8.9g (sat 3.1g, mono 3.4g, poly 1.5g); PROTEIN 23.8g; CARB 13g; fiber 2g; CHOL 54mg; IRON 1.1mg; SODIUM 632mg; CALC 46mg

TECHNIQUE
....

Perfectly Seared Scallops: The inexperienced or hurried cook will barely heat the pan before adding oil and placing the scallops in the pan for a sear. Next comes … nothing. Silence. No sizzle. A hot pan is essential for searing scallops (and sautéing vegetables or creating a great crust on meat, fish, and poultry). It also helps prevent food from sticking. And be sure to add the oil when the pan is hot, just before adding the scallops. Otherwise, it will smoke, and that's bad for the oil. Patting the scallops dry before cooking also helps ensure a great seared crust.

Gnocchi with Shrimp, Asparagus, and Pesto

One pot, one food processor, 20 minutes: This is weeknight pizzazz at its best.

Mince the garlic and shred the Parm while the gnocchi and shrimp cook. Hands-on time: 20 min. Total time: 20 min.

2 quarts plus 1 tablespoon water, divided

1 (16-ounce) package vacuum-packed gnocchi

4 cups (1-inch) slices asparagus (about 1 pound)

1 pound peeled and deveined large shrimp, coarsely chopped

1 cup basil leaves

2 tablespoons pine nuts, toasted

2 tablespoons grated fresh Parmesan cheese

2 teaspoons fresh lemon juice

2 teaspoons bottled minced garlic

4 teaspoons extra-virgin olive oil

1. Bring 2 quarts water to a boil in a Dutch oven. Add gnocchi to pan; cook 4 minutes or until done (gnocchi will rise to surface). Remove gnocchi with a slotted spoon; place in a large bowl. Add asparagus and shrimp to pan; cook 5 minutes or until shrimp are done. Drain. Add shrimp mixture to gnocchi.

2. Place remaining 1 tablespoon water, basil, and next 4 ingredients (through garlic) in a food pro-cessor; process until smooth, scraping sides. Drizzle oil through food chute with food processor on; process until well blended. Add basil mixture to shrimp mixture; toss to coat. Serve immediately.

Serves 4 (serving size: 2 cups).

CALORIES 355; FAT 9.3g (sat 1.6g, mono 4.5g, poly 2.5g); PROTEIN 26.5g; CARB 42.7g; FIBER 3g; CHOL 170mg; IRON 5.7mg; SODIUM 747mg; CALC 108mg

Baked Shrimp with Feta

Quick, tangy, great with orzo.

Hands-on time: 14 min. Total time: 35 min.

1 tablespoon fresh lemon juice

1½ pounds large shrimp, peeled and deveined

1 teaspoon olive oil

½ cup chopped onion

1 garlic clove, minced

2 tablespoons bottled clam juice

1 tablespoon white wine

½ teaspoon dried oregano

¼ teaspoon freshly ground black pepper

1 (14.5-ounce) can diced tomatoes, drained

Cooking spray

½ cup (2 ounces) crumbled feta cheese

2 tablespoons chopped fresh flat-leaf parsley

1. Preheat oven to 450°.
2. Combine lemon juice and shrimp in a large bowl; toss well. Heat a large nonstick skillet over medium-high heat. Add oil to pan; swirl to coat. Add onion to pan; sauté 1 minute, stirring constantly. Add garlic; sauté 1 minute, stirring constantly. Add clam juice and next 4 ingredients (through tomatoes); bring to a boil. Reduce heat, and simmer 5 minutes. Stir in shrimp mixture. Place mixture in an 11 x 7-inch glass or ceramic baking dish coated with cooking spray. Sprinkle cheese evenly over mixture. Bake at 450° for 12 minutes or until shrimp are done and cheese melts. Sprinkle with parsley; serve immediately.

Serves 4 (serving size: 1 cup).

CALORIES 253; FAT 7.1g (sat 2.8g, mono 1.9g, poly 1.4g); PROTEIN 37.5g; CARB 8.1g; FIBER 1.6g; CHOL 271mg; IRON 4.7mg; SODIUM 516mg; CALC 182mg

Seafood Risotto

A dinner for two that needs just salad, bread, and a crisp white wine.

Bay scallops are those tiny scallops that, when absolutely fresh, can be so sweet. They're good here because you're not looking for the classic brown sear, as you would with large sea scallops. Instead, you want soft, tender tidbits that cook gently in the risotto. Hands-on time: 29 min. Total time: 37 min.

- 2 cups fat-free, lower-sodium chicken broth
- 1 (8-ounce) bottle clam juice
- 2 teaspoons butter
- ¼ cup chopped shallots
- ½ cup uncooked Arborio rice
- ⅛ teaspoon saffron threads, crushed
- 1 tablespoon fresh lemon juice
- ½ cup grape tomatoes, halved
- 4 ounces medium shrimp, peeled and deveined
- 4 ounces bay scallops
- 2 tablespoons whipping cream

Chopped fresh parsley (optional)

1. Bring broth and clam juice to a simmer in a medium saucepan (do not boil). Keep warm over low heat.
2. Melt butter in a large saucepan over medium heat. Add shallots to pan; cook 2 minutes or until tender, stirring frequently. Add rice and saffron to pan; cook 30 seconds, stirring constantly. Add lemon juice to pan; cook 15 seconds, stirring constantly. Stir in ½ cup hot broth mixture; cook 2 minutes or until liquid is nearly absorbed, stirring constantly. Add remaining broth mixture, ½ cup at a time, stirring constantly until each portion of broth is absorbed before adding the next (about 18 minutes total).
3. Stir in tomatoes; cook 1 minute. Stir in shrimp and scallops; cook 4 minutes or until shrimp and scallops are done, stirring occasionally. Remove from heat; stir in cream. Sprinkle with parsley, if desired.

Serves 2 (serving size: about 1¼ cups).

CALORIES 400; FAT 10.1g (sat 4.9g, mono 2.6g, poly 1.1g); PROTEIN 30.2g; CARB 49.1g; FIBER 2.6g; CHOL 118mg; IRON 2.8mg; SODIUM 520mg; CALC 89mg

GLOBAL FLAVORS

Saffron: The most expensive spice for a reason. The saffron threads are dried stigmas from a flower that contains only three, which must be hand picked. To release the flavor from the saffron threads, you need to soak them in liquid. The intense flavor and aroma goes a long way, and you can get too much of a good thing; it leaves a medicinal taste if you add too much.

Spicy Shrimp and Grits

Our speedy weeknight version of the Southern favorite.

Pour the bacon drippings into a cup; measure 2 teaspoons and pour back into pan to cook shrimp. This recipe offers options for how to spice up the dish: Use hot pepper sauce for bright, vinegary heat, or chipotle chiles for a fruity, smoky burn. Hands-on time: 18 min. Total time: 20 min.

- 3 cups low-fat milk
- 1 cup water
- 1 tablespoon butter
- ¼ teaspoon black pepper, divided
- ⅛ teaspoon salt, divided
- 1 cup uncooked quick-cooking grits
- ½ cup (2 ounces) grated fresh Parmesan cheese
- 4 applewood-smoked bacon slices
- 1 pound peeled, deveined large shrimp
- 1 cup thinly vertically sliced white onion
- 2 cups grape tomatoes, halved
- 1 teaspoon hot pepper sauce or chopped chipotle chile, canned in adobo sauce
- ⅛ teaspoon ground or crushed red pepper
- ¼ cup green onion strips

1. Combine milk, 1 cup water, butter, ⅛ teaspoon black pepper, and dash of salt in a saucepan over medium-high heat. Bring to a simmer; gradually add grits, stirring constantly with a whisk. Reduce heat to medium; cook 4 minutes or until thick, stirring occasionally. Remove from heat; stir in cheese.
2. While grits cook, cook bacon in a large nonstick skillet over medium heat until crisp. Remove bacon from pan, reserving 2 teaspoons drippings; crumble bacon. Add shrimp to drippings in pan; cook 2 minutes on each side or until done. Remove shrimp from pan.

Add white onion to pan; sauté 1 minute. Stir in bacon, tomatoes, remaining ⅛ teaspoon black pepper, and remaining dash of salt; sauté 2 minutes, stirring occasionally. Add shrimp, pepper sauce, and red pepper; cook 1 minute or until shrimp are heated. Serve over grits; sprinkle with green onions.

Serves 4 (serving size: 1 cup grits, about 1½ cups shrimp mixture, and 1 tablespoon green onions).

CALORIES 520; FAT 16.5g (sat 7.7g, mono 5.2g, poly 1.9g); PROTEIN 41.9g; CARB 50g; FIBER 2.5g; CHOL 210mg; IRON 5mg; SODIUM 778mg; CALC 474mg

Pan-Fried Shrimp with Creole Mayonnaise
Because everyone longs for a seafood basket every once in a while, without the day's worth of fat you get at the fish shack.

Add more hot sauce to the mayo if your family likes fire. Serve with cucumber-tomato salad, coleslaw, or oven-baked fries. Hands-on time: 14 min. Total time: 18 min.

½　cup all-purpose flour

1¼　teaspoons salt-free Creole seasoning, divided

⅛　teaspoon salt

¼　cup fat-free milk

¾　cup dry breadcrumbs

1½　pounds peeled and deveined large shrimp

3　tablespoons olive oil, divided

2　tablespoons canola mayonnaise

1　teaspoon Worcestershire sauce

¼　teaspoon hot sauce

1. Combine flour, 1 teaspoon Creole seasoning, and salt in a shallow dish. Pour milk into a shallow dish. Place breadcrumbs in a shallow dish. Dredge shrimp in flour mixture; dip in milk. Dredge shrimp in breadcrumbs; shake off excess breading.

2. Heat a large nonstick skillet over medium-high heat. Add 1½ tablespoons oil to pan; swirl to coat. Add half of shrimp; cook 2 minutes on each side or until done. Repeat procedure with remaining oil and remaining shrimp.

3. Combine mayonnaise, remaining ¼ teaspoon Creole seasoning, Worcestershire, and hot sauce in a small bowl, stirring with a whisk. Serve Creole mayonnaise with shrimp.

Serves 4 (serving size: about 5 ounces shrimp and 2 teaspoons Creole mayonnaise).

CALORIES 427; FAT 19.5g (sat 2.5g, mono 11.3g, poly 4g); PROTEIN 38.4g; CARB 22g; FIBER 0.9g; CHOL 261mg; IRON 4.7mg; SODIUM 511mg; CALC 111mg

Lemon-Mint Bulgur Risotto with Garlic Shrimp

Proof that the risotto method works nicely with grains other than rice.

You may know chewy bulgur from tabbouleh, but when it's cooked like risotto, the whole grain releases starch and sticks together for something altogether different. Hands-on time: 28 min. Total time: 38 min.

3	cups water
¾	teaspoon salt, divided
2	tablespoons olive oil, divided
¾	cup finely chopped green onions
1	cup uncooked bulgur
4	cups torn spinach
⅓	cup chopped fresh mint
1	tablespoon grated lemon rind
2	tablespoons fresh lemon juice
4	garlic cloves, minced
¼	teaspoon freshly ground black pepper
1	pound medium shrimp, peeled and deveined

Lemon wedges (optional)

1. Combine 3 cups water and ½ teaspoon salt in a medium saucepan; bring to a simmer (do not boil). Keep warm over low heat.
2. Heat a medium sauté pan over medium heat. Add 1 tablespoon oil to pan; swirl to coat. Add green onions; cook 1 minute, stirring constantly. Add bulgur; cook 2 minutes, stirring constantly. Add warm salted water, ½ cup at a time, stirring frequently until each portion of warm salted water is absorbed before adding the next (about 20 minutes total). Remove from heat. Add spinach, mint, rind, and juice; stir until spinach wilts. Keep warm.

3. Heat a medium nonstick skillet over medium-high heat. Add remaining 1 tablespoon oil to pan; swirl to coat. Add garlic; sauté 30 seconds. Add remaining ¼ teaspoon salt, pepper, and shrimp; sauté 2 minutes or until shrimp are done. Divide risotto evenly among 4 small bowls or plates, and arrange shrimp evenly over risotto. Garnish with lemon wedges, if desired.

Serves 4 (serving size: about ¾ cup risotto and 3 ounces shrimp).

CALORIES 323; FAT 9.3g (sat 1.4g, mono 5.3g, poly 1.7g); PROTEIN 28.5g; CARB 32.5g; FIBER 8.3g; CHOL 172mg; IRON 4.9mg; SODIUM 650mg; CALC 130mg

4

FISH & SHELLFISH

TECHNIQUE

Peel and Devein Shrimp: For most, but not all, recipes, peel and devein shrimp before cooking them.

1. Peel off the outer shell, and, depending on the recipe, pull off the tail or leave it intact.

2. Using a paring knife, cut about ¼ inch deep along the outer edge of the shrimp's back.

3. Remove the vein that runs along the back using the tip of the knife.

Marinated Shrimp
We cooked this up as a fresh picnic starter.

But it's also a bright, light main dish. Be careful not to overcook the shrimp—you want them just barely done so they won't become tough as they marinate. You can reserve some of the feathery fennel fronds for a pretty garnish. Hands-on time: 40 min. Total time: 8 hr. 43 min.

3	pounds large shrimp, unpeeled
3	quarts water
1	cup (3-inch) julienne-cut yellow bell pepper
1	cup thinly sliced fennel bulb
⅔	cup thinly sliced shallots
3	garlic cloves, thinly sliced
1	teaspoon grated lemon rind
½	cup fresh lemon juice
1	teaspoon kosher salt
1	teaspoon mustard seeds
1	teaspoon fennel seeds
½	teaspoon sugar
½	teaspoon crushed red pepper
⅓	cup extra-virgin olive oil
4	bay leaves

1. Peel and devein shrimp, leaving tails intact; discard shells.
2. Bring 3 quarts water to a boil in a Dutch oven. Add shrimp; cook 3 minutes or just until shrimp turn pink. Drain and rinse with cold water; drain. Place shrimp in a large bowl. Add bell pepper, fennel bulb, shallots, and garlic; toss to combine.
3. Combine rind and next 6 ingredients (through red pepper) in a medium bowl, stirring with a whisk. Gradually add oil, stirring constantly with a whisk. Stir in bay leaves. Combine oil mixture and shrimp mixture in a large zip-top plastic bag; toss well to coat. Seal and marinate in refrigerator at least 8 hours or up to 24 hours, turning bag occasionally. Discard bay leaves.

Serves 8 (serving size: about 1½ cups).

CALORIES 289; FAT 12.2g (sat 1.8g, mono 7.1g, poly 2.1g); PROTEIN 35.5g; CARB 8.2g; FIBER 1.1g; CHOL 259mg; IRON 4.6mg; SODIUM 501mg; CALC 109mg

Wine Pairing
This bright, tangy dish deserves an equally bright and light summery wine. Spanish albariño is a refreshing summer seafood classic. Look for a screw-cap to take on your picnic.

SUSTAINABILITY NOTE
Shrimp: Look for the Marine Stewardship Council stamp to ensure you're making an ecofriendly choice. U.S.-farmed shrimp or wild northern shrimp from Canada are the best options. Avoid other imported wild and farmed species.

Lemongrass and Garlic Shrimp
Like the best street food skewers, from your own backyard. Make sure the grill is very hot.

Look for lemongrass in Asian markets and many grocery stores; it's like a reedy, super-fragrant first cousin to lemon peel. Substitute 1 teaspoon grated lemon rind for the lemongrass in a pinch.
Hands-on time: 12 min. Total time: 59 min.

¼ cup sugar

3 tablespoons canola oil

2 tablespoons fish sauce

1 fresh lemongrass stalk, trimmed and coarsely chopped

1 large garlic clove, coarsely chopped

36 jumbo Tiger shrimp, peeled and deveined (about 2 pounds)

1. Place first 5 ingredients in a food processor or mini chopper; process until lemongrass is finely chopped. Transfer sugar mixture to a large zip-top plastic bag. Add shrimp; seal and marinate in refrigerator 45 minutes.
2. Preheat grill to high heat.

3. Remove shrimp from bag; discard marinade. Thread 6 shrimp onto each of 6 (12-inch) skewers. Place skewers on grill rack; grill 2 minutes on each side or until done.

Serves 4 (serving size: 9 shrimp).

CALORIES 314; FAT 9.2g (sat 1.1g, mono 3.7g, poly 3.1g); PROTEIN 46.4g; CARB 9g; FIBER 0g; CHOL 345mg; IRON 5.6mg; SODIUM 621mg; CALC 120mg

TECHNIQUE

How to Chop Lemongrass: The citrusy and floral qualities in lemongrass are hidden under the tough outer layer.

1. Trim the top reedy section and root end of the lemongrass.

2. Peel and discard the tough and dry outer layers.

3. To release aromatic oils, place the flat side of the knife against the stalk; pound the knife.

4. Chop or mince trimmed and pounded lemongrass stalk, depending on the recipe.

Crab Eggs Benedict

A mock hollandaise sauce, made from mayonnaise and buttermilk, replaces the traditional clarified butter.

Big chunks of sweet lump crabmeat drenched in creamy egg yolk are a welcome, fancier change from the traditional Canadian bacon. Serve with steamed asparagus. Hands-on time: 15 min. Total time: 21 min.

⅓ cup low-fat buttermilk

⅓ cup canola mayonnaise

½ teaspoon grated lemon rind

1 tablespoon fresh lemon juice

1½ teaspoons Dijon mustard

¼ teaspoon freshly ground black pepper

1½ teaspoons butter

1 tablespoon white wine vinegar

8 large eggs

4 English muffins, halved and toasted

8 ounces fresh lump crabmeat, shell pieces removed

Cracked black pepper

2 tablespoons chopped fresh chives (optional)

1 tablespoon chopped fresh tarragon (optional)

1. Combine first 6 ingredients in a small saucepan over low heat, stirring well with a whisk. Add butter; stir until butter melts. Keep warm.

2. Add water to a large skillet, filling two-thirds full. Bring to a boil; reduce heat, and simmer. Add 1 tablespoon vinegar. Break each egg into a custard cup, and pour gently into pan. Cook 3 minutes or until desired degree of doneness.

Place 1 muffin, cut sides up, on each of 4 plates, and divide crab among muffins. Remove eggs from pan using a slotted spoon. Gently place 1 egg on each muffin half. Top each serving with about 3 tablespoons sauce. Sprinkle with cracked pepper. Garnish with chives and tarragon, if desired.

Serves 4.

CALORIES 503; FAT 28.2g (sat 5.7g, mono 12.4g, poly 5.7g); PROTEIN 32.1g; CARB 29.5g; FIBER 1.9g; CHOL 478mg; IRON 4.8mg; SODIUM 711mg; CALC 127mg

Crab Cakes with Spicy Rémoulade

Crab cake lovers are fierce about the ratio of crab to filler. Our light cakes put the crab forward—and lose calories and fat—by using just enough mayo and breadcrumbs to hold the mixture together.

Plus, we skip the deep-fryer and sauté in oil to ensure crunch. For a milder rémoulade, omit the ground red pepper. An arugula or baby greens salad with a simple olive oil-lemon dressing is a nice accompaniment.
Hands-on time: 20 min. Total time: 20 min.

Crab cakes:

- 1 pound jumbo lump crabmeat, shell pieces removed
- 2 tablespoons finely chopped green bell pepper
- 1½ tablespoons canola mayonnaise
- ¼ teaspoon freshly ground black pepper
- 2 green onions, finely chopped (about ¼ cup)
- 1 large egg, lightly beaten
- 1 cup panko (Japanese breadcrumbs), divided
- 2 tablespoons canola oil, divided

Rémoulade:

- ¼ cup canola mayonnaise
- 2 teaspoons minced shallots
- 1 teaspoon chopped fresh tarragon
- 1 teaspoon chopped fresh flat-leaf parsley
- 1½ teaspoons Dijon mustard
- ¾ teaspoon capers, chopped
- ¾ teaspoon white wine vinegar
- ¼ teaspoon ground red pepper

1. To prepare crab cakes, drain crabmeat on several layers of paper towels. Combine crabmeat, bell pepper, and next 4 ingredients (through egg) in a large bowl, stirring gently to combine. Stir in ¼ cup panko. Place remaining ¾ cup panko in a shallow dish.

2. Divide crab mixture into 8 equal portions. Shape 4 portions into ¾-inch-thick patties; dredge patties in panko. Heat a large nonstick skillet over medium-high heat. Add 1 tablespoon oil to pan; swirl to coat. Add dredged patties to pan; cook 3 minutes on each side or until golden. Remove from pan; keep warm. Repeat procedure with remaining crab mixture, panko, and oil.

3. To prepare rémoulade, combine ¼ cup mayonnaise and remaining ingredients in a small bowl. Serve rémoulade with crab cakes.

Serves 4 (serving size: 2 crab cakes and about 2 tablespoons sauce).

CALORIES 320; FAT 17g (sat 1.2g, mono 6.7g, poly 5g); PROTEIN 26.8g; CARB 11.7g; FIBER 0.9g; CHOL 166mg; IRON 1.5mg; SODIUM 555mg; CALC 133mg

SUSTAINABILITY NOTE

Crab: The crab population in U.S. waters on both coasts and in the Gulf of Mexico is healthy, making many varieties of this premium shellfish sustainable. Best choices include Dungeness crab from the Pacific Coast states and stone crab from the Atlantic and Gulf. American king crab is a good choice, but avoid imported king crab.

Chapter 9

Vegetarian

Entrées

5:
an

America was, from birth, a meat-centric country, though gardens thrived across the land and vegetable cookery is deeply rooted in our regional cuisines. Now we're in the blush of a deep love affair with the carrot, the beet, the bouquet of kale, and the heirloom tomato. Farmers' markets charge for earthy gems what we paid for prime beef not long ago. The crunchy-granola rep of vegetarianism has fallen away, as top-notch chefs work wonders with the fresh and the local. The evidence is deliciously simple: The more plants you eat, the healthier you're likely to be. Our vegetarian mains may include eggs and dairy.

Two Potato and Beet Hash with Poached Eggs and Greens

A beautiful dish of contrasts: Earthy-sweet hash pairs with bitter greens and rich eggs.

Hands-on time: 25 min. Total time: 54 min.

2 tablespoons extra-virgin olive oil, divided
1 cup finely chopped onion
2 cups cubed peeled Yukon gold potato (about ¾ pound)
2 cups cubed peeled sweet potato (about ¾ pound)
1 tablespoon chopped fresh sage, divided
3 garlic cloves, minced
1 cup cubed peeled cooked beets (about ½ pound)
½ teaspoon salt, divided
½ teaspoon black pepper, divided
5 teaspoons red wine vinegar, divided
4 large eggs
½ teaspoon Dijon mustard
6 cups torn frisée or curly endive

1. Heat a large nonstick skillet over medium-high heat. Add 1 tablespoon oil; swirl to coat. Add onion; sauté 5 minutes or until tender, stirring frequently. Add potatoes, 2 teaspoons sage, and garlic, and cook 25 minutes or until potatoes are tender, stirring occasionally. Stir in beets, ¼ teaspoon salt, and ¼ teaspoon pepper; cook 10 minutes, stirring occasionally.

2. Add water to a large skillet, filling two-thirds full. Bring to a boil; reduce heat, and simmer. Add 1 tablespoon vinegar. Break each egg into a custard cup, and pour gently into pan. Cook 3 minutes or until desired degree of doneness. Remove eggs from pan using a slotted spoon. Sprinkle ½ teaspoon sage evenly over eggs.

3. Combine remaining 1 tablespoon oil, 2 teaspoons vinegar, ¼ teaspoon salt, ¼ teaspoon pepper, ½ teaspoon sage, and mustard in a large bowl, stirring with a whisk. Add frisée; toss to coat. Serve with hash and eggs.

Serves 4 (serving size: about 1 cup hash, 1 poached egg, and about 1½ cups frisée).

CALORIES 329; FAT 11.5g (sat 2.3g, mono 6.9g, poly 1.9g); PROTEIN 11.7g; CARB 45.5g; FIBER 8.1g; CHOL 180mg; IRON 3.6mg; SODIUM 472mg; CALC 124mg

Vegetarian Moussaka

Chewy bulgur stands in for meat, but the soul of the classic remains. Heady spices reign over tangy tomatoes and a smooth white sauce.

Tastes great, more filling: The eggplant and bulgur pack this dish with fiber. Hands-on time: 37 min. Total time: 1 hr. 42 min.

3   peeled eggplants, cut into ½-inch-thick slices (about 2½ pounds)

2   tablespoons extra-virgin olive oil, divided

Cooking spray

2   cups chopped onion

4   garlic cloves, minced

½   cup uncooked bulgur

¼   teaspoon ground allspice

¼   teaspoon ground cinnamon

⅛   teaspoon ground cloves

2   cups organic vegetable broth

2   teaspoons chopped fresh oregano

1   (14.5-ounce) can no-salt-added diced tomatoes, undrained

1   tablespoon butter

2   tablespoons all-purpose flour

1   cup 1% low-fat milk

2   tablespoons finely grated fresh Romano cheese

¼   teaspoon salt

1   large egg, lightly beaten

1. Preheat broiler.

2. Brush eggplant slices with 1 tablespoon oil. Place half of eggplant on a foil-lined baking sheet coated with cooking spray; broil 5 inches from heat for 5 minutes on each side or until browned. Repeat procedure with remaining eggplant. Set eggplant aside.

3. Heat a large skillet over medium-high heat. Add remaining 1 tablespoon oil to pan; swirl to coat. Add chopped onion to pan; sauté 8 minutes, stirring frequently. Add garlic; sauté 1 minute. Add bulgur; cook 3 minutes or until bulgur is lightly toasted, stirring frequently. Add allspice, cinnamon, and cloves; cook 1 minute, stirring constantly. Stir in broth, oregano, and tomatoes. Bring to a boil; reduce heat, and simmer 20 minutes or until thick, stirring occasionally.

4. Melt butter in a saucepan over medium heat. Add flour; cook 1 minute, stirring constantly with a whisk until well blended. Gradually add milk, stirring constantly with a whisk. Bring to a boil; reduce heat to medium-low, and simmer 5 minutes or until thick, stirring frequently. Stir in cheese and salt. Remove from heat, and cool slightly. Add egg, stirring well with a whisk.

5. Preheat oven to 350°.

6. Arrange half of eggplant in an 11 x 7-inch glass or ceramic baking dish coated with cooking spray. Spread bulgur mixture evenly over eggplant; arrange remaining eggplant over bulgur mixture. Top with milk mixture. Bake at 350° for 40 minutes; remove from oven. Increase oven temperature to 475°. Return dish to oven 4 minutes or until top is browned. Let stand 10 minutes before serving.

Serves 4.

CALORIES 343; FAT 13.1g (sat 4.2g, mono 6.4g, poly 1.3g); PROTEIN 11.4g; CARB 47.8g; FIBER 13.4g, CHOL 57mg; IRON 2.3mg; SODIUM 583mg; CALC 203mg

Cheesy Polenta with Mushroom Sauté

Each bite has you spooning through meaty mushrooms, then cracking that cheesy crust to reach velvety polenta.

While fontal or fontina cheese was our first choice, Parmesan or provolone is another option.

Hands-on time: 20 min. Total time: 20 min.

2	tablespoons olive oil
2	(4-ounce) packages exotic mushroom blend, chopped
1	(8-ounce) package presliced cremini mushrooms
1	teaspoon minced fresh thyme
½	teaspoon minced fresh oregano
3	garlic cloves, chopped
⅓	cup organic vegetable broth
2	teaspoons fresh lemon juice
⅛	teaspoon black pepper
2	cups 2% reduced-fat milk
1½	cups organic vegetable broth
¾	cup instant polenta
1	cup (4 ounces) shredded fontal or fontina cheese, divided
¼	teaspoon salt

1. Heat a large skillet over high heat. Add oil to pan; swirl to coat. Add mushrooms; sauté 4 minutes, stirring frequently. Add herbs and garlic; sauté 1 minute, stirring constantly. Stir in ⅓ cup broth, juice, and pepper.

2. Bring milk and 1½ cups broth to a boil. Stir in polenta; cook 4 minutes, stirring constantly. Stir in half of cheese and salt.

Divide polenta among 4 gratin dishes, and top with remaining cheese. Broil 5 minutes. Top each serving with ½ cup mushrooms.

Serves 4 (serving size: 1 gratin).

CALORIES 377; FAT 18g (sat 7.9g, mono 8.1g, poly 1.3g); PROTEIN 16.9g; CARB 30.5g; FIBER 4.6g; CHOL 42mg; IRON 1.2mg; SODIUM 710mg; CALC 322mg

Onion Tart 🌿

The essence of French onion soup in a flaky pastry shell.

Hands-on time: 19 min. Total time: 1 hr. 10 min.

1	tablespoon olive oil
2	tablespoons chopped fresh thyme
½	teaspoon kosher salt
¼	teaspoon black pepper
2½	pounds onion, sliced
½	(14.1-ounce) package refrigerated pie dough
¼	cup (1 ounce) crumbled reduced-fat feta cheese
¼	cup (1 ounce) shredded reduced-fat Swiss cheese
1	large egg, lightly beaten
2	tablespoons water

1. Preheat oven to 425°.

2. Heat a large nonstick skillet over medium-high heat. Add oil to pan; swirl to coat. Add thyme and next 3 ingredients (through onion), and cook 20 minutes, stirring occasionally.

3. Roll dough out on a parchment paper–lined baking sheet. Sprinkle feta cheese in center, leaving a 1½-inch border; top with onion mixture. Sprinkle with Swiss cheese. Fold piecrust border up and over onion mixture, pleating as you go, leaving a 6-inch-wide opening. Combine egg and 2 tablespoons water; brush over dough. Bake at 425° for 25 minutes or until golden. Cool 10 minutes.

Serves 4 (serving size: 1 wedge).

CALORIES 402; FAT 18.9g (sat 6.7g, mono 6.8g, poly 3.7g); PROTEIN 7.6g; CARB 51.4g; FIBER 5g; CHOL 13mg; IRON 0.8mg; SODIUM 606mg; CALC 146mg

Goat Cheese and Roasted Corn Quesadillas 🌿🌾

How do you make the basic quesadilla better? Start with corn tortillas for deeper flavor, then fill with caramelized corn and tangy goat cheese.

If you have fresh cilantro on hand, chop 2 tablespoons, and stir it into the salsa for a burst of extra flavor.
Hands-on time: 24 min. Total time: 24 min.

1	cup fresh corn kernels (about 1 large ear)
⅔	cup (5 ounces) goat cheese, softened
8	(6-inch) corn tortillas
¼	cup chopped green onions (about 1 green onion)
10	tablespoons bottled salsa verde, divided
1	tablespoon canola oil, divided

1. Heat a large nonstick skillet over medium-high heat. Add corn; sauté 2 minutes or until browned. Place corn in a small bowl. Add goat cheese to corn; stir until well blended. Divide corn mixture evenly among 4 tortillas; spread to within ¼ inch of sides. Sprinkle each tortilla with 1 tablespoon green onions. Drizzle each with 1½ teaspoons salsa; top with remaining 4 tortillas.

2. Heat pan over medium-high heat. Add 1½ teaspoons oil to pan; swirl to coat. Place 2 quesadillas in pan. Cook quesadillas 1½ minutes on each side or until golden. Remove from pan; keep warm. Wipe pan clean with paper towels. Repeat procedure with remaining oil and quesadillas. Cut each quesadilla into 4 wedges. Serve with remaining salsa.

Serves 4 (serving size: 4 wedges and 2 tablespoons salsa).

CALORIES 270; FAT 13.1g (sat 5.6g, mono 4.8g, poly 2.2g); PROTEIN 9.9g; CARB 28.6g; FIBER 3.2g; CHOL 16mg; IRON 1mg; SODIUM 435mg; CALC 75mg

Onion Tart

Artichoke and Goat Cheese Strata

The iconic make-ahead brunch casserole, reimagined with Provençal flavors.

Make-ahead instructions: Prepare through Step 2, cover, and chill. Before baking, let the bread mixture stand at room temperature 10 minutes while the oven preheats. Then assemble and bake. The cook time will increase by about 10 minutes. Garnish with parsley for a hit of vibrant green. Hands-on time: 21 min. Total time: 1 hr. 43 min.

1 teaspoon olive oil

½ cup finely chopped shallots (about 1 large)

1 (10-ounce) package frozen artichoke hearts, thawed

2 garlic cloves, minced

½ teaspoon dried herbes de Provence

1¾ cups 1% low-fat milk

½ teaspoon freshly ground black pepper

¼ teaspoon salt

4 large eggs

⅓ cup (about 1½ ounces) grated Parmigiano-Reggiano cheese

½ (1-pound) loaf country-style white bread, cut into 1-inch cubes (about 5 cups)

Cooking spray

¾ cup (3 ounces) crumbled goat cheese

1. Heat a large nonstick skillet over medium heat. Add oil to pan; swirl to coat. Add shallots; cook 2 minutes, stirring frequently. Stir in artichoke and garlic; cook 8 minutes or until artichoke begins to brown, stirring occasionally. Remove from heat; stir in herbes de Provence. Cool 10 minutes.

2. Combine milk and next 3 ingredients (through eggs) in a large bowl, stirring with a whisk. Add Parmigiano-Reggiano cheese and bread; toss gently to combine. Stir in artichoke mixture; let stand 20 minutes.

3. Preheat oven to 375°.

4. Spoon half of bread mixture into a 2-quart glass or ceramic baking dish coated with cooking spray. Sprinkle with half of goat cheese; top with remaining bread mixture. Sprinkle with remaining half of goat cheese.

Bake at 375° for 50 minutes or until browned and bubbly.

Serves 6.

CALORIES 286; FAT 10.7g (sat 5.1g, mono 3.4g, poly 0.9g); PROTEIN 16.8g; CARB 31.1g; FIBER 2.7g; CHOL 139mg; IRON 2.5mg; SODIUM 561mg; CALC 272mg

Lentil-Barley Burgers with Fiery Fruit Salsa
A modern take on the veggie burger, no bun needed.

Fresh fruit, vegetables, barley, and lentils fill this hearty entrée with fiber. Pureed lentils bind the mixture, and whole lentils offer texture. Serve with lime wedges for added zest. Hands-on time: 33 min. Total time: 2 hr.

Salsa:

- ¼ cup finely chopped pineapple
- ¼ cup finely chopped mango
- ¼ cup finely chopped tomatillo
- ¼ cup halved grape tomatoes
- 1 tablespoon fresh lime juice
- 1 serrano chile, minced

Burgers:

- 1½ cups water
- ½ cup dried lentils
- 4 tablespoons canola oil, divided
- 1 cup chopped onion
- ¼ cup grated carrot
- 4 garlic cloves, minced
- 2 tablespoons tomato paste
- 1½ teaspoons ground cumin
- ¾ teaspoon dried oregano
- ½ teaspoon chili powder
- ¾ teaspoon salt, divided
- ¾ cup cooked pearl barley

- ½ cup panko (Japanese breadcrumbs)
- ¼ cup finely chopped fresh parsley
- ½ teaspoon coarsely ground black pepper
- 2 large egg whites
- 1 large egg

1. To prepare salsa, combine first 6 ingredients; cover and refrigerate.

2. To prepare burgers, combine 1½ cups water and lentils in a saucepan; bring to a boil. Cover, reduce heat, and simmer 25 minutes or until lentils are tender. Drain. Place half of lentils in a large bowl. Place remaining lentils in a food processor; process until smooth. Add processed lentils to whole lentils in bowl.

3. Heat a large nonstick skillet over medium-high heat. Add 1 tablespoon oil to pan; swirl to coat. Add onion and carrot; sauté 6 minutes or until tender, stirring occasionally. Add garlic; cook 1 minute, stirring constantly. Add tomato paste, cumin, oregano, chili powder, and ¼ teaspoon salt; cook 1 minute, stirring constantly. Add onion mixture to lentils. Add remaining ½ teaspoon salt, barley, and next 5 ingredients (through egg); stir well. Cover and refrigerate 1 hour or until firm.

4. Divide mixture into 8 portions, shaping each into a ½-inch-thick patty. Heat a large nonstick skillet over medium-high heat. Add 1½ tablespoons oil; swirl to coat. Add 4 patties; cook 3 minutes on each side or until browned. Repeat procedure with remaining 1½ tablespoons oil and 4 patties. Serve with salsa.

Serves 4 (serving size: 2 patties and ¼ cup salsa).

CALORIES 346; FAT 16.4g (sat 1.5g, mono 9.4g, poly 4.4g); PROTEIN 12.7g; CARB 39.4g; FIBER 9.5g; CHOL 53mg; IRON 3.9mg; SODIUM 538mg; CALC 61mg

5

VEGETARIAN ENTRÉES

NUTRITION MADE EASY

Lentils: Quick and easy to cook, these legumes have a mild, earthy flavor that serves as an almost blank canvas for seasonings. The beauty of the little lentil is there's no need to presoak, but do rinse and pick out stones before cooking. Brown lentils are the most common and quickest-cooking, but there are other varieties, including green ones that are slightly peppery, and yellow, red, or orange ones that break down to a soft, creamy consistency (they're often labeled "dal"). All pack in fiber, folic acid, and protein.

Spinach Pie with Goat Cheese, Raisins, and Pine Nuts 🌿
The pleasure of this dish—a twist on Greek spanakopita— is crunching through that fragile, super-crisp phyllo.

Working with phyllo causes many cooks stress, but no need. The key to paper-thin results is proper thawing, which means thinking ahead: Set a closed package of frozen phyllo dough in the refrigerator overnight, or ideally for 24 hours. To prevent opened dough from drying during the layering process, cover with wax paper and a damp towel. Hands-on time: 20 min. Total time: 2 hr. 10 min.

⅓ cup olive oil, divided

2 cups minced onion (about 1 large)

5 (9-ounce) packages fresh spinach

½ cup golden raisins

2 cups (8 ounces) crumbled goat cheese

⅓ cup pine nuts, toasted

½ teaspoon kosher salt

¼ teaspoon ground black pepper

12 sheets frozen phyllo dough, thawed

Cooking spray

1. Preheat oven to 400°.
2. Heat a large Dutch oven over medium heat. Add 3 tablespoons oil to pan; swirl to coat. Add onion to pan; cook 5 minutes or until browned, stirring occasionally. Add spinach, 1 bag at a time, and cook 3 minutes or until spinach wilts, stirring frequently. Simmer spinach mixture 40 minutes or until liquid evaporates. Stir in raisins. Remove from heat; cool completely. Stir in cheese, nuts, salt, and pepper.
3. Press 1 phyllo sheet into bottom and up sides of a 13 x 9-inch glass or ceramic baking dish coated with cooking spray (cover remaining dough to prevent drying); lightly coat phyllo with cooking spray. Repeat procedure with 7 phyllo sheets. Spread spinach mixture in an even layer onto phyllo. Place 1 phyllo sheet on a large cutting board or work surface (cover remaining dough to keep from drying); lightly brush with 1½ teaspoons oil. Repeat procedure with remaining 3 phyllo sheets and remaining 1½ tablespoons oil. Place phyllo layer over spinach mixture; tuck in sides to enclose spinach fully. Bake at 400° for 30 minutes. Remove from oven; let stand 15 minutes.

Serves 8 (serving size: 1 piece).

CALORIES 363; FAT 21.8g (sat 6.6g, mono 9.9g, poly 3.6g); PROTEIN 14.9g; CARB 31.9g; FIBER 6.4g; CHOL 13mg; IRON 5.3mg; SODIUM 480mg; CALC 300mg

Wine Pairing
Take a big fat Greek holiday and pair this savory pastry with assyrtiko, a dry, minerally white wine made on the Greek island of Santorini.

Eggplant Parmesan

All the cheesy-gooey-saucy deliciousness you'd expect from the Italian-American classic—and you save a whopping 700 calories and 22 grams of saturated fat per serving.

Regular panko got soggy when we tried it, so make sure you use whole-wheat panko. (Bonus: whole grains!) The panko barely browns, but it creates a perfectly crisp coating.

Hands-on time: 25 min. Total time: 1 hr. 45 min.

Eggplant:

- 2 large eggs, lightly beaten
- 1 tablespoon water
- 2 cups whole-wheat panko (Japanese breadcrumbs)
- ¼ cup (1 ounce) grated fresh Parmigiano-Reggiano cheese
- 2 (1-pound) eggplants, peeled and cut crosswise into ½-inch-thick slices

Cooking spray

Filling:

- ½ cup torn fresh basil
- ¼ cup (1 ounce) grated fresh Parmigiano-Reggiano cheese
- ½ teaspoon crushed red pepper
- ¼ teaspoon salt
- 3 garlic cloves, minced
- 1 (16-ounce) carton part-skim ricotta cheese
- 1 large egg, lightly beaten

Remaining ingredients:

- 1 (24-ounce) jar premium pasta sauce
- ¼ teaspoon salt
- 8 ounces thinly sliced mozzarella cheese
- ¾ cup (3 ounces) finely grated fontina cheese

1. Preheat oven to 375°.

2. To make eggplant, combine 2 eggs and 1 tablespoon water in a shallow dish. Combine panko and ¼ cup Parmigiano-Reggiano in a second shallow dish. Dip eggplant in egg mixture; dredge in panko mixture, pressing gently to adhere and shaking off excess. Place eggplant slices 1 inch apart on baking sheets coated with cooking spray. Bake at 375° for 30 minutes or until golden, turning once and rotating baking sheets after 15 minutes.

3. To make filling, combine basil and next 6 ingredients (through egg).

4. To assemble, spoon ½ cup pasta sauce in bottom of a 13 x 9-inch glass or ceramic baking dish coated with cooking spray. Layer half of eggplant slices over pasta sauce. Sprinkle eggplant with ¼ teaspoon salt. Top with about ¾ cup pasta sauce; spread half of ricotta mixture over sauce, and top with a third of the mozzarella and ¼ cup fontina. Repeat layers once, ending with about 1 cup pasta sauce. Cover tightly with aluminum foil coated with cooking spray. Bake at 375° for 35 minutes. Remove foil; top with remaining third of mozzarella and ¼ cup fontina. Bake at 375° for 10 minutes or until sauce is bubbly and cheese melts; cool 10 minutes.

Serves 10 (serving size: 1 slice).

CALORIES 318; FAT 15.1g (sat 8.2g, mono 2.7g, poly 0.6g); PROTEIN 19.3g; CARB 26.8g; FIBER 4.8g; CHOL 99mg; IRON 1.6mg; SODIUM 655mg; CALC 365mg

TECHNIQUE

Panko Breading: Too much or too little of the panko coating will prevent you from getting the coveted crispy "oven-fried" effect that is the crux of this dish. Here's how to get the crumb count just right.

1. Give the eggplant a quick dip in the egg wash; let the excess drip off.

2. Gently press the panko onto the slice to help it adhere.

Parmesan Flans with Tomatoes and Basil 🌿

The dessert custard goes savory—no gimmick, but instead a silky, delicate entrée crowned by summer's sweetest tomatoes.

Garnish with fresh shaved Parmigiano-Reggiano to make this dish beautiful. Pair it with a chilled soup, salad, and white wine for a light meal. Hands-on time: 12 min. Total time: 39 min.

Cooking spray

3　tablespoons all-purpose flour

1　cup 1% low-fat milk

3　large eggs, lightly beaten

3　large egg whites, lightly beaten

¾　cup (3 ounces) finely grated Parmigiano-Reggiano cheese

¼　teaspoon freshly ground black pepper, divided

⅛　teaspoon salt

2　cups chopped seeded tomato

Dash of salt

¼　cup small basil leaves

1. Preheat oven to 375°.
2. Coat 4 (6-ounce) custard cups or ramekins with cooking spray. Place 3 tablespoons flour in a medium bowl. Gradually add milk to bowl, stirring constantly with a whisk until blended. Add eggs and egg whites; stir well. Add Parmigiano-Reggiano, ⅛ teaspoon pepper, and ⅛ teaspoon salt; stir well. Divide mixture evenly among prepared custard cups. Place custard cups in a 9-inch square glass or ceramic baking dish; add hot water to pan to a depth of 1 inch. Bake at 375° for 25 minutes or until puffy and set.

3. Combine tomato, dash of salt, and dash of pepper in a medium bowl. Loosen edges of flans with a knife or rubber spatula. Place a plate, upside down, on top of each cup; invert onto plates. Spoon ½ cup tomato mixture over each flan. Top each serving with 1 tablespoon basil; sprinkle flans evenly with remaining dash of pepper.

Serves 4.

CALORIES 223; FAT 10.9g (sat 5.3g, mono 3.4g, poly 0.9g); PROTEIN 19.1g; CARB 12.5g; FIBER 1.3g; CHOL 180mg; IRON 1.5mg; SODIUM 561mg; CALC 345mg

Bibimbop 🌿

A thrilling combination of rice and vegetables, this signature Korean dish is worth the effort.

As you prepare each component, place the hot food on a jelly-roll pan, and keep in a warm oven.
Hands-on time: 50 min. Total time: 1 hr. 24 min.

8 ounces extra-firm tofu, drained

⅓ cup water

¼ cup apple cider vinegar

2 teaspoons sugar, divided

2 teaspoons minced garlic, divided

1 teaspoon minced peeled fresh ginger, divided

¼ teaspoon crushed red pepper

1 cup julienne-cut carrot

2 tablespoons lower-sodium soy sauce

3 tablespoons plus 2 teaspoons dark sesame oil, divided

3 cups hot cooked short-grain rice

1 cup fresh bean sprouts

1 (5-ounce) package sliced shiitake mushroom caps

1 (9-ounce) package fresh baby spinach

1 teaspoon unsalted butter

4 large eggs

4 teaspoons Korean chili paste

¼ teaspoon kosher salt

1. Cut tofu into ¾-inch-thick slices. Place tofu slices in a single layer on several layers of paper towels; cover with additional paper towels. Let tofu stand 30 minutes to drain, pressing down occasionally.
2. While tofu stands, combine ⅓ cup water, vinegar, 1 teaspoon sugar, ½ teaspoon garlic, ½ teaspoon ginger, and crushed red pepper in a small saucepan. Bring to a boil. Add carrot, and remove from heat; let stand 30 minutes. Drain.
3. Remove tofu from paper towels, and cut into ¾-inch cubes. Place tofu cubes in a medium bowl. Combine remaining 1 teaspoon sugar, ½ teaspoon garlic, remaining ½ teaspoon ginger, soy sauce, and 1 tablespoon sesame oil in a small bowl, stirring with a whisk. Add 1 tablespoon soy sauce mixture to tofu; toss gently. Let stand 15 minutes.
4. While tofu stands, heat a 10-inch cast-iron skillet over high heat 4 minutes. Add 1 tablespoon sesame oil; swirl to coat. Add rice to pan in a single layer; cook 1 minute (do not stir). Remove from heat; let stand 20 minutes.
5. Heat a large nonstick skillet over medium-high heat. Add 1 teaspoon oil; swirl to coat. Add 1½ teaspoons soy sauce mixture and bean sprouts to pan; sauté 1 minute. Remove sprouts from pan; keep warm. Add 1 teaspoon oil to pan; swirl to coat. Add mushrooms to pan; sauté 2 minutes. Stir in 1½ teaspoons soy sauce mixture; sauté 1 minute. Remove mushrooms from pan; keep warm. Add 2 teaspoons oil to pan; swirl to coat. Add tofu to pan; sauté 7 minutes or until golden brown. Remove tofu from pan; keep warm. Add remaining 1 teaspoon oil to pan; swirl to coat. Add remaining 1 teaspoon garlic and remaining 1 tablespoon soy sauce mixture; sauté 30 seconds. Add spinach to pan; sauté 1 minute or until spinach wilts. Remove spinach from pan; keep warm. Reduce heat to medium. Melt butter in pan. Crack eggs into pan; cook 4 minutes or until whites are set. Remove from heat.
6. Place ¾ cup rice in each of 4 shallow bowls. Top each serving evenly with carrots, sprouts, mushrooms, tofu, and spinach. Top each serving with 1 egg and 1 teaspoon chili paste. Sprinkle evenly with salt.

Serves 4 (serving size: 1 bowl).

CALORIES 502; FAT 23.4g (sat 4.5g, mono 9.9g, poly 7.1g); PROTEIN 20.9g; CARB 56.4g; FIBER 6.1g, CHOL 214mg; IRON 6.8mg; SODIUM 698mg; CALC 199mg

Arugula and Fontina Soufflé 🌿

The virtue of any good soufflé is its airy softness. Each bite here is like a fluffy cloud—spiked with peppery greens and earthy cheese.

Hands-on time: 18 min. Total time: 1 hr. 8 min.

Cooking spray
½ cup dry breadcrumbs
6 ounces trimmed arugula (about 9 cups)
1.5 ounces all-purpose flour (about ⅓ cup)
½ teaspoon salt
⅛ teaspoon ground nutmeg
⅛ teaspoon ground red pepper
⅛ teaspoon freshly ground black pepper
1¼ cups 1% low-fat milk
½ cup (2 ounces) shredded fontina cheese
1 large egg yolk, lightly beaten
6 large egg whites
Dash of cream of tartar

1. Preheat oven to 425°; place a rimmed baking sheet in oven.
2. Lightly coat a 2-quart soufflé dish with cooking spray; sprinkle breadcrumbs evenly over dish.
3. Cook arugula in boiling water 15 seconds or until wilted, and drain in a sieve, pressing until barely moist. Finely chop; place in a large bowl.
4. Weigh or lightly spoon flour into a dry measuring cup; level with a knife. Combine flour, salt, nutmeg, red pepper, and black pepper in a medium, heavy saucepan over medium heat. Gradually add milk, stirring constantly with a whisk; bring to a boil. Cook 1 minute or until thick and bubbly. Remove from heat; let stand 5 minutes. Add cheese; stir until smooth. Stir in arugula and egg yolk.
5. Place egg whites and cream of tartar in a large mixing bowl; beat with a mixer at high speed until medium peaks form (do not overbeat). Gently stir one-fourth of egg white mixture into arugula mixture; gently fold in remaining egg white mixture. Spoon into prepared soufflé dish. Place dish on preheated baking sheet; place in 425° oven. Immediately reduce oven temperature to 350°. Bake at 350° for 45 minutes or until puffed, golden, and set. Serve immediately.

Serves 6.

CALORIES 154; FAT 5.1g (sat 2.5g, mono 1.5g, poly 0.5g); PROTEIN 10.8g; CARB 16g; FIBER 0.9g; CHOL 50mg; IRON 1.4mg; SODIUM 437mg; CALC 178mg

Asparagus and Gruyère variation: 🌿
Substitute ¾ pound asparagus for arugula. Cook asparagus in boiling water 4 minutes; drain and rinse with cold water. Cut a 1-inch tip from each asparagus spear; finely chop stalks. Substitute 1 teaspoon dry mustard for ground red pepper. Substitute ½ cup (2 ounces) shredded Gruyère for fontina. Stir in asparagus tips and chopped asparagus with cheese.

Serves 6.

CALORIES 165; FAT 5.3g (sat 2.5g, mono 1.6g, poly 0.4g); PROTEIN 11.9g; CARB 17.5g; FIBER 1.7g; CHOL 49mg; IRON 1.6mg; SODIUM 387mg; CALC 191mg

Spinach and Feta variation: 🌿
Substitute 10 ounces baby spinach (about 8 cups) for the arugula. Substitute ½ cup (2 ounces) crumbled feta cheese for the shredded fontina. Stir in 2 teaspoons chopped fresh dill with cheese.

Serves 6.

CALORIES 143; FAT 4.1g (sat 2.1g, mono 1.1g, poly 0.3g); PROTEIN 10.1g; CARB 16.5g; FIBER 1.5g; CHOL 47mg; IRON 2.1mg; SODIUM 490mg; CALC 167mg

Asparagus, Tomato, and Onion Farinata 🌿

Made with chickpea flour, this Italian-style crust is high fiber, high protein, and gluten free.

Hands-on time: 42 min. Total time: 1 hr. 22 min.

1   pint cherry tomatoes, halved

4   tablespoons olive oil, divided

2¼ teaspoons chopped fresh rosemary, divided

⅜   teaspoon freshly ground black pepper, divided

3.18 ounces chickpea (garbanzo bean) flour (about ¾ cup)

1   cup water

½   teaspoon salt

2½ cups thinly vertically sliced yellow onion

⅛   teaspoon crushed red pepper

3   garlic cloves, chopped

1   cup (1-inch) slices asparagus

2   tablespoons shaved pecorino Romano cheese

1   teaspoon fresh lemon juice

2   teaspoons balsamic vinegar

4   cups baby arugula

3   tablespoons pine nuts, toasted

1. Preheat oven to 450°.

2. Combine tomatoes, 1½ teaspoons oil, ¼ teaspoon rosemary, and ⅛ teaspoon black pepper in a small bowl, tossing to coat. Arrange tomatoes in a single layer on a jelly-roll pan; bake at 450° for 20 minutes, stirring once. Cool slightly.

3. Weigh or lightly spoon flour into a dry measuring cup; level with a knife. Combine flour, 1 cup water, 1 tablespoon oil, remaining 2 teaspoons rosemary, salt, and remaining ¼ teaspoon black pepper in a large bowl, stirring with a whisk until smooth. Let stand 30 minutes.

4. Place a 10-inch cast-iron skillet in oven.

5. Heat a large skillet over medium-high heat. Add 1½ teaspoons oil; swirl to coat. Add onion. Cover, and cook 8 minutes or until tender, stirring occasionally. Stir in red pepper and garlic. Cook, uncovered, 18 minutes or until onions are golden, stirring frequently. Remove from heat; stir in asparagus.

6. Carefully remove cast-iron pan from oven. Add 1 tablespoon oil; swirl to coat. Stir batter once; pour batter into pan. Bake at 450° for 20 minutes. Top evenly with onion mixture and tomatoes. Bake an additional 12 minutes or until center of dough is set. Remove from oven; let stand 10 minutes. Sprinkle evenly with cheese. Cut into 4 wedges.

7. Combine remaining 1 tablespoon oil, juice, and vinegar in a medium bowl, stirring with a whisk. Add arugula; toss gently to coat. Arrange 1 cup arugula on each of 4 plates; sprinkle each serving with about 2 teaspoons nuts. Serve with farinata.

Serves 4.

CALORIES 321; FAT 20.5g (sat 2.9g, mono 11.7g, poly 4.5g); PROTEIN 9.8g; CARB 27.2g; FIBER 6g; CHOL 2mg; IRON 3.1mg; SODIUM 358mg; CALC 110mg

Tofu Fried Rice

A fast version of a take-out classic: American-style fried rice is paired with peas and carrots and crisped cubes of tofu.

Hands-on time: 20 min. Total time: 20 min.

- 2 cups uncooked instant rice
- 2 tablespoons canola oil, divided
- 1 (14-ounce) package reduced-fat firm tofu, drained and cut into (½-inch) cubes
- 2 large eggs, lightly beaten
- 1 cup (½-inch-thick) slices green onions
- 1 cup frozen peas and carrots, thawed
- 4 garlic cloves, minced
- 1 teaspoon minced peeled fresh ginger
- 2 tablespoons sake (rice wine)
- 3 tablespoons lower-sodium soy sauce
- 1 tablespoon hoisin sauce
- ½ teaspoon dark sesame oil

Thinly sliced green onions (optional)

1. Cook rice according to package directions, omitting salt and fat.

2. Heat a large nonstick skillet over medium-high heat. Add 1 tablespoon oil; swirl to coat. Add tofu; cook 4 minutes or until lightly browned, stirring occasionally. Remove from pan. Add eggs to pan; cook 1 minute or until done, breaking egg into small pieces. Remove from pan. Add remaining 1 tablespoon oil to pan; swirl to coat. Add 1 cup onions, peas and carrots, garlic, and ginger; sauté 2 minutes, stirring frequently.

3. Combine sake, soy sauce, hoisin sauce, and sesame oil. Add cooked rice to pan; cook 2 minutes, stirring constantly. Add tofu, egg, and soy sauce mixture; cook 30 seconds, stirring constantly. Garnish with sliced green onions, if desired.

Serves 4 (serving size: 1½ cups).

CALORIES 378; FAT 11g (sat 1.8g, mono 4.4g, poly 4.1g); PROTEIN 15.8g; CARB 50.6g; FIBER 3.2g; CHOL 106mg; IRON 3.8mg; SODIUM 629mg; CALC 79mg

Quinoa and Potato Croquettes 🌿 🌾

Banish all memories of those dry little croquettes from childhood. These babies are moist mashed potato and quinoa cakes, jazzed up with jalapeño, cumin, and cilantro.

Serve with coleslaw and dollop with salsa and sour cream. Hands-on time: 17 min. Total time: 50 min.

1   (12-ounce) baking potato
2   cups water
1   cup uncooked quinoa, rinsed
¾   teaspoon salt
2   teaspoons canola oil
½   cup thinly sliced green onions
⅓   cup chopped fresh cilantro
1   jalapeño pepper, seeded and finely chopped
1   teaspoon ground cumin
½   teaspoon dried oregano
½   teaspoon freshly ground black pepper
2   garlic cloves, minced
½   cup 1% low-fat cottage cheese, drained
½   cup (2 ounces) finely shredded extra-sharp cheddar cheese
1   large egg, lightly beaten
1   cup panko (Japanese breadcrumbs)
Cooking spray

1. Pierce potato with a fork, and place on paper towels in microwave oven. Microwave at HIGH 5 minutes or until fork pierces potato easily, turning potato after 3 minutes. Wrap in a towel; let stand 5 minutes. Peel and mash potato.
2. Bring 2 cups water to a boil in a saucepan; add quinoa and salt. Reduce heat, and simmer 15 minutes; drain.
3. Heat a large skillet over medium-high heat. Add 2 teaspoons oil to pan; swirl to coat. Add onions, cilantro, and jalapeño to pan; sauté 1 minute. Add cumin, oregano, black pepper, and garlic; sauté 1 minute. Combine potato, quinoa, onion mixture, cottage cheese, and cheddar cheese in a bowl, stirring well. Let stand 5 minutes; stir in egg.
4. Shape potato mixture into 15 patties. Carefully dredge each patty in panko. Place on a baking sheet. Cover and chill 10 minutes.
5. Heat skillet over medium heat. Coat pan with cooking spray. Add 8 patties to pan; cook 2 minutes on each side or until golden brown. Keep warm. Repeat procedure with remaining 7 patties.

Serves 5 (serving size: 3 croquettes).

CALORIES 322; FAT 9.3g (sat 3.3g, mono 2.2g, poly 1.8g); PROTEIN 14.2g; CARB 44.7g; FIBER 4.4g, CHOL 53mg; IRON 2.4mg; SODIUM 576mg; CALC 134mg

NUTRITION MADE EASY

Quinoa: A whole grain that isn't a grain? Yes, that's the case with quinoa, which counts as a whole grain but is technically a seed, making it a gluten-free food with all the benefits of other whole grains. Most quinoa is prerinsed to remove the bitter coating, but it won't hurt to rinse it yourself to make sure. The nutty seed cooks quickly, and you can tell when it's done because the germ of the kernel sticks out like a little white tail.

Spinach and Smoked Gouda Quiche 🌿

The trick here is to pull the quiche from the oven when it's still a bit wiggly in the middle for the creamiest, most custardy texture.

Of course, if you like a firmer texture, just bake five minutes more than we recommend. Making the crust takes time, but it's absolutely worth it for this savory pie. Hands-on time: 25 min. Total time: 2 hr. 36 min.

Crust:

6	tablespoons butter, softened
2	tablespoons 1% low-fat milk
¼	teaspoon salt
1	large egg yolk
5.6	ounces all-purpose flour (about 1¼ cups)

Filling:

1	tablespoon extra-virgin olive oil
½	cup thinly sliced green onions
3	cups fresh baby spinach
1	cup 1% low-fat milk
¾	cup (3 ounces) grated smoked Gouda cheese
¾	teaspoon salt
Dash of grated nutmeg	
3	large eggs

1. To prepare crust, place butter in a large bowl; beat with a mixer at medium speed until light and fluffy. Combine 2 tablespoons milk, ¼ teaspoon salt, and egg yolk in a small bowl; stir well with a whisk. Add milk mixture to butter, 1 tablespoon at a time, beating well after each addition. Weigh or lightly spoon flour into dry measuring cups; level with a knife. Add flour to milk mixture; beat just until combined. Press mixture into a 4-inch circle on plastic wrap; cover. Chill 1 hour.

2. Preheat oven to 350°.

3. Unwrap and place chilled dough on a lightly floured surface. Roll dough into a 10-inch circle. Fit dough into a 9-inch pie plate. Freeze 15 minutes. Bake at 350° for 25 minutes or until lightly browned. Cool.

4. To prepare filling, heat a large skillet over medium-high heat. Add oil to pan; swirl to coat. Add onions; sauté 5 minutes or until tender. Add spinach; sauté 2 minutes.

5. Combine 1 cup milk and next 4 ingredients (through eggs) in a bowl, stirring well with a whisk. Stir in spinach mixture. Pour filling into crust. Bake at 350° for 35 minutes.

Serves 10 (serving size: 1 wedge).

CALORIES 205; FAT 12.9g (sat 6.8g, mono 4.3g, poly 0.8g); PROTEIN 7.3g; CARB 15.4g; FIBER 1.1g; CHOL 113mg; IRON 1.5mg; SODIUM 405mg; CALC 120mg

Rösti Casserole with Baked Eggs 🌿
The Swiss take on smothered-covered hash browns, baked into a cheesy casserole.

Greek yogurt adds a tangy tickle to shredded potatoes and turnips; creamy eggs and nutty Gruyère balance the tang. Serve with a colorful mixed greens salad. Hands-on time: 16 min. Total time: 54 min.

1¼ cups plain fat-free Greek yogurt

2 tablespoons all-purpose flour

1½ cups grated peeled turnip (about 8 ounces)

1¼ cups (5 ounces) shredded Gruyère cheese

¼ cup chopped fresh chives

¼ cup olive oil

1 tablespoon butter, melted

1¼ teaspoons salt

½ teaspoon freshly ground black pepper

¼ teaspoon grated whole nutmeg

1 (30-ounce) package frozen shredded hash brown potatoes, thawed

Cooking spray

8 large eggs

Chopped fresh chives (optional)

Freshly ground black pepper (optional)

1. Preheat oven to 400°.

2. Combine yogurt and flour in a large bowl, stirring well. Add turnip and next 8 ingredients (through potatoes) to yogurt mixture. Spread potato mixture evenly into a 13 x 9–inch glass or ceramic baking dish coated with cooking spray. Bake at 400° for 30 minutes or until bubbly. Remove from oven.

With the back of a spoon, make 8 indentations in top of potato mixture. Crack 1 egg into each indentation. Return dish to oven. Bake at 400° for 8 minutes or until egg whites are firm and yolks barely move when pan is touched. Cut into 8 pieces. Garnish with chives and black pepper, if desired. Serve immediately.

Serves 8 (serving size: 1 piece).

CALORIES 354; FAT 18.1g (sat 6.4g, mono 9g, poly 1.9g); PROTEIN 18g; CARB 27.3g; FIBER 2.1g; CHOL 203mg; IRON 1.2mg; SODIUM 562mg; CALC 240mg

Red Lentil Dal with Charred Onions 🌿
An Indian classic with toasted spices, smoky onions, and soupy lentils.

Serve over white or brown basmati rice to complete the meal and soak up the sauce.
Hands-on time: 17 min. Total time: 1 hr. 3 min.

1 tablespoon olive oil, divided

1 medium onion, cut into ¼-inch-thick slices

1 teaspoon mustard seeds

½ teaspoon coriander seeds

½ teaspoon cumin seeds

1 whole clove

¼ teaspoon ground cinnamon

⅛ teaspoon ground cardamom

1 small dried hot red chile

1 tablespoon minced peeled fresh ginger

1 garlic clove, minced

4 cups organic vegetable broth

1 cup dried small red lentils

1 (14.5-ounce) can no-salt-added diced tomatoes, undrained

¼ cup chopped fresh cilantro

1 tablespoon fresh lime juice

1. Heat a large heavy cast-iron skillet over medium-high heat. Add 1 teaspoon oil to pan; swirl to coat. Add onion to pan; cook 2 minutes or until charred. Carefully turn over onion, and cook 4 minutes or until blackened and charred. Remove from heat. Coarsely chop; set aside.
2. Combine mustard seeds, coriander seeds, cumin seeds, and clove in a small skillet over medium heat. Cook 1½ minutes or until fragrant, stirring frequently. Remove from heat. Place mustard mixture, cinnamon, cardamom, and chile in a spice or coffee grinder; pulse until ground.
3. Heat a small Dutch oven over medium-high heat. Add remaining 2 teaspoons oil to pan; swirl to coat. Add ginger and garlic to pan; sauté 1 minute. Stir in spice mixture; sauté 1 minute. Add broth, lentils, and tomatoes to pan; bring to a boil. Cover, reduce heat, and simmer 30 minutes, stirring occasionally. Uncover; add onion, and cook 10 minutes. Stir in cilantro and juice.

Serves 5 (serving size: 1⅓ cups).

CALORIES 208; FAT 3.9g (sat 0.4g, mono 2.2g, poly 0.4g); PROTEIN 11.8g; CARB 32.9g; FIBER 7.8g; CHOL 0mg; IRON 2.8mg; SODIUM 495mg; CALC 46mg

Beer Pairing
India Pale Ale, a hopped-up version of a pale ale beer, has an extra dose of fresh, citrusy, slightly bitter hops that complements classic Indian fare.

VEGETARIAN ENTRÉES

Gyoza with Soy-Citrus Sauce

Mushroom-stuffed dumplings are sautéed and then steamed for authentic crispy-chewy textures.

Speed the process by chopping the filling in the food processor and using purchased gyoza skins.
Hands-on time: 17 min. Total time: 50 min.

- 1 tablespoon minced peeled fresh ginger
- 2 tablespoons lower-sodium soy sauce, divided
- 5 teaspoons peanut oil, divided
- ½ teaspoon grated orange rind
- 1 teaspoon fresh orange juice
- ⅛ teaspoon crushed red pepper
- 8 ounces shiitake mushrooms, stemmed and chopped
- 8 ounces button mushrooms, chopped
- 2 green onions, cut into 2-inch pieces
- 2 garlic cloves
- 6 ounces chopped fresh spinach
- 28 gyoza skins
- ½ cup organic vegetable broth, divided
- ⅓ cup fresh orange juice
- 2 teaspoons rice vinegar

Fresh chives (optional)

1. Place ginger, 1 tablespoon soy sauce, 2 teaspoons oil, orange rind, 1 teaspoon orange juice, red pepper, mushrooms, green onions, and garlic cloves in a food processor, and process until finely chopped.

2. Heat a large nonstick skillet over medium heat. Add 1 teaspoon oil to pan; swirl to coat. Add mushroom mixture and spinach to pan; cook 10 minutes or until liquid evaporates, stirring frequently. Remove from pan; cool slightly.

3. Moisten edges of gyoza skin with water, working with 1 gyoza skin at a time (cover remaining skins to prevent drying). Spoon about 1 tablespoon spinach mixture into center of circle. Fold in half, pinching edges together to seal.

Place dumpling, seam side up, on a baking sheet (cover loosely with a towel to prevent drying). Repeat procedure with remaining wrappers and filling.

4. Wipe pan clean with paper towels. Heat pan over medium-high heat. Add 1 teaspoon oil to pan; swirl to coat. Add half of dumplings to pan; cook 2 minutes on each side or until lightly browned. Remove from pan; keep warm. Repeat procedure with remaining 1 teaspoon oil and remaining dumplings. Add ¼ cup broth, ⅓ cup juice, remaining 1 tablespoon soy sauce, and vinegar to pan; bring to a boil. Place dipping sauce in a small bowl.

5. Add remaining ¼ cup broth to pan; bring to a boil. Add dumplings; cover and cook 2 minutes or until tender. Remove from pan. Serve with dipping sauce; top with chives, if desired.

Serves 4 (serving size: 7 dumplings and 2 tablespoons sauce).

CALORIES 223; FAT 6.7g (sat 1.1g, mono 2.8g, poly 2.2g); PROTEIN 9.5g; CARB 32.5g; FIBER 3.1g; CHOL 7mg; IRON 3.4mg; SODIUM 622mg; CALC 84mg

Indian-Style Tofu and Cauliflower 🌿

A variation on the great Indian dish *aloo gobi*, with tofu standing in for the potatoes.

Toasting the spices is the absolute key to profound flavor. Brown mustard seeds are hotter and smaller than the more common yellow seeds. Hands-on time: 14 min. Total time: 1 hr. 16 min.

1   (14-ounce) package firm water-packed tofu, drained

1   medium onion, cut into 6 wedges

2   tablespoons canola oil

1   teaspoon brown mustard seeds

¾   teaspoon cumin seeds

2   teaspoons curry powder

4   garlic cloves

1   (½-inch) piece fresh ginger, peeled and coarsely chopped

4   cups cauliflower florets (about 1¼ pounds)

¼   cup water

1   teaspoon salt

1   (14.5-ounce) can diced tomatoes, undrained

4½   cups hot cooked basmati rice

¼   cup plain fat-free yogurt

¼   cup chopped fresh cilantro

1. Place tofu on several layers of paper towels. Cover tofu with several more layers of paper towels; top with a cast-iron or other heavy skillet. Let stand 30 minutes. Discard paper towels. Cut tofu into ½-inch cubes.

2. Place onion in a food processor; pulse until finely chopped. Heat a large skillet over medium heat. Add oil to pan; swirl to coat. Add mustard seeds and cumin seeds; cook 10 seconds or until mustard seeds begin to pop. Add chopped onion and curry powder; cook 10 minutes, stirring frequently. Increase heat to medium-high; cook 2 minutes or until onion is golden, stirring constantly.

3. Place garlic and ginger in food processor; process until a smooth paste forms. Stir garlic mixture into onion mixture; sauté 1 minute, stirring constantly. Stir in tofu, cauliflower, ¼ cup water, salt, and tomatoes; bring to a simmer. Cover, reduce heat to medium-low, and cook 15 minutes. Uncover, increase heat to medium, and simmer 10 minutes or until cauliflower is tender.

4. Spoon ¾ cup rice onto each of 6 plates; top each serving with 1 cup tofu mixture. Spoon 2 teaspoons yogurt over each serving; sprinkle with cilantro.

Serves 6.

CALORIES 312; FAT 8.8g (sat 0.8g, mono 5.5g, poly 1.5g); PROTEIN 12.5g; CARB 47.6g; FIBER 5g; CHOL 0mg; IRON 3.5mg; SODIUM 517mg; CALC 187mg

Fall Vegetable Curry 🌿

Madras curry powder is worlds away from the slightly musty regular stuff—it's brighter, more fragrant, and packs much more heat.

Serve over hot cooked basmati rice or whole-wheat couscous. Hands-on time: 13 min. Total time: 25 min.

1½   teaspoons olive oil

1   cup diced peeled sweet potato

1   cup small cauliflower florets

¼   cup thinly sliced yellow onion

2   teaspoons Madras curry powder

½   cup organic vegetable broth

¼   teaspoon salt

1   (15-ounce) can organic chickpeas (garbanzo beans), rinsed and drained

1   (14.5-ounce) can no-salt-added diced tomatoes, undrained

2   tablespoons chopped fresh cilantro

½   cup plain 2% reduced-fat Greek yogurt

1. Heat a large nonstick skillet over medium-high heat. Add oil to pan; swirl to coat. Add potato to pan; sauté 3 minutes, stirring occasionally. Decrease heat to medium. Add cauliflower, onion, and curry powder; cook 1 minute, stirring constantly. Add broth and next 3 ingredients (through tomatoes); bring to a boil. Cover, reduce heat, and simmer 10 minutes or until vegetables are tender, stirring occasionally. Sprinkle with cilantro; serve with yogurt.

Serves 4 (serving size: 1 cup curry and 2 tablespoons yogurt).

CALORIES 231; FAT 3.9g (sat 0.9g, mono 1.6g, poly 0.9g); PROTEIN 10.4g; CARB 40.8g; FIBER 8.6g; CHOL 2mg; IRON 2.5mg; SODIUM 626mg; CALC 106mg

GLOBAL FLAVORS

Madras Curry Powder: Blending more than a dozen spices, including fenugreek, coriander, cumin, turmeric, peppers, ginger, and garlic, creates a vibrantly flavored blend that varies depending on the producer. Packaged Madras curry powder is a good shortcut choice for those just trying Indian food, and to speed up weeknight dinners.

Tofu Steaks with Red Pepper–Walnut Sauce 🌿

Here's a little bit of East meets West: three–step breaded crispy tofu with an almost-romesco sauce.

The herb marinade does double duty as the base for the Mediterranean-style dipping sauce. Serve with a side salad and orzo tossed with some extra chopped fresh herbs and fresh mozzarella.

Hands-on time: 30 min. Total time: 2 hr.

1 (14-ounce) package water-packed reduced-fat extra-firm tofu
¼ cup finely chopped fresh basil
¼ cup water
2 tablespoons chopped fresh parsley
1 tablespoon chopped fresh thyme
2 tablespoons white wine vinegar
1 tablespoon Dijon mustard
½ teaspoon crushed red pepper
¼ teaspoon salt
8 garlic cloves, minced
½ cup all-purpose flour
½ cup egg substitute
2 cups panko (Japanese breadcrumbs)
2 tablespoons olive oil
3 tablespoons chopped walnuts, toasted
1 (12-ounce) bottle roasted red bell peppers, drained

1. Cut tofu crosswise into 4 slices. Place tofu slices on several layers of heavy-duty paper towels; cover with additional paper towels. Let stand 30 minutes, pressing down occasionally.

2. Combine basil and next 8 ingredients (through garlic) in a large zip-top plastic bag. Add tofu to bag; seal. Marinate in refrigerator 1 hour, turning bag occasionally.

3. Place flour in a shallow dish. Place egg substitute in another shallow dish. Place panko in another shallow dish.

4. Remove tofu from marinade, reserving remaining marinade. Working with 1 tofu piece at a time, dredge tofu in flour, shaking off excess. Dip tofu in egg substitute, allowing excess to drip off. Coat tofu completely with panko, pressing lightly to adhere. Set aside. Repeat procedure with remaining tofu, flour, egg substitute, and panko.

5. Heat a large nonstick skillet over medium-high heat. Add oil to pan; swirl to coat. Add tofu to pan; reduce heat to medium, and cook 4 minutes on each side or until browned. Remove tofu from pan, and keep warm.

6. Place reserved marinade, walnuts, and bell peppers in a blender; process until smooth (about 2 minutes). Pour bell pepper mixture into pan; cook over medium-high heat 2 minutes or until thoroughly heated. Serve with tofu.

Serves 4 (serving size: 1 tofu piece and about ⅓ cup sauce).

CALORIES 291; FAT 15.1g (sat 1.3g, mono 6.4g, poly 5.9g); PROTEIN 15.9g; CARB 23g; FIBER 3.5g; CHOL 0mg; IRON 2.8mg; SODIUM 513mg; CALC 74mg

Tempeh and Green Bean Stir-Fry with Peanut Sauce 🌿
Tempeh's soy-nut quality and considerable chew are matched with a spice-spiked peanut sauce.

Tempeh is a textured, high-protein soy product that originated in Indonesia; we love it, but substitute extra-firm tofu if you want subtler flavor and softer texture. Everything is cooked in one skillet using different techniques—stir-frying, steaming, and glazing—to bring out the best in each ingredient.

Hands-on time: 25 min. Total time: 31 min.

Peanut sauce:

- ¼ cup water
- 1 tablespoon brown sugar
- 3 tablespoons natural-style, chunky peanut butter
- 1 teaspoon Sriracha (hot chile sauce)
- 1 teaspoon lower-sodium soy sauce

Stir-fry:

- 2 teaspoons brown sugar
- 5 teaspoons lower-sodium soy sauce
- 1 teaspoon Sriracha
- 4 garlic cloves, chopped
- 5 teaspoons sesame oil, divided
- 1 (8-ounce) package organic tempeh, cut into ⅓-inch strips
- 2 cups thinly sliced carrot

- 1 cup (2-inch) strips red bell pepper
- 1 pound green beans, trimmed
- ½ cup water
- ¾ cup thinly sliced green onions, divided
- 6 ounces fresh bean sprouts

1. To prepare peanut sauce, combine first 5 ingredients in a medium bowl, stirring well with a whisk. Set aside.

2. To prepare stir-fry, combine 2 teaspoons sugar and next 3 ingredients (through garlic) in a small bowl, stirring with a whisk.

3. Heat a large heavy skillet over medium-high heat. Add 1 tablespoon sesame oil to pan; swirl to coat. Add tempeh and half of soy sauce mixture; stir-fry 5 minutes or until tempeh is golden brown. Remove tempeh mixture from pan, and keep warm. Add

remaining 2 teaspoons oil to pan; swirl to coat. Add carrot, bell pepper, and green beans to pan; stir-fry 3 minutes. Add ½ cup water; reduce heat to medium. Cover and simmer 5 minutes or until beans are crisp-tender. Stir in remaining half of soy sauce mixture, tempeh mixture, half of onions, and bean sprouts; cook 2 minutes or until sprouts are tender. Serve with peanut sauce and remaining half of onions.

Serves 4 (serving size: 2 cups tempeh mixture, 2 tablespoons peanut sauce, and 1½ tablespoons green onions).

CALORIES 357; FAT 18.3g (sat 2.9g, mono 7.1g, poly 6.7g); PROTEIN 18.4g; CARB 35.2g; FIBER 8.2g; CHOL 0mg; IRON 4mg; SODIUM 353mg; CALC 158mg

GLOBAL FLAVORS

Sriracha: The squeeze bottle with the green twist top and white strutting rooster is the breakout-celebrity Asian hot sauce of record and can be found in just about every food store across the country. It's genuinely hot, but the sweet-garlic balance works in dishes where other thinner, vinegar-based sauces might be too acidic. This is ketchup all grown up and ready to boogie with Asian dishes, as well as many foods on the grill.

Summer Lemon-Vegetable Risotto 🌿
Dare we suggest that vegetables upstage the rice in this produce-packed risotto? We do; they do.

Smart technique: Reserving some of the cooking liquid to stir in after the risotto comes off the heat ensures that you end up with the creamy texture you expect. Hands-on time: 46 min. Total time: 57 min.

- 8 ounces asparagus, trimmed and cut into 1-inch pieces
- 8 ounces sugar snap peas, trimmed and cut in half
- 5 teaspoons extra-virgin olive oil, divided
- 1 (8-ounce) zucchini, halved lengthwise and cut into ½-inch-thick slices
- 1 (8-ounce) yellow squash, halved lengthwise and cut into ½-inch-thick slices
- 4¾ cups organic vegetable broth
- ½ cup finely chopped shallots
- 1 cup uncooked Arborio rice
- ¼ cup dry white wine
- ½ cup (2 ounces) grated fresh pecorino Romano cheese
- ¼ cup chopped fresh chives
- 1 teaspoon grated lemon rind
- 2 tablespoons fresh lemon juice
- 1 tablespoon unsalted butter
- ¼ teaspoon salt

1. Bring a large saucepan of water to a boil. Add asparagus and peas; cook 3 minutes or until crisp-tender. Drain and rinse under cold water.
2. Heat a large nonstick skillet over medium-high heat. Add 2 teaspoons oil to pan; swirl to coat. Add zucchini and squash to pan; cook 7 minutes or until lightly browned, stirring occasionally. Set aside.
3. Bring broth to a simmer in a medium saucepan (do not boil). Keep warm over low heat.
4. Heat a Dutch oven over medium heat. Add remaining 1 tablespoon oil; swirl to coat. Add shallots; cook 3 minutes or until tender, stirring occasionally. Stir in rice; cook 1 minute, stirring constantly. Stir in wine; cook until liquid is absorbed (about 30 seconds), stirring constantly. Stir in 1 cup broth; cook 5 minutes or until liquid is nearly absorbed, stirring constantly. Reserve ¼ cup broth. Add remaining broth, ½ cup at a time, stirring constantly until each portion of broth is absorbed before adding the next (about 22 minutes). Stir in vegetables; cook 1 minute or until thoroughly heated. Remove from heat; stir in reserved ¼ cup broth and remaining ingredients.

Serves 4 (serving size: 1½ cups).

CALORIES 395; FAT 12.3g (sat 4.7g, mono 4.9g, poly 0.8g); PROTEIN 10.6g; CARB 56.2g; FIBER 7.1g; CHOL 18mg; IRON 3.1mg; SODIUM 512mg; CALC 191mg

Wine Pairing
A dry, bright Italian wine such as a good Soave classic or a Verdicchio is a wonderful pair for this risotto.

Potato, Turnip, and Spinach Baeckeoffe 🌿
Our meatless riff on a classic French casserole is as warming and soul-satisfying as comfort food gets.

"Baeckeoffe" means "baker's oven" in the German-Alsatian dialect, as it was traditionally made in a dish brought to the local baker to cook in his big oven. Classic versions are loaded with meat, but our vegetarian version is equally hearty and rich. Hands-on time: 35 min. Total time: 2 hr. 5 min.

4 teaspoons canola oil, divided

1 pound sliced mushroom caps

2 garlic cloves, minced

1 cup white wine

2 tablespoons chopped fresh flat-leaf parsley

1 large thyme sprig

¾ teaspoon freshly ground black pepper, divided

2 tablespoons ⅓-less-fat cream cheese

4 cups vertically sliced onion (about 2 medium)

Cooking spray

1 (8-ounce) Yukon gold potato, peeled and cut into ¼-inch-thick slices

2 cups packed baby spinach leaves

½ teaspoon salt, divided

1 (6-ounce) turnip, peeled and cut into ⅛-inch-thick slices

1½ teaspoons chopped fresh tarragon

3 tablespoons heavy whipping cream

½ cup (2 ounces) shredded Gruyère cheese

1. Preheat oven to 350°.

2. Heat a large nonstick skillet over medium-high heat. Add 2 teaspoons oil to pan; swirl to coat. Add mushrooms to pan; sauté 2 minutes or until lightly browned. Stir in garlic; sauté 30 seconds. Add wine; cook 2 minutes. Add parsley, thyme, and ¼ teaspoon pepper. Cover, reduce heat, and simmer 10 minutes. Uncover and cook 6 minutes or until liquid almost evaporates. Remove from heat; discard thyme. Add cream cheese, stirring until cheese melts. Remove mushroom mixture from pan. Wipe pan clean with paper towels.

3. Heat pan over medium-high heat. Add remaining 2 teaspoons oil to pan; swirl to coat. Add onion; sauté 5 minutes, stirring frequently. Reduce heat to medium; continue cooking 15 minutes or until deep golden brown, stirring frequently. Set aside.

4. Coat a 6-cup glass or ceramic baking dish with cooking spray. Arrange potato slices in dish; top with spinach. Sprinkle ¼ teaspoon salt and ¼ teaspoon pepper evenly over spinach. Spoon mushroom mixture over pepper; arrange turnip slices over mushroom mixture. Top with caramelized onions; sprinkle with remaining ¼ teaspoon salt, remaining ¼ teaspoon pepper, and tarragon. Pour cream over tarragon; sprinkle evenly with Gruyère cheese. Cover and bake at 350° for 40 minutes. Uncover and bake an additional 20 minutes or until vegetables are tender and cheese begins to brown.

Serves 4 (serving size: about 1¼ cups).

CALORIES 278; FAT 15.7g (sat 6.7g, mono 5.6g, poly 1.9g); PROTEIN 10.8g; CARB 24.2g; FIBER 4.2g; CHOL 36mg; IRON 1.6mg; SODIUM 435mg; CALC 203mg

5

VEGETARIAN ENTRÉES

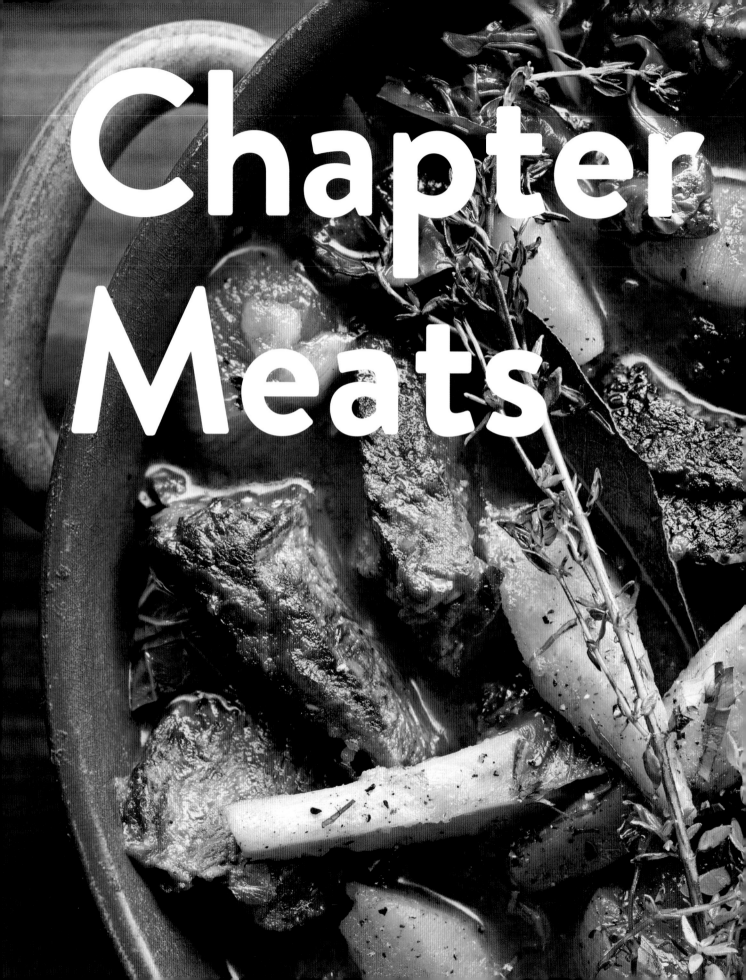

Chapter
Meats

6:

Beef Pot Roast with Turnip Greens, page 178

In the era of right-sized meat portions, the dishes that satisfy are those that capitalize on the flavor and characteristics of the cuts you're using. When you're cooking with less fat in the pan and—in the case of a grass-fed beefsteak, for example—less fat in the meat, cooking techniques come to the fore. We have learned a lot about meat over the years, about slow-cooking tough cuts, quick-cooking other cuts, incorporating techniques and flavors from around the world, and even adding a bit of butter for steakhouse-quality satisfaction.

Beef Tenderloin with Horseradish-Chive Sauce

There's a lot to love about the lemony bite of this creamy sauce, matched with a lean, tender cut.

If you manage to have any left over, make a sandwich with thinly sliced beef on toasted sourdough bread with the horseradish-chive sauce and arugula. Hands-on time: 13 min. Total time: 48 min.

1	(2-pound) beef tenderloin, trimmed
1	tablespoon olive oil
1½	teaspoons coarsely ground black pepper
¾	teaspoon kosher salt
⅔	cup light sour cream
2	tablespoons chopped fresh chives
3	tablespoons prepared horseradish
1	teaspoon fresh lemon juice
1	teaspoon Dijon mustard
⅛	teaspoon kosher salt

1. Preheat oven to 450°.

2. Heat a large skillet over medium-high heat. Rub beef with oil; coat all sides with pepper and ¾ teaspoon salt. Add beef to pan; cook 3 minutes, browning on all sides.

3. Place beef on a broiler pan. Bake at 450° for 25 minutes or until a thermometer registers 125°. Remove from oven; let stand 10 minutes before slicing.

4. Combine sour cream and next 5 ingredients (through ⅛ teaspoon salt); serve with beef.

Serves 8 (serving size: 3 ounces beef and about 1½ tablespoons sauce).

CALORIES 210; FAT 10.1g (sat 4.1g, mono 3.9g, poly 0.5g); PROTEIN 25.7g; CARB 2.4g; FIBER 0.3g; CHOL 67mg; IRON 1.7mg; SODIUM 310mg; CALC 21mg

Cheesy Meat Loaf Minis

Diced white cheddar makes this comfort food seem more indulgent than it actually is—fewer than 300 calories per serving.

Serve with a salad or mashed potatoes. To make fresh breadcrumbs, place torn bread in a food processor; pulse 10 times or until fine crumbs form. Hands-on time: 15 min. Total time: 40 min.

½   cup fresh breadcrumbs (about 1 ounce)

Cooking spray

1   cup chopped onion

2   garlic cloves, chopped

½   cup ketchup, divided

¾   cup (3 ounces) diced white cheddar cheese

¼   cup chopped fresh parsley

2   tablespoons grated Parmesan cheese

1   tablespoon prepared horseradish

1   tablespoon Dijon mustard

¾   teaspoon dried oregano

¼   teaspoon salt

¼   teaspoon freshly ground black pepper

1½   pounds ground sirloin

1   large egg, lightly beaten

1. Preheat oven to 425°.

2. Heat a large skillet over medium-high heat. Add breadcrumbs to pan; cook 3 minutes or until toasted, stirring frequently. Remove from pan; set aside.

3. Heat pan over medium-high heat. Coat pan with cooking spray. Add onion and garlic; sauté 3 minutes, stirring frequently. Combine onion mixture, breadcrumbs, ¼ cup ketchup, and next 10 ingredients (through egg). Shape into 6 (4 x 2–inch) loaves on a broiler pan coated with cooking spray; spread remaining ¼ cup ketchup evenly over loaves. Bake at 425° for 25 minutes or until done.

Serves 6 (serving size: 1 meat loaf).

CALORIES 256; FAT 11.6g (sat 5.7g, mono 3.9g, poly 0.9g); PROTEIN 28.5g; CARB 11.2g; FIBER 0.9g; CHOL 112mg; IRON 2.6mg; SODIUM 620mg; CALC 159mg

Mongolian Beef

This is a classic dish from the Chinese-American repertoire—Mongolian in name only, but delectable with tons of green onions and a gingery-garlicky brown sauce.

Serve this lightly spiced dish over wide rice noodles to catch all the sauce. Hands-on time: 20 min. Total time: 20 min.

2	tablespoons lower-sodium soy sauce
1	teaspoon sugar
1	teaspoon cornstarch
2	teaspoons dry sherry
2	teaspoons hoisin sauce
1	teaspoon rice vinegar
1	teaspoon chile paste with garlic (such as sambal oelek)
¼	teaspoon salt
2	teaspoons peanut oil
1	tablespoon minced peeled fresh ginger
1	tablespoon minced fresh garlic
1	pound sirloin steak, cut across grain into thin slices
16	medium-sized green onions, cut into 2-inch pieces

1. Combine first 8 ingredients, stirring until smooth.

2. Heat a large nonstick skillet over medium-high heat. Add peanut oil to pan; swirl to coat. Add ginger, garlic, and beef; sauté 2 minutes or until beef is browned. Add green onion pieces; sauté 30 seconds, stirring constantly.

Add soy sauce mixture to pan; cook 1 minute or until thick, stirring constantly.

Serves 4 (serving size: 1 cup).

CALORIES 237; FAT 10.5g (sat 3.5g, mono 4.3g, poly 1.1g); PROTEIN 26g; CARB 9.1g; FIBER 1.7g; CHOL 60mg; IRON 2.7mg; SODIUM 517mg; CALC 67mg

6

MEATS

CHOICE INGREDIENT

Cornstarch: Cornstarch is gluten free and has twice the thickening power of flour. When swapping it for flour, use half the amount called for in the recipe. Cornstarch yields a translucent rather than opaque sauce and generally doesn't lump if you gradually stir it into cold liquid to make a slurry before adding to the hot liquid.

Beef Pot Roast with Turnip Greens

Slightly bitter greens, parsnips, and cipollini onions: Here's our new favorite interpretation of the Sunday dinner classic.

Cipollini are small, flat Italian onions. If you can't find them, substitute pearl onions. Other large, full-flavored greens like mustard greens or kale will work as well. Beef cuts that require a slow and moist cooking method go by many names: blade roast, cross rib roast, seven-bone pot roast, arm pot roast, and boneless chuck roast. Hands-on time: 38 min. Total time: 8 hr. 38 min.

¾ cup all-purpose flour

1 (3-pound) boneless chuck roast, trimmed

1 teaspoon kosher salt

½ teaspoon freshly ground black pepper

1 tablespoon olive oil

1 pound fresh turnip greens, trimmed and coarsely chopped

3 cups (2-inch) diagonally cut parsnips (about 1 pound)

3 cups cubed peeled Yukon gold potatoes (about 1 pound)

2 cups cipollini onions, peeled and quartered

2 tablespoons tomato paste

1 cup dry red wine

1 (14-ounce) can fat-free, lower-sodium beef broth

1 tablespoon black peppercorns

4 thyme sprigs

3 garlic cloves, crushed

2 bay leaves

1 bunch fresh flat-leaf parsley

Fresh thyme sprigs (optional)

1. Place flour in a shallow dish. Sprinkle beef evenly with salt and pepper; dredge in flour. Heat a large skillet over medium-high heat. Add oil to pan; swirl to coat. Add beef; sauté 10 minutes, browning on all sides. Place turnip greens in a 6-quart electric slow cooker; top with parsnips, potatoes, and onions. Transfer beef to slow cooker. Add tomato paste to pan; cook 30 seconds, stirring constantly. Stir in wine and broth; bring to a boil, scraping pan to loosen browned bits. Cook 1 minute, stirring constantly. Pour broth mixture into slow cooker.

2. Place peppercorns and next 4 ingredients (through parsley) on a double layer of cheesecloth. Gather edges of cheesecloth together; secure with twine. Add cheesecloth bundle to slow cooker. Cover and cook on LOW 8 hours or until beef and vegetables are tender. Discard cheesecloth bundle. Remove roast from slow cooker; slice. Serve with vegetable mixture and cooking liquid. Garnish with thyme sprigs, if desired.

Serves 12 (serving size: 3 ounces beef, ¾ cup vegetable mixture, and ⅓ cup sauce).

CALORIES 424; FAT 21.3g (sat 8.1g, mono 9.4g, poly 0.9g); PROTEIN 33g; CARB 23.5g; FIBER 2.9g; CHOL 99mg; IRON 3.8mg; SODIUM 348mg; CALC 90mg

NUTRITION MADE EASY

Meat Labels: Nutrition information is available for all meats in the meat department, but it might not always be where you'd expect to find it. Factory-packed or branded meats and processed meats (like hot dogs) arrive at the store with standard on-pack labels. For meat that is butchered and packaged in grocery stores, the nutrition information may be displayed on a poster or in a brochure rather than on the package. Ground and chopped meats are required to have on-pack labels. If a label says "80% lean/20% fat," that means the ground meat is 20% fat by weight—considerably more than 20% of calories from fat.

Cabernet Short Ribs with Parmesan Polenta

Don't skip the gremolata. It melds all the elements and adds bright notes to a hearty dish.

Larger ribs will obviously take longer in the oven to get fork-tender, and one of the big ones will be a serving. To safely know when the sauce has reduced to 2 cups, pour into a 4-cup measuring cup to avoid a nasty splash. Return for more cooking if you have too much. Serve a good cabernet with this rich, simple yet grand dish. Hands-on time: 30 min. Total time: 2 hr. 21 min.

Ribs:

16 (3-ounce) bone-in beef short ribs, trimmed

⅝ teaspoon kosher salt

½ teaspoon freshly ground black pepper

2 teaspoons olive oil, divided

1 cup chopped onion

¾ cup chopped shallots

½ cup chopped carrot

½ cup chopped celery

6 garlic cloves, sliced

1 rosemary sprig

2½ cups cabernet sauvignon or other dry red wine

1¼ cups lower-sodium beef broth

1 teaspoon all-purpose flour

2 teaspoons water

1 tablespoon balsamic vinegar

Gremolata:

⅓ cup chopped fresh flat-leaf parsley

½ teaspoon grated lemon rind

1 garlic clove, minced

Polenta:

3 cups fat-free milk

1 cup water

⅝ teaspoon kosher salt

⅛ teaspoon freshly ground black pepper

1 cup quick-cooking polenta

¼ cup (1 ounce) grated fresh Parmigiano-Reggiano cheese

1. To prepare ribs, sprinkle ribs with ⅝ teaspoon salt and ½ teaspoon black pepper. Heat a large Dutch oven over medium-high heat. Add 1 teaspoon oil to pan; swirl to coat. Add 8 ribs; sauté 6 minutes, turning to brown on all sides. Remove ribs. Repeat procedure with remaining 1 teaspoon oil and 8 ribs. Add onion and next 5 ingredients (through rosemary) to pan; sauté 3 minutes, stirring constantly. Add wine to pan; bring to a boil, scraping pan to loosen browned bits. Cook 13 minutes or until reduced to 2 cups.

2. Preheat oven to 350°.

3. Add broth to pan; bring to a boil. Return ribs to pan. Cover and bake at 350° for 1½ hours, turning ribs after 45 minutes. Remove ribs from pan; strain cooking liquid through a fine sieve over a bowl. Discard solids. Skim fat; discard. Return cooking liquid to pan. Combine flour and 2 teaspoons water in a small bowl, stirring well. Add to pan; bring to a boil, and cook 11 minutes or until reduced to about 1 cup. Stir in vinegar.

4. To prepare gremolata, combine parsley, lemon rind, and minced garlic.

5. To prepare polenta, combine milk, 1 cup water, ⅝ teaspoon salt, and ⅛ teaspoon black pepper in a saucepan; bring to a boil over medium heat. Slowly stir in polenta; cook 5 minutes or until thick, stirring frequently. Stir in cheese. Place ½ cup polenta in each of 8 shallow bowls; top each with 2 ribs, 2 tablespoons sauce, and about 2 teaspoons gremolata.

Serves 8.

CALORIES 483; FAT 19.1g (sat 7.7g, mono 7.9g, poly 0.7g); PROTEIN 34.3g; CARB 29g; FIBER 2.2g; CHOL 85mg; IRON 5.2mg; SODIUM 694mg; CALC 210mg

MEATS

Dijon and Herb–Crusted Standing Beef Rib Roast
Simple, perfectly seasoned, and absolutely stunning.

There are certain celebrations that call for a showstopping, centerpiece roast. This is an indulgence, a special-occasion dish. Thankfully, with sensible portions, the calories, saturated fat, and sodium all stay within reason. Round out the meal with an abundance of vegetables. Hands-on time: 35 min. Total time: 6 hr.

1 (5-pound) standing rib roast, trimmed
2 (1-ounce) slices white bread
1 teaspoon salt
½ teaspoon freshly ground black pepper
Cooking spray
½ cup chopped fresh basil
½ cup chopped fresh parsley
¼ cup Dijon mustard
1 teaspoon chopped fresh thyme
3 garlic cloves, minced

1. Let roast stand at room temperature 1 hour.
2. Place bread in a food processor; pulse 10 times or until fine crumbs measure ¾ cup. Heat a small skillet over medium heat. Add breadcrumbs to pan; cook 12 minutes or until toasted, stirring frequently. Cool 5 minutes.
3. Preheat oven to 200°.
4. Sprinkle roast with salt and pepper. Heat a large skillet over medium-high heat. Coat pan with cooking spray. Add roast to pan; cook 5 minutes, browning on all sides. Remove roast from pan. Combine basil and next 4 ingredients (through garlic) in a bowl; spread mustard mixture over roast. Pat breadcrumbs onto roast. Place roast on rack of a roasting pan coated with cooking spray; place rack in pan.

5. Bake roast at 200° for 3½ hours or until a thermometer registers 135° or until desired degree of doneness. Let stand 20 minutes before slicing.

Serves 12 (serving size: about 3½ ounces).

CALORIES 229; FAT 13.9g (sat 5.4g, mono 5.7g, poly 0.6g); PROTEIN 22.2g; CARB 2.3g; FIBER 0.3g; CHOL 103mg; IRON 1.8mg; SODIUM 298mg; CALC 27mg

Wine Pairing
A spectacular main dish calls for an equally memorable wine pairing. This beef rib roast is even more delicious with an excellent-quality French Bordeaux or California cabernet sauvignon.

TECHNIQUE

Taking the Chill Off Meat: If you pop meat straight from the fridge into the oven or onto the grill, uneven cooking can result. Meats will cook more evenly if you allow them to stand at room temperature for 15 minutes to an hour (depending on the size of the cut). That way you'll avoid the bull's-eye effect with red meats, in which the middle is rare (or even raw) while the outside is well done. It's less of a problem with smaller cuts like chicken breasts—though even those benefit from resting at room temperature for 5 to 10 minutes before cooking. This is the sort of practice that, while easily overlooked, can produce the admirable results that signal a great cook at work.

Pan-Seared Grass-Fed Strip Steak

This method creates a succulent, buttery steak with a perfectly caramelized crust. The juices form a rich sauce.

We developed this recipe after buying half a grass-fed cow and noticing that quick-cooking alone couldn't coax enough beefy flavor from an expensive cut; it was dry. A little butter gives lean meat a flavor boost without adding much total fat. Warning: Smoky! Keep the exhaust fan on high, or, even better, cook in a skillet on a hot outdoor grill. Hands-on time: 10 min. Total time: 51 min.

2	(12-ounce) lean, grass-fed New York strip steaks
1	teaspoon kosher salt
¾	teaspoon freshly ground black pepper
1	tablespoon olive oil
2	tablespoons butter
2	thyme sprigs
2	garlic cloves, crushed

1. Let steaks stand at room temperature 30 minutes.

2. Sprinkle salt and pepper evenly over steaks. Heat a large cast-iron skillet over high heat. Add oil to pan; swirl to coat. Add steaks to pan; cook 3 minutes on each side or until browned. Reduce heat to medium-low; add butter, thyme, and garlic to pan. Carefully grasp pan handle using an oven mitt or folded dish towel. Tilt pan toward you so butter pools; cook 1½ minutes, basting steaks with butter constantly. Remove steaks from pan; cover loosely with foil. Let stand 10 minutes. Reserve butter mixture.

3. Cut steak diagonally across grain into thin slices. Discard thyme and garlic; spoon reserved butter mixture over steak.

Serves 6 (serving size: 3 ounces beef and ¾ teaspoon butter mixture).

CALORIES 197; FAT 10.2g (sat 4.4g, mono 2.2g, poly 0.7g); PROTEIN 26.3g; CARB 0.3g; FIBER 0g; CHOL 73mg; IRON 2.1mg; SODIUM 410mg; CALC 13mg

NUTRITION MADE EASY

Grass-Fed Beef: All cattle graze on pasture for the first six months to a year of their lives. Most American cattle then finish at a feedlot, consuming a mix of corn, soy, grains, and other supplements, plus hormones and antibiotics. This growth-spurt formula can get the cow to slaughter weight up to a year faster than a grass-fed animal and enhances fat marbling.

Eating exclusively from a pasture gives grass-fed meat a leaner profile, and it can be lower in saturated fat and higher in good fats, including omega-3s. However, when we sent beef to a lab, we found that the differences weren't universal or dramatic. The bigger issues are environmental and humanitarian—the energy required for intensive feedlot practices and whether it matters to you how an animal lives before slaughter.

Cajun Steak Frites with Kale

A modern, healthy approach to the steak dinner includes a prudent portion of herb-rubbed meat, crispy oven fries, and a hearty serving of earthy greens.

If you synchronize your cooking, this one-dish meal comes together in a little over an hour. Don't get excited and turn the fries before they're browned on the bottom, or they will become a pile of mushy potatoes. Garlic salt won't brown and turn bitter in the high heat of the oven, as could happen to fresh garlic. Hands-on time: 25 min. Total time: 1 hr. 5 min.

Frites:

- 1 pound baking potatoes, cut lengthwise into ¼-inch-thick strips
- 1 tablespoon olive oil
- 1 teaspoon hot sauce
- ¾ teaspoon dried thyme
- ¼ teaspoon garlic salt

Cooking spray

Steak:

- 1 (1-pound) flank steak, trimmed
- ¼ teaspoon salt
- ¼ teaspoon garlic powder
- ¼ teaspoon dried thyme
- ¼ teaspoon dried oregano
- ⅛ teaspoon ground cumin
- ⅛ teaspoon paprika
- ⅛ teaspoon chili powder
- ⅛ teaspoon ground red pepper
- ⅛ teaspoon freshly ground black pepper

Kale:

- 1 tablespoon olive oil
- 1 garlic clove, minced
- 1 pound kale, stemmed and shredded
- ¼ cup water
- 1 teaspoon red wine vinegar
- ¼ teaspoon salt
- ¼ teaspoon freshly ground black pepper

1. Preheat oven to 500°.
2. To prepare frites, heat a large baking sheet in oven 5 minutes. Combine potatoes, 1 tablespoon oil, and hot sauce in a large bowl. Add ¾ teaspoon thyme and garlic salt to potato mixture; toss to combine. Remove preheated pan from oven. Coat pan with cooking spray. Arrange potatoes in a single layer on prepared pan. Bake at 500° for 40 minutes or until crisp, turning once after 20 minutes. Remove from oven; cover and keep warm.
3. Preheat broiler.
4. To prepare steak, let steak stand at room temperature 15 minutes. Combine ¼ teaspoon salt and next 8 ingredients (through ⅛ teaspoon black pepper); sprinkle both sides of steak with spice blend. Place steak on a broiler pan coated with cooking spray, and broil 6 minutes on each side or until desired degree of doneness. Cover and let rest 5 minutes. Cut steak diagonally across grain into thin slices.
5. To prepare kale, heat a large skillet over medium heat. Add 1 tablespoon oil and minced garlic to pan; cook 1 minute, stirring constantly. Add kale and ¼ cup water to pan; cover and cook 5 minutes or until tender. Remove from heat; stir in vinegar, salt, and black pepper. Arrange 1 cup kale and 3 ounces steak on each of 4 plates; divide frites evenly among servings.

Serves 4.

CALORIES 369; FAT 14.3g (sat 3.9g, mono 7.6g, poly 1.3g); PROTEIN 28.1g; CARB 32.7g; FIBER 4.6g; CHOL 45mg; IRON 4.2mg; SODIUM 459mg; CALC 149mg

Easy Braised Brisket

A super-simple recipe with the surprising addition of tangy kalamatas to enhance the meatiness.

Serve over rice or mashed potatoes, or with crusty bread. If you have fresh oregano, use 1 tablespoon in place of dried. Hands-on time: 25 min. Total time: 4 hr.

1   (2½-pound) beef brisket, trimmed
¾   teaspoon salt
¼   teaspoon freshly ground black pepper
Cooking spray
1½ cups chopped onion
1   teaspoon dried oregano
½   cup water
⅓   cup chopped pitted kalamata olives
1   (14.5-ounce) can diced tomatoes, undrained

1. Sprinkle brisket evenly with salt and pepper. Heat a large Dutch oven over medium-high heat. Coat pan with cooking spray. Add brisket to pan, and cook 10 minutes, browning on all sides. Remove brisket from pan. Add onion and oregano to pan; sauté 3 minutes, stirring frequently.

2. Return brisket to pan; add ½ cup water. Cover; reduce heat, and simmer 2 hours. Add olives and tomatoes; cover and cook 1 hour.

3. Remove brisket from pan; let stand 5 minutes. Cut brisket against grain into thin slices; return brisket slices to pan. Cover and cook over medium-low heat 30 minutes.

Serves 8 (serving size: about 3½ ounces brisket and about ⅓ cup sauce).

CALORIES 224; FAT 7.3g (sat 2.3g, mono 3.7g, poly 0.5g); PROTEIN 31.4g; CARB 6g; FIBER 1g; CHOL 58mg; IRON 3.2mg; SODIUM 557mg; CALC 42mg

Beer Pairing

Beef brisket is classic with a nutty brown ale, but you can highlight the kalamata olives with a red ale, a clean, dry brew that gets its color from roasted barley.

TECHNIQUE
....

Slicing Meat Against the Grain: For tender slices, look at the meat to determine the direction of the grain (the muscle fibers), and cut across the grain, not with it. This is particularly important with tougher cuts such as flank steak or skirt steak, in which the grain is also quite obvious. But it's also a good practice even with more tender cuts, such as standing rib roast, or even poultry.

Carne Asada Tacos with Avocado Pico de Gallo

If you haven't tried skirt steak, prepare to have your world rocked. It's one of the richest, beefiest cuts.

When you have a very long piece of steak, it's OK to cut it into smaller pieces so they'll fit in the pan; just be sure to slice against the grain once it's cooked. If you don't have a gas stove to cook the tortillas, char them slightly in a grill pan over high heat. Hands-on time: 24 min. Total time: 3 hr. 36 min.

¼ cup fresh lime juice (about 2 medium limes)

1 (1-pound) skirt steak, trimmed

1 teaspoon ground cumin

¾ teaspoon kosher salt, divided

½ teaspoon ground red pepper

Cooking spray

1 cup diced seeded plum tomato

¼ cup diced onion

3 tablespoons finely chopped fresh cilantro

1 tablespoon diced seeded jalapeño pepper

1 tablespoon fresh lime juice

1 garlic clove, minced

¾ cup diced avocado (about 1 medium)

8 corn tortillas

Lime wedges (optional)

1. Combine ¼ cup juice and steak in a shallow dish. Sprinkle cumin, ½ teaspoon salt, and red pepper over both sides of steak. Cover and marinate in refrigerator 3 hours.
2. Heat grill pan over high heat. Coat pan with cooking spray. Add steak to pan; cook 3 minutes on each side or until desired degree of doneness. Let stand at least 10 minutes. Cut steak into ½-inch pieces.

3. Combine tomato and next 5 ingredients (through garlic) in a bowl. Gently stir in avocado and remaining ¼ teaspoon salt.
4. Heat tortillas over gas flame 15 seconds on each side or until charred on edges. Divide steak evenly among tortillas. Top with pico de gallo. Serve with lime wedges, if desired.

Serves 4 (serving size: 2 tacos and ¼ cup pico de gallo).

CALORIES 372; FAT 15.8g (sat 4.1g, mono 8.4g, poly 1.6g); PROTEIN 27.6g; CARB 32.6g; FIBER 5g; CHOL 50mg; IRON 4mg; SODIUM 505mg; CALC 115mg

Sirloin Skewers with Grilled Vegetable Couscous and Fiery Pepper Sauce

A North African–style sauce with cumin, caraway, and red pepper adds fragrant warmth to this dish.

Prepare the sauce up to one day ahead. If you prefer, blacken the bell peppers on the grill instead of in the oven. Make them first to allow time to steam. Hands-on time: 15 min. Total time: 1 hr. 11 min.

Pepper sauce:

4	red bell peppers
½	cup fresh cilantro leaves
¼	cup extra-virgin olive oil
3	tablespoons fresh lemon juice
1½	teaspoons ground coriander
1½	teaspoons ground cumin
½	teaspoon kosher salt
½	teaspoon caraway seeds
½	teaspoon crushed red pepper

Couscous:

1	cup water
1	cup fat-free, lower-sodium chicken broth
1	bay leaf
2	cups uncooked couscous
8	ounces eggplant, cut lengthwise into ½-inch-thick slices
8	ounces squash, cut lengthwise into ½-inch-thick slices
8	ounces zucchini, cut lengthwise into ½-inch-thick slices
4	green onions, trimmed
	Cooking spray

Skewers:

1½	pounds top sirloin steak, cut into 1-inch cubes
¾	teaspoon freshly ground black pepper
½	teaspoon kosher salt

1. Preheat broiler.
2. To prepare pepper sauce, cut bell peppers in half lengthwise; discard seeds and membranes. Place bell pepper halves, skin sides up, on a foil-lined baking sheet; flatten with hand. Broil 12 minutes or until blackened. Place in a paper bag, and fold to close tightly. Let stand 20 minutes. Peel. Place peppers and next 8 ingredients (through crushed red pepper) in a blender; process until smooth.
3. Preheat grill to medium-high heat.
4. To prepare couscous, combine 1 cup water, broth, and bay leaf in a medium saucepan; bring to a boil. Stir in couscous; cover. Remove from heat; let stand 10 minutes. Fluff with a fork; discard bay leaf.
5. Arrange eggplant and next 3 ingredients (though green onions) on grill rack coated with cooking spray; grill 3 minutes on each side or until vegetables are tender and

well marked. Remove from heat; coarsely chop vegetables. Combine ½ cup pepper sauce, couscous, and chopped vegetables in a large bowl; toss gently. Keep warm.
6. To prepare skewers, thread beef onto 12 (7-inch) skewers. Lightly coat beef with cooking spray; sprinkle with black pepper and ½ teaspoon salt. Place skewers on grill rack coated with cooking spray; grill 8 minutes or until desired degree of doneness, turning once. Serve with couscous mixture and remaining sauce.

Serves 6 (serving size: 2 skewers, about 1⅓ cups couscous mixture, and about ¼ cup sauce).

CALORIES 526; FAT 15.4g (sat 3.3g, mono 9.3g, poly 1.4g); PROTEIN 36.7g; CARB 58.5g; FIBER 8.2g; CHOL 49mg; IRON 3.7mg; SODIUM 461mg; CALC 75mg

Simmered Cabbage with Beef, Shan Style

This is one of the most delicious dishes we tested in 2011—a sublime Southeast Asian riff on beef and cabbage from Naomi Duguid.

Slow simmering like this is favored in northern Thailand and among the Shan people in Myanmar. Ingredients that have been combined with very little water and little or no oil are cooked under a tightly sealed lid. The result is ethereal. Hands-on time: 17 min. Total time: 37 min.

2 tablespoons peanut oil

1 cup thinly vertically sliced shallots

1 teaspoon salt

1 teaspoon turmeric

½ teaspoon ground red pepper

¼ pound ground sirloin

4 cups finely shredded cabbage (about 1 small head)

1 cup thin plum tomato wedges (about 2 medium)

⅓ cup coarsely chopped unsalted, dry-roasted peanuts

1. Heat a wok or Dutch oven over medium heat. Add oil to pan; swirl to coat. Add shallots, salt, turmeric, and red pepper; cook 3 minutes or until shallots are tender, stirring frequently. Add beef; cook 2 minutes or until beef begins to brown. Add cabbage and tomato; toss well to combine. Reduce heat to medium-low; cover and cook 10 minutes or until cabbage wilts. Stir in peanuts; cover and cook 10 minutes or until cabbage is tender.

Serves 4 (serving size: 1 cup).

CALORIES 238; FAT 15.9g (sat 3.2g, mono 7.4g, poly 4.3g); PROTEIN 10.9g; CARB 15.7g; FIBER 3.4g; CHOL 18mg; IRON 2.1mg; SODIUM 629mg; CALC 59mg

6

MEATS

NUTRITION MADE EASY

Lean Beef Choices: Familiarize yourself with our go-to leaner beef options. With these cuts that boast less fat, cooking method is everything. Here's a quick guide.

Brisket: A fibrous cut that takes well to slow braising, roasting, and smoking on a low-heat grill.

Flank steak: A versatile recipe workhorse—just make sure to slice it thinly against the grain, or it will be too chewy.

NY strip: A classic grilling or pan-frying steak with full flavor.

Skirt steak: More tender than flank steak, this cut is great for fajitas, tacos, or stir-fries.

Chuck roast: It may be called a roast, but its toughness demands low, moist heat. Stewing and braising are best.

Ground sirloin: Especially good when mixed with ingredients to keep it moist, as in meat loaf, or cooked into soups or saucy dishes.

Tenderloin: Comparatively lean for a tender cut. You'll get the best results with grilling, roasting, sautéing, or broiling. Don't overcook; it dries out easily.

Top round: While often cut like a steak, top round is tough and is best in dishes like pot roast that cook longer over low heat.

Top sirloin: Slightly less tender than a strip steak, this cut can still handle high heat in a kebab cooked on the grill or broiled.

Spice-Rubbed Pork Chops with Apple-Cranberry Chutney

The pork-and-applesauce combo is updated with chipotle, ginger, and tart cranberries.

Serve with asparagus or haricots verts. Hands-on time: 16 min. Total time: 41 min.

Chutney:

- 1 tablespoon butter
- 5 cups (¼-inch) cubed apple (about 3 apples)
- ¼ cup dried cranberries
- 3 tablespoons brown sugar
- 3 tablespoons cider vinegar
- 2 teaspoons minced peeled fresh ginger
- ¼ teaspoon salt
- ¼ teaspoon dry mustard
- ⅛ teaspoon ground allspice

Pork:

- ¾ teaspoon ground chipotle chile pepper

- ½ teaspoon salt
- ½ teaspoon garlic powder
- ½ teaspoon ground coriander
- ¼ teaspoon freshly ground black pepper
- 4 (4-ounce) boneless center-cut loin pork chops, trimmed

Cooking spray

1. To prepare chutney, melt butter in a nonstick skillet over medium-high heat. Add apple; sauté 4 minutes or until lightly browned, stirring frequently. Add cranberries and next 6 ingredients (through allspice); bring to a boil.

Reduce heat, and simmer 8 minutes or until apples are tender, stirring occasionally.
2. To prepare pork, heat a grill pan over medium-high heat. Combine chipotle and next 4 ingredients (through black pepper); sprinkle over pork. Coat grill pan with cooking spray. Add pork to pan; cook 4 minutes on each side or until done. Serve with chutney.

Serves 4 (serving size: 1 chop and about ⅓ cup chutney).

CALORIES 321; FAT 9.6g (sat 4.2g, mono 3.6g, poly 0.7g); PROTEIN 24.4g; CARB 34.6g; FIBER 2.4g; CHOL 72mg; IRON 1.1mg; SODIUM 520mg; CALC 45mg

Pan-Roasted Pork Loin with Leeks

This easy dish became a consistent staff favorite after Giuliano Hazan shared it with us back in 2001.

It's served with a supple sauce made from the melted leeks with which the meat simmers.
Hands-on time: 18 min. Total time: 2 hr. 35 min.

4	large leeks (about 2¼ pounds)
½	cup water
1	tablespoon butter, divided
½	teaspoon salt, divided
½	teaspoon black pepper, divided
1	(2-pound) boneless pork loin, trimmed
½	cup dry white wine
	Chopped fresh parsley (optional)

1. Remove roots and tough upper leaves from leeks. Cut each leek in half lengthwise. Cut each half crosswise into ½-inch-thick slices (about 6 cups). Soak in cold water to loosen dirt.

2. Combine leeks, ½ cup water, 1 teaspoon butter, ¼ teaspoon salt, and ¼ teaspoon pepper in a large Dutch oven or deep sauté pan over medium-high heat. Cook 10 minutes or until leek wilts. Pour leek mixture into a bowl.

3. Melt remaining 2 teaspoons butter in pan over medium-high heat; swirl to coat. Add pork to pan; cook 5 minutes, turning to brown on all sides. Add remaining ¼ teaspoon salt, remaining ¼ teaspoon pepper, and wine to pan; cook 15 seconds, scraping pan to loosen browned bits. Return leek mixture to pan. Cover, reduce heat, and simmer 2 hours or until pork is tender. Remove pork from pan. Increase heat to reduce leek sauce if too watery. Cut pork into ¼-inch-thick slices. Serve with leek mixture. Garnish with chopped parsley, if desired.

Serves 6 (serving size: about 3 ounces pork and about 2½ tablespoons leek mixture).

CALORIES 246; FAT 10.7g (sat 4.2g, mono 4.4g, poly 1.1g); PROTEIN 24.8g; CARB 12.1g; FIBER 1g; CHOL 73mg; IRON 2.8mg; SODIUM 306mg; CALC 60mg

Wine Pairing
Pork is a versatile meat that pairs well with red and white wine. Highlight the earthy leek sauce with torrontés, an aromatic white from Argentina.

Tacos al Pastor with Grilled Pineapple Salsa

Ancho, chipotle, and fresh jalapeños are a nice introduction to Mexican chile alchemy.

Both the meat and fruit get the smoky grill treatment in these delicious tacos. Serve with a tart salad of lettuce tossed with lime juice and oil; soften the flavor with chunks of rich avocado.
Hands-on time: 34 min. Total time: 1 hr. 8 min.

Pork:

1   **chipotle chile, canned in adobo sauce**

1   **tablespoon olive oil**

1   **(1-pound) pork tenderloin, trimmed**

1   **tablespoon chopped fresh oregano**

2   **teaspoons ancho chile powder**

½   **teaspoon ground cumin**

½   **teaspoon kosher salt**

¼   **teaspoon freshly ground black pepper**

Cooking spray

Salsa:

4   **(½-inch-thick) slices fresh pineapple**

¼   **cup fresh cilantro leaves**

3   **tablespoons thinly sliced red onion**

3   **tablespoons fresh lime juice**

¼   **teaspoon kosher salt**

½   **jalapeño pepper, thinly sliced**

Remaining ingredients:

8   **(6-inch) corn tortillas**

8   **lime wedges**

1. To prepare pork, preheat grill to high heat.

2. Mince chipotle chile. Combine chipotle and oil in a small bowl; rub evenly over pork. Combine oregano and next 4 ingredients (through black pepper); sprinkle evenly over pork. Let pork stand 30 minutes. Place pork on grill rack coated with cooking spray; grill 6 minutes on each side or until a thermometer registers 145°. Remove pork from grill; let stand 5 minutes. Coarsely chop pork; keep warm.

3. To prepare salsa, place pineapple on grill rack coated with cooking spray; grill 5 minutes on each side. Coarsely chop pineapple; place in a medium bowl. Add cilantro and next 4 ingredients (through jalapeño); toss to combine.

4. Warm tortillas according to package directions. Place 2 tortillas on each of 4 plates; divide pork evenly among tortillas. Top each taco with about 3 tablespoons salsa. Serve with lime wedges.

Serves 4 (serving size: 2 tacos and 2 lime wedges).

CALORIES 305; FAT 7.1g (sat 1.3g, mono 3.4g, poly 1.3g); PROTEIN 26.6g; CARB 36.9g; FIBER 4.7g; CHOL 74mg; IRON 1.7mg; SODIUM 513mg; CALC 51mg

Pork with Tangy Shallot Sauce

Three steps to porky perfection: Braise meat until tender, sauté until crisp, and glaze to caramelize.

The piquant, sour sauce (fruity habanero, orange, lime) is inspired by a Haitian condiment. Serve with rice and pan-fried plantains. Garnish with cilantro leaves and lime wedges. Hands-on time: 45 min. Total time: 14 hr. 54 min.

1	habanero pepper
¾	cup fresh orange juice (about 3 large oranges)
6	tablespoons fresh lime juice, divided
3	tablespoons minced shallots
2	tablespoons minced fresh garlic
1	tablespoon Dijon mustard
1	tablespoon honey
1½	teaspoons salt
4	thyme sprigs
3	pounds boneless pork shoulder, trimmed and cut into 1½-inch pieces
2	cups fat-free, lower-sodium chicken broth
½	cup thinly sliced shallots
1	teaspoon cider vinegar
1	teaspoon freshly ground black pepper
1	tablespoon canola oil

1. Cut habanero in half. Seed one half of pepper, and leave seeds in other half. Mince both pepper halves. Combine minced habanero, orange juice, ¼ cup lime juice, minced shallots, and next 5 ingredients (through thyme) in a large bowl; stir with a whisk. Add pork; toss to coat. Cover and chill 12 to 24 hours.

2. Place pork and marinade in a Dutch oven over medium-high heat. Add broth; bring to a boil. Cover, reduce heat, and simmer 1½ hours or until meat is tender. Remove pork from pan with a slotted spoon, reserving cooking liquid. Strain cooking liquid through a sieve into a bowl; discard solids. Place a large zip-top plastic bag in a bowl. Pour reserved cooking liquid into bag, and let stand 5 minutes. Snip off 1 bottom corner of bag; drain liquid into a medium saucepan, stopping before fat layer reaches opening. Discard fat. Set ½ cup cooking liquid aside to glaze pork.

3. Place saucepan with cooking liquid over medium-high heat; bring to a boil. Cook 20 minutes or until reduced to about 1 cup. Add sliced shallots, vinegar, black pepper, and 1 tablespoon lime juice. Cover and keep warm.

4. Heat a large nonstick skillet over medium heat. Add oil to pan; swirl to coat. Add pork; cook 10 minutes, turning to brown well on all sides. Add reserved ½ cup cooking liquid and remaining 1 tablespoon lime juice. Increase heat to medium-high; cook 4 minutes or until liquid nearly evaporates, stirring occasionally. Place pork in a bowl; pour sauce over pork.

Serves 10 (serving size: about 3 ounces pork and 2 tablespoons sauce).

CALORIES 223; FAT 8.8g (sat 2.6g, mono 4.2g, poly 1.2g); PROTEIN 27.3g; CARB 7.3g; FIBER 0.3g; CHOL 75mg; IRON 1.4mg; SODIUM 550mg; CALC 33mg

Roast Pork Tenderloin with Plum Barbecue Sauce
A fusion BBQ sauce: Asian and Southern, sweet and vinegary.

Once it's cooked, set aside 2½ cups sauce to serve with the pork, and use the rest to baste as it cooks.
Hands-on time: 15 min. Total time: 1 hr. 5 min.

Sauce:

- 2 tablespoons canola oil
- 1 cup chopped onion
- 2 garlic cloves, finely chopped
- ¼ cup packed brown sugar
- ¼ cup rice wine vinegar
- ¼ cup ketchup
- 2 tablespoons lower-sodium soy sauce
- 2 teaspoons dry mustard
- 1 teaspoon ground ginger
- ½ teaspoon freshly ground black pepper
- ⅛ teaspoon crushed red pepper
- 2 whole cloves
- 1½ pounds black plums, quartered and pitted
- 1 star anise

Pork:

- 2 tablespoons canola oil
- 2 (1-pound) pork tenderloins, trimmed
- ½ teaspoon salt
- ½ teaspoon freshly ground black pepper

1. Heat a large saucepan over medium-high heat. Add 2 tablespoons oil to pan; swirl to coat. Add onion and garlic; sauté 5 minutes, stirring constantly. Add sugar and next 10 ingredients (through star anise); bring to a boil. Reduce heat, and simmer, partially covered, 30 minutes or until plums break down and sauce thickens, stirring occasionally. Discard cloves and anise.
2. Preheat oven to 450°.
3. Heat a large skillet over medium-high heat. Add 2 tablespoons oil to pan; swirl to coat. Sprinkle pork evenly with salt and ½ teaspoon black pepper. Add pork to pan, and sauté 7 minutes, browning on all sides.

4. Transfer pork to a foil-lined jelly-roll pan; coat with ½ cup plum sauce. Roast pork at 450° for 15 minutes. Remove pork from oven. Turn pork over; coat with an additional ½ cup plum sauce. Roast 7 minutes or until a thermometer registers 145°. Remove from pan; let stand 10 minutes. Slice crosswise. Serve with remaining plum sauce.

Serves 8 (serving size: 3 ounces pork and about ⅓ cup sauce).

CALORIES 378; FAT 10.3g (sat 1.6g, mono 5.6g, poly 2.4g); PROTEIN 25.2g; CARB 50.7g; FIBER 4.7g; CHOL 62mg; IRON 2mg; SODIUM 417mg; CALC 22mg

Wine Pairing
The sweet and spicy plum sauce is a natural match with gewürztraminer, a slightly sweet white wine with opulent floral and spice aromas.

Grilled Pork Chops with Shallot Butter

Chops are herb-rubbed and grilled, then dabbed with a citrus-herb butter.

Allow the butter to come to room temperature before spreading over the pork. You can also combine the oil and herbs a couple of hours in advance, and rub onto the meat before grilling. Hands-on time: 11 min. Total time: 37 min.

8 (7-ounce) bone-in center-cut pork chops

1 teaspoon salt, divided

¾ teaspoon freshly ground black pepper

2 tablespoons extra-virgin olive oil

2 teaspoons finely chopped fresh chives

1 teaspoon finely chopped fresh thyme

1 teaspoon finely chopped fresh rosemary

3 garlic cloves, minced

2 tablespoons butter, softened

2½ teaspoons minced shallots

¼ teaspoon grated lemon rind

1. Preheat grill to medium-high heat.

2. Sprinkle both sides of pork evenly with ½ teaspoon salt and pepper. Combine oil and next 4 ingredients (through garlic), stirring well. Rub oil mixture evenly over both sides of pork. Place pork on grill rack; grill 5 minutes on each side or until a thermometer registers 145°. Remove pork from grill; let stand 5 minutes. Sprinkle with remaining ½ teaspoon salt.

3. Combine butter, shallots, and rind, stirring well. Spread about 1 teaspoon butter mixture over each pork chop; let pork stand 5 minutes.

Serves 8 (serving size: 1 pork chop).

CALORIES 208; FAT 12.2g (sat 4.5g, mono 5.9g, poly 0.9g); PROTEIN 22.5g; CARB 0.7g; FIBER 0.1g; CHOL 68mg; IRON 0.7mg; SODIUM 360mg; CALC 28mg

Blue Cheese–Stuffed Pork Chops with Pears

Pear and blue cheese are mighty fine on their own, but they're gorgeous with pork.

Serve with Haricots Verts with Warm Bacon Vinaigrette (page 312) to showcase fall produce.
Hands-on time: 24 min. Total time: 24 min.

4 (4-ounce) boneless center-cut loin pork chops, trimmed

½ cup (2 ounces) crumbled blue cheese

½ teaspoon kosher salt, divided

½ teaspoon freshly ground black pepper, divided

1½ teaspoons olive oil

1½ teaspoons butter

1 ripe pear, cored and cut into 16 wedges

1. Cut a horizontal slit through thickest portion of each pork chop to form a pocket. Stuff 2 tablespoons blue cheese into each pocket. Sprinkle ¼ teaspoon salt and ¼ teaspoon pepper evenly over both sides of pork. Heat a large nonstick skillet over medium-high heat. Add oil to pan; swirl to coat. Add pork to pan; sauté 3 minutes on each side or until desired degree of doneness. Remove pork from pan; let stand 5 minutes.

2. Melt butter in pan. Add pear to pan. Sprinkle pear with remaining ¼ teaspoon salt and remaining ¼ teaspoon pepper; sauté 4 minutes or until lightly browned, stirring occasionally. Serve with pork.

Serves 4 (serving size: 1 stuffed pork chop and 4 pear wedges).

CALORIES 246; FAT 13g (sat 5.5g, mono 1g, poly 4.8g); PROTEIN 24.4g; CARB 7.3g; FIBER 1.4g; CHOL 81mg; IRON 0.8mg; SODIUM 493mg; CALC 98mg

Spiced Pork Tenderloin with Sautéed Apples

Sweet, aromatic spices coat the tenderloin, while apples cook with savory shallots and thyme.

Serve with a spinach salad. Hands-on time: 10 min. Total time: 20 min.

⅜   teaspoon salt

¼   teaspoon ground coriander

¼   teaspoon freshly ground black pepper

⅛   teaspoon ground cinnamon

⅛   teaspoon ground nutmeg

1   pound pork tenderloin, trimmed and cut crosswise into 12 pieces

Cooking spray

2   tablespoons butter

2   cups thinly sliced Braeburn or Gala apple

⅓   cup thinly sliced shallots

⅛   teaspoon salt

¼   cup apple cider

1   teaspoon fresh thyme leaves

1. Heat a large cast-iron skillet over medium-high heat. Combine first 5 ingredients; sprinkle evenly over pork. Coat pan with cooking spray. Add pork to pan; cook 3 minutes on each side or until desired degree of doneness. Remove pork from pan; keep warm.

2. Melt butter in pan; swirl to coat. Add apple, shallots, and ⅛ teaspoon salt; sauté 4 minutes or until apple starts to brown. Add apple cider to pan; cook 2 minutes or until apple is crisp-tender. Stir in thyme leaves. Serve apple mixture with pork.

Serves 4 (serving size: 3 pork medallions and about ½ cup apple mixture).

CALORIES 234; FAT 9.7g (sat 5g, mono 3.2g, poly 0.7g); PROTEIN 24.4g; CARB 12.3g; FIBER 1.5g; CHOL 89mg; IRON 1.7mg; SODIUM 394mg; CALC 18mg

Fruit and Walnut–Stuffed Pork Loin

A plum, sour cherry, and apricot fruit trio within and a crispy crust outside: It's simpler than it looks and grand for guests.

The dried fruits are rehydrated in a blend of orange-flavored liqueur and red wine. Use orange juice and chicken broth if you don't want alcohol. Hands-on time: 30 min. Total time: 1 hr. 44 min.

½ cup dry red wine

¼ cup dried sour cherries

¼ cup chopped dried apricots

¼ cup chopped dried plums

2 tablespoons Triple Sec (orange-flavored liqueur)

⅓ cup finely chopped walnuts

2 tablespoons chopped shallots

1¼ teaspoons salt, divided

½ teaspoon grated lemon rind

2 (1-ounce) slices French bread

1 teaspoon chopped fresh thyme

¼ teaspoon freshly ground black pepper

2 garlic cloves, minced

1 (2½-pound) boneless center-cut pork loin roast, trimmed

2 tablespoons Dijon mustard

Cooking spray

1. Preheat oven to 400°.

2. Combine first 5 ingredients in a medium microwave-safe bowl; microwave at HIGH 2 minutes. Let stand 10 minutes or until fruit is plump. Drain mixture through a sieve, reserving fruit mixture. Combine fruit mixture, walnuts, shallots, ¼ teaspoon salt, and rind.

3. Place ¾ teaspoon salt, bread, and next 3 ingredients (through garlic) in a food processor; process until fine crumbs form.

4. Cut pork in half lengthwise, cutting to, but not through, other side; open halves, laying pork flat. Starting from center, cut each half lengthwise, cutting to, but not through, other side; open halves, laying pork flat. Place pork between 2 sheets of plastic wrap; pound to an even thickness. Discard plastic wrap. Spread fruit mixture over pork, leaving a ½-inch border. Roll up pork, jelly-roll fashion, starting with one long side. Secure at 1- to 2-inch intervals with twine. Sprinkle outside of pork evenly with remaining ¼ teaspoon salt; brush evenly with mustard. Sprinkle breadcrumb mixture over pork; press gently to adhere. Place pork on a broiler pan coated with cooking spray. Bake at 400° for 45 minutes or until a thermometer registers 145°. Let pork stand 10 minutes. Remove twine. Cut into 16 (½-inch-thick) slices.

Serves 8 (serving size: 2 slices).

CALORIES 323; FAT 12.4g (sat 3.7g, mono 4.5g, poly 3.1g); PROTEIN 29.7g; CARB 18.9g; FIBER 1.4g; CHOL 79mg; IRON 1.9mg; SODIUM 573mg; CALC 41mg

TECHNIQUE

Stuffing Pork Tenderloin and Loin: This works with many combinations of cheeses, herbs, and fruits.

1. Slice tenderloin or loin in half lengthwise; cut each half lengthwise. Open halves, laying pork flat.

2. Pound pork to an even thickness. Slide segments of kitchen twine beneath the pork at 1- to 2-inch intervals.

3. Spread the filling evenly over the pork, leaving a ½-inch border along edges.

4. Staring with long end, roll up, jelly-roll style, tucking in filling as you go. Secure with twine.

Slow-Cooker Char Siu Pork Roast

Time rather than labor perfects this tender Chinese version of barbecue pork.

Serve with sticky or long-grain white rice and stir-fried vegetables. Hands-on time: 20 min.
Total time: 10 hr. 50 min.

¼ cup lower-sodium soy sauce
¼ cup hoisin sauce
3 tablespoons ketchup
3 tablespoons honey
2 teaspoons minced fresh garlic
2 teaspoons grated peeled fresh ginger
1 teaspoon dark sesame oil
½ teaspoon five-spice powder
2 pounds boneless Boston butt pork roast, trimmed
½ cup fat-free, lower-sodium chicken broth

1. Combine first 8 ingredients in a small bowl, stirring well with a whisk. Place in a large zip-top plastic bag. Add pork to bag; seal. Marinate in refrigerator at least 2 hours, turning occasionally.
2. Place pork and marinade in an electric slow cooker. Cover and cook on LOW 8 hours.
3. Remove pork from slow cooker using a slotted spoon; keep warm.

4. Add broth to sauce in slow cooker. Cover and cook on LOW 30 minutes or until sauce thickens. Shred pork with 2 forks; serve with sauce.

Serves 8 (serving size: 3 ounces pork and ¼ cup sauce).

CALORIES 227; FAT 9.5g (sat 3.1g, mono 3.9g, poly 1.1g); PROTEIN 21.6g; CARB 12.7g; FIBER 0.4g; CHOL 73mg; IRON 1.7mg; SODIUM 561mg; CALC 30mg

6

MEATS

Hoppin' John with Mustard Greens

Ham-flavored beans and rice, a traditional New Year's dish in the South, is rich in fiber and the goodness of greens.

Double down on the Southern groove and serve with corn bread. Look for fresh black-eyed peas in the produce department, or cook frozen ones for this one-dish meal. Hands-on time: 16 min.
Total time: 51 min.

2 cups water
2 tablespoons whole-grain Dijon mustard
1 teaspoon salt
¼ teaspoon dried thyme
2 tablespoons olive oil
3½ cups chopped onion
1 cup uncooked long-grain white rice
⅔ cup finely chopped ham
4 garlic cloves, minced
4 cups cooked black-eyed peas

4 cups chopped trimmed mustard greens

1. Combine first 4 ingredients, stirring with a whisk; set aside.
2. Heat a Dutch oven over medium-high heat. Add oil to pan; swirl to coat. Add onion to pan; sauté 6 minutes, stirring frequently. Add rice, ham, and garlic; sauté 2 minutes, stirring frequently. Stir in water mixture; bring to a boil. Cover, reduce heat, and simmer 15 minutes. Add peas and greens;

cover and cook 5 minutes. Stir; cover and cook 5 minutes or until greens and rice are tender.

Serves 6 (serving size: about 1⅓ cups).

CALORIES 389; FAT 7g (sat 1.4g, mono 4.1g, poly 1g); PROTEIN 18.2g; CARB 63.6g; FIBER 11g; CHOL 14mg; IRON 5.1mg; SODIUM 502mg; CALC 109mg

Argentinean Pork

Tenderloin pairs beautifully with an herb-packed sauce based on classic South American chimichurri.

Serve with mashed potatoes and garnish with fresh cilantro and grated lemon rind. Hands-on time: 20 min. Total time: 1 hr. 30 min.

6 tablespoons extra-virgin olive oil, divided

1 cup fresh parsley leaves, divided

⅔ cup fresh cilantro leaves, divided

½ teaspoon ground cumin

¼ teaspoon crushed red pepper

1 (1-pound) pork tenderloin, trimmed

¾ teaspoon kosher salt, divided

½ teaspoon freshly ground black pepper

Cooking spray

1 tablespoon fresh oregano leaves

1 tablespoon fresh lemon juice

1 tablespoon sherry vinegar

2 garlic cloves, chopped

1 shallot, chopped

1. Combine 2 tablespoons oil, ¼ cup parsley, ⅓ cup cilantro, cumin, and red pepper in a shallow dish. Add pork. Cover and marinate in refrigerator 1 hour, turning once.
2. Preheat grill to medium-high heat.
3. Sprinkle pork with ½ teaspoon salt and black pepper. Place pork on grill rack coated with cooking spray; grill 8 minutes. Turn pork over; grill 7 minutes or until a thermometer registers 145°. Remove pork from grill. Let stand 5 minutes. Slice pork crosswise.
4. Place remaining ¾ cup parsley, remaining ⅓ cup cilantro, remaining ¼ teaspoon salt, oregano, and next 4 ingredients (through shallot) in a food processor; pulse 10 times. Drizzle remaining ¼ cup oil through food chute with processor on; process until well blended. Serve with pork.

Serves 4 (serving size: 3 ounces pork and 2 tablespoons sauce).

CALORIES 319; FAT 23g (sat 3.6g, mono 15.7g, poly 2.6g); PROTEIN 24.5g; CARB 2.9g; FIBER 0.7g; CHOL 74mg; IRON 2.4mg; SODIUM 430mg; CALC 39mg

Wine Pairing
A fruity, rustic malbec from Argentina is a geographically apropos complement to the meaty pork and fresh chimichurri.

MEATS

Savory Bread Puddings with Ham and Cheddar

A dessert favorite moves to breakfast and wakes up with cheddar, ham, sour cream, and green onions.

Preparing the puddings in individual ramekins gives them a dressier feel and shortens cook time.
Hands-on time: 22 min. Total time: 42 min.

8   ounces multigrain bread with seeds, cut into ¾-inch cubes

Cooking spray

¾   cup (3 ounces) shredded sharp cheddar cheese, divided

¼   cup chopped green onions, divided

¾   cup fat-free milk

¼   cup fat-free, lower-sodium chicken broth

⅛   teaspoon freshly ground black pepper

3   ounces lower-sodium ham, minced

2   large egg yolks, lightly beaten

3   large egg whites

4   teaspoons reduced-fat sour cream

1. Preheat oven to 375°.

2. Place bread cubes on a jelly-roll pan; coat with cooking spray. Bake at 375° for 10 minutes or until lightly toasted, turning once. Remove from oven; cool.

3. Combine bread, ½ cup cheese, 3 tablespoons onions, and next 5 ingredients (through egg yolks) in a large bowl. Place egg whites in a small bowl; beat with a mixer at high speed until foamy (about 30 seconds). Gently fold egg whites into bread mixture.

4. Spoon about 1 cup bread mixture into each of 4 (7-ounce) ramekins coated with cooking spray. Divide remaining ¼ cup cheese and remaining 1 tablespoon onions evenly among ramekins. Bake at 375° for 20 minutes or until lightly browned. Top each serving with 1 teaspoon sour cream.

Serves 4 (serving size: 1 bread pudding).

CALORIES 272; FAT 11.2g (sat 5g, mono 3.3g, poly 0.6g); PROTEIN 18.5g; CARB 28.4g; FIBER 8.6g; CHOL 140mg; IRON 2mg; SODIUM 536mg; CALC 400mg

Wine Pairing

Classic mimosas made with Champagne and orange juice add sparkle to this a.m. meal. Dress up these drinks with a splash of grenadine and a strawberry garnish over the rim.

Quick Cassoulet

That's right, a quicker version of a French meat-and-bean masterpiece that can take two days. It's not as complex, but the spirit of the dish is here.

A variety of meats adds depth, and the medley of sausages (versus traditional large hunks of slow-cooking meats) cuts the cook time to around an hour without sacrificing flavor. Of course, if you prefer, use all one type of sausage. Open some great red wine, and chase this course with a salad of bitter greens. Hands-on time: 29 min. Total time: 1 hr. 22 min.

2½ tablespoons olive oil, divided

3 (4-inch) pork sausages, sliced (about 6 ounces)

3 (4-inch) lamb sausages, sliced (about 6½ ounces)

3 (4-inch) duck sausages, sliced (about 6½ ounces)

Cooking spray

1 cup finely chopped onion

½ cup finely chopped carrot

½ cup finely chopped celery

2 tablespoons minced fresh garlic

½ teaspoon freshly ground black pepper

¼ teaspoon salt

½ cup dry white wine

¼ cup cognac or brandy

2 cups fat-free, lower-sodium chicken broth

1 tablespoon chopped fresh thyme

3 (15-ounce) cans unsalted cannellini beans, rinsed and drained

2 bay leaves

1 (14.5-ounce) can no-salt-added diced tomatoes, drained

Dash of ground cloves

1 (4-ounce) piece French bread baguette

1. Preheat oven to 325°.

2. Heat a large Dutch oven over medium heat. Add 1 tablespoon oil to pan; swirl to coat. Add sausages; cook 8 minutes, stirring frequently. Remove sausages from pan using a slotted spoon; drain. Wipe pan with paper towels to absorb remaining oil, leaving browned bits on bottom of pan. Coat pan with cooking spray. Add onion and next 5 ingredients (through salt); cook 8 minutes, stirring occasionally. Add wine and cognac; bring to a boil. Cook 10 minutes or until liquid almost evaporates, scraping pan to loosen browned bits.

3. Add broth and next 5 ingredients (through ground cloves) to vegetable mixture. Return sausages to pan; stir to combine. Bring mixture to a boil; remove from heat. Discard bay leaves. Bake at 325° for 30 minutes.

4. Place bread in a food processor; pulse 10 times or until fine crumbs measure 2 cups. Heat a large nonstick skillet over medium-high heat. Add crumbs to pan; sauté 3 minutes or until lightly browned, stirring frequently. Drizzle with remaining 1½ tablespoons oil; sauté 2 minutes or until crumbs are golden, stirring frequently.

5. Remove cassoulet from oven; sprinkle with crumbs. Bake at 325° for 10 minutes.

Serves 8 (serving size: about 1½ cups).

CALORIES 440; FAT 28.2g (sat 9.4g, mono 13.4g, poly 4.5g); PROTEIN 16.2g; CARB 27.5g; FIBER 5.6g; CHOL 67mg; IRON 4.2mg; SODIUM 770mg; CALC 58mg

Lamb Shanks Braised with Tomato

Braised meats benefit from simple recipes, the key being low, slow, undisturbed cooking.

This cooking method breaks down the loads of connective tissue found in lamb shanks, rendering them tender and succulent. Serve over polenta. Hands-on time: 15 min. Total time: 2 hr. 30 min.

Cooking spray

4   (12-ounce) lamb shanks, trimmed

½   teaspoon salt

¼   teaspoon freshly ground black pepper

4   garlic cloves, minced

¾   cup dry red wine

2   (14.5-ounce) cans diced tomatoes with basil, garlic, and oregano, undrained

¼   cup chopped fresh parsley

1. Heat a large Dutch oven over medium-high heat. Coat pan with cooking spray. Sprinkle lamb with salt and pepper. Add lamb to pan, and cook 4 minutes on each side or until browned. Remove from pan. Add garlic to pan; sauté 15 seconds. Add wine; cook 2 minutes, scraping pan to loosen browned bits. Stir in tomatoes; cook 2 minutes. Return lamb to pan. Cover, reduce heat, and simmer 1 hour. Turn lamb over; simmer 1 hour or until meat is done and very tender.

2. Place lamb on a plate; cover loosely with foil. Skim fat from surface of sauce. Bring to a boil; cook 10 minutes or until thick. Return lamb to pan; cook 4 minutes or until lamb is thoroughly heated. Stir in parsley.

Serves 4 (serving size: 1 shank and ¾ cup sauce).

CALORIES 254; FAT 11.4g (sat 4.8g, mono 4.8g, poly 0.8g); PROTEIN 25.9g; CARB 11.7g; FIBER 3.5g; CHOL 89mg; IRON 2.9mg; SODIUM 439mg; CALC 64mg

Chermoula-Marinated Lamb Loin Chops

A North African garlic-coriander spice paste is the key to this bold, simple lamb dish.

Less expensive loin chops cook quickly to a nice pinkness. It pairs beautifully with a simply dressed salad.
Hands-on time: 20 min. Total time: 8 hr. 26 min.

¼ cup finely chopped fresh cilantro

2 tablespoons finely chopped fresh flat-leaf parsley

2 tablespoons minced onion

2 tablespoons fresh lemon juice

1 tablespoon extra-virgin olive oil

¾ teaspoon smoked paprika

½ teaspoon ground coriander

2 garlic cloves, minced

8 (4-ounce) lamb loin chops, trimmed

¼ teaspoon salt

¼ teaspoon freshly ground black pepper

2 teaspoons canola oil

Cooking spray

1. Combine first 8 ingredients in a large zip-top plastic bag. Add lamb; seal and marinate in refrigerator 8 hours or overnight.
2. Preheat oven to 450°.
3. Remove lamb from bag; discard marinade. Sprinkle both sides of lamb evenly with salt and pepper. Heat a large nonstick skillet over medium-high heat. Add canola oil to pan; swirl to coat. Add half of lamb to pan; cook 2 minutes or until browned. Transfer lamb, browned sides up, to a broiler pan coated with cooking spray. Repeat procedure with remaining lamb. Bake lamb at 450° for 6 minutes or until desired degree of doneness.

Serves 4 (serving size: 2 lamb chops).

CALORIES 265; FAT 15g (sat 4.1g, mono 8.3g, poly 1.1g); PROTEIN 28.9g; CARB 1.9g; FIBER 0.4g; CHOL 91mg; IRON 2.1mg; SODIUM 229mg; CALC 26mg

Wine Pairing

Sweet, opulent Australian shiraz is a consummate match with lamb, and the wine's subtle spices highlight the spices in the sweet-and-savory marinade.

6

MEATS

TEST KITCHEN SECRET

Preparing Lamb Loin Chops: These affordable, versatile chops are quick-cooking, so they're great for weeknight meals. For best flavor and looks, sear them to create a beautiful brown crust and finish them in the oven.

Lamb Shoulder Braised with Spring Vegetables, Green Herbs, and White Wine

Spring is the season for *navarin*, a light stew of vegetables with lamb and herbs.

You may need to call ahead to order lamb shoulder from your butcher. Ask if they have grass-fed meat from a local producer. Hands-on time: 31 min. Total time: 2 hr. 35 min.

1½ tablespoons butter

2 small onions, cut into 8 wedges

6 garlic cloves, crushed

2 pounds lamb shoulder, trimmed and cut into 1½-inch pieces

3 cups fruity white wine (such as riesling)

1 teaspoon salt

½ teaspoon freshly ground black pepper

1 tablespoon chopped fresh oregano

1 tablespoon chopped fresh flat-leaf parsley

2 teaspoons chopped fresh rosemary

½ pound small red potatoes, halved

½ pound turnips, peeled and cut into 1-inch cubes

½ pound carrots, peeled and cut into 1-inch pieces

½ pound asparagus, trimmed and cut into 2-inch pieces

1. Melt butter in a Dutch oven over medium-high heat. Add onion to pan; sauté 4 minutes, stirring frequently. Add garlic; sauté 1 minute, stirring constantly. Spoon onion mixture into a large bowl. Add half of lamb to pan; sauté 4 minutes, turning to brown on all sides. Remove from pan; add to onion mixture. Repeat procedure with remaining lamb.

2. Add wine to pan, scraping pan to loosen browned bits. Return lamb mixture to pan; sprinkle with salt and pepper. Combine oregano, parsley, and rosemary. Add half of herb mixture to pan; bring to a boil. Cover, reduce heat, and simmer 1½ hours or until lamb is tender. Add potatoes, turnips, and carrots to pan; cover and cook 40 minutes or until tender. Add asparagus; cook 5 minutes or until asparagus is tender. Stir in remaining herb mixture.

Serves 8 (serving size: 1¼ cups).

CALORIES 325; FAT 12.6g (sat 5.3g, mono 4.7g, poly 1.1g); PROTEIN 34.3g; CARB 17.2g; FIBER 3.6g; CHOL 110mg; IRON 4.2mg; SODIUM 448mg; CALC 75mg

Rosemary Lamb Rib Chops

This most delicate and tender cut of lamb shouldn't hide behind powerful flavors. We give it a proper sear and just a hint of seasoning.

Sweet potatoes and a salad with bitter greens and apple make a good partner for the meat.
Hands-on time: 16 min. Total time: 22 min.

1½ teaspoons chopped fresh rosemary
½ teaspoon salt
¼ teaspoon freshly ground black pepper
1 garlic clove, minced
8 (3-ounce) lamb rib chops, trimmed
2 teaspoons olive oil

1. Combine first 4 ingredients in a small bowl; sprinkle evenly over lamb, rubbing to coat.
2. Heat a large skillet over medium-high heat. Add oil to pan; swirl to coat. Add lamb; cook 3 minutes on each side or until desired degree of doneness. Remove lamb from pan; let stand 5 minutes.

Serves 4 (serving size: 2 lamb chops).

CALORIES 157; FAT 9.7g (sat 3g, mono 4.6g, poly 0.9g); PROTEIN 16g; CARB 0.4g; FIBER 0.1g; CHOL 52mg; IRON 1.4mg; SODIUM 344mg; CALC 12mg

Kibbeh Meatballs with Spiced Yogurt Sauce

Middle Eastern torpedo-shaped meatballs get a lower-fat treatment with pan-frying.

The versatile sauce is a Mediterranean version of ranch dressing: garlicky and full of cucumber crunch.
Hands-on time: 21 min. Total time: 1 hr. 45 min.

1½ cups plain fat-free Greek yogurt
1 cup shredded seeded cucumber
½ teaspoon ground cumin
½ teaspoon minced fresh garlic
⅛ teaspoon salt
⅛ teaspoon freshly ground black pepper
¾ cup uncooked bulgur
2 cups cold water
1 pound lean ground lamb (20% fat)
¼ cup minced shallots
¼ cup minced fresh parsley

¾ teaspoon salt
½ teaspoon ground cumin
½ teaspoon ground allspice
½ teaspoon ground cinnamon
¼ teaspoon ground red pepper
1 tablespoon olive oil

1. Combine first 6 ingredients in a bowl; chill.
2. Combine bulgur and 2 cups water in a medium bowl. Let stand 30 minutes; drain bulgur through a fine sieve, pressing out excess liquid. Place bulgur, lamb, and next 7 ingredients (through red pepper)
in a food processor; process just until smooth. Cover and chill 30 minutes. Shape lamb mixture into 20 (2½-inch-long) football-shaped meatballs.
3. Heat a nonstick skillet over medium-high heat. Add oil to pan; swirl to coat. Add meatballs; cook 12 minutes, browning on all sides. Serve with sauce.

Serves 10 (serving size: 2 meatballs and 3 tablespoons sauce).

CALORIES 161; FAT 7.7g (sat 2.7g, mono 3.6g, poly 0.6g); PROTEIN 12.2g; CARB 10.8g; FIBER 2.3g; CHOL 30mg; IRON 1.1mg; SODIUM 248mg; CALC 43mg

Chapter
Poultry

7:

Old-Fashioned Chicken Potpie, page 235

Chicken is the go-to "protein" (as chefs call it) for American cooks in a hurry, and in our Test Kitchen we have stuffed, paillarded, fricasseed, breaded, poached, and pan-fried hundreds of thousands of chicken breasts—the leanest meat on the bird, and a versatile foil for global sauces and flavors. A 4-ounce cooked skinless portion (6 ounces, raw) contains only 182 calories, and only a quarter of its 4 grams of fat are saturated. It makes all the difference to buy the best breasts, taken from chickens that still taste like chicken, and then cook with care lest they turn to rubber. And make sure to try the richer thighs—not as fatty as you might think, and tasty.

Meyer Lemon Chicken Piccata

The caper-dotted classic gets a beautiful, light update, fragrant with the perfume of Meyer lemons.

If Meyer lemons are unavailable, put 3 tablespoons orange juice in a 1-cup glass measuring cup, and add enough lemon juice to reach ⅓ cup juice for the recipe. Hands-on time: 36 min. Total time: 36 min.

2 (8-ounce) skinless, boneless chicken breast halves

½ teaspoon kosher salt

¼ teaspoon black pepper

¼ cup all-purpose flour

2 tablespoons unsalted butter, divided

⅓ cup sauvignon blanc or other crisp, tart white wine

½ cup fat-free, lower-sodium chicken broth

⅓ cup fresh Meyer lemon juice (about 3 lemons)

2 tablespoons capers, rinsed and drained

¼ cup chopped fresh flat-leaf parsley

1. Split chicken breast halves in half horizontally to form 4 cutlets. Place each cutlet between 2 sheets of heavy-duty plastic wrap; pound to ¼-inch thickness using a meat mallet or small heavy skillet. Sprinkle cutlets evenly with salt and pepper. Place flour in a shallow dish; dredge cutlets in flour.

2. Melt 1 tablespoon butter in a large skillet over medium-high heat. Add 2 cutlets to pan; sauté 2 minutes. Turn cutlets over; sauté 1 minute. Remove cutlets from pan. Repeat procedure with remaining 1 tablespoon butter and 2 cutlets.

3. Add wine to pan; bring to a boil, scraping pan to loosen browned bits. Cook 1 minute or until liquid almost evaporates. Stir in broth; bring to a boil. Cook until broth mixture is reduced to 2 tablespoons (about 4 minutes). Stir in juice and capers. Serve over chicken. Sprinkle with parsley.

Serves 4 (serving size: 1 cutlet, 2 tablespoons sauce, and 1 tablespoon parsley).

CALORIES 214; FAT 7.3g (sat 4.1g, mono 1.9g, poly 0.6g); PROTEIN 27.5g; CARB 8.5g; FIBER 0.6g; CHOL 81mg; IRON 1.6mg; SODIUM 502mg; CALC 26mg

Chicken and Mushrooms with Marsala Wine Sauce

The earthy depth of porcini and shiitake mushrooms is balanced by the bright pop of the cherry tomatoes and the subtle sweetness of the wine.

Drape over mashed potatoes, polenta, or egg noodles for a complete meal. Hands-on time: 17 min. Total time: 1 hr. 5 min.

½ cup dried porcini mushrooms (about ½ ounce)

4 (6-ounce) skinless, boneless chicken breast halves

4 teaspoons all-purpose flour, divided

⅝ teaspoon salt, divided

¼ teaspoon freshly ground black pepper

2 tablespoons olive oil, divided

½ cup chopped onion

¼ teaspoon crushed red pepper

5 garlic cloves, thinly sliced

1½ cups thinly sliced shiitake mushroom caps (about 4 ounces)

1½ cups thinly sliced button mushrooms (about 4 ounces)

1 teaspoon dried oregano

½ cup dry Marsala

⅔ cup fat-free, lower-sodium chicken broth

1 cup halved cherry tomatoes

¼ cup small fresh basil leaves

1. Place porcini mushrooms in a small bowl; cover with boiling water. Cover and let stand 30 minutes or until tender. Drain and rinse; drain well. Thinly slice.

2. Place each chicken breast half between 2 sheets of heavy-duty plastic wrap; pound chicken to ½-inch thickness using a meat mallet or small heavy skillet. Combine 3 teaspoons flour, ¼ teaspoon salt, and black pepper in a shallow dish. Dredge chicken in flour mixture.

3. Heat a large stainless-steel skillet over medium-high heat. Add 1 tablespoon oil to pan; swirl to coat. Add chicken; cook 3 minutes on each side or until done. Remove chicken from pan; cover and keep warm.

4. Heat remaining 1 tablespoon oil in pan over medium-high heat. Add onion, red pepper, and garlic; sauté 2 minutes or until onion is lightly browned. Add remaining ⅜ teaspoon salt; porcini, shiitake, and button mushrooms; and oregano. Sauté 6 minutes or until mushrooms release moisture and darken. Sprinkle with remaining 1 teaspoon flour; cook 1 minute, stirring constantly. Stir in wine; cook 1 minute. Add broth; bring to a boil. Reduce heat, and simmer 1 minute. Add chicken and tomatoes; cook 2 minutes or until thoroughly heated, turning chicken once. Sprinkle with basil.

Serves 4 (serving size: 1 chicken breast half and about ½ cup sauce).

CALORIES 384; FAT 10g (sat 1.6g, mono 5.9g, poly 1.6g); PROTEIN 48.2g; CARB 20.3g; FIBER 4.8g; CHOL 99mg; IRON 6.1mg; SODIUM 570mg; CALC 50mg

CHOICE INGREDIENT

Porcini Mushrooms: These are a rare treat if found fresh, but they are most often available in dried form, where their flavor is super-concentrated. Rehydration restores the meaty earthiness that makes them so desirable. Soak in boiling water for about half an hour to soften them. Don't discard the flavor-infused liquid—it can further build the mushroom essence in the dish (strain it to get rid of any gritty bits).

Parmesan Chicken Paillards with Cherry Tomato Sauce

Success with such a simple recipe comes down to the best ingredients—crumbly aged cheese and good sherry vinegar.

Paillards are boneless, skinless chicken breasts pounded flat and sautéed. A crust of Parmesan adds flavor. Serve with green beans and orzo with parsley. Hands-on time: 16 min. Total time: 34 min.

4	(6-ounce) skinless, boneless chicken breast halves
½	teaspoon kosher salt, divided
½	teaspoon freshly ground black pepper, divided
¼	cup (1 ounce) grated fresh Parmigiano-Reggiano cheese
1	tablespoon all-purpose flour
2	tablespoons olive oil, divided
½	cup finely chopped onion
¼	cup fat-free, lower-sodium chicken broth
1	tablespoon sherry vinegar
2	cups quartered cherry tomatoes
1	teaspoon fresh oregano

1. Place each chicken breast half between 2 sheets of heavy-duty plastic wrap; pound to ½-inch thickness using a meat mallet or small heavy skillet. Sprinkle chicken with ¼ teaspoon salt and ¼ teaspoon pepper. Combine cheese and flour in a shallow dish. Dredge 1 side of each chicken breast half in cheese mixture.

2. Heat a large nonstick skillet over medium-high heat. Add 2 teaspoons oil to pan; swirl to coat. Add 2 chicken breast halves, cheese sides down; cook 4 minutes on each side or until done. Repeat procedure with 2 teaspoons oil and remaining 2 chicken breast halves. Remove from pan; keep warm.

3. Add remaining 2 teaspoons oil to pan; swirl to coat. Add onion; sauté 2 minutes, stirring frequently. Stir in broth and vinegar; cook 1 minute or until liquid almost evaporates. Add tomatoes, remaining ¼ teaspoon salt, remaining ¼ teaspoon pepper, and oregano; cook 2 minutes.

Serves 4 (serving size: 1 chicken breast half and about ⅓ cup tomato mixture).

CALORIES 300; FAT 10.4g (sat 2.4g, mono 5.9g, poly 1.3g); PROTEIN 42.5g; CARB 6.7g; FIBER 1.4g; CHOL 102mg; IRON 1.7mg; SODIUM 476mg; CALC 93mg

TEST KITCHEN SECRET

The Best Breasts to Buy: For best flavor, look for humanely raised, fresh (not frozen) chicken that has not been "marinated"—code for a 15% saline injection, which can make chicken taste salty or broth-like. To us, air-chilling the bird is important. Many mass-produced birds are chilled in cold water, which waters down the flavor. Air-chilled birds taste rich and almost gamey, and our tasters deemed them worth the extra cost. The bottom line: Although this can be an economy meat, money spent on premium quality pays off with real chicken flavor.

Walnut and Rosemary Oven-Fried Chicken

Fast, easy, and terrifically crunchy: the taste of fried chicken for fewer than 300 calories.

It's versatile, too—use as a stand-alone entrée, perch atop salads, or use as a base for chicken Parmesan. Add kid appeal with a honey-mustard dipping sauce. Hands-on time: 12 min. Total time: 25 min.

¼ cup low-fat buttermilk

2 tablespoons Dijon mustard

4 (4-ounce) chicken cutlets

⅓ cup panko (Japanese breadcrumbs)

⅓ cup finely chopped walnuts

2 tablespoons grated fresh Parmigiano-Reggiano cheese

¾ teaspoon minced fresh rosemary

¼ teaspoon kosher salt

¼ teaspoon freshly ground black pepper

Cooking spray

Rosemary leaves (optional)

1. Preheat oven to 425°.

2. Combine buttermilk and mustard in a shallow dish, stirring with a whisk. Add chicken to buttermilk mixture, turning to coat.

3. Heat a small skillet over medium-high heat. Add panko to pan; cook 3 minutes or until golden, stirring frequently. Combine panko, nuts, and next 4 ingredients (through pepper) in a shallow dish. Remove chicken from buttermilk mixture; discard buttermilk mixture. Dredge chicken in panko mixture.

4. Place a wire rack on a large baking sheet; coat rack with cooking spray. Arrange chicken on rack; coat chicken with cooking spray. Bake at 425° for 13 minutes or until chicken is done. Garnish with rosemary leaves, if desired.

Serves 4 (serving size: 1 cutlet).

CALORIES 227; FAT 8.9g (sat 1.5g, mono 1.4g, poly 5g); PROTEIN 29.6g; CARB 6g; FIBER 0.9g; CHOL 68mg; IRON 1.2mg; SODIUM 344mg; CALC 60mg

Lemony Chicken Saltimbocca

Saltimbocca means "jump in the mouth"—apt for a fast dish that marries woodsy sage, bright lemon, and salty prosciutto.

Serve over a bed of angel hair pasta or polenta. Hands-on time: 11 min. Total time: 19 min.

4 (4-ounce) chicken cutlets

⅛ teaspoon salt

12 fresh sage leaves

2 ounces very thinly sliced prosciutto, cut into 8 thin strips

4 teaspoons extra-virgin olive oil, divided

⅓ cup fat-free, lower-sodium chicken broth

¼ cup fresh lemon juice

½ teaspoon cornstarch

Lemon wedges (optional)

1. Sprinkle chicken evenly with salt. Place 3 sage leaves on each cutlet; wrap 2 prosciutto slices around each cutlet, securing sage leaves in place.

2. Heat a large skillet over medium heat. Add 1 tablespoon oil to pan; swirl to coat. Add chicken to pan; cook 2 minutes on each side or until done. Remove chicken from pan; keep warm.

3. Combine broth, juice, and cornstarch in a small bowl; stir with a whisk until smooth. Add cornstarch mixture and remaining 1 teaspoon oil to pan; bring to a boil, stirring constantly. Cook 1 minute or until slightly thick, stirring constantly with a whisk. Spoon sauce over chicken. Serve with lemon wedges, if desired.

Serves 4 (serving size: 1 cutlet and 2 tablespoons sauce).

CALORIES 202; FAT 7.5g (sat 1.5g, mono 4.3g, poly 0.9g); PROTEIN 30.5g; CARB 2.3g; FIBER 0.2g; CHOL 77mg; IRON 1.1mg; SODIUM 560mg; CALC 18mg

Wine Pairing
This flavor-packed chicken needs a simple wine. Oregon pinot gris is light, with refreshing fruit that highlights the dish's flavors rather than overpowering them.

NUTRITION MADE EASY

Dark or White, Skin or Skinned? It's true that dark meat is more caloric than white. But if you're consistently choosing light meat out of nutrition fidelity, you may want to reconsider. A 6-ounce serving of dark-meat turkey, for example, contains only 40 more calories than an equal amount of white meat. Let taste be your guide, not the numbers.

As for skin, there's good news there, too. Fifty-five percent of the fat in chicken skin is monounsaturated—the heart-healthy kind of fat. When it comes to that gorgeous Thanksgiving turkey, with its mahogany, crisped skin, know that each ounce of cooked skin contains just 3 grams of saturated fat—about the same as 1¼ teaspoons of butter. Not a deal breaker, in other words, and for most of us, an essential indulgence.

Chicken Puttanesca

What's not to love: olives, garlic, red pepper, capers, and anchovy in a feisty bird version of the pasta standard.

Serve with angel hair pasta. Remove leftover anchovies from the can; place in an airtight container. Cover anchovies with extra-virgin olive oil, and refrigerate. Hands-on time: 10 min. Total time: 20 min.

1½ tablespoons olive oil, divided

4 (4-ounce) skinless, boneless chicken cutlets

¼ cup minced fresh onion

3 garlic cloves, minced

2 cups chopped tomato

¼ cup sliced green olives

1 tablespoon chopped fresh oregano

1½ teaspoons capers, chopped

½ teaspoon crushed red pepper

¼ teaspoon salt

1 canned anchovy fillet, chopped

1. Heat a large nonstick skillet over medium-high heat. Add 1 tablespoon oil to pan; swirl to coat. Add chicken; cook 5 minutes or until done, turning once. Remove chicken from pan; keep warm. Add remaining 1½ teaspoons oil, onion, and garlic to pan; sauté 1 minute. Add tomato and next 6 ingredients (through anchovy). Bring to a simmer; cook 9 minutes or until slightly thick, stirring occasionally. Serve chicken with sauce.

Serves 4 (serving size: 1 chicken cutlet and about ⅓ cup sauce).

CALORIES 241; FAT 9.9g (sat 1.1g, mono 5.8g, poly 1.5g); PROTEIN 30.9g; CARB 6.6g; FIBER 1.4g; CHOL 87mg; IRON 1.2mg; SODIUM 602mg; CALC 33mg

Korean Meatballs

A quick buzz in the food processor turns chicken breasts into ground meat that's ready to marry with the Korean flavor trinity—sweetness, garlic, and salty soy.

Serve meatballs with store-bought kimchi and these quick-pickled cucumbers to add heat and tang to the meal. Slice 1 English cucumber crosswise into thin rounds; combine with 2 crushed garlic cloves. Combine 1 cup rice vinegar, ¾ cup water, 2 tablespoons sugar, and ½ teaspoon salt; microwave at HIGH 2 minutes or until boiling. Pour vinegar mixture over cucumber mixture; stir in 1 tablespoon sambal oelek (ground fresh chile paste). Cover and chill at least 4 hours. Hands-on time: 20 min. Total time: 32 min.

2 tablespoons brown sugar

2 tablespoons canola oil

8 garlic cloves

3 tablespoons lower-sodium soy sauce

¼ teaspoon salt

1 pound skinless, boneless chicken breasts, cut into 1-inch pieces

Cooking spray

1. Preheat oven to 400°.
2. Place brown sugar, oil, and garlic in a food processor; process until finely ground. Add soy sauce, salt, and chicken; process until finely ground. Divide chicken mixture into 20 equal portions. With moist hands, shape each portion into a ball.
3. Heat a large cast-iron skillet over medium-high heat. Add 10 meatballs to pan; sauté 4 minutes, turning to brown meatballs on all sides. Arrange browned meatballs on a jelly-roll pan coated with cooking spray. Repeat procedure with remaining meatballs. Bake at 400° for 5 minutes or until done.

Serves 4 (serving size: 5 meatballs).

CALORIES 225; FAT 9.7g (sat 1.3g, mono 5g, poly 2.7g); PROTEIN 23.9g; CARB 9.7g; FIBER 0.2g; CHOL 63mg; IRON 1.2mg; SODIUM 606mg; CALC 30mg

Chicken Puttanesca

Sautéed Chicken with Sage Browned Butter

When butter goes beyond melted to browned, gorgeous flavors bloom: toasty caramel-like, milky, and rich.

Thin, pounded cutlets cook in a flash and remain supremely tender and juicy. After cooking the chicken, use the tasty browned bits left behind in the pan as the base for a speedy sauce. The autumnal flavors of butter and sage would pair nicely with roasted butternut squash or mashed sweet potatoes.

Hands-on time: 25 min. Total time: 25 min.

4   (6-ounce) skinless, boneless chicken breast halves

¼   teaspoon salt

¼   teaspoon freshly ground black pepper

Cooking spray

½   cup all-purpose flour

3   tablespoons butter

2   sage sprigs

1   tablespoon minced shallots

1   teaspoon chopped fresh thyme

2   tablespoons fresh lemon juice

Fresh sage leaves (optional)

1. Place each breast half between 2 sheets of plastic wrap; pound to ¼-inch thickness. Sprinkle evenly with salt and pepper. Heat a large skillet over medium-high heat; coat with cooking spray. Place flour in a shallow dish; dredge chicken in flour. Add chicken to pan; sauté 4 minutes on each side or until done. Remove chicken from pan.

2. Add butter and sage sprigs to pan; cook over medium heat until butter browns. Discard sage. Add shallots and thyme; cook 30 seconds. Add lemon juice; cook 30 seconds. Serve with chicken. Garnish with sage leaves, if desired.

Serves 4 (serving size: 1 chicken breast half and 1 tablespoon sauce).

CALORIES 326; FAT 11.1g (sat 6.1g, mono 2.8g, poly 0.9g); PROTEIN 41.1g; CARB 13.1g; FIBER 0.5g; CHOL 122mg; IRON 2mg; SODIUM 320mg; CALC 26mg

Chicken Satay

The authentic taste of an Indonesian street-food favorite, using supermarket ingredients and the power of char-grilling.

Serve with rice noodles tossed with cilantro, sesame seeds, and dark sesame oil; top with thinly sliced cucumber. If using a gas grill, preheat it during the last 20 minutes of marinating. Hands-on time: 27 min. Total time: 1 hr. 27 min.

⅓ cup unsalted, dry-roasted peanuts

1 tablespoon toasted cumin seeds

2 tablespoons fresh lime juice

1 tablespoon dark sesame oil

1 teaspoon toasted coriander seeds

2 garlic cloves

1 shallot, peeled

⅓ cup light coconut milk

3 tablespoons brown sugar

1 tablespoon grated peeled fresh ginger

¼ teaspoon ground turmeric

1 serrano chile, stem removed

6 skinless, boneless chicken thighs, cut into 36 pieces

½ teaspoon salt

1. Combine first 7 ingredients in a food processor; process until smooth. Add coconut milk and next 4 ingredients (through serrano chile); process until smooth. Spoon peanut mixture into a large zip-top plastic bag. Add chicken to bag; seal and marinate in refrigerator 1 hour, turning after 30 minutes.

2. Preheat grill to medium-high heat.

3. Remove chicken from bag; discard marinade. Thread chicken evenly onto 12 (6-inch) skewers; sprinkle evenly with salt. Grill 6 minutes on each side or until chicken is done.

Serves 4 (serving size: 3 skewers).

CALORIES 300; FAT 15.2g (sat 2.7g, mono 6.1g, poly 4.7g); PROTEIN 24.6g; CARB 17.5g; FIBER 2.1g; CHOL 86mg; IRON 2.2mg; SODIUM 508mg; CALC 51mg

Beer Pairing
A malty, nutty brown ale highlights the aromatic spices and peanuts in the marinade.

7

POULTRY

Mark Bittman's Chicken, Mustard Greens, and Gruyère Quesadillas

Our "Less Meat, More Flavor" columnist uses only enough cheese to bind the ingredients—leaving room for more vegetables and bits of meat for savory highlights.

Baking yields crispy, flaky quesadillas and allows you to cook more at one time. Hands-on time: 26 min. Total time: 26 min.

2 tablespoons olive oil, divided

½ teaspoon freshly ground black pepper, divided

⅛ teaspoon kosher salt

2 skinless, boneless chicken thighs (about 5 ounces), chopped

4 cups chopped stemmed mustard greens

1 tablespoon minced fresh garlic

Dash of kosher salt

¼ teaspoon grated lemon rind

4 (6-inch) 100% whole-wheat tortillas

¼ cup (1 ounce) grated Gruyère cheese

1. Preheat oven to 400°.

2. Heat a large skillet over medium-high heat. Add 1 tablespoon oil to pan; swirl to coat. Sprinkle ¼ teaspoon pepper and ⅛ teaspoon salt evenly over chicken; toss to coat. Add chicken to pan; cook 2 minutes or until browned, stirring occasionally. Add greens, garlic, and dash of salt; cook 3 minutes or until greens wilt, stirring frequently. Stir in remaining ¼ teaspoon pepper and rind.

3. Brush remaining 1 tablespoon oil over a jelly-roll pan; arrange tortillas in a single layer on pan. Sprinkle 1 tablespoon cheese evenly over each tortilla; top each tortilla with about ⅔ cup chicken mixture. Bake at 400° for 5 minutes or until cheese begins to melt. Remove pan from oven; carefully fold each tortilla in half, pressing gently to close. Bake quesadillas an additional 10 minutes or until browned and crisp, turning carefully after 5 minutes.

Serves 2 (serving size: 2 quesadillas).

CALORIES 476; FAT 22.9g (sat 5.2g, mono 12.2g, poly 2.4g); PROTEIN 25.3g; CARB 41.3g; FIBER 8g; CHOL 74mg; IRON 5mg; SODIUM 736mg; CALC 400mg

NUTRITION MADE EASY

Whole-Wheat Tortillas: The calories, fat, fiber, and sodium vary depending on the brand, as does the flavor. Check labels to select the highest-fiber/lowest-sodium options, and sample until you find your favorite. If the flour is 100% whole-wheat, you've added another whole grain to your diet.

Chicken Fricassee with Orzo

Here, the lean meat is enriched with a splash of cream, diced ham, and garlic.

This is one of those dishes that'll become a go-to meal because it's so easy and family-pleasing.
Hands-on time: 15 min. Total time: 40 min.

4 (6-ounce) skinless, boneless chicken breast halves

½ teaspoon salt

¼ teaspoon freshly ground black pepper

2 teaspoons butter

¾ cup chopped green onions

½ cup diced carrot

½ cup diced ham

2 garlic cloves, minced

1 cup fat-free, lower-sodium chicken broth

½ cup dry white wine

⅓ cup heavy whipping cream

2 cups hot cooked orzo (about 1 cup uncooked rice-shaped pasta)

¼ cup chopped fresh parsley
Parsley sprigs (optional)

1. Sprinkle chicken evenly with salt and pepper. Melt butter in a large nonstick skillet over medium-high heat. Add chicken to pan; sauté 3 minutes on each side or until browned. Remove from pan; cover and keep warm.

2. Add onions, carrot, ham, and garlic to pan; sauté 4 minutes or until lightly browned, stirring frequently. Stir in broth and wine, scraping pan to loosen browned bits. Return chicken to pan; bring to a boil. Cover, reduce heat, and simmer 10 minutes or until chicken is done. Remove chicken from pan with a slotted spoon; keep warm. Decrease heat to medium. Add cream to pan; cook, uncovered, 8 minutes. Spoon ½ cup orzo onto each of 4 plates. Top each serving with 1 chicken breast half, ⅓ cup sauce, and 1 tablespoon chopped parsley. Garnish with parsley sprigs, if desired.

Serves 4.

CALORIES 505; FAT 13.6g (sat 6.9g, mono 3.8g, poly 1.1g); PROTEIN 50.3g; CARB 37.2g; FIBER 2.6g; CHOL 141mg; IRON 2.2mg; SODIUM 682mg; CALC 64mg

Chicken Enchilada Casserole

Less fussy than traditional rolled enchiladas and just as delicious. Budget-friendly, too.

Frozen corn means you can make this all year, but in season you can use fresh. Hands-on time: 50 min. Total time: 1 hr. 5 min.

Cooking spray

4 **bone-in chicken thighs, skinned**

⅓ **cup chopped fresh cilantro, divided**

1 **cup frozen corn kernels, thawed**

⅓ **cup (3 ounces) ⅓-less-fat cream cheese, softened**

½ **teaspoon ground red pepper**

½ **teaspoon ground cumin**

¼ **teaspoon kosher salt**

¼ **teaspoon freshly ground black pepper**

2 **cups chopped onion, divided**

6 **garlic cloves, minced and divided**

1 **cup fat-free, lower-sodium chicken broth**

⅔ **cup salsa verde**

¼ **cup water**

2 **tablespoons chopped pickled jalapeño pepper**

9 **(6-inch) corn tortillas**

¼ **cup (1 ounce) shredded sharp cheddar cheese**

1. Preheat oven to 425°.
2. Heat a large ovenproof skillet over medium-high heat. Coat pan with cooking spray. Add chicken to pan; sauté 4 minutes on each side. Place pan in oven; bake at 425° for 10 minutes or until chicken is done. Remove chicken from pan; let stand 15 minutes. Remove meat from bones; shred. Discard bones. Place chicken in a medium bowl. Add 1½ tablespoons cilantro, corn, and next 5 ingredients (through black pepper) to chicken; toss to combine.
3. Return pan to medium-high heat. Add ½ cup onion; sauté 5 minutes, stirring occasionally. Add 3 garlic cloves; sauté 30 seconds, stirring constantly. Add onion mixture to chicken mixture; stir to combine.
4. Combine remaining 1½ cups onion, remaining 3 garlic cloves, broth, salsa, ¼ cup water, and jalapeño in a medium saucepan over medium-high heat; bring to a boil. Reduce heat, and simmer 15 minutes, stirring occasionally. Remove from heat; let stand 10 minutes. Carefully pour mixture into a blender; add 2 tablespoons cilantro. Process until smooth.

5. Heat a large skillet over medium-high heat. Add 2 tortillas, and cook 1½ minutes on each side. Remove tortillas from pan; repeat procedure with remaining tortillas. Cut tortillas into quarters.
6. Spread ½ cup salsa mixture in bottom of an 8-inch square glass or ceramic baking dish coated with cooking spray. Arrange 12 tortilla quarters over salsa mixture. Spoon half of chicken mixture over tortillas. Repeat layers, ending with tortillas. Pour remaining salsa mixture over tortillas; sprinkle evenly with cheddar cheese. Bake at 425° for 15 minutes or until bubbly and lightly browned. Top with remaining cilantro.

Serves 4 (serving size: about 1¾ cups).

CALORIES 371; FAT 12.4g (sat 5g, mono 2.9g, poly 1.8g); PROTEIN 23.1g; CARB 45.3g; FIBER 5.4g; CHOL 80mg; IRON 1.5mg; SODIUM 759mg; CALC 141mg

GLOBAL FLAVORS
....
Salsa Verde: This green salsa gets its color from tomatillos and cilantro. Use as a dip for chips, or incorporate into enchiladas, burritos, and other traditional Mexican dishes. Canned or bottled versions add quick acidity to saucy dishes like chili.

Kung Pao Chicken

Cooking in sesame oil and topping with peanuts maximizes the nutty flavors.

Rice is a natural accompaniment; make it richer by using canned light coconut milk in place of a third of the water. Hands-on time: 27 min. Total time: 27 min.

2 tablespoons dark sesame oil

1 cup chopped onion

2 garlic cloves, minced

1 pound skinless, boneless chicken thighs, cut into 1-inch pieces

¾ cup cold water

3 tablespoons lower-sodium soy sauce

2 teaspoons cornstarch

1 teaspoon brown sugar

1 to 1½ teaspoons crushed red pepper

½ teaspoon minced peeled fresh ginger

1 cup thinly sliced red bell pepper (about 1 large pepper)

1 cup snow peas, trimmed

2 tablespoons chopped unsalted, dry-roasted peanuts

1. Heat a large skillet over medium-high heat. Add oil to pan; swirl to coat. Add onion; sauté 3 minutes or until softened, stirring frequently. Add garlic; sauté 30 seconds, stirring constantly. Add chicken; sauté 3 minutes or until chicken begins to brown, stirring occasionally.

2. Combine ¾ cup cold water and next 5 ingredients (through ginger), stirring with a whisk until sugar dissolves. Add water mixture to pan; bring to a boil. Add bell pepper and snow peas to pan; cook 2 minutes or until vegetables are crisp-tender and sauce thickens. Sprinkle with peanuts.

Serves 4 (serving size: 1 cup).

CALORIES 275; FAT 13.8g (sat 2.6g, mono 5.3g, poly 4.8g); PROTEIN 25.3g; CARB 11.9g; FIBER 2.2g; CHOL 94mg; IRON 2mg; SODIUM 502mg; CALC 41mg

Bistro Braised Chicken

If you usually bypass meaty, rich chicken thighs, this dish will bring them back into rotation.

They're inexpensive, have a rich flavor that's just shy of gamey, and stay moist no matter how you cook them. Sticky-sweet dried plums and tangy Dijon add incomparable richness to this French-style meal.
Hands-on time: 13 min. Total time: 1 hr.

1	tablespoon butter, divided
8	(4-ounce) bone-in chicken thighs, skinned
1	cup thinly sliced carrot
¾	cup chopped onion
½	cup thinly sliced celery
8	pitted dried plums, chopped
½	teaspoon dried thyme
¼	teaspoon dried sage
2	teaspoons Dijon mustard
1	(14-ounce) can fat-free, lower-sodium chicken broth
¾	cup water
⅜	teaspoon salt
½	teaspoon freshly ground black pepper
4	cups hot cooked egg noodles

1. Melt 1 teaspoon butter in a large skillet over medium heat. Add chicken to pan; cook 6 minutes, browning on both sides. Remove chicken from pan; keep warm.

2. Add remaining 2 teaspoons butter to pan; swirl until butter melts. Add carrot, onion, celery, and dried plums; cook 4 minutes or until vegetables begin to soften, stirring frequently. Stir in thyme and sage; cook 30 seconds. Stir in mustard. Add broth and ¾ cup water, scraping pan to loosen browned bits; bring to a simmer.

3. Return chicken to pan. Cover, reduce heat, and simmer 35 minutes. Uncover, increase heat to medium-high, and simmer until sauce is reduced by half (about 10 minutes). Stir in salt and pepper. Serve over noodles.

Serves 4 (serving size: 1 cup egg noodles, 2 chicken thighs, and about ½ cup vegetable mixture).

CALORIES 483; FAT 11.5g (sat 4.3g, mono 3.9g, poly 1.8g); PROTEIN 36.9g; CARB 57.3g; FIBER 5g; CHOL 189mg; IRON 3.7mg; SODIUM 692mg; CALC 76mg

Wine Pairing

Pair this dish with a French viognier, a floral, full-bodied white wine that's heavy enough for the dark meat but won't overpower the delicious sauce.

Roasted Moroccan-Spiced Chicken with Grapes

Though we usually call for removing skin from dark-meat chicken, here it stays on for delicious flavor, crispy texture, and extra richness. The serving size is small, so saturated fat isn't a problem.

The grapes will soften and collapse soon after removing them from the oven, so serve right away. A side of hot cooked bulgur or whole-wheat couscous would complete the meal nicely. Hands-on time: 32 min. Total time: 52 min.

1½   cups sliced yellow onion

4   large carrots, quartered lengthwise and cut into ½-inch pieces (about 3 cups)

5   teaspoons olive oil, divided

¾   teaspoon kosher salt, divided

½   teaspoon freshly ground black pepper, divided

½   teaspoon ground cumin

½   teaspoon ground coriander

¼   teaspoon ground cinnamon

⅛   teaspoon ground red pepper

4   bone-in, skin-on chicken thighs, trimmed (about 1½ pounds)

3   cups seedless red grapes

¼   cup picholine olives, pitted

2   tablespoons chopped fresh flat-leaf parsley

1. Place 2 jelly-roll pans in oven. Preheat oven to 450°.

2. Combine onion, carrot, and 1 tablespoon oil in a medium bowl; toss well. Arrange carrot mixture on 1 preheated pan; sprinkle with ¼ teaspoon salt. Bake at 450° for 10 minutes.

3. Combine ⅜ teaspoon salt, ¼ teaspoon black pepper, and next 4 ingredients (through red pepper) in a small bowl. Sprinkle spice mixture evenly over chicken. Heat a small skillet over medium-high heat. Add

1 teaspoon oil to pan; swirl to coat. Add chicken to pan, skin sides down; cook 5 minutes or until browned and skin is crisp. Remove chicken from pan. Add chicken to vegetable mixture, skin sides up. Bake at 450° for 20 minutes or until chicken is done and vegetables are tender.

4. Combine remaining 1 teaspoon oil, grapes, remaining ¼ teaspoon black pepper, remaining ⅛ teaspoon salt, and olives in a medium bowl; toss well. Place grape mixture on remaining

preheated jelly-roll pan. Bake at 450° for 15 minutes or until grapes are charred and beginning to soften, stirring occasionally. Place ½ cup vegetable mixture and ½ cup grape mixture on each of 4 plates. Top each serving with 1 chicken thigh. Sprinkle with parsley.

Serves 4.

CALORIES 406; FAT 23.3g (sat 5.4g, mono 12.4g, poly 4.3g); PROTEIN 18.6g; CARB 33g; FIBER 4.2g; CHOL 79mg; IRON 2.1mg; SODIUM 661mg; CALC 68mg

Chicken Biryani

If you like the chicken-and-rice combination but crave a new approach, try this Indian classic, fragrant with saffron, cardamom, ginger, and cinnamon.

Whole-milk yogurt keeps its creamy texture when cooked; don't substitute low-fat yogurt, which will curdle. Try Madras curry powder for more punch. Hands-on time: 20 min. Total time: 1 hr. 4 min.

3 cups water

1¼ teaspoons salt, divided

¼ teaspoon saffron threads, crushed

1½ cups uncooked basmati rice

1 (3-inch) cinnamon stick

1 tablespoon canola oil

1 pound skinless, boneless chicken thighs, cut into bite-sized pieces

1 cup chopped onion

2 teaspoons curry powder

1 teaspoon minced peeled fresh ginger

½ teaspoon ground cardamom

⅛ teaspoon ground red pepper

2 garlic cloves, minced

2 serrano chiles, seeded and minced

1 cup plain whole-milk yogurt

½ cup golden raisins

½ cup chopped dry-roasted cashews

¼ cup fresh cilantro leaves

1. Bring 3 cups water, ¾ teaspoon salt, and saffron to a boil in a medium saucepan. Add rice and cinnamon stick to pan. Cover, reduce heat, and simmer 20 minutes or until liquid is absorbed. Discard cinnamon stick.

2. Heat a large nonstick skillet over medium-high heat. Add oil to pan; swirl to coat. Sprinkle chicken with ¼ teaspoon salt. Add chicken to pan; sauté 5 minutes or until lightly browned. Remove chicken from pan; cover and keep warm.

3. Add onion and remaining ¼ teaspoon salt to pan. Cover, reduce heat to low, and cook 10 minutes or until lightly browned, stirring occasionally. Add curry and next 5 ingredients (through serrano chiles); cook 3 minutes, stirring frequently. Add yogurt to pan; cook 3 minutes or until slightly thick, stirring constantly with a whisk. Add chicken and raisins; cook 4 minutes or until thoroughly heated. Add rice; stir to combine. Sprinkle with cashews and cilantro.

Serves 6 (serving size: 1⅓ cups).

CALORIES 435; FAT 12.7g (sat 3.2g, mono 5.1g, poly 3.2g); PROTEIN 22.8g; CARB 59.2g; FIBER 1.9g; CHOL 68mg; IRON 2.3mg; SODIUM 651mg; CALC 84mg

Spicy Honey-Brushed Chicken Thighs

Sweet, spicy, and sticky-delicious, these thighs get barbecue-like flavor with the convenience of the broiler.

Serve with typical 'cue fixings: corn on the cob, baked beans, and slaw. Or, play off the cumin and lean in a Southwestern direction with yellow rice and black beans. Hands-on time: 6 min. Total time: 20 min.

2 teaspoons garlic powder

2 teaspoons chili powder

1 teaspoon ground cumin

1 teaspoon paprika

¾ teaspoon salt

½ teaspoon ground red pepper

8 skinless, boneless chicken thighs

Cooking spray

6 tablespoons honey

2 teaspoons cider vinegar

1. Preheat broiler.

2. Combine first 6 ingredients in a large bowl. Add chicken to bowl; toss to coat. Place chicken on a broiler pan coated with cooking spray. Broil 5 minutes on each side.

3. Combine honey and vinegar in a small bowl, stirring well. Remove chicken from oven; brush ¼ cup honey mixture over chicken. Broil 1 minute. Remove from oven and turn over. Brush chicken with remaining honey mixture. Broil an additional 1 minute or until chicken is done.

Serves 4 (serving size: 2 chicken thighs).

CALORIES 321; FAT 11g (sat 3g, mono 4.1g, poly 2.5g); PROTEIN 28g; CARB 27.9g; FIBER 0.6g; CHOL 99mg; IRON 2.1mg; SODIUM 528mg; CALC 84mg

POULTRY

Old-Fashioned Chicken Potpie

Sometimes you just want pure, homey comfort. Our version hits all the flaky, creamy, potato-rich notes of the classic but is much lighter in calories and sodium.

Homemade piecrust takes a bit of time to make, but the buttery flavor is worth it. Make individual potpies by spooning servings into 12-ounce ramekins. Divide dough into 8 portions, and roll to fit. Have fun with the presentation—make some lattice-topped, cut out shapes in others, or make standard steam vents.

Hands-on time: 23 min. Total time: 1 hr. 58 min.

Crust:

6.75 ounces all-purpose flour (about 1½ cups), divided

¼ teaspoon salt

7 tablespoons unsalted butter, chilled

5 tablespoons ice water

Filling:

2 teaspoons unsalted butter

1 cup chopped carrot

½ cup chopped onion

1 teaspoon chopped fresh thyme

3 cups fat-free, lower-sodium chicken broth

2⅓ cups cubed red potato (about 1 pound)

1.5 ounces (about ⅓ cup) all-purpose flour

⅓ cup water

2 cups diced cooked rotisserie chicken

1 cup frozen petite peas

½ teaspoon salt

¼ teaspoon freshly ground black pepper

Cooking spray

2 teaspoons 1% low-fat milk

1. To prepare crust, weigh or lightly spoon 6.75 ounces (about 1½ cups) flour into dry measuring cups; level with a knife. Combine 6.75 ounces (about 1½ cups) flour and ¼ teaspoon salt in a large bowl; cut in 7 tablespoons butter with a pastry blender or 2 knives until mixture resembles coarse meal. Add 5 tablespoons ice water; stir just until moist. Press mixture gently into a 5-inch circle; cover with plastic wrap. Chill 15 minutes. Roll dough into a 12 x 8–inch rectangle on a lightly floured surface. Chill dough until ready to use.

2. Preheat oven to 400°.

3. To prepare filling, melt 2 teaspoons butter in a Dutch oven over medium-high heat. Add carrot, onion, and thyme; cook 8 minutes or until vegetables are soft. Add broth and potato; bring to a boil. Cover and simmer 10 minutes. Combine flour and ⅓ cup water in a small bowl; stir with a whisk until smooth. Return potato mixture to a boil. Slowly drizzle flour mixture into potato mixture, stirring constantly. Cook 1 minute or until mixture thickens.

Stir in chicken, peas, ½ teaspoon salt, and pepper. Spoon chicken mixture into an 11 x 7-inch glass or ceramic baking dish coated with cooking spray. Place dough on top of chicken mixture, pressing to edge of dish. Cut 4 slits in top of crust to allow steam to escape. Gently brush crust with milk. Bake at 400° for 50 minutes or until golden and bubbly. Let stand 10 minutes.

Serves 8 (serving size: about 1½ cups).

CALORIES 310; FAT 12.6g (sat 7.3g, mono 3.3g, poly 0.8g); PROTEIN 20.2g; CARB 35.7g; FIBER 3.1g; CHOL 55mg; IRON 2.2mg; SODIUM 522mg; CALC 30mg

POULTRY

Classic Roast Chicken

Here's one of our Test Kitchen discoveries: Reversing the usual roasting technique makes for a moister bird.

This chicken starts at moderate heat and finishes at high heat, as opposed to the usual high-heat start and low-heat finish. Be sure to turn on your vent: The final blast may generate some smoke. Allow the chicken to stand at least 10 minutes before you slice it so the juices redistribute throughout the meat.
Hands-on time: 30 min. Total time: 1 hr. 30 min.

1   **(4-pound) whole roasting chicken**

2   **teaspoons unsalted butter, softened**

1½   **teaspoons minced fresh thyme**

1   **teaspoon paprika**

1   **teaspoon ground coriander**

2   **teaspoons extra-virgin olive oil**

¾   **teaspoon salt**

¼   **teaspoon freshly ground black pepper**

2   **garlic cloves, minced**

3   **shallots, peeled and halved**

3   **fresh thyme sprigs**

1   **lemon, quartered**

1. Preheat oven to 350°.

2. Discard giblets and neck from chicken. Starting at neck cavity, loosen skin from breasts and drumsticks by inserting fingers, gently pushing between skin and meat.

3. Combine butter and next 7 ingredients (through garlic) in a small bowl. Rub mixture under loosened skin and over flesh; rub over top of skin. Tie ends of legs together with twine. Lift wing tips up and over back; tuck under chicken. Place chicken, breast side up, on a rack; place rack in roasting pan. Place shallots, thyme sprigs, and lemon in cavity of chicken.

4. Bake at 350° for 45 minutes. Increase oven temperature to 450° (do not remove chicken); bake at 450° for 15 minutes or until a thermometer inserted in meaty part of leg registers 165°. Remove chicken from pan; let stand 10 minutes. Discard skin. Carve chicken.

Serves 4 (serving size: 1 breast half or 1 leg-thigh quarter).

CALORIES 278; FAT 13.6g (sat 4.1g, mono 5.7g, poly 2.5g); PROTEIN 35.7g; CARB 0.9g; FIBER 0.3g; CHOL 111mg; IRON 1.9mg; SODIUM 563mg; CALC 23mg

7

POULTRY

TECHNIQUE

Roasting a Whole Chicken: A timer and meat thermometer are two essentials for a perfect bird.

1. Simply cross the legs and tie them together with kitchen twine. Next, lift the wing tips up, and tuck them under the bird. Once it's cooked, discard the twine, and the chicken will hold this tidy shape.

2. Place the chicken on a rack in a roasting pan. Elevating the bird allows air to circulate and promotes even browning. Stuff the cavity with fruits, vegetables, and herbs.

3. Cooking to the proper temperature is the most critical step. Insert a thermometer into the meaty part of the leg (avoiding the bone). When the temperature reaches 165°, pull the bird from the oven. Let rest 10 minutes.

Grilled Chicken with Sriracha Glaze

Sriracha—that thick, sweet Thai chile sauce now found in pretty much any grocery store—has become the darling of the condiment world. Here, it adds fire to a sweet glaze for grilled leg quarters.

Dense, bone-in chicken leg-thigh quarters benefit from long, slow cooking over indirect heat. This method also prevents the sweet glaze from burning. Customize the glaze according to what you have on hand; try pineapple preserves or apple jelly in place of mango jam, or hot pepper sauce instead of Sriracha. Serve with a simple slaw of cabbage, carrots, lime juice, and sugar. Hands-on time: 16 min. Total time: 1 hr. 48 min.

⅔   cup mango jam

2   tablespoons finely chopped fresh chives

2   tablespoons rice vinegar

2   tablespoons Sriracha (hot chile sauce)

1   tablespoon olive oil

4   (12-ounce) bone-in chicken leg-thigh quarters, skinned

½   teaspoon kosher salt

¼   teaspoon freshly ground black pepper

1. Prepare grill for indirect grilling. If using a gas grill, heat one side to medium-high heat and leave one side with no heat. If using a charcoal grill, arrange hot coals on either side of charcoal grate, leaving an empty space in the middle.

2. Combine mango jam, chives, vinegar, and Sriracha, stirring until smooth. Reserve ¼ cup mango mixture; set aside.

3. Brush oil evenly over chicken. Sprinkle chicken with salt and pepper.

4. Carefully remove grill rack. Place a disposable aluminum foil pan on unheated part of grill. Carefully return grill rack to grill. Place chicken on grill rack over unheated part. Brush chicken with about 2 tablespoons remaining mango mixture. Close lid; grill 1½ hours or until a thermometer inserted into meaty part of thigh registers 165°, turning chicken and brushing with about 2 tablespoons mango mixture every 20 minutes. Transfer chicken to a platter. Drizzle chicken with reserved ¼ cup mango mixture.

Serves 4 (serving size: 1 leg-thigh quarter and 1 tablespoon mango mixture).

CALORIES 326; FAT 10.4g (sat 2.3g, mono 4.7g, poly 2.1g); PROTEIN 38.7g; CARB 18.2g; FIBER 2.7g; CHOL 154mg; IRON 4.5mg; SODIUM 515mg; CALC 102mg

Fantastic Bourbon Smoked Chicken

After Steven Raichlen sent us this recipe in 2011, we declared it the most beautiful and best-tasting bird we'd ever had.

Applewood chips work well for this dish because they have a lighter, more elegant flavor than hickory or mesquite. This chicken is so wonderfully moist and flavorful, it really doesn't need embellishment. But if you want a barbecue sauce, find one with less than 300mg of sodium per serving. Hands-on time: 20 min. Total time: 20 hr. 35 min.

- 2 quarts water
- 9 tablespoons bourbon, divided
- ¼ cup packed dark brown sugar
- 3 tablespoons kosher salt
- 2 quarts ice water
- 1 tablespoon black peppercorns
- 1 tablespoon coriander seeds
- 3 bay leaves
- 3 garlic cloves, peeled
- 1 small onion, quartered
- 1 small Fuji apple, cored and quartered
- 1 lemon, quartered
- 1 (4-pound) whole chicken
- 2 cups applewood chips
- ½ teaspoon freshly ground black pepper
- Cooking spray
- 1 tablespoon butter, melted

1. Combine 2 quarts water, ½ cup bourbon, sugar, and salt in a large Dutch oven; bring to a boil, stirring until salt and sugar dissolve. Add 2 quarts ice water and next 7 ingredients (through lemon); cool to room temperature. Add chicken to brine; cover and refrigerate 18 hours, turning chicken occasionally.
2. Soak wood chips in water for 1 hour; drain.
3. Remove chicken from brine; pat dry with paper towels. Strain brine through a sieve; discard brine, and reserve 2 apple quarters, 2 lemon quarters, 2 onion quarters, and garlic. Discard remaining solids. Sprinkle chicken cavity with black pepper; add reserved solids to chicken cavity. Lift wing tips up and over back; tuck under chicken. Tie legs.
4. Remove grill rack, and set aside. Prepare grill for indirect grilling, heating one side to high heat and leaving one side with no heat. Pierce bottom of a disposable aluminum foil pan several times with the tip of a knife. Place pan on heat element on heated side of grill; add 1 cup wood chips to pan. Place another disposable aluminum foil pan (do not pierce pan) on unheated side of grill. Pour 2 cups water in pan. Let chips stand 15 minutes or until smoking; reduce heat to medium-low. Maintain temperature at 275°.

5. Coat grill rack with cooking spray; place on grill. Place chicken, breast side up, on grill rack over foil pan on unheated side of grill. Combine remaining 1 tablespoon bourbon and butter; baste chicken with bourbon mixture. Close lid; cook 2 hours at 275° or until thermometer inserted into meaty part of thigh registers 165°. Add remaining 1 cup wood chips halfway through cooking time. Place chicken on a platter; cover with foil. Let stand 15 minutes. Discard skin before serving.

Serves 4 (serving size: about 5 ounces chicken).

CALORIES 299; FAT 12.6g (sat 4.4g, mono 4.3g, poly 2.3g); PROTEIN 35.8g; CARB 6.2g; FIBER 1g; CHOL 114mg; IRON 1.8mg; SODIUM 560mg; CALC 30mg

Easy Coq au Vin

Our quicker stovetop version of a traditional oven-braised dish yields the same moist, fork-tender dark-meat chicken with luscious red wine sauce.

Mushrooms and pearl onions are cooked separately until golden and added to the sauce at the end for texture. Serve with noodles, rice, or boiled potatoes. Hands-on time: 26 min. Total time: 1 hr. 44 min.

4 applewood-smoked bacon slices, cut into 1-inch pieces

4 chicken drumsticks, skinned

4 chicken thighs, skinned

½ teaspoon freshly ground black pepper, divided

⅛ teaspoon kosher salt

1 cup finely chopped onion

½ cup finely chopped celery

½ cup finely chopped carrot

1 teaspoon finely chopped fresh thyme

4 garlic cloves, minced

2 bay leaves

1 tablespoon no-salt-added tomato paste

1 (750-milliliter) bottle red wine

2 cups fat-free, lower-sodium chicken broth

1 tablespoon extra-virgin olive oil

8 ounces button mushrooms, quartered

6 ounces frozen pearl onions

¼ cup chopped fresh flat-leaf parsley

1. Cook bacon in a large, deep skillet over medium heat until crisp. Remove bacon from pan. Reserve 2 tablespoons drippings in pan. Sprinkle chicken with ¼ teaspoon pepper and salt. Add chicken to drippings in pan, and cook 5 minutes on each side or until browned. Remove chicken from pan.

2. Add chopped onion and next 5 ingredients (through bay leaves) to pan; cook 5 minutes. Add tomato paste to pan, and cook 1 minute. Stir in wine; bring to a boil. Cook 10 minutes or until reduced by half, stirring occasionally. Return chicken to pan. Add broth; bring to a simmer. Cover and simmer 35 minutes or until chicken is done, turning after 20 minutes. Remove chicken from pan; cover.

3. Heat a large heavy skillet over medium heat. Add oil to pan; swirl to coat. Add mushrooms and pearl onions to pan; sprinkle with remaining ¼ teaspoon pepper. Cook 10 minutes or until golden, stirring occasionally. Remove from heat.

4. Place chicken cooking liquid over medium-high heat; bring to a boil. Cook until reduced by half (about 10 minutes). Discard bay leaves. Stir in mushroom mixture. Return chicken to pan; simmer 5 minutes or until heated. Sprinkle with parsley and bacon.

Serves 4 (serving size: 1 thigh, 1 drumstick, and about 1 cup sauce).

CALORIES 319; FAT 13.2g (sat 3.6g, mono 4.1g, poly 1.8g); PROTEIN 33.9g; CARB 16.1g; FIBER 2.7g; CHOL 115mg; IRON 3.2mg; SODIUM 692mg; CALC 78mg

Wine Pairing

Burgundy or Oregon pinot noir, a light, earthy red, calls out the root vegetables and mushrooms in this rich and rustic meal.

Apple-Poblano Whole Roast Turkey

A hint of Southwest spice and chile heat blend with sweet apples for a crowd-pleasing change from traditional turkey.

Brining is the key to a moist bird. Hands-on time: 40 min. Total time: 16 hr. 6 min.

- 8 cups water
- 8 cups apple cider
- ½ cup packed brown sugar
- ⅓ cup kosher salt
- 2 tablespoons black peppercorns, crushed
- 1 jalapeño pepper, quartered lengthwise
- 1 (12-pound) organic fresh turkey
- 1 tablespoon brown sugar
- 1 teaspoon kosher salt
- ¾ teaspoon dried oregano
- ½ teaspoon ground cumin
- ½ teaspoon freshly ground black pepper
- ½ teaspoon ground red pepper
- ¼ teaspoon ground coriander
- 3 Gala apples, quartered and divided
- 2 poblano chiles, quartered, seeded, and divided
- 1 cup cilantro leaves

Cooking spray

- 3 cups water
- 3 cups fat-free, lower-sodium chicken broth, divided
- 2 tablespoons unsalted butter
- 2 cups chopped onion
- 5 garlic cloves, crushed
- 1.1 ounces all-purpose flour (about ¼ cup)
- 1 cup apple cider
- 3 tablespoons chopped fresh cilantro
- 2 tablespoons fresh lime juice

1. Combine first 6 ingredients, stirring well.

2. Remove giblets and neck from turkey; reserve neck and giblets. Trim excess fat. Place a turkey-sized oven bag inside a second bag to form a double thickness. Place bags in a large stockpot. Place turkey inside inner bag. Add brine. Secure bags with several twist ties. Refrigerate 12 to 24 hours.

3. Preheat oven to 500°.

4. Remove turkey from bags; discard brine. Pat turkey dry. Starting at neck cavity, loosen skin from breast and drumsticks by inserting fingers, gently pushing between skin and meat. Combine 1 tablespoon sugar and next 6 ingredients (through coriander) in a small bowl. Rub spice mixture under loosened skin over flesh. Place 1 apple quarter and 1 poblano quarter in the neck cavity; close skin flap. Arrange 5 apple quarters, 1 poblano quarter, and 1 cup cilantro leaves in body cavity. Secure legs with kitchen twine. Arrange turkey, neck, and giblets on the rack of a roasting pan coated with cooking spray. Arrange remaining 6 apple quarters and 6 poblano quarters in bottom of roasting pan coated with cooking spray. Place rack with turkey in pan. Roast at 500° for 30 minutes.

5. Reduce oven temperature to 350° (do not remove turkey from oven). Place a foil tent over turkey breast. Pour 3 cups water in bottom of pan.

6. Bake turkey at 350° for 40 minutes. Rotate turkey, and baste with ¾ cup broth. Roast for 30 minutes; rotate turkey. Baste with ¾ cup broth. Roast 20 minutes or until a thermometer inserted in thickest part of thigh registers 165°. Remove from oven. Place turkey, breast side down, on a jelly-roll pan or cutting board. Cover and let stand, covered, 30 minutes. Serve breast side up. Chop giblets. Discard neck.

7. Strain pan drippings through a sieve into a bowl; discard solids. Melt butter in a large saucepan over medium-high heat. Add onion to pan; sauté 5 minutes or until translucent, stirring frequently. Stir in reserved chopped giblets and garlic; sauté 2 minutes, stirring constantly. Weigh or lightly spoon flour into a dry measuring cup; level with a knife. Sprinkle flour over onion mixture; sauté 2 minutes, stirring frequently. Add drippings, remaining 1½ cups broth, and 1 cup apple cider; bring to a boil. Reduce heat, and simmer until reduced to 3 cups (about 15 minutes). Strain through a sieve over a bowl; discard solids. Stir in chopped cilantro and lime juice. Discard turkey skin; carve turkey. Serve with gravy.

Serves 12 (serving size: 6 ounces turkey and about ¼ cup gravy).

CALORIES 302; FAT 3.4g (sat 1.7g, mono 0.5g, poly 0.8g); PROTEIN 55g; CARB 9.7g; FIBER 0.6g; CHOL 154mg; IRON 3.1mg; SODIUM 620mg; CALC 31mg

POULTRY

Apple and Cranberry Turkey Roulade

This dish really streamlines the holiday meal: Apple-cranberry stuffing takes the place of cranberry sauce, and the roulade is much easier to carve than a whole turkey.

Stuff, roll, and tie the tenderloins a day ahead. Let them stand at room temperature for 20 minutes before cooking. If you can't find turkey tenderloins, use skinless, boneless turkey breast halves. For tips on cutting and stuffing tenderloins, see page 200. Hands-on time: 33 min. Total time: 1 hr. 45 min.

2	slices center-cut bacon, chopped
1	cup chopped onion
1	teaspoon chopped fresh rosemary
1	teaspoon salt, divided
¾	teaspoon freshly ground black pepper, divided
1½	cups fat-free, lower-sodium chicken broth, divided
3	cups chopped peeled Granny Smith apple (about 2 medium)
½	cup dried cranberries
3	(12-ounce) turkey tenderloins
2	teaspoons canola oil
3	fresh rosemary sprigs
1	tablespoon all-purpose flour

1. Preheat oven to 325°.
2. Cook bacon in a large skillet over medium heat 7 minutes or until bacon begins to brown, stirring occasionally. Stir in onion, chopped rosemary, ¼ teaspoon salt, and ¼ teaspoon pepper; cook 8 minutes or until onion begins to brown, stirring occasionally. Stir in 1 cup broth, apple, and cranberries. Bring to a boil. Reduce heat, and simmer 15 minutes or until liquid evaporates and apple is almost tender, stirring occasionally. Remove from heat, and cool slightly. Set aside 1 cup apple mixture.
3. Slice tenderloins in half lengthwise, cutting to, but not through, other side. Open halves, laying tenderloins flat. Place each tenderloin between 2 sheets of heavy-duty plastic wrap; pound to ½-inch thickness using a meat mallet or small heavy skillet. Discard plastic wrap.
4. Sprinkle remaining ¾ teaspoon salt and ½ teaspoon black pepper evenly over both sides of tenderloins. Spread ⅓ cup apple mixture over each tenderloin; roll up, jelly-roll fashion, starting with long sides. Secure at 2-inch intervals with twine.
5. Heat a large Dutch oven over medium-high heat. Add oil to pan; swirl to coat. Add tenderloins; cook 6 minutes, turning to brown on all sides. Add remaining ½ cup broth and rosemary sprigs; bring to a boil. Cover and bake at 325° for 25 minutes or until a thermometer inserted in thickest portion registers 165°. Remove tenderloins from pan; let stand 10 minutes. Remove twine, and slice crosswise into ½-inch-thick slices.
6. Strain cooking liquid through a fine sieve over a bowl; discard solids. Combine flour and ¼ cup cooking liquid, stirring with a whisk until smooth. Return flour mixture and remaining cooking liquid to pan. Stir in reserved 1 cup apple mixture; bring to a boil. Cook 1 minute or until thick, stirring constantly. Serve with turkey.

Serves 8 (serving size: about 2 turkey slices and ¼ cup sauce).

CALORIES 220; FAT 3.3g (sat 0.8g, mono 0.6g, poly 0.9g); PROTEIN 33.2g; CARB 12.8g; FIBER 1.4g; CHOL 82mg; IRON 1.8mg; SODIUM 486mg; CALC 23mg

Wine Pairing
Riesling is an ideal holiday white wine because it plays nicely with a variety of dishes, including this gorgeous, fruity turkey showstopper.

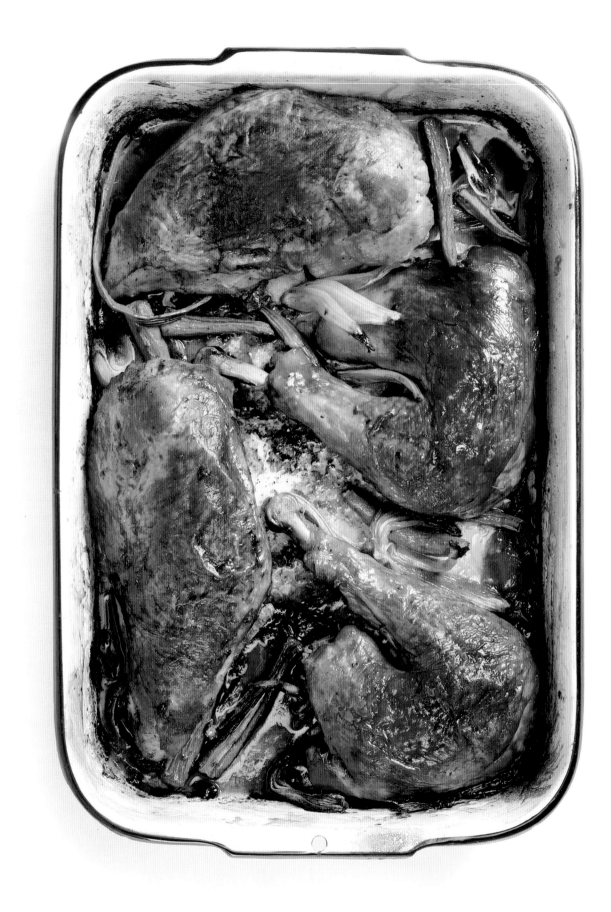

Slow-Roasted Turkey with Cream Gravy

To ensure turkey perfection, this method takes a cue from chefs: The bird is cut into parts before roasting low and slow.

Sure, you won't be able to parade a whole bird through the dining room, but you will be lauded for the succulent results. If breaking down the turkey seems tricky, have your butcher do it.

Hands-on time: 30 min. Total time: 10 hr.

1   (12-pound) fresh or frozen whole turkey, thawed
1   tablespoon kosher salt
10 cups cold water
4   celery stalks, quartered and divided
2   medium onions, peeled, quartered, and divided
2   carrots, quartered and divided
½   cup heavy whipping cream, divided
1½ teaspoons freshly ground black pepper
2   tablespoons cornstarch

1. Remove giblets and neck from turkey; set aside. Discard liver. Place turkey, breast side up, on a cutting board. Pull legs away from body; using a boning knife, cut through skin at leg joint. Using both hands, turn leg quarter away from body until joint pops out of socket. When flesh and joint are exposed, place knife firmly against joint to make cut. Cut through joint to remove leg quarters; set aside. Remove wings along joint; reserve wings. Using kitchen shears, cut along backbone on both sides from tail to neck to remove backbone; reserve backbone. Place breast, meat side down, on a cutting board. Using a large, heavy knife, cut breast in half lengthwise.

2. Place breast halves and leg quarters in a large bowl; sprinkle with salt. Cover and chill 8 hours or overnight.

3. Combine reserved giblets, wings, and backbone in a large Dutch oven. Add 10 cups water, 8 celery pieces, 4 onion quarters, and 4 carrot pieces. Bring to a boil over medium-high heat. Reduce heat, and simmer 5 hours or until mixture measures 8 cups. Cool to room temperature. Cover and chill stock 8 hours or overnight.

4. Skim solidified fat from surface of stock; discard fat. Return stock to high heat; bring to a boil. Boil 30 minutes or until stock measures 3 cups. Strain mixture through a sieve, reserving stock. Discard solids.

5. Remove turkey from refrigerator; let stand at room temperature 30 minutes.

6. Preheat oven to 325°.

7. Arrange turkey pieces, skin sides up, in a roasting pan; arrange remaining 8 celery pieces, remaining 4 onion quarters, and remaining 4 carrot pieces in pan. Brush turkey skin with 2 tablespoons cream; sprinkle with pepper. Bake at 325° for 1½ hours or until a thermometer inserted in thickest part of breast registers 165°, basting every 30 minutes with

2½ tablespoons stock. Remove from oven. Place breast halves and leg quarters on a jelly-roll pan or cutting board. Cover and let stand 30 minutes. Discard skin.

8. Add 1 cup stock to bottom of roasting pan, scraping to loosen browned bits from bottom of pan. Place a zip-top plastic bag inside a 2-cup glass measure. Pour drippings into bag; let stand 10 minutes (fat will rise to top). Seal bag; carefully snip off 1 bottom corner of bag. Strain drippings through a sieve into a medium saucepan, stopping before fat layer reaches opening; discard fat and solids. Add remaining 1½ cups stock to pan; bring to a boil over medium-high heat. Combine remaining 6 tablespoons cream and cornstarch in a bowl, stirring with a whisk until smooth. Add cream mixture to stock mixture, stirring with a whisk. Boil 1 minute or until slightly thick, stirring constantly. Serve gravy with turkey.

Serves 12 (serving size: about 5 ounces turkey and 3 tablespoons gravy).

CALORIES 254; FAT 7.4g (sat 3.5g, mono 1.9g, poly 1.2g); PROTEIN 42.2g; CARB 2g; FIBER 0.2g; CHOL 153mg; IRON 2.8mg; SODIUM 581mg; CALC 37mg

Smoked Turkey Breast with Pomegranate-Thyme Glaze

Late November may not be prime time for grilling in all parts of the country, but adding smoke and fire to your Thanksgiving bird is worth the momentary chill.

Or, make this your new summer backyard-barbecue showpiece. The whole turkey breast cooks relatively quickly over an indirect fire, but it's still plenty big to feed a crowd. Hands-on time: 30 min. Total time: 2 hr. 55 min.

2 cups cherry or applewood chips

1 (6-pound) whole bone-in turkey breast

1 tablespoon chopped fresh thyme, divided

2 teaspoons kosher salt, divided

1 teaspoon freshly ground black pepper

3 garlic cloves, thinly sliced

1 teaspoon olive oil

1 large shallot, finely chopped

1½ cups pomegranate juice

¼ cup sugar

Cooking spray

1. Soak wood chips in water 1 hour; drain well.

2. Trim excess fat from turkey. Loosen skin from breast by inserting fingers, gently pushing between skin and meat. Combine 2 teaspoons thyme, 1½ teaspoons salt, pepper, and garlic, stirring well. Rub thyme mixture under loosened skin.

3. Heat a small saucepan over medium-high heat. Add oil to pan; swirl to coat. Add remaining 1 teaspoon thyme, remaining ½ teaspoon salt, and shallots; sauté 2 minutes, stirring frequently. Add juice and sugar; bring to a boil. Reduce heat, and simmer 15 minutes or until syrupy and reduced to about ½ cup. Remove from heat.

4. To prepare turkey for indirect grilling, remove grill rack. Preheat grill to medium-high heat using both burners. After preheating, turn left burner off (leave right burner on). Place 1 cup wood chips on heat element on right side. Place a disposable aluminum foil pan on heat element on left (unheated) side. Pour 2 cups water in pan. Coat grill rack with cooking spray; place on grill. Place turkey on grill rack covering left burner. Cover and grill 1 hour and 20 minutes or until a thermometer registers 165°, turning halfway through cooking time. Add remaining 1 cup wood chips halfway through cooking time; brush turkey with half of pomegranate mixture during last 5 minutes of cooking. Place turkey on a platter. Let stand 30 minutes. Discard skin. Serve with remaining pomegranate mixture.

Serves 8 (serving size: 6 ounces turkey and about 1½ teaspoons sauce).

CALORIES 349; FAT 2.2g (sat 0.6g, mono 0.7g, poly 0.5g); PROTEIN 64.3g; CARB 14.3g; FIBER 0.1g; CHOL 176mg; IRON 3.5mg; SODIUM 597mg; CALC 39mg

NUTRITION MADE EASY

Pomegranate Juice: A little sweet, a little tart, and a whole lot of healthy. Polyphenols are cancer-fighting antioxidants. One glass of pomegranate juice has the same polyphenol content as two glasses of red wine, four glasses of cranberry juice, or 10 cups of green tea. It's also an excellent source of vitamin C, potassium, and calcium.

Turkey and Wild Mushroom Hash Cakes

Perfect for leftovers: A few extra ingredients turn turkey and mashed potatoes into crunchy-creamy-cheesy patties.

Rotisserie or leftover chicken can easily stand in for the turkey. Reach into the fridge and grab cranberry sauce to serve on the side. Hands-on time: 30 min. Total time: 45 min.

4   teaspoons canola oil, divided

2   cups chopped shiitake mushroom caps (about 4 ounces)

1   garlic clove, minced

2   cups chopped cooked turkey breast (about 10 ounces)

2   cups leftover mashed potatoes or packaged mashed potatoes

¾   cup panko (Japanese breadcrumbs), divided

½   cup (2 ounces) shredded cheddar cheese

⅓   cup thinly sliced green onions

1½   tablespoons finely chopped fresh thyme

¼   teaspoon salt

¼   teaspoon freshly ground black pepper

1. Heat a large nonstick skillet over medium-high heat. Add 1 teaspoon oil; swirl to coat. Add mushrooms and garlic to pan; sauté 5 minutes or until tender, stirring frequently. Combine mushroom mixture, turkey, potatoes, ¼ cup panko, and next 5 ingredients (through pepper) in a large bowl. Divide mixture into 8 equal portions, shaping each into a ½-inch-thick patty. Refrigerate 10 minutes. Dredge patties in remaining ½ cup panko.

2. Wipe pan clean with paper towels. Heat pan over medium-high heat. Add 1½ teaspoons oil to pan; swirl to coat. Add 4 patties; cook 2 minutes on each side. Repeat procedure with remaining 1½ teaspoons oil and remaining 4 patties.

Serves 4 (serving size: 2 patties).

CALORIES 356; FAT 14.2g (sat 6.1g, mono 3.1g, poly 1.5g); PROTEIN 29.2g; CARB 26.5g; FIBER 3g; CHOL 84mg; IRON 2.3mg; SODIUM 502mg; CALC 153mg

Mushroom and Sausage Ragù with Polenta

Cream cheese and butter stirred into polenta creates an inviting base for a savory, chunky sauce.

Cook the polenta while the ragù simmers so everything will be ready and hot at the same time.
Hands-on time: 21 min. Total time: 49 min.

1½ tablespoons olive oil, divided

8 ounces hot turkey Italian sausage

½ cup chopped onion

1 pound cremini mushrooms, sliced

2 large garlic cloves, minced

¼ teaspoon kosher salt, divided

1 (14.5-ounce) can no-salt-added diced tomatoes, undrained

2½ cups fat-free, lower-sodium chicken broth

1½ cups water

1 cup uncooked polenta

½ cup (4 ounces) ⅓-less-fat cream cheese

1 tablespoon unsalted butter

1. Heat a skillet over medium-high heat. Add 1½ teaspoons oil to pan; swirl to coat. Remove sausage from casings. Add sausage to pan; sauté 3 minutes or until browned, stirring to crumble. Remove sausage from pan.

2. Add remaining 1 tablespoon oil to pan; swirl to coat. Add onion; sauté 3 minutes, stirring occasionally. Add mushrooms; sauté 4 minutes, stirring occasionally. Add garlic; sauté 1 minute, stirring constantly. Stir in sausage, ⅛ teaspoon salt, and tomatoes; bring to a simmer. Reduce heat to medium; simmer 15 minutes.

3. Bring broth and 1½ cups water to a boil in a medium saucepan. Add polenta to pan, stirring well.

Reduce heat to medium; simmer 20 minutes or until thick, stirring occasionally. Stir in remaining ⅛ teaspoon salt, cream cheese, and butter. Serve with sausage mixture.

Serves 4 (serving size: 1 cup polenta and 1 cup ragù).

CALORIES 428; FAT 18.7g (sat 8.4g, mono 8.5g, poly 1.4g); PROTEIN 18.2g; CARB 46g; FIBER 4.6g; CHOL 53mg; IRON 3.3mg; SODIUM 796mg; CALC 74mg

Wine Pairing

This savory dish calls for a wine with good acidity and a touch of earthiness to highlight the mushrooms. Try a Chianti Classico, a Tuscan red with hints of cherries and earthy spices.

TECHNIQUE

Mincing Garlic: Choose heads of garlic that are firm and free of dark spots and green shoots. Garlic needs to be crushed or chopped to release its flavor.

1. Place unpeeled garlic clove on cutting board. Using the flat side of a chef's knife, press down hard using the heel of your hand until the papery skin cracks or breaks open.

2. Remove skin and cut off tough bottom portion of garlic. Make thin, lengthwise cuts through garlic clove, then cut strips crosswise.

Turkey Cabbage Cups

Cool, crisp napa cabbage leaves cradle spicy-herby filling in this quick and easy take on the flavor-packed Southeast Asian dish *larb*.

Ground chicken and green cabbage are fine stand-ins for turkey and napa cabbage. Hands-on time: 22 min. Total time: 22 min.

1	teaspoon grated peeled fresh ginger
1¼	pounds ground turkey
½	cup thinly sliced green onions
1	tablespoon brown sugar
2	tablespoons chopped fresh cilantro
2	tablespoons chopped fresh mint
2	tablespoons fresh lime juice
1½	tablespoons fish sauce
2	teaspoons olive oil
1	teaspoon dark sesame oil
1	jalapeño pepper, finely chopped
12	large napa (Chinese) cabbage leaves (about 8 ounces)
¼	cup chopped unsalted, dry-roasted peanuts

1. Heat a large nonstick skillet over medium heat. Add ginger and turkey to pan; cook 7 minutes or until turkey is done, stirring frequently. Drain turkey mixture; place in a large bowl. Add green onions and next 8 ingredients (through jalapeño); toss well. Spoon ⅓ cup turkey mixture into each cabbage leaf. Top with peanuts.

Serves 4 (serving size: 3 filled cabbage cups).

CALORIES 267; FAT 13.6g (sat 3.7g, mono 6.4g, poly 2.7g); PROTEIN 30.3g; CARB 7.6g; FIBER 1.4g; CHOL 89mg; IRON 1.8mg; SODIUM 637mg; CALC 111mg

NUTRITION MADE EASY

Ground Turkey: There are a number of options available, so read the label to be sure you get what you want. The leanest, labeled "ground turkey breast," is white meat only, with no skin and about 3% fat. Regular "ground turkey" is made from white and dark meat with some skin and is about 10% fat (similar to ground round)—its richness works best here. Frozen ground turkey is usually all dark meat with skin and is 15% fat, similar to ground sirloin.

Sausage and Cheese Breakfast Casserole

Pop a prepared casserole in the oven and let it bake while you sip coffee—that's the way to wake up on a lazy Sunday.

Or, prepare individual servings in 8-ounce ramekins and bake for 30 minutes. This breakfast casserole is much lower in fat than most. Find turkey breakfast sausage in the freezer section, or in the fresh poultry area. If you buy turkey sausage links, remove the casings and proceed with the recipe. Garnish with fresh chives. Hands-on time: 18 min. Total time: 9 hr. 43 min.

1   teaspoon canola oil

12   ounces turkey breakfast sausage

2   cups 1% low-fat milk

2   cups egg substitute

1   teaspoon dry mustard

½   teaspoon freshly ground black pepper

¼   teaspoon salt

¼   teaspoon ground red pepper

3   large eggs

16   (1-ounce) slices white bread

1   cup (4 ounces) finely shredded reduced-fat extra-sharp cheddar cheese

Cooking spray

1. Heat a large nonstick skillet over medium-high heat. Add oil to pan; swirl to coat. Add sausage to pan; cook 5 minutes or until browned, stirring to crumble. Remove from heat; cool.

2. Combine milk and next 6 ingredients (through eggs) in a large bowl, stirring with a whisk.

3. Trim crusts from bread; cut into 1-inch cubes. Add bread cubes, sausage, and cheese to milk mixture, stirring to combine. Pour mixture into a 13 x 9–inch glass or ceramic baking dish or 3-quart casserole dish coated with cooking spray, spreading evenly. Cover and chill 8 hours or overnight.

4. Preheat oven to 350°.

5. Remove casserole from refrigerator; let stand 30 minutes. Bake at 350° for 45 minutes or until set and lightly browned. Let stand 10 minutes.

Serves 12 (serving size: about 1 cup).

CALORIES 245; FAT 9.2g (sat 3.7g, mono 2g, poly 1.3g); PROTEIN 18.5g; CARB 20.4g; FIBER 0.8g; CHOL 84mg; IRON 2.5mg; SODIUM 609mg; CALC 185mg

Chapter Pasta &

8: Pizza

Take dough, boil it or bake it, add sauces and toppings: This is the simple formula for pasta and pizza in Europe, and for flatbreads and noodle dishes all the way to Japan and China. It's some of the most soul-satisfying food in the world. Markets burst with hundreds of noodle varieties, fresh and dried. No need for giant portions, and no need, in the case of Italian dishes, to freight a serving with staggering amounts of cheese. Stripped back to glorious essentials, this is the definition of healthy cooking: seasonal, simple, exuberant—and even better when paired with a glass of healthy wine.

Fettuccine with Olive Oil, Garlic, and Red Pepper

Simple, simple, simply delicious!

The trick for a perfect bowl of *aglio e olio* (garlic and oil) is to cook the garlic just enough to coax its flavor into the oil without burning it. Garlic gets brown and bitter in just a second, so use moderate heat and be watchful. Hands-on time: 19 min. Total time: 28 min.

- ¼ cup extra-virgin olive oil, divided
- 3 garlic cloves, minced
- ½ teaspoon crushed red pepper
- 6 quarts water
- 3¼ teaspoons kosher salt, divided
- 8 ounces uncooked fettuccine
- ½ cup (2 ounces) grated fresh Parmesan cheese
- ⅓ cup coarsely chopped fresh flat-leaf parsley

1. Heat a large skillet over medium heat. Add 2 tablespoons oil to pan; swirl to coat. Add garlic; cook 30 seconds or until fragrant, stirring constantly. Stir in pepper. Remove from heat.

2. Bring 6 quarts water and 1 tablespoon salt to a boil in a large pot. Add pasta; cook 8 minutes or until almost tender. Drain pasta in a colander over a bowl, reserving ½ cup cooking liquid. Add hot pasta, reserved cooking liquid, remaining ¼ teaspoon salt, and cheese to garlic mixture. Increase heat to medium-high; cook 2 minutes or until pasta is al dente, stirring occasionally. Remove from heat; sprinkle with parsley. Place 1½ cups pasta on each of 4 plates; drizzle each serving with 1½ teaspoons olive oil.

Serves 4.

CALORIES 397; FAT 19g (sat 4.6g, mono 11.3g, poly 2.5g); PROTEIN 13.2g; CARB 44g; FIBER 2.1g; CHOL 12mg; IRON 2.4mg; SODIUM 559mg; CALC 180mg

Linguine with 5-Minute Lemony Ricotta

The first time you taste homemade ricotta out of your microwave is a eureka moment that makes you wonder who won the Nobel Prize for this.

Acid and heat separate the milky curds, and lemon peel stirred in at the end makes it liltingly aromatic. It's fabulous right off a spoon. Timing varies depending on microwave power, though, so start with just four minutes, and check texture. You're looking for curds that, before draining, are fluffy and delicate. They'll firm up a bit. Hands-on time: 30 min. Total time: 50 min.

2	cups 2% reduced-fat milk
½	cup plain whole-milk Greek yogurt
2	teaspoons cider vinegar
1½	teaspoons grated lemon rind
1	teaspoon kosher salt, divided
8	ounces uncooked linguine
1	tablespoon olive oil
2	small yellow squash, chopped
1	small zucchini, chopped
1	pint grape tomatoes, halved
4	garlic cloves, coarsely chopped
⅓	cup fat-free, lower-sodium chicken broth
½	teaspoon freshly ground black pepper
¼	cup small fresh mint leaves

1. Combine first 3 ingredients in a microwave-safe 1-quart liquid measuring cup; microwave at HIGH 4 minutes. Stir to form small curds. Strain through a sieve lined with a double layer of cheesecloth; let stand 5 minutes. Discard liquid. Scrape cheese mixture into a small bowl; stir in rind and ¼ teaspoon salt.

2. Cook pasta according to package directions, omitting salt and fat; drain.

3. Heat a large skillet over medium-high heat. Add oil to pan; swirl to coat. Add squash and zucchini to pan, and sauté 1 minute. Add ¼ teaspoon salt, tomatoes, and garlic; sauté 4 minutes, stirring frequently. Add broth and pasta to pan; cook 2 minutes or until thoroughly heated, tossing to combine. Place 2 cups pasta mixture in each of 4 shallow bowls; sprinkle evenly with remaining ½ teaspoon salt and pepper. Top each serving with 2 tablespoons cheese mixture and 1 tablespoon mint. Serve immediately.

Serves 4.

CALORIES 372; FAT 9.8g (sat 4.6g, mono 3.2g, poly 0.6g); PROTEIN 15.9g; CARB 56.5g; FIBER 4.1g; CHOL 15mg; IRON 2.6mg; SODIUM 587mg; CALC 212mg

Whole-Wheat Pasta with Sausage, Leeks, and Fontina
Whole-wheat pasta has a chewy, slightly rough texture that matches nicely with these hearty ingredients.

Flavors and textures jumble up in every bite. Hands-on time: 15 min. Total time: 37 min.

6   quarts water

2⅜   teaspoons salt, divided

1   pound uncooked whole-wheat penne or rigatoni

1   tablespoon olive oil

1   (4-ounce) link sweet Italian sausage

2   cups chopped leek

4   cups shredded Savoy cabbage (about 9½ ounces)

1   cup fat-free, lower-sodium chicken broth

¼   teaspoon freshly ground black pepper

½   cup (2 ounces) shredded fontina cheese

1. Bring 6 quarts water and 2 teaspoons salt to a boil in a large stockpot. Add pasta; cook 8 minutes or until almost al dente, stirring occasionally. Drain.

2. Heat a Dutch oven over medium-high heat. Add oil to pan; swirl to coat. Remove casing from sausage. Add sausage to pan; cook 2 minutes or until lightly browned, stirring to crumble. Add leek; cook 2 minutes or until leek is soft, stirring frequently. Add cabbage; cook 2 minutes or until cabbage wilts, stirring frequently. Add remaining ⅜ teaspoon salt, broth, and pepper; bring to a boil. Reduce heat, and simmer 15 minutes or until vegetables are very tender.

3. Add pasta to sausage mixture, tossing to coat. Bring to a boil; reduce heat, and cook 1 minute, stirring constantly, or until pasta is al dente. Remove from heat; stir in cheese. Serve immediately.

Serves 6 (serving size: 1⅔ cups).

CALORIES 385; FAT 8.9g (sat 3.2g, mono 3.8g, poly 1.2g); PROTEIN 17.3g; CARB 64.3g; FIBER 8.3g; CHOL 18mg; IRON 3.8mg; SODIUM 609mg; CALC 119mg

Bucatini with Green Peas and Pancetta

The cured-pork flavor of the best pancetta is worth hunting down from a good specialty shop. Just a little makes a dish sing.

Buy extra pancetta to store in the freezer for flavoring sauces, soups, and other pasta tosses. Use frozen green peas, thawed, if fresh are unavailable. Bucatini is a thick, spaghetti-like pasta with a hollow center. If you can't find it, substitute linguine. Hands-on time: 30 min. Total time: 45 min.

3	tablespoons extra-virgin olive oil, divided
½	cup chopped pancetta (about 2 ounces)
¼	cup finely chopped shallots
1¼	cups shelled green peas (about 1½ pounds unshelled)
1	garlic clove, minced
¼	cup dry white wine
2	teaspoons chopped fresh thyme
6	quarts water
1	tablespoon kosher salt
8	ounces uncooked bucatini pasta
⅜	teaspoon kosher salt
¼	teaspoon freshly ground black pepper
½	cup (2 ounces) grated fresh Parmigiano-Reggiano cheese

1. Heat a large skillet over medium heat. Add 1 tablespoon oil to pan; swirl to coat. Add pancetta; cook 10 minutes or until browned and crisp, stirring occasionally. Remove pancetta from pan, reserving 1 tablespoon drippings in pan; set pancetta aside. Add shallots to pan; cook 4 minutes or until tender, stirring occasionally. Add peas and garlic; cook 1 minute, stirring occasionally. Add wine and thyme. Increase heat to medium-high. Bring to a boil; cook until liquid reduces to 2 tablespoons (about 3 minutes). Remove from heat.
2. Bring 6 quarts water and 1 tablespoon salt to a boil in a large pot. Add pasta; cook 8 minutes or until al dente. Drain pasta in a colander over a bowl, reserving ½ cup cooking liquid. Add pasta, remaining 2 tablespoons oil,

⅜ teaspoon salt, and pepper to pea mixture; toss well. Stir in reserved cooking liquid. Place about 1¼ cups pasta mixture in each of 4 shallow bowls. Sprinkle pancetta evenly over pasta; top each serving with 2 tablespoons cheese.

Serves 4.

CALORIES 403; FAT 16.8g (sat 4.3g, mono 7.5g, poly 1.6g); PROTEIN 13.5g; CARB 51.1g; FIBER 4.2g; CHOL 12mg; IRON 2.8mg; SODIUM 604mg; CALC 64mg

Wine Pairing
Green, peppery grüner veltliner from Austria is savory and refreshing with this veggie-rich pasta dish.

Summer Pappardelle with Tomatoes, Arugula, and Parmesan

Warm lemon-garlic dressing gently wilts the peppery greens and coats softened tomatoes in this bright pasta toss.

If your cooked pasta clumps together, here's a save: Rinse the pasta quickly under hot water, drain again thoroughly, and then toss with the tomato mixture and arugula. Use a large skillet so you can mix everything together right in the pan, as chefs like to do—and it's one less bowl to wash.

Hands-on time: 10 min. Total time: 20 min.

9 ounces uncooked pappardelle (wide ribbon pasta)

2 tablespoons extra-virgin olive oil

¼ teaspoon crushed red pepper

3 garlic cloves, thinly sliced

1½ cups halved yellow tear-drop cherry tomatoes (pear-shaped)

1½ cups halved grape tomatoes

2¼ teaspoons fresh lemon juice

⅝ teaspoon salt

5 cups loosely packed trimmed arugula

⅓ cup (1½ ounces) shaved fresh Parmesan cheese

2 bacon slices, cooked and crumbled

1. Cook pasta according to package directions, omitting salt and fat. Drain; keep warm.

2. Heat a large nonstick skillet over medium heat. Add oil to pan; swirl to coat. Add pepper and garlic; cook 1 minute or until garlic is fragrant, stirring constantly. Add tomatoes; cook 45 seconds or just until heated, stirring gently. Remove pan from heat; stir in juice and salt. Combine pasta, arugula, and tomato mixture in a large bowl, tossing to coat. Top with cheese and bacon.

Serves 4 (serving size: 2 cups).

CALORIES 388; FAT 12.5g (sat 3.5g, mono 6.6g, poly 1.1g); PROTEIN 15.2g; CARB 55.7g; FIBER 3.8g; CHOL 10mg; IRON 3.1mg; SODIUM 683mg; CALC 189mg

Farfalle with Creamy Wild Mushroom Sauce 🌿
Our goal was an ultra-creamy sauce, and this dish delivers.

The exotic mushroom blend, usually a combination of shiitake, cremini, and oyster mushrooms, is sold in 8-ounce packages. If it's not available, you can use all cremini mushrooms. Hands-on time: 10 min. Total time: 21 min.

1　pound uncooked farfalle (bow tie pasta)

1　tablespoon canola oil

½　cup chopped onion

⅓　cup finely chopped shallots

1　tablespoon minced fresh garlic

1½　teaspoons salt, divided

12　ounces presliced exotic mushroom blend

¼　teaspoon freshly ground black pepper

¼　cup dry white wine

⅔　cup heavy whipping cream

½　cup (2 ounces) grated fresh Parmigiano-Reggiano cheese

2　tablespoons chopped fresh parsley

Minced fresh parsley (optional)

1. Cook pasta according to package directions, omitting salt and fat; drain.

2. Heat a large nonstick skillet over medium-high heat. Add oil to pan; swirl to coat. Add onion, shallots, garlic, 1 teaspoon salt, mushrooms, and pepper to pan; cook 12 minutes or until liquid evaporates and mushrooms are tender, stirring occasionally. Add wine; cook 2 minutes or until liquid evaporates, stirring occasionally. Remove from heat.

3. Add cooked pasta, cream, cheese, and 2 tablespoons parsley, tossing gently to coat. Stir in remaining ½ teaspoon salt. Garnish with minced fresh parsley, if desired. Serve immediately.

Serves 8 (serving size: 1¼ cups).

CALORIES 343; FAT 11.9g (sat 6.1g, mono 3.8g, poly 0.8g); PROTEIN 12.1g; CARB 47.4g; FIBER 2.3g; CHOL 32mg; IRON 2.3mg; SODIUM 565mg; CALC 124mg

Wine Pairing

An aged Champagne is spicy and complex with notes of toasty bread and stewed fruits that make an incredible marriage with the creamy mushroom sauce.

TECHNIQUE

A Pasta-Cooking Primer: Tips for making the best noodles ever.

1. Use a Dutch oven or a stockpot to allow the pasta to move freely in the boiling water; this ensures it cooks evenly. Use 4 to 6 quarts of water to cook spaghetti and other "long" pastas, or 1 pound of shaped pasta.

2. You can salt the water to deepen the flavor—use 2 teaspoons to 1 tablespoon salt for each full pot of water. While this will add some sodium to the final dish, most of the sodium drains off.

3. Bring the water to a rolling boil, and add the pasta. Once the pasta has been added, be sure to stir to prevent it from sticking to the bottom and clumping. Begin timing when water returns to boil.

4. Use a timer to let you know when to taste the pasta; sample to determine if it's al dente. Long pasta will have a white dot in the center; in round pasta, there will be a faint but clear white ring around the center.

Chicken Spaghetti
Retro comfort food—wonderful.

Here, we break the processed cheese rule (we rarely use it) because it lends a creaminess to the sauce that we just otherwise couldn't achieve. It's a nostalgic flavor and texture throwback. Hands-on time: 60 min. Total time: 60 min.

7 cups boiling water, divided

½ ounce dried porcini mushrooms (about ½ cup)

8 ounces uncooked spaghetti

2¼ teaspoons kosher salt, divided

2 tablespoons extra-virgin olive oil, divided

3 (6-ounce) skinless, boneless chicken breast halves, cut into bite-sized pieces

½ teaspoon freshly ground black pepper

2 tablespoons butter

8 ounces cremini mushrooms, sliced

2 teaspoons minced fresh garlic

3 tablespoons all-purpose flour

1¼ cups fat-free, lower-sodium chicken broth

1¼ cups 2% reduced-fat milk

4 ounces processed cheese, cubed

⅓ cup (3 ounces) ⅓-less-fat cream cheese

½ cup (2 ounces) Gruyère cheese, shredded

1½ cups frozen English peas, thawed

⅓ cup finely chopped fresh chives

1½ ounces French bread, torn into pieces

1. Combine 1 cup boiling water and porcini mushrooms in a small bowl; let stand 20 minutes. Drain in a colander over a bowl, reserving ½ cup soaking liquid. Chop porcini.
2. Cook pasta in remaining 6 cups boiling water with 2 teaspoons salt until al dente; drain. Rinse pasta with cold water; drain.
3. Heat a large saucepan over medium-high heat. Add 1 tablespoon oil to pan; swirl to coat. Sprinkle chicken with remaining ¼ teaspoon salt and pepper. Add chicken to pan; sauté 5 minutes, turning to brown on all sides. Remove chicken from pan. Melt butter in pan. Add cremini mushrooms and garlic to pan; sauté 3 minutes, stirring frequently. Add flour; sauté 1 minute, stirring constantly.

4. Arrange rack in middle of oven. Preheat broiler.
5. Combine reserved porcini liquid, broth, and milk. Gradually add broth mixture to flour mixture in pan, stirring constantly; bring to a boil. Reduce heat, and cook 1 minute or until slightly thick. Stir in processed cheese and cream cheese. Remove from heat; stir until smooth. Stir in Gruyère. Add porcini, pasta, chicken, peas, and chives; toss. Scrape pasta mixture into a broiler-safe 13 x 9–inch glass or ceramic baking dish.
6. Place bread in a food processor; drizzle with remaining 1 tablespoon oil. Process until coarse crumbs form. Sprinkle crumb mixture evenly over pasta mixture. Place dish on middle rack in oven; broil 6 minutes or until golden.

Serves 8 (serving size: about 1½ cups).

CALORIES 413; FAT 16.4g (sat 7.9g, mono 5g, poly 1.2g); PROTEIN 29g; CARB 36g; FIBER 3.1g; CHOL 75mg; IRON 2.8mg; SODIUM 583mg; CALC 228mg

PASTA & PIZZA

Creamy, Light Macaroni and Cheese

We set out to make a serious dent in the calorie and fat content of good old mac and cheese, while preserving the creamy comfort-food texture.

Solution: Butternut squash. Combined with milk and Greek yogurt, it adds rich flavor, sneaks in a vegetable, and gives color to a three-cheese sauce that contains no cheddar. Hands-on time: 1 hr. Total time: 1 hr. 25 min.

3 cups cubed peeled butternut squash (about 1 [1-pound] squash)

1¼ cups fat-free, lower-sodium chicken broth

1½ cups fat-free milk

2 garlic cloves, peeled

2 tablespoons plain fat-free Greek yogurt

1 teaspoon kosher salt

½ teaspoon freshly ground black pepper

1¼ cups (5 ounces) shredded Gruyère cheese

1 cup (4 ounces) grated pecorino Romano cheese

¼ cup (1 ounce) finely grated fresh Parmigiano-Reggiano cheese, divided

1 pound uncooked cavatappi

Cooking spray

1 teaspoon olive oil

½ cup panko (Japanese breadcrumbs)

2 tablespoons minced fresh parsley

1. Preheat oven to 375°.

2. Combine first 4 ingredients in a medium saucepan; bring to a boil over medium-high heat. Reduce heat to medium, and simmer until squash is tender when pierced with a fork, about 25 minutes. Remove from heat.

3. Place hot squash mixture in a blender. Add yogurt, salt, and pepper. Remove center piece of blender lid (to allow steam to escape); secure blender lid on blender. Place a clean towel over opening in blender lid (to avoid splatters). Blend until smooth. Place blended squash mixture in a bowl; stir in Gruyère, pecorino Romano, and 2 tablespoons Parmigiano-Reggiano until combined.

4. Cook pasta according to package directions, omitting salt and fat; drain well. Add pasta to squash mixture; stir until combined. Spread mixture evenly into a 13 x 9–inch glass or ceramic baking dish coated with cooking spray.

5. Heat a medium skillet over medium heat. Add oil to pan; swirl to coat. Add panko; cook 2 minutes or until golden brown. Remove from heat; stir in remaining 2 tablespoons Parmigiano-Reggiano cheese. Sprinkle evenly over pasta mixture. Lightly coat topping with cooking spray.

6. Bake at 375° for 25 minutes or until bubbly. Sprinkle with parsley; serve immediately.

Serves 8 (serving size: 1⅓ cups).

CALORIES 390; FAT 10.9g (sat 6.1g, mono 2.1g, poly 0.4g); PROTEIN 19.1g; CARB 53.9g; FIBER 3.2g; CHOL 31mg; IRON 2.4mg; SODIUM 589mg; CALC 403mg

TECHNIQUE

Butternut Squash "Béchamel": To retain as much cheese as possible for both flavor and nonnegotiable gooey texture, the traditional buttery, heavy sauce gets a boost from butternut squash.

1. Boil the squash with milk, broth, and garlic to help marry the sweet and savory flavors for an intensely rich base. No roux, no clumps, no mess.

2. Puree the butternut mixture until smooth. Thick Greek yogurt adds tang and richness.

3. Stir the three cheeses into the pureed butternut sauce while it's still warm to ensure they all melt evenly.

4. Use a pasta shape that holds on to the sauce. Great options are cavatappi, because of its corkscrew shape and grooved ridges, and penne rigate.

Butternut Squash, Caramelized Onion, and Spinach Lasagna 🍃
Sage and butternut bring out the best in each other.

Caramelized onions, fontina cheese, and sautéed spinach complete the fall festival of flavors. A béchamel-style sauce creams the dish up. Hands-on time: 1 hr. 15 min. Total time: 2 hr.

6 cups (½-inch) cubed peeled butternut squash

2 tablespoons extra-virgin olive oil, divided

2 tablespoons chopped fresh sage

1 teaspoon kosher salt, divided

½ teaspoon freshly ground black pepper

12 garlic cloves, unpeeled (about 1 head)

Cooking spray

1 large onion, vertically sliced

2 tablespoons water

2 (9-ounce) packages fresh spinach

5 cups 1% low-fat milk, divided

1 bay leaf

1 thyme sprig

5 tablespoons all-purpose flour

1½ cups (6 ounces) shredded fontina cheese, divided

⅜ teaspoon ground red pepper

¼ teaspoon grated whole nutmeg

9 no-boil lasagna noodles

1. Preheat oven to 425°.
2. Combine squash, 1 tablespoon oil, sage, ½ teaspoon salt, black pepper, and garlic in a large bowl; toss to coat. Arrange squash mixture on a baking sheet coated with cooking spray. Bake at 425° for 30 minutes or until squash is tender. Cool slightly; peel garlic. Place squash and garlic in a bowl; partially mash with a fork.
3. Heat a large Dutch oven over medium-high heat. Add remaining 1 tablespoon oil to pan; swirl to coat. Add onion; sauté 4 minutes. Reduce heat to medium-low; continue cooking 20 minutes or until golden brown, stirring frequently. Place onion in a bowl.
4. Add 2 tablespoons water and spinach to Dutch oven; increase heat to high. Cover and cook 2 minutes or until spinach wilts. Drain in a colander; cool. Squeeze excess liquid from spinach. Add spinach to onions.
5. Heat 4½ cups milk, bay leaf, and thyme in a medium saucepan over medium-high heat. Bring to a boil; remove from heat. Let stand 10 minutes. Discard bay leaf and thyme. Return pan to medium heat. Combine remaining ½ cup milk and flour in a small bowl. Add milk mixture to pan, stirring with a whisk until blended. Bring to a boil; reduce heat, and simmer 5 minutes or until thick, stirring constantly. Remove from heat; stir in remaining ½ teaspoon salt, 1¼ cups cheese, red pepper, and nutmeg.
6. Spread ½ cup milk mixture in bottom of a 13 x 9-inch glass or ceramic baking dish coated with cooking spray. Arrange 3 noodles over milk mixture; top with half of squash mixture, half of spinach mixture, and ¾ cup milk mixture. Repeat layers, ending with noodles. Spread remaining milk mixture over noodles. Bake at 425° for 30 minutes; remove from oven. Sprinkle with remaining ¼ cup cheese.
7. Preheat broiler.
8. Broil 2 minutes or until cheese melts and is lightly browned. Let stand 10 minutes before serving.

Serves 8 (serving size: 1 piece).

CALORIES 360; FAT 11.9g (sat 5.4g, mono 4.7g, poly 1g); PROTEIN 16.6g; CARB 50g; FIBER 6.5g; CHOL 31mg; IRON 4mg; SODIUM 576mg; CALC 406mg

8

PASTA & PIZZA

Baked Pasta with Sausage, Tomatoes, and Cheese
Easy, cheesy, sausage-y, and good.

It's a perfect pasta dish for busy weeknights. For a gluten-free version, try brown rice penne. Garnish with small fresh basil leaves. Hands-on time: 17 min. Total time: 50 min.

5   quarts water
1   (1-pound) package uncooked ziti (short tube-shaped pasta)
1   pound hot turkey Italian sausage links
1   cup chopped onion
2   garlic cloves, minced
1   tablespoon tomato paste
¼   teaspoon black pepper
2   (14.5-ounce) cans no-salt-added petite-cut tomatoes, undrained
¼   cup chopped fresh basil
Cooking spray

1   cup (4 ounces) shredded fresh mozzarella cheese
1   cup (4 ounces) grated fresh Parmesan cheese

1. Preheat oven to 350°.
2. Bring 5 quarts water to a boil in a large stockpot. Add pasta; cook 2 minutes short of package directions (pasta should be almost al dente). Drain pasta; set aside.
3. Remove casings from sausage. Cook sausage, onion, and garlic in a large nonstick skillet over medium heat until browned, stirring to crumble. Add tomato paste, pepper, and tomatoes; bring to a boil.

Cover; reduce heat, and simmer 10 minutes, stirring occasionally.
4. Combine cooked pasta, sausage mixture, and basil. Place half of pasta mixture in a 4-quart glass or ceramic casserole dish coated with cooking spray. Top with half of mozzarella and half of Parmesan. Repeat layers. Bake at 350° for 25 minutes or until bubbly.

Serves 8 (serving size: 1½ cups).

CALORIES 434; FAT 13.3g (sat 6.2g, mono 3.3g, poly 1.8g); PROTEIN 28.5g; CARB 51g; FIBER 3.1g; CHOL 68mg; IRON 3.4mg; SODIUM 660mg; CALC 293mg

Hearty Lasagna

A straightforward crowd-pleaser in the Italian-American style. Fresh herbs make all the difference.

Fat-free ricotta in the filling allows you to splurge on gooey, full-fat provolone in the layers.
Hands-on time: 30 min. Total time: 2 hr. 58 min.

¾	pound ground round
1	tablespoon olive oil
1	cup chopped onion
3	garlic cloves, minced
2	(28-ounce) cans whole tomatoes, undrained and chopped
½	cup fresh basil, divided
¼	cup chopped fresh parsley, divided
¼	cup fresh oregano, divided
1	teaspoon sugar
¼	teaspoon freshly ground black pepper
¼	cup (1 ounce) grated fresh Parmesan cheese
1	(32-ounce) carton fat-free ricotta cheese
1	large egg white, lightly beaten
	Cooking spray
12	cooked lasagna noodles
2	cups (8 ounces) shredded Italian provolone cheese
	Fresh oregano sprigs (optional)

1. Cook meat in a large saucepan over medium heat until browned, stirring to crumble. Drain; set aside. Wipe pan with paper towels. Heat pan over medium heat. Add oil to pan; swirl to coat. Add onion and garlic to pan; cook 5 minutes, stirring frequently. Return meat to pan. Remove tomatoes from can using a slotted spoon, reserving juices. Crush tomatoes. Stir tomatoes, juices, ¼ cup basil, 2 tablespoons parsley, 2 tablespoons oregano, sugar, and pepper into garlic mixture; bring to a boil. Reduce heat, and simmer 45 minutes. Remove from heat.

2. Preheat oven to 350°.

3. Combine remaining ¼ cup basil, remaining 2 tablespoons parsley, remaining 2 tablespoons oregano, Parmesan, ricotta, and egg white in a bowl; set aside.

4. Spread ¾ cup tomato mixture in bottom of a 13 x 9-inch glass or ceramic baking dish coated with cooking spray. Arrange 4 noodles over tomato mixture; top with half of ricotta mixture, 2 cups tomato mixture, and ⅔ cup provolone. Repeat layers, ending with noodles. Spread remaining tomato mixture over noodles. Cover; bake at 350° for 1 hour. Sprinkle with remaining provolone; bake, uncovered, 15 minutes. Let stand 10 minutes before serving. Garnish with oregano, if desired.

Serves 12

CALORIES 345; FAT 16g (sat 8.5g, mono 5.2g, poly 0.7g); PROTEIN 23.5g; CARB 25.7g; FIBER 2.1g; CHOL 56mg; IRON 2.5mg; SODIUM 603mg; CALC 424mg

TEST KITCHEN SECRET

Chopping Herbs: To chop parsley (or cilantro) quickly, don't pick leaves from the bunch. Instead, wash and dry the bunch while it's still bound together. Then make a diagonal cut (to avoid the thicker stems in the center) from the top of the bunch to chop off roughly the amount you'll need.

Vegetarian Bolognese with Whole-Wheat Penne 🌿 🌾
The Parmigiano-Reggiano rind simmers with the sauce, infusing it with deep, savory umami taste.

Wrap unused cheese rinds in heavy-duty plastic wrap or zip-top plastic bags, and save to season soups, stews, or tomato sauces. Garnish with small fresh basil leaves. Hands-on time: 12 min. Total time: 1 hr. 10 min.

¼ cup dried porcini mushrooms (about ¼ ounce)

1 tablespoon olive oil

1½ cups finely chopped onion

½ cup finely chopped carrot

½ cup finely chopped celery

1 (8-ounce) package cremini mushrooms, finely chopped

½ cup dry red wine

¼ cup warm water

½ teaspoon salt

½ teaspoon freshly ground black pepper

1 (28-ounce) can organic crushed tomatoes with basil, undrained

1 (2-inch) piece Parmigiano-Reggiano cheese rind

12 ounces uncooked whole-wheat penne (tube-shaped pasta)

½ cup (2 ounces) shaved Parmigiano-Reggiano cheese

1. Place dried mushrooms in a spice or coffee grinder; process until finely ground.

2. Heat a large saucepan over medium-high heat. Add oil to pan; swirl to coat. Add onion, carrot, celery, and cremini mushrooms to pan; sauté 10 minutes, stirring frequently. Add wine; simmer 2 minutes or until liquid almost evaporates. Add ¼ cup warm water and next 4 ingredients (through cheese rind). Stir in ground porcini. Cover, reduce heat, and simmer 40 minutes. Keep warm. Remove rind; discard.

3. Cook pasta according to package directions, omitting salt and fat; drain. Place 1 cup pasta in each of 6 bowls. Top each serving with ¾ cup sauce and about 1 tablespoon cheese.

Serves 6.

CALORIES 334; FAT 7.2g (sat 2.1g, mono 2.5g, poly 1.9g); PROTEIN 14.8g; CARB 57.7g; FIBER 9.7g; CHOL 9mg; IRON 3.3mg; SODIUM 542mg; CALC 156mg

Spaghetti with Pork Bolognese

The rich sauce uses pork two ways, ground and salt-cured. It has old-world depth—but it's less rich.

A little liquid remaining in your sauce helps coat the pasta. This version differs from other Italian tomato sauces because it gets its flavor from a soffrito—sautéed finely chopped onion, celery, carrots, and garlic.
Hands-on time: 17 min. Total time: 1 hr. 48 min.

1½ tablespoons extra-virgin olive oil

2 cups finely chopped onion

½ cup finely chopped carrot (about 1 medium)

½ cup finely chopped celery (about 1 stalk)

1½ teaspoons chopped garlic

¾ teaspoon kosher salt, divided

1 bay leaf

1 pound ground pork tenderloin

¾ pound ground pork

2 ounces pancetta, finely diced

¼ cup tomato paste

2 cups chopped plum tomato (about ½ pound)

1½ cups organic vegetable broth

1 cup dry white wine

1 cup 1% low-fat milk

⅛ teaspoon grated whole nutmeg

1 (2-ounce) piece Parmigiano-Reggiano cheese rind

1 (3-inch) cinnamon stick

½ teaspoon freshly ground black pepper

8 cups hot cooked spaghetti (about 1 pound uncooked)

½ cup (2 ounces) grated fresh Parmigiano-Reggiano cheese

½ cup chopped fresh parsley

1. Heat a large Dutch oven over medium heat. Add oil to pan; swirl to coat. Add onion, carrot, celery, garlic, ¼ teaspoon salt, and bay leaf to pan; cook 8 minutes or until vegetables are tender, stirring occasionally. Increase heat to medium-high. Add ground pork tenderloin, ground pork, pancetta, and ¼ teaspoon salt to pan; sauté 8 minutes or until pork loses its pink color. Stir in tomato paste; cook 1 minute. Add tomato and next 5 ingredients (through rind) to pan; bring to a boil. Reduce heat, and simmer 45 minutes. Add cinnamon; simmer 30 minutes or until most of liquid evaporates. Discard bay leaf, rind, and cinnamon stick; stir in remaining ¼ teaspoon salt and pepper. Arrange 1 cup pasta on each of 8 plates; top each serving with about ¾ cup sauce, 1 tablespoon cheese, and 1 tablespoon parsley.

Serves 8.

CALORIES 512; FAT 18g (sat 6.8g, mono 6.8g, poly 1.6g); PROTEIN 34.5g; CARB 51.4g; FIBER 4.5g; CHOL 79mg; IRON 4mg; SODIUM 696mg; CALC 205mg

Wine Pairing

This thick, meaty sauce calls for a red wine with high acidity to cut the richness and amplify the delicious spices. Try an Italian sangiovese.

Linguine with Clam Sauce

As if they have tiny individual timers, littleneck clams pop open when done.

Use the larger amount of red pepper for a zestier dish. One serving of this dish delivers your daily iron needs. Hands-on time: 10 min. Total time: 20 min.

¼ cup extra-virgin olive oil, divided
2 garlic cloves, minced
⅓ cup clam juice
¼ cup chopped fresh flat-leaf parsley
½ to ¾ teaspoon crushed red pepper
½ teaspoon salt
¼ teaspoon freshly ground black pepper
3 dozen littleneck clams
8 cups hot cooked linguine (about 1 pound uncooked pasta)

1. Heat a large skillet over medium heat. Add 2 tablespoons oil to pan; swirl to coat. Add garlic to pan; cook 2 minutes or until golden, stirring frequently. Stir in clam juice and next 5 ingredients (through clams). Cover and cook 10 minutes or until clams open. Discard any unopened shells.

2. Place pasta in a large bowl. Add remaining 2 tablespoons oil; toss well to coat. Add clam mixture to pasta; toss well.

Serves 6 (serving size: 1⅓ cups pasta mixture and 6 clams).

CALORIES 442; FAT 11.2g (sat 1.7g, mono 6.7g, poly 1.3g); PROTEIN 25.1g; CARB 59.9g; FIBER 2.6g; CHOL 39mg; IRON 18.7mg; SODIUM 491mg; CALC 74mg

Pasta with Fresh Tomato-Basil Sauce

For extra color, choose a cheery multicolored mix of cherry tomatoes or a combination of cherry and wee pear tomatoes.

The sauce is good with long pasta, but you can also try penne, gemelli, or farfalle. Hands-on time: 10 min. Total time: 15 min.

1 (9-ounce) package refrigerated fresh fettuccine
2 tablespoons olive oil
3 garlic cloves, minced
4 cups cherry tomatoes, halved
½ teaspoon salt
1 cup fresh basil leaves, torn
¼ teaspoon freshly ground black pepper
½ cup (2 ounces) shaved Parmigiano-Reggiano cheese

1. Cook pasta according to package directions, omitting salt and fat. Drain; place pasta in a large bowl.
2. Heat a medium saucepan over medium heat. Add oil to pan; swirl to coat. Add garlic to pan; cook 1 minute, stirring frequently. Add tomatoes and salt; cover and cook 4 minutes. Remove from heat; stir in basil and pepper. Add tomato mixture to pasta; toss well to combine. Top with cheese.

Serves 4 (serving size: about 1½ cups pasta and about 2 tablespoons cheese).

CALORIES 343; FAT 13.3g (sat 4.2g, mono 6.2g, poly 1.1g); PROTEIN 14.8g; CARB 43.4g; FIBER 3.7g; CHOL 51mg; IRON 2.6mg; SODIUM 541mg; CALC 201mg

Pasta with Fresh
Tomato-Basil Sauce

Shrimp Fettuccine Alfredo
Refrigerated fresh pasta turns this into a light, 30-minute version of the classic.

To cut fat and maintain creamy goodness, we replaced heavy cream and butter with half-and-half and lower-fat cream cheese. The sauce can seize up a bit as it stands. If so, add reserved pasta water at the end until you reach the perfect consistency. Hands-on time: 14 min. Total time: 30 min.

- 1 (9-ounce) package refrigerated fresh fettuccine
- 1 pound peeled and deveined medium shrimp
- 2 green onions, chopped
- 2 garlic cloves, minced
- 2 teaspoons olive oil
- ½ cup (2 ounces) grated fresh Parmigiano-Reggiano cheese
- ⅓ cup half-and-half
- 3 tablespoons (1½ ounces) ⅓-less-fat cream cheese
- ¼ teaspoon freshly ground black pepper
- 2 tablespoons chopped fresh parsley

1. Cook pasta according to package directions, omitting salt and fat. Drain pasta in a colander over a bowl, reserving ¼ cup cooking liquid. Combine shrimp, onions, and garlic in a bowl.
2. Heat a large skillet over medium-high heat. Add oil to pan; swirl to coat. Add shrimp mixture to pan; sauté 4 minutes or until shrimp are done, stirring occasionally. Remove from pan; keep warm.
3. Reduce heat to medium heat. Add reserved cooking liquid, Parmigiano-Reggiano, half-and-half, cream cheese, and pepper to pan; cook 2 minutes or until cheeses melt. Combine pasta, cheese mixture, and shrimp mixture. Sprinkle with parsley.

Serves 4 (serving size: about 1 cup).

CALORIES 442; FAT 14.3g (sat 6.1g, mono 3.1g, poly 1.2g); PROTEIN 37.4g; CARB 40g; FIBER 2.1g; CHOL 200mg; IRON 3.2mg; SODIUM 565mg; CALC 256mg

Penne with Pesto
Our light-but-true version of the classic sauce.

Avoid packing basil leaves when you measure them so you don't use too much—a common mistake with pesto that results in an unbalanced sauce. Hands-on time: 10 min. Total time: 22 min.

- 4 cups fresh basil leaves
- ¼ cup pine nuts
- ¼ cup extra-virgin olive oil
- ¼ teaspoon salt
- 2 garlic cloves, peeled
- ½ cup (2 ounces) grated fresh Parmesan cheese
- 2 tablespoons grated fresh Romano cheese
- 2 cups uncooked penne (about 8 ounces)

1. Place first 5 ingredients in a food processor; process until finely minced. Place in a large bowl. Stir in cheeses until blended.
2. Cook pasta according to package directions, omitting salt and fat. Drain in a colander over a bowl, reserving 3 tablespoons cooking liquid. Add pasta and reserved cooking liquid to pesto, tossing to coat.

Serves 4 (serving size: about 1 cup).

CALORIES 427; FAT 20.2g (sat 5.5g, mono 10.4g, poly 2.8g); PROTEIN 17g; CARB 45.1g; FIBER 2g; CHOL 18mg; IRON 3.6mg; SODIUM 613mg; CALC 308mg

Fettuccine with Mushrooms and Hazelnuts

Butter-browned nuts, sage, and mixed mushrooms make this an earthy treat.

Look for blanched hazelnuts, which should have most or all of their skins removed.

Hands-on time: 14 min. Total time: 18 min.

- 1 (9-ounce) package refrigerated fresh fettuccine
- 1 tablespoon butter
- ¼ cup chopped blanched hazelnuts
- 1 tablespoon olive oil
- 4 garlic cloves, thinly sliced
- 3 (4-ounce) packages presliced exotic mushroom blend
- ½ teaspoon salt, divided
- ¼ teaspoon freshly ground black pepper
- 2 teaspoons chopped fresh sage
- ½ cup (2 ounces) shaved Parmigiano-Reggiano cheese
- 2 tablespoons finely chopped chives

1. Cook pasta according to package directions, omitting salt and fat. Drain in a colander over a bowl, reserving ¾ cup cooking liquid.

2. Melt butter in a large nonstick skillet over medium-high heat. Add hazelnuts to pan; sauté 3 minutes or until toasted and fragrant, stirring frequently. Remove from pan with a slotted spoon. Add oil to pan; swirl to coat. Add garlic and mushrooms to pan; sprinkle with ¼ teaspoon salt and pepper. Sauté mushroom mixture 5 minutes; stir in sage. Add pasta, reserved cooking liquid, and remaining ¼ teaspoon salt to pan; toss well to combine. Remove from heat; top with cheese, toasted hazelnuts, and chives.

Serves 4 (serving size: about 1½ cups pasta mixture, 2 tablespoons cheese, and 1 tablespoon hazelnuts).

CALORIES 364; FAT 16.5g (sat 5.7g, mono 7.6g, poly 1.2g); PROTEIN 16.8g; CARB 40.2g; FIBER 3.2g; CHOL 56mg; IRON 2.4mg; SODIUM 563mg; CALC 204mg

CHOICE INGREDIENT

Parmigiano-Reggiano Cheese: Buy in small blocks, and look for bumpy, crystalline texture. Keep fresher longer by giving it breathing room: Wrap loosely in wax or parchment paper, and then cover with plastic wrap and refrigerate.

Soy-Citrus Scallops with Soba Noodles

Robust Japanese buckwheat noodles and seared scallops get coated with a marinade that has been reduced to a glaze.

Serve with still-crunchy snow peas or sugar snap peas. You can toss them right in with the noodles.
Hands-on time: 10 min. Total time: 20 min.

3	tablespoons lower-sodium soy sauce
1	tablespoon fresh orange juice
1	tablespoon rice vinegar
1	tablespoon honey
½	teaspoon minced peeled fresh ginger
¼	teaspoon chili garlic sauce
1	tablespoon dark sesame oil, divided
1	pound large sea scallops
4	cups hot cooked soba (about 6 ounces uncooked buckwheat noodles)
⅛	teaspoon salt
¼	cup thinly sliced green onions

1. Combine first 6 ingredients and 1 teaspoon oil in a shallow baking dish. Add scallops to dish in a single layer; marinate 4 minutes on each side.

2. Heat a large skillet over medium-high heat. Add remaining 2 teaspoons oil to pan; swirl to coat. Remove scallops from dish, reserving marinade. Add scallops to pan; sauté 1 minute on each side or until almost done. Remove scallops from pan; keep warm. Place reserved marinade in pan; bring to a boil. Return scallops to pan; cook 1 minute.

3. Combine noodles, salt, and onions in a large bowl. Place 1 cup noodle mixture on each of 4 plates. Top each serving with about 3 scallops; drizzle with 1 tablespoon sauce.

Serves 4.

CALORIES 315; FAT 4.5g (sat 0.6g, mono 1.5g, poly 1.5g); PROTEIN 28g; CARB 42.7g; FIBER 1.9g; CHOL 37mg; IRON 1.3mg; SODIUM 653mg; CALC 41mg

8

PASTA & PIZZA

CHOICE INGREDIENT

Long Pasta Alternatives: One hundred percent durum semolina spaghetti and its various long cousins—made from a high-protein, high-gluten wheat for beautiful al dente texture—are the best choices for many pasta purposes. But there are more alternatives than ever.

Veggie-enhanced spaghetti: Dried vegetable powders add color but only trace vitamins and minerals. Buy if you like the flavor and color, but know that it doesn't offer any vegetables.

Whole-wheat spaghetti: The nutty, slightly sweet flavor and chewy texture pair well with a robust, chunky sauce. It's tops for fiber and counts as a serving of whole grains.

Soba noodles: A tasty, thin buck-wheat noodle that isn't wheat but is usually blended with wheat, so it's not always gluten free. They can be high in sodium, so check the labels.

Gluten-free brown rice spaghetti: If you have a gluten intolerance, this pasta is one of your whole-grain options.

Udon noodles: A thick, ropy Japanese wheat noodle that stands up well in a rich, savory broth.

Spicy Malaysian-Style Stir-Fried Noodles 🌿

Sweet bean sauce—a salty-sugary brew of fermented soybeans and flavorings—mixes with fiery chile paste for some serious flavor.

Versions of this popular dish are called *mee goreng* in Malaysia, Singapore, and Indonesia. Look for the sweet bean sauce and the chewy noodles (which are sometimes frozen) at Asian markets. Toggle the chile paste for more or less heat. Hands-on time: 15 min. Total time: 33 min.

1 (14-ounce) package water-packed extra-firm tofu, drained

1 (1-pound) package fresh Chinese egg noodles

2 tablespoons dark sesame oil

4 garlic cloves, minced

¼ teaspoon salt

4 heads baby bok choy, trimmed and cut crosswise into 2-inch-thick strips

1 tablespoon sugar

3 tablespoons chile paste with garlic (such as sambal oelek)

2 tablespoons fresh lime juice

2 tablespoons sweet bean sauce

2 tablespoons lower-sodium soy sauce

1. Place tofu on several layers of paper towels. Cover with several more layers of paper towels; top with a cast-iron skillet or other heavy pan. Let stand 30 minutes. Cut tofu into ½-inch cubes.

2. Cook noodles in a large saucepan of boiling water 3 minutes or until al dente; drain in a colander over a bowl, reserving 1 cup cooking liquid. Wipe pan with paper towels.

3. Heat pan over medium heat. Add oil to pan; swirl to coat. Add garlic to pan; cook 30 seconds, stirring constantly. Add salt and bok choy; cook 30 seconds, stirring constantly. Stir in ½ cup reserved cooking liquid; bring to a boil. Reduce heat, and cook 4 minutes.

4. Combine sugar and next 4 ingredients (through soy sauce), stirring with a whisk. Add sugar mixture, noodles, and remaining ½ cup cooking liquid to pan; cook 30 seconds or until thoroughly heated, tossing to coat. Add tofu; toss gently to combine. Serve immediately.

Serves 6 (serving size: 1⅔ cups).

CALORIES 359; FAT 9.5g (sat 1.4g, mono 2.6g, poly 4.2g); PROTEIN 15.1g; CARB 53g; FIBER 2.1g; CHOL 17mg; IRON 3.4mg; SODIUM 617mg; CALC 65mg

Sesame Noodles with Broccoli 🌿 🌾

Open, sesame: Tahini (sesame seed paste) in the sauce and toasted seeds as a garnish deliver lots of healthy oils and nutty flavor.

Toast seeds in a dry skillet over medium heat for about 5 minutes, stirring frequently, to bring out the flavor. Mix it up by adding shrimp, flank steak, pork tenderloin, or sautéed cubed tofu.
Hands-on time: 14 min. Total time: 20 min.

Sauce:

2	tablespoons tahini (sesame seed paste)
2	tablespoons water
2	tablespoons rice wine vinegar
2	tablespoons lower-sodium soy sauce
1½	tablespoons dark sesame oil
2	teaspoons honey
¼	teaspoon salt
½	teaspoon grated peeled fresh ginger
½	teaspoon chile paste with garlic (such as sambal oelek)
2	garlic cloves, minced

Noodles:

8	ounces uncooked whole-wheat spaghetti
5	cups broccoli florets
2	cups matchstick-cut carrots
¾	cup thinly sliced green onions
⅓	cup chopped fresh cilantro
3	tablespoons sesame seeds, toasted
⅛	teaspoon salt

1. To prepare sauce, combine first 10 ingredients in a small bowl, stirring with a whisk.

2. To prepare noodles, cook pasta in a large pot of boiling water 5 minutes, omitting salt and fat. Add broccoli to pan; cook 1 minute. Add carrots to pan; cook 1 minute. Drain; place pasta and vegetables in a large bowl. Sprinkle with onions and next 3 ingredients (through salt). Drizzle with sauce; toss well. Serve immediately.

Serves 4 (serving size: 2 cups).

CALORIES 400; FAT 13.2g (sat 1.9g, mono 4.8g, poly 5.7g); PROTEIN 14.7g; CARB 63.1g; FIBER 13.3g; CHOL 0mg; IRON 4.2mg; SODIUM 578mg; CALC 120mg

Wine Pairing
A crisp, dry Rueda, a white wine from Spain made mostly from the verdejo grape, cuts the rich nuttiness of the tahini while complementing the broccoli.

8

PASTA & PIZZA

Curry-Spiced Udon Noodles 🌿

Mild curry is a popular flavor for noodle dishes and soups in Japan. Fresh lemongrass and ginger perk this riff right up.

Store-bought red curry paste, now common, is bold and convenient. Use only the lower bulb of the lemongrass stalk, and remove the tough outer leaves before chopping. You can also shred it with a fine Microplane grater. Thick, chewy udon noodles are worth seeking out, but in a pinch, you can sub spaghetti. Hands-on time: 20 min. Total time: 35 min.

8 ounces dry udon noodles (thick, round Japanese wheat noodles)

4 teaspoons peanut oil, divided

2 cups julienne-cut carrot

2 cups julienne-cut red bell pepper

1 cup julienne-cut green bell pepper

4 cups thinly sliced shiitake mushroom caps (about 8 ounces)

3 tablespoons chopped peeled fresh lemongrass

1 tablespoon grated peeled fresh ginger

1 tablespoon red curry paste

2 teaspoons ground cumin

1 teaspoon ground turmeric

8 garlic cloves, minced

1 cup organic vegetable broth

½ cup water

2 teaspoons lower-sodium soy sauce

¼ teaspoon kosher salt

3 green onions, thinly sliced

⅓ cup cilantro leaves

¼ cup chopped dry-roasted, unsalted cashews

1. Cook noodles according to package directions, omitting salt and fat. Set noodles aside; keep warm.

2. Heat a large nonstick skillet over medium-high heat. Add 2 teaspoons oil to pan; swirl to coat. Add carrot to pan; sauté 2 minutes, stirring frequently. Add bell peppers; sauté 2 minutes, stirring frequently. Remove carrot mixture from pan.

3. Heat remaining 2 teaspoons oil in pan over medium-high heat; swirl to coat. Add mushrooms to pan; sauté 2 minutes, stirring occasionally. Add lemongrass and next 5 ingredients (through garlic); cook 1 minute, stirring constantly. Add broth, ½ cup water, soy sauce, and salt. Bring to a boil; cover, reduce heat, and simmer 2 minutes or until slightly thick. Add noodles, carrot mixture, and onions; cook 2 minutes, tossing to combine. Divide noodle mixture evenly among 4 bowls; top with cilantro and cashews.

Serves 4 (serving size: 1½ cups noodle mixture, about 4 teaspoons cilantro, and 1 tablespoon cashews).

CALORIES 402; FAT 10.8g (sat 1.7g, mono 4.5g, poly 2.3g); PROTEIN 12.7g; CARB 66g; FIBER 8.5g; CHOL 0mg; IRON 4.4mg; SODIUM 555mg; CALC 77mg

Shrimp Pad Thai

This dish is a Thai-restaurant standby, but worth making at home, especially if you can put your hands on some excellent shrimp.

To avoid mushy noodles, undercook them a bit—they continue to absorb liquid from the sauce during the stir-fry action. Heat lovers will want to lace the bowl with a bit of extra Sriracha. Hands-on time: 25 min. Total time: 25 min.

8 ounces uncooked flat rice noodles (pad Thai noodles)

2 tablespoons dark brown sugar

2 tablespoons lower-sodium soy sauce

1½ tablespoons fish sauce

1½ tablespoons fresh lime juice

1 tablespoon Sriracha or chili garlic sauce

3 tablespoons canola oil

1 cup (2-inch) sliced green onions

8 ounces peeled and deveined large shrimp

5 garlic cloves, minced

1 cup fresh mung bean sprouts

¼ cup chopped unsalted, dry-roasted peanuts

3 tablespoons thinly sliced fresh basil

1. Cook noodles according to package directions; drain.

2. Combine sugar and next 4 ingredients (through Sriracha) in a small bowl.

3. Heat a large skillet or wok over medium-high heat. Add oil to pan; swirl to coat. Add onions, shrimp, and garlic; stir-fry 2 minutes or until shrimp are almost done. Add cooked noodles; toss to combine. Stir in sauce; cook 1 minute, stirring constantly to combine. Arrange about 1 cup noodle mixture on each of 4 plates; top each serving with ¼ cup bean sprouts, 1 tablespoon peanuts, and about 2 teaspoons basil.

Serves 4.

CALORIES 462; FAT 16.1g (sat 1.6g, mono 9.1g, poly 4.8g); PROTEIN 15.8g; CARB 64.3g; FIBER 2.6g; CHOL 86mg; IRON 3.7mg; SODIUM 779mg; CALC 90mg

Lo Mein with Tofu

A great starter dish for the tofu-wary: Pan-frying firm tofu gives crispy edges, and the sauce savors it up.

Cabbage, carrots, and bean sprouts add crunch and color. Although lo mein is traditionally made with Chinese egg noodles, here we substitute whole-wheat linguine. Hands-on time: 23 min. Total time: 51 min.

1   (14-ounce) package firm water-packed tofu, drained and cut crosswise into 4 (1-inch-thick) pieces

8   ounces uncooked whole-wheat linguine

1   teaspoon dark sesame oil

½   teaspoon salt, divided

¼   teaspoon freshly ground black pepper, divided

2   tablespoons canola oil, divided

3   tablespoons oyster sauce

1½ tablespoons mirin (sweet rice wine)

1½ tablespoons lower-sodium soy sauce

1   teaspoon rice vinegar

¾   cup vertically sliced onion

2   cups shredded cabbage

2   cups peeled, thinly diagonally cut carrot

2   large garlic cloves, thinly sliced

1½ cups fresh mung bean sprouts

¼   cup chopped green onions

1. Place tofu in a single layer on several layers of paper towels. Cover tofu with several more layers of paper towels; top with a cast-iron skillet or other heavy pan. Let stand 30 minutes.

2. Cook pasta in boiling water 8 minutes or until al dente; drain. Combine pasta, sesame oil, ¼ teaspoon salt, and ⅛ teaspoon pepper; toss. Set aside.

3. Sprinkle remaining ¼ teaspoon salt and remaining ⅛ teaspoon pepper evenly over tofu. Heat a large cast-iron skillet over medium-high heat. Add 1 tablespoon canola oil to pan; swirl to coat. Add tofu to pan; cook 4 minutes on each side or until golden. Remove from pan; cut into bite-sized pieces. Combine oyster sauce and next 3 ingredients (through vinegar) in a small bowl, stirring well.

4. Heat a wok or cast-iron skillet over medium-high heat. Add remaining 1 tablespoon canola oil to pan; swirl to coat. Add vertically sliced onion; stir-fry 2 minutes or until lightly browned. Add cabbage, carrot, and garlic; stir-fry 2 minutes or until cabbage wilts. Reduce heat to medium; stir in tofu and vinegar mixture, tossing to coat. Add pasta and bean sprouts; toss. Cook 2 minutes or until thoroughly heated. Sprinkle with green onions.

Serves 4 (serving size: 1¾ cups).

CALORIES 397; FAT 15.4g (sat 1.3g, mono 8.8g, poly 4.1g); PROTEIN 18.2g; CARB 55.1g; FIBER 9g; CHOL 0mg; IRON 4mg; SODIUM 736mg; CALC 248mg

Pizza: It's All About the Crust

A good pie depends on good crust, which begins with a dough in which the gluten has been well established so it can be stretched thin. Things then move to the oven, which should be very hot to produce rapid browning and blistering. Ideally, you'd make your own dough—and be rewarded with complex flavor and perfect texture, whether cracker thin or chewy. Real-life time constraints may prevent that, but there's good news for the busy: Purchased dough can be almost as good.

Store-Bought Fresh Pizza Dough

In the roster of shortcut ingredients, a ball of fresh pizza dough is an all-star. In as little as 30 minutes, you can make a fantastic pie with crispy-chewy, deliciously browned crust that's just as good as what you'd find at many pizza joints. Fresh dough, from the supermarket bakery section or from your local pizzeria, is our favorite to work with, though prepared crusts can work when you're in a real time crunch. A little advice: If the dough

starts retracting and fighting you as you shape it, cover it and walk away; let it relax for 5 to 10 minutes, and it'll be more cooperative when you come back to it.

Quick Tip: Chilled dough from the store needs time to rest at room temperature; this allows the gluten to relax. If you don't have the 15 to 30 minutes it takes, use your microwave. Place the dough in a microwave-safe bowl, and microwave at HIGH 30 seconds or at MEDIUM (50% power) 45 seconds to 1 minute.

Prepared Pizza Crusts

Prebaked crusts will significantly cut your prep time, and our toppings will still taste great on them. A couple of tips: They may be higher in sodium than our homemade crusts, so if sodium is a concern, use less added salt in the recipe. They will also likely require a different baking time and temperature, so heed the package guidelines.

Wild Mushroom Pizza with Truffle Oil 🌿

Truffle oil takes this pizza to a wonderful place.

Taking just 30 minutes to rise and double in size, this is a quick homemade pizza dough. Hands-on time: 27 min. Total time: 1 hr. 29 min.

1	teaspoon sugar
1	package quick-rise yeast (about 2¼ teaspoons)
½	cup warm water (100° to 110°)
6.7	ounces all-purpose flour, divided (about 1½ cups)
½	teaspoon salt, divided
	Cooking spray
2	teaspoons cornmeal
2	teaspoons olive oil
2	cups thinly sliced shiitake mushroom caps (about 4 ounces)
2	cups sliced cremini mushrooms (about 4 ounces)
1½	cups (¼-inch-thick) slices portobello mushrooms (about 4 ounces)
⅔	cup (about 2½ ounces) grated fontina cheese, divided
2	teaspoons chopped fresh thyme
½	teaspoon truffle oil
¼	cup (1 ounce) grated fresh Parmesan cheese
¼	teaspoon sea salt

1. Dissolve sugar and yeast in ½ cup warm water in a large bowl; let stand 5 minutes. Weigh or lightly spoon flour into dry measuring cups; level with a knife. Add 5.6 ounces flour (about 1¼ cups) and ¼ teaspoon salt to yeast mixture; stir until a soft dough forms. Turn dough out onto a lightly floured surface. Knead until smooth and elastic (about 10 minutes); add enough of remaining 1.1 ounces flour (about ¼ cup), 1 tablespoon at a time, to prevent dough from sticking to hands (dough will feel tacky).

2. Place dough in a large bowl coated with cooking spray; cover surface of dough with plastic wrap lightly coated with cooking spray. Cover and let rise in a warm place (85°), free from drafts, 30 minutes or until doubled in size. (Gently press two fingers into dough. If indentation remains, dough has risen enough.) Punch dough down; cover and let stand 5 minutes. Line a baking sheet with parchment paper; sprinkle with cornmeal. Roll dough into a 12-inch circle on a floured surface. Place dough on prepared baking sheet. Crimp edges of dough with fingers to form a rim; let rise 10 minutes.

3. Preheat oven to 475°.

4. While dough rises, heat a large nonstick skillet over medium heat. Add olive oil to pan; swirl to coat. Add remaining ¼ teaspoon salt and mushrooms; cook 7 minutes or until mushrooms soften and moisture almost evaporates, stirring frequently.

5. Sprinkle ¼ cup fontina evenly over dough; arrange mushroom mixture evenly over fontina. Sprinkle with thyme; drizzle evenly with truffle oil. Sprinkle remaining fontina and Parmesan cheese evenly over top. Bake at 475° for 15 minutes or until crust is lightly browned. Slide pizza onto a cutting board; sprinkle with sea salt. Cut into 8 slices. Serve immediately.

Serves 4 (serving size: 2 slices).

CALORIES 331; FAT 10.6g (sat 4.9g, mono 4.2g, poly 0.8g); PROTEIN 14.8g; CARB 42.8g; FIBER 3.1g; CHOL 25mg; IRON 3.5mg; SODIUM 693mg; CALC 180mg

---

CHOICE INGREDIENT

Truffle Oil: Truffle oil is an instant way to add earthy depth to a dish. Ounce-for-ounce, it's expensive, but a little goes a long way. Look for small 2- or 3-ounce bottles, which are less likely to go bad before you use up the oil. Keep very cool, or store in the fridge. Black truffle oil is more mushroomy, while white oil is rather heady and pungent. Delicious on a mushroom pizza, it's also fantastic drizzled over soup, tossed with pasta, or stirred into a savory sauté.

Pepperoni Deep-Dish Pizza

Here's your knife, fork, and two napkins kind of deep-dish pie, invented at Pizzeria Uno in Chicago more than 60 years ago.

We retained all the gooey-cheesy-crusty deliciousness of this dish while lightening it significantly. Part-skim mozzarella cheese and a modest amount of flavor-packed pepperoni keep saturated fat low. Making your own pizza dough and sauce reins in the sodium. Hands-on time: 22 min. Total time: 26 hr. 11 min.

1 cup warm water (100° to 110°), divided

12 ounces bread flour (about 2½ cups)

1 package dry yeast (about 2¼ teaspoons)

4 teaspoons olive oil

½ teaspoon kosher salt

Cooking spray

1¼ cups (5 ounces) shredded part-skim mozzarella cheese

1½ cups Basic Pizza Sauce

2 ounces pepperoni slices

2 tablespoons grated Parmigiano-Reggiano cheese

1. Pour ¾ cup warm water in the bowl of a stand mixer with dough hook attached. Weigh or lightly spoon flour into dry measuring cups; level with a knife. Add flour to ¾ cup water; mix until combined. Cover and let stand 20 minutes. Combine remaining ¼ cup water and yeast in a small bowl; let stand 5 minutes or until bubbly. Add yeast mixture, oil, and salt to flour mixture; mix 5 minutes or until a soft dough forms. Place dough in a large bowl coated with cooking spray; cover surface of dough with plastic wrap lightly coated with cooking spray. Refrigerate 24 hours.
2. Remove dough from refrigerator. Cover and let stand 1 hour or until dough comes to room temperature. Punch dough down. Roll dough out to a 14 x 11–inch rectangle on a lightly floured surface. Press dough into bottom and partially up sides

of a 13 x 9–inch metal baking pan coated with cooking spray. Cover dough loosely with plastic wrap.
3. Place a baking sheet in oven on bottom rack. Preheat oven to 450°.
4. Remove plastic wrap from dough. Arrange ¾ cup mozzarella evenly over dough; top with Basic Pizza Sauce, pepperoni, Parmigiano-Reggiano, and remaining ½ cup mozzarella. Place pan on baking sheet in oven; bake at 450° for 25 minutes or until crust is golden. Cut pizza into 6 rectangles.

Serves 6 (serving size: 1 rectangle).

CALORIES 404; FAT 16.3g (sat 5.9g, mono 7.8g, poly 1.5g); PROTEIN 16.9g; CARB 47.1g; FIBER 2.7g; CHOL 26mg; IRON 3.9mg; SODIUM 607mg; CALC 244mg

BASIC PIZZA SAUCE

San Marzano tomatoes are traditionally used in Neapolitan pizza sauce. We like their balanced sweet-acidic quality.

2 tablespoons extra-virgin olive oil

5 garlic cloves, minced

1 (28-ounce) can San Marzano tomatoes, undrained

½ teaspoon kosher salt

½ teaspoon dried oregano

1. Heat a medium saucepan over medium heat. Add oil to pan; swirl to coat. Add garlic to pan; cook 1 minute, stirring frequently. Remove tomatoes from can using a slotted spoon, reserving juices. Crush tomatoes. Stir tomatoes, juices, salt, and oregano into garlic mixture; bring to a boil. Reduce

heat, and simmer 30 minutes, stirring occasionally.

Serves 6 (serving size: about ⅓ cup).

CALORIES 66; FAT 4.7g (sat 0.7g, mono 3.3g, poly 0.6g); PROTEIN 1.2g; CARB 6.2g; FIBER 1.4g; CHOL 0mg; IRON 1.4mg; SODIUM 175mg; CALC 48mg

Roasted Vegetable and Ricotta Pizza 🌿

Let the market be your guide—use any color bell pepper, onion, or summer squash.

Roasted vegetables and creamy ricotta are a beautiful combination. Hands-on time: 20 min. Total time: 1 hr.

1   **pound refrigerated fresh pizza dough**

2   **cups sliced cremini mushrooms**

1   **cup (¼-inch-thick) slices zucchini**

¼   **teaspoon black pepper**

1   **medium-sized yellow bell pepper, sliced**

1   **medium-sized red onion, cut into thick slices**

5½   **teaspoons olive oil, divided**

1   **tablespoon yellow cornmeal**

⅓   **cup tomato sauce**

1   **cup (4 ounces) shredded part-skim mozzarella cheese**

½   **teaspoon crushed red pepper**

⅓   **cup part-skim ricotta cheese**

2   **tablespoons small fresh basil leaves**

1. Position an oven rack in lowest setting; place a pizza stone on rack. Preheat oven to 500°.

2. Remove dough from refrigerator. Cover and let stand, 30 minutes.

3. Combine mushrooms and next 4 ingredients (through onion) in a large bowl. Drizzle with 1½ tablespoons oil; toss to coat. Arrange vegetables on a jelly-roll pan. Bake at 500° for 15 minutes.

4. Punch dough down. Sprinkle a lightly floured baking sheet with cornmeal; roll dough into a 15-inch circle on prepared baking sheet. Brush dough with remaining 1 teaspoon oil. Spread sauce over dough, leaving a ½-inch border. Sprinkle ½ cup mozzarella over sauce; top with vegetables. Sprinkle remaining ½ cup mozzarella and red pepper over vegetables. Dollop with ricotta. Slide pizza onto preheated pizza stone. Bake at 500° for 11 minutes or until crust is golden. Sprinkle with basil. Cut pizza into 12 slices.

Serves 6 (serving size: 2 slices).

CALORIES 347; FAT 11.1g (sat 3.7g, mono 4.4g, poly 2g); PROTEIN 14.8g; CARB 48.5g; FIBER 2.7g; CHOL 15mg; IRON 3mg; SODIUM 655mg; CALC 193mg

Wine Pairing

Light, bright, and ever-so-slightly bubbly, vinho verde ("green wine") from Portugal is an ideal quaffer with this light veggie pizza.

Four Cheese Pizza

Premium ricotta—which has a creamy texture and rich, full flavor—takes this into really delicious territory.

Hands-on time: 15 min. Total time: 25 hr. 55 min.

1 cup warm water (100° to 110°), divided

10 ounces bread flour (about 2 cups plus 2 tablespoons)

1 package dry yeast (about 2¼ teaspoons)

7 teaspoons olive oil, divided

½ teaspoon kosher salt

Cooking spray

1 tablespoon yellow cornmeal

2 tablespoons chopped garlic

⅓ cup (about 3 ounces) part-skim ricotta cheese

1¼ ounces taleggio cheese, thinly sliced

¼ cup (1 ounce) crumbled Gorgonzola cheese

¼ cup (1 ounce) finely grated fresh Parmigiano-Reggiano cheese

2 tablespoons chopped fresh chives

1. Pour ¾ cup warm water in the bowl of a stand mixer with dough hook attached. Weigh or lightly spoon flour into dry measuring cups and spoons; level with a knife. Add flour to ¾ cup water; mix until combined. Cover and let stand 20 minutes. Combine remaining ¼ cup water and yeast in a small bowl; let stand 5 minutes or until bubbly. Add yeast mixture, 4 teaspoons oil, and salt to flour mixture; mix 5 minutes or until a soft dough forms. Place dough in a large bowl coated with cooking spray; cover surface of dough with plastic wrap lightly coated with cooking spray. Refrigerate 24 hours.

2. Remove dough from refrigerator. Cover and let stand 1 hour or until dough comes to room temperature. Punch dough down. Roll dough out to a 12-inch circle on a lightly floured baking sheet, without raised sides, sprinkled with cornmeal. Crimp edges to form a ½-inch border. Cover dough loosely with plastic wrap.

3. Position an oven rack in lowest setting. Place a pizza stone on rack. Preheat oven to 550°. Preheat stone 30 minutes before baking dough.

4. Remove plastic wrap from dough. Combine remaining 1 tablespoon oil and garlic; gently brush garlic mixture evenly over dough, leaving a ½-inch border. Spread ricotta evenly over dough; arrange taleggio and Gorgonzola evenly over ricotta. Top with Parmigiano-Reggiano. Slide pizza onto preheated pizza stone, using a spatula as a guide. Bake at 550° for 10 minutes or until crust is golden. Cut pizza into 10 wedges; sprinkle with chives.

Serves 5 (serving size: 2 wedges).

CALORIES 370; FAT 14.1g (sat 5.2g, mono 6.7g, poly 1.4g); PROTEIN 14.6g; CARB 45.7g; FIBER 1.9g; CHOL 22mg; IRON 1.2mg; SODIUM 344mg; CALC 174mg

Barbecue Chicken Pizza

The contrast of tangy tomato chutney, savory chicken, and sharp cheddar cheese garners rave reviews for this simple, six-ingredient pizza.

If you can't find tomato chutney, use store-bought barbecue sauce to replicate the savory-and-sweet flavor. Hands-on time: 9 min. Total time: 25 min.

1   (10-ounce) Italian cheese-flavored thin pizza crust

¾   cup tomato chutney

2   cups chopped roasted skinless, boneless chicken breasts (about 2 breasts)

⅔   cup diced plum tomato

¾   cup (3 ounces) shredded extra-sharp white cheddar cheese

⅓   cup chopped green onions

1. Preheat oven to 450°.
2. Place crust on a baking sheet. Bake at 450° for 3 minutes. Remove from oven; spread chutney over crust, leaving a ½-inch border. Arrange chicken over chutney; sprinkle tomato, cheese, and onions evenly over chicken.

Bake at 450° for 9 minutes or until cheese melts. Cut pizza into 6 wedges.

Serves 6 (serving size: 1 wedge).

CALORIES 300; FAT 8.5g (sat 3.9g, mono 2.9g, poly 1g); PROTEIN 21.3g; CARB 35.2g; FIBER 1.2g; CHOL 48mg; IRON 1.7mg; SODIUM 622mg; CALC 247mg

NUTRITION MADE EASY

Pizza Portions: Pizza is so easy to enjoy that before you know it, you may have eaten half of the pie. But when bread meets cheese, sauce, and meat, sodium ratchets up, as do calories. So proper portioning, as with any calorie-dense food, is important. Think of pizza as your entrée—give it the same amount of space on your plate, and serve a big salad on the side.

Pizza Margherita 🌿
For this ultra-simple pizza, use the best fresh mozzarella and basil available.

The thin, lightly crisp yet chewy crust is blistered and bubbly. Fresh mozzarella may exude water as it cooks, making for a soggy crust. To prevent that, pat the slices dry with paper towels before placing them on the pizza. Hands-on time: 20 min. Total time: 25 hr. 55 min.

1 cup warm water (100° to 110°), divided

10 ounces bread flour (about 2 cups plus 2 tablespoons)

1 package dry yeast (about 2¼ teaspoons)

4 teaspoons olive oil

¾ teaspoon kosher salt, divided

Cooking spray

1 tablespoon yellow cornmeal

¾ cup Basic Pizza Sauce (page 288)

1¼ cups (5 ounces) thinly sliced fresh mozzarella cheese

⅓ cup small fresh basil leaves

1. Pour ¾ cup warm water in the bowl of a stand mixer with dough hook attached. Weigh or lightly spoon flour into dry measuring cups and spoons; level with a knife. Add flour to ¾ cup water; mix until combined. Cover and let stand 20 minutes. Combine remaining ¼ cup water and yeast in a small bowl; let stand 5 minutes or until bubbly. Add yeast mixture, oil, and ½ teaspoon salt to flour mixture; mix 5 minutes or until a soft dough forms. Place dough in a large bowl coated with cooking spray; cover surface of dough with plastic wrap lightly coated with cooking spray. Refrigerate 24 hours.

2. Remove dough from refrigerator. Cover and let stand 1 hour or until dough comes to room temperature. Punch dough down. Roll dough into a 12-inch circle on a lightly floured baking sheet, without raised sides, sprinkled with cornmeal. Crimp edges to form a ½-inch border. Cover dough loosely with plastic wrap.

3. Position an oven rack in the lowest setting. Place a pizza stone on rack. Preheat oven to 550°. Preheat pizza stone 30 minutes before baking dough.

4. Remove plastic wrap from dough. Sprinkle dough with remaining ¼ teaspoon salt. Spread Basic Pizza Sauce evenly over dough, leaving a ½-inch border. Arrange cheese slices evenly over pizza. Slide pizza onto preheated pizza stone, using a spatula as a guide. Bake at 550° for 11 minutes or until crust is golden. Cut pizza into 10 wedges; sprinkle evenly with basil.

Serves 5 (serving size: 2 wedges).

CALORIES 421; FAT 10.9g (sat 4.7g, mono 4.7g, poly 1g); PROTEIN 16.9g; CARB 62.8g; FIBER 6.5g; CHOL 22mg; IRON 4.4mg; SODIUM 754mg; CALC 267mg

Wine Pairing
Though this pizza originates in Naples, a southern Italian red is too heavy for the delicate flavors of fresh mozzarella and basil. Instead, try a light, high-acid northern Italian red like Valpolicella.

Bacon, Tomato, and Arugula Pizza

Everything we love about a BLT, pizza-fied.

To make your leftovers taste like the first batch, store the arugula mixture in a separate container.
Hands-on time: 9 min. Total time: 40 min.

1 pound refrigerated fresh pizza dough

Cooking spray

5 applewood-smoked bacon slices

2 cups grape tomatoes, halved lengthwise

½ teaspoon crushed red pepper

1 tablespoon yellow cornmeal

½ cup lower-sodium marinara sauce

¾ cup (3 ounces) shredded part-skim mozzarella cheese

1 cup baby arugula

1 teaspoon extra-virgin olive oil

½ teaspoon white wine vinegar

1. Preheat oven to 450°.
2. Place dough in a bowl coated with cooking spray; cover and let stand 15 minutes.
3. Cook bacon in a skillet over medium heat until crisp. Remove bacon; crumble. Add tomatoes and pepper to drippings in pan; cook 2 minutes, stirring occasionally.
4. Sprinkle a baking sheet with cornmeal; roll dough into a 12-inch circle on prepared baking sheet. Spread sauce evenly over dough, leaving a ½-inch border. Top with tomatoes and bacon. Sprinkle cheese over top. Bake at 450° on bottom oven rack 17 minutes or until crust is golden. Combine arugula, oil, and vinegar in a bowl; top pizza with arugula mixture.

Serves 6 (serving size: 1 slice).

CALORIES 314; FAT 9.1g (sat 4.5g, mono 2.1g, poly 2.1g); PROTEIN 13.5g; CARB 50.2g; FIBER 2.1g; CHOL 17mg; IRON 2.5mg; SODIUM 770mg; CALC 124mg

Spicy Sausage and Mushroom Pizza

Cooking the onion, mushroom, bell pepper, and Italian sausage together melds all the good flavors while softening up the vegetables.

Serve with an arugula salad with thinly sliced red onion and this lemony dressing: Combine 2 tablespoons extra-virgin olive oil, ½ teaspoon grated lemon rind, 1 tablespoon fresh lemon juice, and ¼ teaspoon salt, stirring with a whisk. Hands-on time: 7 min. Total time: 36 min.

1 pound refrigerated fresh pizza dough

Cooking spray

2 teaspoons olive oil

4 ounces hot turkey Italian sausage

1 cup thinly sliced onion

1 (8-ounce) package presliced mushrooms

1 cup diced red or green bell pepper

1 tablespoon yellow cornmeal

½ cup lower-sodium marinara sauce

½ cup (2 ounces) shredded part-skim mozzarella cheese

¼ cup (1 ounce) grated fresh Parmigiano-Reggiano cheese

1. Preheat oven to 450°.

2. Place dough in a bowl coated with cooking spray; cover and let stand 15 minutes.

3. Heat a large nonstick skillet over medium-high heat. Add oil to pan; swirl to coat. Remove casings from sausage. Add sausage to pan; cook 3 minutes, stirring to crumble. Add onion and mushrooms; sauté 4 minutes. Add bell pepper; sauté 2 minutes.

4. Sprinkle a baking sheet with cornmeal; roll dough into a 12-inch circle on prepared baking sheet. Spread sauce over dough, leaving a ½-inch border. Top with sausage mixture. Sprinkle cheeses over sausage mixture. Bake at 450° on bottom oven rack 17 minutes or until crust is golden.

Serves 6 (serving size: 1 slice).

CALORIES 330; FAT 9g (sat 2.1g, mono 1.9g, poly 1.7g); PROTEIN 15.6g; CARB 52.4g; FIBER 2.6g; CHOL 22mg; IRON 3.2mg; SODIUM 751mg; CALC 134mg

8

PASTA & PIZZA

Honey-Wheat Pizza with Pear-Prosciutto Salad

We like to make a lot of what we call salad pizzas—topping baked crust with a beautiful, fresh salad. This is a salty, fruity, delicious example.

A showy, crimson-skinned pear is beautiful here, but any pear variety you like will work.
Hands-on time: 24 min. Total time: 2 hr. 8 min.

1	cup warm water (100° to 110°)
1	tablespoon honey
2	tablespoons extra-virgin olive oil, divided
1½	teaspoons dry yeast
9	ounces all-purpose flour (about 2 cups)
2.38	ounces whole-wheat flour (about ½ cup)
¾	teaspoon kosher salt
	Cooking spray
1½	cups (6 ounces) crumbled goat cheese
1	tablespoon cornmeal
4	cups fresh mâche or baby spinach
2	teaspoons chopped fresh thyme
2	teaspoons fresh lemon juice
½	teaspoon freshly ground black pepper
3	ounces very thinly sliced prosciutto, chopped
2	ripe Starkrimson or red Bartlett pears, cored and thinly sliced

1. Combine 1 cup warm water, honey, and 1 teaspoon oil in a small bowl, stirring with a whisk. Stir in yeast; let stand 10 minutes. Weigh or lightly spoon flours into dry measuring cups; level with a knife. Place flours and salt in a food processor; pulse 2 times or until blended. Add yeast mixture, pulsing to combine (dough will feel sticky). Turn dough out onto a floured surface; knead lightly 3 to 4 times.

2. Place dough in a large bowl coated with cooking spray, turning to coat top. Cover and let rise in a warm place (85°), free from drafts, 1 hour or until doubled in size. (Gently press two fingers into dough. If indentation remains, dough has risen enough.) Punch dough down; cover and let rest 10 minutes.

3. Preheat oven to 450°.

4. Place a baking sheet in oven. Roll dough into a 14-inch circle on a floured surface. Brush dough evenly with 1 tablespoon oil, and sprinkle evenly with cheese. Place dough on a baking sheet sprinkled with cornmeal. Transfer dough carefully to preheated pan; bake at 450° for 12 minutes or until crust is crisp and golden. Combine remaining 2 teaspoons oil, mâche, and next 5 ingredients (through pears); toss to combine. Arrange salad over crust.

Serves 6 (serving size: 1 slice).

CALORIES 393; FAT 12.7g (sat 5.2g, mono 5.3g, poly 0.9g); PROTEIN 18.1g; CARB 56.8g; FIBER 5.3g; CHOL 21mg; IRON 3.7mg; SODIUM 559mg; CALC 95mg

Wine Pairing

The honeyed notes in the crust and sweet pear salad marry well with chenin blanc, a floral, honeyed white wine with refreshing acidity.

PASTA & PIZZA

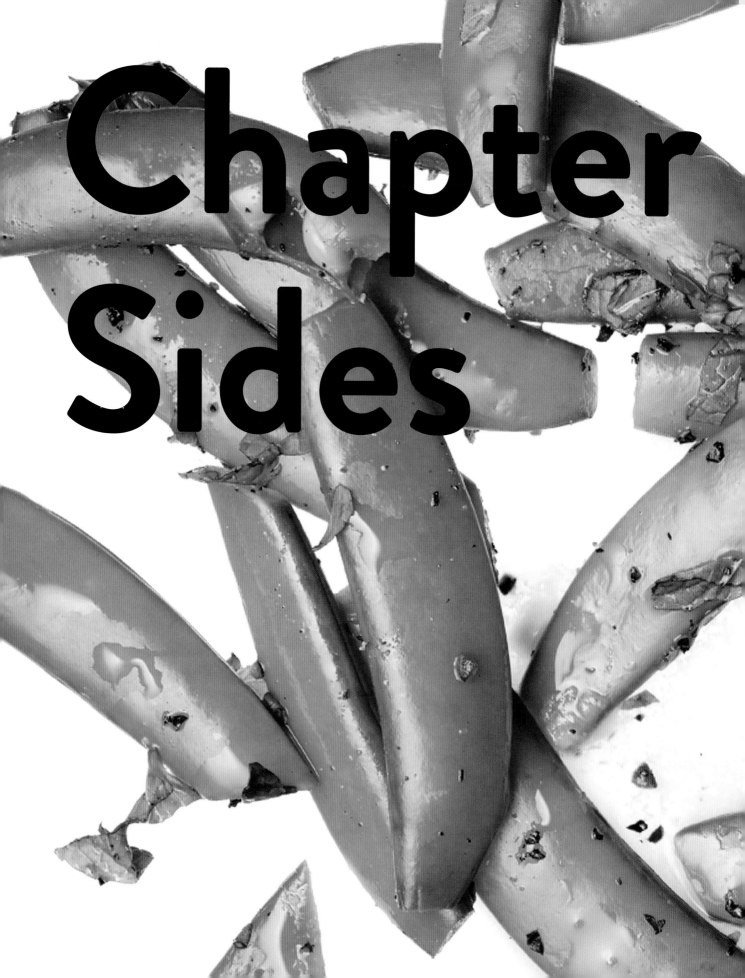

Chapter

Sides

9:

Steamed Sugar Snap Peas, page 319

The keys to a healthy diet—more variety, more plants, smaller portions of meat—bring us squarely here. It's time to move the periphery of the plate to the center; think of sides as a series of healthy entrées, mezze-style. When the farmers' markets are at their peak, in fact, you can dispense with an entrée altogether and serve a plateful of vivid sides. Along with perfectly cooked seasonal vegetables, there are lots of whole-grain choices here—and don't forget the humbly delicious potato. Most of the vegetable sides are low in calories, many under 100 per serving and some as low as 30.

Grilled Corn on the Cob with Roasted Jalapeño Butter

A flavored butter takes grilled corn into the stratosphere. Blistered jalapeño chiles mellow, tasting more fruity and "green" than fiery.

You don't need to slather on lots of butter—just a little, combined with honey and oil, is plenty to coat the corn and keep it moist. For a lovely presentation, gently pull the husks away from the cob to remove and discard silks, but don't rip the husks off. Remove one strip from each husk, and use it to tie the husks back; proceed with the recipe. Hands-on time: 25 min. Total time: 39 min.

1 jalapeño pepper
Cooking spray
1½ tablespoons unsalted butter, softened
1 teaspoon grated lime rind
2 teaspoons honey
1 teaspoon canola oil
¼ teaspoon salt
6 ears shucked corn

1. Preheat grill to medium-high heat.
2. Place jalapeño on grill rack coated with cooking spray; cover and grill 10 minutes or until blackened and charred, turning occasionally.
3. Place jalapeño in a paper bag; fold to close tightly. Let stand 5 minutes. Peel and discard skins; cut jalapeño in half lengthwise. Discard stem, seeds, and membranes. Finely chop jalapeño. Combine jalapeño, butter, and next 4 ingredients (through salt) in a small bowl; stir well.
4. Place corn on grill rack. Cover and grill 10 minutes or until lightly charred, turning occasionally. Place corn on serving plate; brush with jalapeño butter.

Serves 6 (serving size: 1 ear).

CALORIES 119; FAT 4.9g (sat 2.1g, mono 1.6g, poly 0.8g); PROTEIN 3g; CARB 19.2g; FIBER 2.5g; CHOL 8mg; IRON 0.5mg; SODIUM 112mg; CALC 3mg

Asparagus with Balsamic Tomatoes 🌿

One of the easiest of all spring vegetables. Some like asparagus crunchy, and some prefer it cooked just a little longer, until silky. There's no rule.

The base recipe is a natural with steak, roasted pork, or chicken. Thick asparagus can be tough and fibrous, while pencil-thin asparagus can overcook in a moment; choose, if you can, stalks that are neither too fat nor too skinny. To quickly trim them, snap one stalk by bending until it breaks. It should snap where the tender and woody parts meet. Using that spear as your guide, line up the rest of the stalks on your board, and slice them all. Hands-on time: 10 min. Total time: 20 min.

1 pound asparagus, trimmed

2 teaspoons extra-virgin olive oil

1½ cups halved grape tomatoes

½ teaspoon minced fresh garlic

2 tablespoons balsamic vinegar

¼ teaspoon salt

3 tablespoons crumbled goat cheese

½ teaspoon freshly ground black pepper

1. Cook asparagus in boiling water 2 minutes or until crisp-tender; drain.

2. Heat a large skillet over medium-high heat. Add oil to pan; swirl to coat. Add tomatoes and garlic to pan; cook 5 minutes, stirring frequently. Stir in vinegar; cook 3 minutes. Stir in salt. Arrange asparagus on a platter; top with tomato mixture. Sprinkle with cheese and pepper.

Serves 4.

CALORIES 69; FAT 3.9g (sat 1.4g, mono 2g, poly 0.3g); PROTEIN 3g; CARB 6.5g; FIBER 2.1g; CHOL 4mg; IRON 1.6mg; SODIUM 181mg; CALC 45mg

Raisin and Pine Nut variation: 🌿
Serve with pork, chicken, or fish. Omit tomatoes, garlic, vinegar, and goat cheese. Cook asparagus as directed in recipe. Cook ⅓ cup sliced red onion and 2 tablespoons pine nuts in oil 4 minutes, stirring frequently. Add 3 tablespoons raisins, 2½ tablespoons orange juice, and 2 teaspoons honey; cook 2 minutes, stirring occasionally. Stir in salt and ¼ teaspoon orange rind. Spoon over asparagus; sprinkle with pepper.

Serves 4.

CALORIES 101; FAT 5.4g (sat 0.6g, mono 2.6g, poly 1.7g); PROTEIN 2.3g; CARB 13.3g; FIBER 1.9g; CHOL 0mg; IRON 1.8mg; SODIUM 150mg; CALC 23mg

Sesame-Ginger Glazed variation: 🌿
Serve with shrimp, scallops, or stir-fried beef. Omit oil, tomatoes, vinegar, salt, cheese, and pepper. Cook asparagus as directed in recipe. Microwave 1 tablespoon lower-sodium soy sauce, 1 teaspoon honey, 1 teaspoon lime juice, 1 teaspoon minced peeled fresh ginger, and garlic at HIGH 2 minutes.

Drizzle over asparagus; sprinkle with 2 teaspoons toasted sesame seeds. Serve with lime wedges.

Serves 4.

CALORIES 31; FAT 0.8g (sat 0.1g, mono 0.3g, poly 0.4g); PROTEIN 1.9g; CARB 5.2g; FIBER 1.5g; CHOL 0mg; IRON 1.6mg; SODIUM 135mg; CALC 32mg

Lemon-Tarragon variation: 🌿
Serve with filet mignon or roast chicken. Omit tomatoes, vinegar, and cheese; decrease pepper to ¼ teaspoon. Cook asparagus as directed in recipe. Combine ⅛ teaspoon lemon rind, 1 tablespoon fresh lemon juice, 2 teaspoons chopped fresh tarragon, garlic, ½ teaspoon minced shallot, ½ teaspoon Dijon mustard, salt, pepper, and oil. Drizzle tarragon mixture over asparagus; toss gently to coat.

Serves 4.

CALORIES 36; FAT 2.4g (sat 0.4g, mono 1.8g, poly 0.2g); PROTEIN 1.4g; CARB 3.1g; FIBER 1.3g; CHOL 0mg; IRON 1.3mg; SODIUM 162mg; CALC 18mg

Roasted Chile-Garlic Broccoli 🌿

Broccoli deserves so much better than the old boil-and-butter routine. Cooking in a superhot oven chars the outside slightly, leaving it tender within.

Chile paste and dark sesame oil move the flavor needle and call for pairing with a robust entrée like grilled salmon, tuna, or beef. Hands-on time: 8 min. Total time: 18 min.

6 cups broccoli florets

2 tablespoons dark sesame oil

2 teaspoons sambal oelek (chile paste with garlic)

½ teaspoon salt

⅛ teaspoon sugar

6 large garlic cloves, coarsely chopped

1. Place a small roasting pan in oven. Preheat oven to 450°.
2. Place broccoli in a large bowl; drizzle with oil, tossing to coat. Add sambal, salt, and sugar to broccoli mixture; toss to coat. Add broccoli mixture to hot roasting pan; arrange in a single layer. Bake at 450° for 5 minutes; remove from oven. Add garlic to pan; stir. Bake an additional 5 minutes or until broccoli is lightly browned.

Serves 4 (serving size: 1¼ cups).

CALORIES 99; FAT 7.2g (sat 1g, mono 2.7g, poly 3g); PROTEIN 3.5g; CARB 7.7g; FIBER 3.2g; CHOL 0mg; IRON 1mg; SODIUM 252mg; CALC 59mg

Indian-Spiced Okra 🌿

No slippery-slimy here. When you leave the pods whole and sauté, as with this classic preparation, the texture is al dente.

Even folks who run from okra enjoy the taste and texture of this highly seasoned dish. We left the seeds in the chile to dial up the heat. Serve with grilled chicken or lamb, or round out a vegetarian dinner with basmati rice and Red Lentil Dal with Charred Onions, page 163. Hands-on time: 7 min. Total time: 15 min.

¾ teaspoon brown mustard seeds

1 tablespoon canola oil

1 teaspoon ground coriander

1 teaspoon finely chopped serrano chile

½ teaspoon kosher salt

¼ teaspoon curry powder

1 pound small to medium okra pods, trimmed

1. Heat a large heavy skillet over medium-high heat; add mustard seeds. Cook 30 seconds or until toasted and fragrant. Add oil and remaining ingredients to pan; cook 1 minute, stirring occasionally. Cover, reduce heat to low, and cook 8 minutes, stirring occasionally. Uncover, increase heat to high, and cook 2 minutes or until okra is lightly browned.

Serves 6 (serving size: ⅔ cup).

CALORIES 47; FAT 2.6g (sat 0.2g, mono 1.4g, poly 0.7g); PROTEIN 1.7g; CARB 5.7g; FIBER 2.7g; CHOL 0mg; IRON 0.7mg; SODIUM 163mg; CALC 66mg

Garlic-Roasted Kale 🌿

Who knew a leaf could be roasted? But roasted kale is amazing—the leaves turn from a dusty dark green to deep emerald with brown-tinged, curly edges that crunch.

Serve this piping hot right out of the oven; the leaves lose their texture as the dish stands.
Hands-on time: 12 min. Total time: 24 min.

3	tablespoons extra-virgin olive oil
½	teaspoon kosher salt
3	garlic cloves, thinly sliced
1½	pounds kale, stems removed and chopped
2	teaspoons sherry vinegar

1. Arrange oven racks in center and lower third of oven. Preheat oven to 425°. Place 2 large jelly-roll pans in oven 5 minutes.

2. Combine first 4 ingredients in a large bowl; toss to coat. Divide kale mixture evenly between hot pans, spreading with a silicone spatula to separate leaves. Bake at 425° for 7 minutes. Stir kale; rotate pans. Bake an additional 5 minutes or until edges of leaves are crisp and kale is tender.

3. Place kale in a large bowl. Drizzle with vinegar; toss to combine. Serve immediately.

Serves 10 (serving size: about ⅔ cup).

CALORIES 72; FAT 4.7g (sat 0.7g, mono 3g, poly 0.8g); PROTEIN 2.3g; CARB 7.1g; FIBER 1.4g; CHOL 0mg; IRON 1.2mg; SODIUM 125mg; CALC 93mg

CHOICE INGREDIENT

The Glory of Hearty Leafy Greens: When choosing these greens, select crisp-feeling leaves that have no signs of yellowing edges, yellow spots, or wilting. Wrap unwashed greens in damp paper towels, and refrigerate in a plastic bag for up to five days. The leaves can trap a lot of dirt, so be sure to rinse several times in a sink or large bowl full of cool water until no dirt or grit remains. Remove and discard the tough, fibrous stems before chopping the leaves.

Beet greens have thin, smooth leaves that are milder and a bit sweeter than most winter greens.

Peppery broccoli rabe has dark-green, rippled leaves and long, sometimes tough stems.

Collard greens' large leaves branch from a thick central stem. These greens require longer cooking for delicate, melt-in-your-mouth texture.

Kale's firm, tight, crinkly leaves have an earthy flavor like cabbage.

Mustard greens have yellowish, light-green leaves, with the smaller ones being the spiciest.

Swiss chard can have red, white, fuchsia, or bright yellow stems. Red or ruby chard is earthier than white-stemmed.

Turnip greens have a strong flavor and benefit from slow braising.

Brussels Sprouts with Bacon

Cooked well, Brussels sprouts are delicious nuggets—crisp-tender, nutty, and faintly sweet, with a pleasing hint of bitterness.

And they match with all sorts of flavors: sesame, citrus peel, nuts, vinegar, and, of course, bacon.

Hands-on time: 8 min. Total time: 20 min.

3   **center-cut bacon slices, finely chopped**

1½   **cups sliced onion**

¼   **teaspoon dried thyme**

⅓   **cup fat-free, lower-sodium chicken broth**

1   **pound Brussels sprouts, trimmed and halved**

1. Heat a large skillet over medium-high heat. Add bacon to pan; cook 7 minutes or until crisp. Remove bacon from pan, reserving 2 teaspoons drippings in pan.
2. Add onion and thyme to pan; sauté 3 minutes, stirring frequently. Add broth and Brussels sprouts; bring to a boil. Cover and simmer 6 minutes or until crisp-tender. Sprinkle with bacon.

Serves 4 (serving size: about 1 cup).

CALORIES 107; FAT 4g (sat 1.7g, mono 1.7g, poly 0.5g); PROTEIN 5.8g; CARB 14.9g; FIBER 5g; CHOL 8mg; IRON 1.7mg; SODIUM 165mg; CALC 59mg

Cauliflower with Garlicky Panko 🌿
Tender cauliflower gets showered with a crunchy, garlic-spiked topping.

Good-for-you olive oil crisps the Japanese-style breadcrumbs and browns the cauliflower. Make extra garlicky topping, and use it to dress up other vegetables, such as Brussels sprouts, broccoli, or green beans. Hands-on time: 13 min. Total time: 28 min.

- 6 cups cauliflower florets
- 2 tablespoons water
- 3 tablespoons olive oil, divided
- ½ cup panko (Japanese breadcrumbs)
- 1 garlic clove, minced
- 1 tablespoon chopped fresh parsley
- ½ teaspoon salt
- ¼ teaspoon freshly ground black pepper

1. Combine cauliflower and 2 tablespoons water in a microwave-safe bowl. Microwave at HIGH 6 minutes or until crisp-tender; drain.
2. Heat a large nonstick skillet over medium-high heat. Add 1½ tablespoons oil to pan; swirl to coat. Add panko to pan, and cook 3 minutes or until toasted, stirring constantly. Remove panko from pan.
3. Add remaining 1½ tablespoons oil and garlic to pan. Add cauliflower to pan; sauté 5 minutes or until golden, stirring occasionally. Add panko, parsley, salt, and pepper; toss to combine.

Serves 8 (serving size: about ⅔ cup).

CALORIES 78; FAT 5.3g (sat 0.7g, mono 3.7g, poly 0.6g); PROTEIN 2g; CARB 6.7g; FIBER 2g; CHOL 0mg; IRON 0.4mg; SODIUM 181mg; CALC 18mg

Roasted Eggplants with Herbs 🌿
A stunning side from Susan Loomis, a longtime resident of France, shows how delicious simplicity can be.

This easy preparation yields irresistible results that will likely upstage the entrée. Use very firm, small eggplants; if they're young and fresh enough, they won't be bitter. Hands-on time: 12 min. Total time: 39 min.

- 4 small eggplants (about 13 ounces)
- 2½ tablespoons extra-virgin olive oil, divided
- ¼ teaspoon fine sea salt
- ⅛ teaspoon freshly ground black pepper
- ⅓ cup chopped fresh basil
- 2 teaspoons chopped fresh sage
- 2 teaspoons chopped fresh rosemary

1. Preheat oven to 450°.
2. Cut each eggplant lengthwise into ¼-inch-thick slices, cutting to, but not through, stem end. Fan eggplants; place on a baking sheet lined with parchment paper. Brush 1½ tablespoons oil evenly over eggplant slices. Bake at 450° for 15 minutes; remove from oven. Press eggplants gently to fan slices. Brush eggplants with 1½ teaspoons oil; sprinkle evenly with salt and pepper. Bake an additional 10 minutes or until flesh is tender and edges are browned and slightly crisp.
3. Drizzle remaining 1½ teaspoons oil evenly over eggplants; sprinkle with herbs.

Serves 4 (serving size: 1 eggplant).

CALORIES 104; FAT 9.2g (sat 1.3g, mono 6.6g, poly 1g); PROTEIN 1.1g; CARB 5.7g; FIBER 3.4g; CHOL 0mg; IRON 0.4mg; SODIUM 122mg; CALC 18mg

Roasted Eggplants
with Herbs

Butternut Squash Casserole with Blue Cheese and Sage 🌿

It's time to bring nutrient-rich squash into frequent use, if you haven't already done so. Its sweet earthy flavor and silky texture sing with pungent blue cheese. Conveniently, it bakes while you cook the rest of the meal.

Here, cubes bake with fragrant sage and pungent blue cheese under a crisp breadcrumb coating. It's a jazzed-up gratin that's completely cream-free. Hands-on time: 18 min. Total time: 47 min.

5   cups (¾-inch) cubed peeled butternut squash (about 2 pounds)
1   (1½-ounce) slice white bread
4   teaspoons olive oil, divided
2   cups thinly sliced onion
1   tablespoon chopped fresh sage
¼   teaspoon salt
¼   teaspoon freshly ground black pepper
Cooking spray
⅓   cup (about 1½ ounces) crumbled blue cheese

1. Preheat oven to 400°.

2. Steam squash, covered, 10 minutes or until tender.

3. Place bread in a food processor; pulse 12 times or until coarse crumbs measure ½ cup. Add 2 teaspoons oil; pulse 5 times or until combined.

4. Heat a large nonstick skillet over medium-high heat. Add remaining 2 teaspoons oil to pan; swirl to coat. Add onion to pan; sauté 5 minutes or until tender, stirring occasionally. Transfer onion mixture to a large bowl. Add squash, sage, salt, and pepper to onion mixture; toss gently to combine. Spoon squash mixture into an 11 x 7-inch glass or ceramic baking dish coated with cooking spray. Bake at 400° for 20 minutes. Sprinkle cheese evenly over squash mixture; sprinkle evenly with breadcrumb mixture. Bake an additional 10 minutes or until cheese melts and crumbs are golden brown.

Serves 6 (serving size: about 1 cup).

CALORIES 142; FAT 5.7g (sat 1.9g, mono 2.8g, poly 0.4g); PROTEIN 3.8g; CARB 21.1g; FIBER 3.2g; CHOL 5mg; IRON 1.1mg; SODIUM 245mg; CALC 120mg

TECHNIQUE

Prepping Butternut Squash: Besides being a great side for simple roast chicken, pork, or beef tenderloin, butternut squash provides more than a day's worth of vitamin A and about half of your daily recommended vitamin C. Select a squash that feels heavy for its size, is firm to the touch, and has no dark or soft spots.

1. Remove the skin with a vegetable peeler, and halve the peeled squash lengthwise.

2. Scoop out the seeds.

3. Slice the squash into strips with a chef's knife, and cut into cubes.

Cilantro and Cumin–Spiced Carrots 🌿
A fresh taste for carrots with a vivid garlic-and-herb vinaigrette to complement the natural sweetness.

This is a delicious alternative to the usual buttery-sugary glaze. If you can't find real baby carrots, simply cut a regular carrot in half crosswise, halve the skinny bottom part lengthwise, and quarter the thicker top section; ta-da—baby carrots! (We're not fond of the whittled-down, clone-like sameness of packaged "baby carrots.") Hands-on time: 20 min. Total time: 20 min.

2   quarts water

1   pound baby carrots, trimmed and halved lengthwise

1   garlic clove, chopped

½   cup chopped fresh cilantro

2   tablespoons chopped fresh dill

1   tablespoon olive oil

1   tablespoon fresh orange juice

½   teaspoon ground cumin

¼   teaspoon kosher salt

1. Bring 2 quarts water to a boil in a saucepan. Add carrots; cook 3 minutes or until crisp-tender. Drain.

2. Place garlic in a food processor; pulse 3 times or until finely chopped. Add cilantro; pulse 3 times or until combined. Add dill and next 4 ingredients (through salt); pulse 3 times or until combined. Spoon dill mixture over carrots; toss gently to coat. Serve warm or at room temperature.

Serves 8 (serving size: about ⅓ cup).

CALORIES 38; FAT 1.9g (sat 0.3g, mono 1.2g, poly 0.2g); PROTEIN 0.5g; CARB 5.2g; FIBER 1.5g; CHOL 0mg; IRON 0.2mg; SODIUM 95mg; CALC 19mg

---

Baby Bok Choy with Soy-Ginger Drizzle 🌿
Beautiful, delicious, ridiculously quick.

The flavor-packed drizzle is based on the Japanese condiment ponzu. No need to cook the stalks and leaves separately. If you can't find baby bok choy, you can use coarsely chopped regular bok choy instead. Hands-on time: 6 min. Total time: 12 min.

1   pound baby bok choy, cut in half lengthwise

1   tablespoon lower-sodium soy sauce

1   tablespoon fresh orange juice

1   teaspoon dark sesame oil

½   teaspoon grated peeled fresh ginger

1. Steam bok choy 5 minutes or until crisp-tender. Combine soy sauce, juice, oil, and ginger; drizzle over bok choy.

Serves 4 (serving size: about 4 ounces bok choy and about 1¾ teaspoons sauce).

CALORIES 27; FAT 1.4g (sat 0.2g, mono 0.5g, poly 0.6g); PROTEIN 2g; CARB 2.8g; FIBER 1.1g; CHOL 0mg; IRON 0.9mg; SODIUM 171mg; CALC 120mg

Haricots Verts with Warm Bacon Vinaigrette

Delicate, slender French beans are punctuated with walnut oil, toasted walnuts, and the welcome salty crunch of bacon.

Haricots verts are thin, fresh French green beans. If you can't find them, substitute regular fresh beans, which you'll need to cook a few minutes longer. You can also use white wine vinegar instead of Champagne for a slightly sharper taste. Hands-on time: 11 min. Total time: 30 min.

- 2 pounds haricots verts, trimmed
- 3 bacon slices, chopped
- ¾ cup finely chopped shallots (about 2 medium)
- 1½ tablespoons toasted walnut oil
- 2 teaspoons Champagne or white wine vinegar
- ¾ teaspoon kosher salt
- 3 tablespoons chopped walnuts, toasted
- 1 tablespoon chopped fresh flat-leaf parsley

1. Cook beans in boiling water 7 minutes or until crisp-tender. Drain and plunge beans into ice water; drain.
2. Cook bacon in a large nonstick skillet over medium heat until crisp. Remove bacon with a slotted spoon, reserving drippings in pan. Add shallots to drippings in pan; cook 5 minutes or until tender. Combine shallots and bacon in a large bowl. Add beans to pan; cook 3 minutes or until thoroughly heated. Add beans, oil, vinegar, and salt to bacon mixture; toss to combine. Sprinkle with walnuts and parsley.

Serves 8 (serving size: about 1 cup).

CALORIES 108; FAT 6.2g (sat 1.1g, mono 0.8g, poly 3g); PROTEIN 4.2g; CARB 11.3g; FIBER 4.2g; CHOL 4mg; IRON 1.5mg; SODIUM 267mg; CALC 51mg

Green Peas with Pancetta

The peas-and-pork equation is immortal. Here, fresh peas burst with sweetness, and a touch of salty pancetta is the perfect accent.

For the freshest, best flavor, purchase and cook peas on the same day. But you can enjoy this dish all year long with tiny frozen peas. Hands-on time: 12 min. Total time: 25 min.

- 1 ounce chopped pancetta (about 3 slices)
- ¾ cup finely chopped white onion
- 1 garlic clove, minced
- 3 cups shelled green peas or frozen petite green peas
- 1 cup fat-free, lower-sodium chicken broth
- 2 teaspoons sugar
- ¼ teaspoon salt
- ¼ cup chopped fresh flat-leaf parsley

1. Heat a large nonstick skillet over medium-high heat. Add pancetta to pan; sauté 5 minutes or until crisp, stirring frequently. Remove pancetta with a slotted spoon, reserving drippings in pan. Add onion and garlic to drippings in pan; sauté 2 minutes or until tender. Add peas, broth, sugar, and salt to pan; simmer 5 minutes or until peas are tender, stirring occasionally. Stir in pancetta and parsley.

Serves 6 (serving size: ½ cup).

CALORIES 92; FAT 1.9g (sat 0.7g, mono 0g, poly 0.1g); PROTEIN 5.1g; CARB 14.1g; FIBER 4.1g; CHOL 3mg; IRON 1.3mg; SODIUM 256mg; CALC 27mg

Haricots Verts with Warm
Bacon Vinaigrette

Spring Vegetable Skillet

Spinach with Raisins and Pine Nuts 🌿

Earthy greens get a sweet lift from the fruit in this classic Catalan combo.

It also works with chard or escarole. Soaking raisins plumps and tenderizes them. To toast pine nuts, place in a small skillet over medium heat; cook until golden, stirring frequently—and keep an eye on the expensive little nuggets, lest they burn. Remove pine nuts from the pan immediately, or they'll overtoast. Use any remaining spinach mixture to top grilled flatbreads or bruschetta. Hands-on time: 14 min. Total time: 30 min.

¼ cup raisins
1 teaspoon olive oil
1 cup chopped onion
2 pounds bagged prewashed spinach
¼ cup pine nuts, toasted
½ teaspoon salt
¼ teaspoon freshly ground black pepper

1. Place raisins in a small bowl; cover with hot water. Let stand 5 minutes or until plump; drain.
2. Heat a Dutch oven over medium heat. Add oil to pan; swirl to coat. Add onion to pan; cook 10 minutes or until tender, stirring occasionally. Add about one-fourth of spinach to pan; cook 3 minutes or until spinach wilts, stirring occasionally. Repeat procedure 3 times with remaining spinach. Stir in raisins, nuts, salt, and pepper.

Serves 10 (serving size: ½ cup).

CALORIES 68; FAT 3g (sat 0.6g, mono 1g, poly 1.2g); PROTEIN 3.5g; CARB 8.4g; FIBER 2.8g; CHOL 0mg; IRON 2.8mg; SODIUM 193mg; CALC 96mg

Spring Vegetable Skillet 🌿

Fresh, in-season vegetables often need little more embellishment than salt, a touch of butter, and fresh herbs.

Delicate sugar snaps are blanched to retain their bite; basil or parsley works in place of tarragon. Hands-on time: 15 min. Total time: 20 min.

16 baby carrots with tops (about 10 ounces)
¾ teaspoon kosher salt, divided
12 ounces sugar snap peas, trimmed
1½ tablespoons butter
1 tablespoon chopped fresh tarragon
¼ teaspoon freshly ground black pepper
1 teaspoon grated lemon rind
1 teaspoon fresh lemon juice

1. Peel carrots, and cut off tops to within 1 inch of carrot; cut in half lengthwise.
2. Place ¼ teaspoon salt in a large saucepan of water; bring to a boil. Add carrots and peas; cook 3 minutes or until crisp-tender. Drain.
3. Melt butter in a large nonstick skillet over medium-high heat. Add vegetables; cook 1 minute, stirring to coat. Stir in remaining ½ teaspoon salt, tarragon, and pepper; cook 1 minute. Remove from heat; stir in rind and juice.

Serves 6 (serving size: ⅔ cup).

CALORIES 69; FAT 2.9g (sat 1.8g, mono 0.7g, poly 0.1g); PROTEIN 1.7g; CARB 8.8g; FIBER 2.8g; CHOL 8mg; IRON 1.2mg; SODIUM 221mg; CALC 58mg

Aromatic Slow-Roasted Tomatoes

As if by magic, all-day slow roasting takes ho-hum winter tomatoes and turns out fruit with summery concentrated sweetness and intense tomato essence.

Serve alongside roast beef or lamb, seared steak, or fish, or make our Slow-Roasted Tomato Sauce (below) and toss it with pasta. Hands-on time: 5 min. Total time: 7 hr. 35 min.

- 1 tablespoon sugar
- 1 tablespoon extra-virgin olive oil
- ½ teaspoon salt
- ½ teaspoon dried basil
- ½ teaspoon dried oregano
- ¼ teaspoon freshly ground black pepper
- 4 pounds plum tomatoes, halved lengthwise (about 16 medium)

Cooking spray

1. Preheat oven to 200°.
2. Combine first 7 ingredients in a large bowl, tossing gently to coat. Arrange tomatoes, cut sides up, on a baking sheet coated with cooking spray. Roast at 200° for 7½ hours.

Serves 8 (serving size: 4 tomato halves).

CALORIES 63; FAT 2.2g (sat 0.3g, mono 1.3g, poly 0.4g); PROTEIN 2g; CARB 10.6g; FIBER 2.8g; CHOL 0mg; IRON 0.7mg; SODIUM 157mg; CALC 26mg

Slow-Roasted Tomato Sauce:
Process slow-roasted tomatoes until smooth; put through a food mill. Heat a medium saucepan over medium heat. Add 2 teaspoons extra-virgin olive oil; swirl to coat. Add 1 large garlic clove, sliced, to pan; cook 2 minutes, stirring constantly. Stir in tomato puree.

Simmer 1 hour or until sauce is reduced to 1¾ cups, stirring occasionally.

Serves 6 (serving size: about ⅓ cup).

CALORIES 98; FAT 4.4g (sat 0.6g, mono 2.9g, poly 0.6g); PROTEIN 2.7g; CARB 14.3g; FIBER 3.7g; CHOL 0mg; IRON 0.9mg; SODIUM 209mg; CALC 35mg

Roasted Baby Summer Squash with Caper Gremolata 🌿
Scalloped pattypan squash and baby zucchini are simply exquisite, their subtle flavor lifted by the briny zip of capers.

If you can't find pattypan squash or baby zucchini, use regular zucchini or yellow squash, and cut into chunks. Hands-on time: 19 min. Total time: 34 min.

Gremolata:
- ¼ cup chopped fresh flat-leaf parsley
- 1 teaspoon grated lemon rind
- 2 tablespoons fresh lemon juice
- 1 tablespoon capers
- 2 teaspoons extra-virgin olive oil
- 1 garlic clove, minced

Squash:
- 4 cups multicolored baby pattypan squash, halved lengthwise
- 3 cups baby zucchini, trimmed
- 2 teaspoons extra-virgin olive oil
- ¼ teaspoon kosher salt
- ¼ teaspoon freshly ground black pepper

1. Preheat oven to 475°.

2. To prepare gremolata, combine first 6 ingredients in a small bowl; set aside.

3. To prepare squash, combine pattypan squash, zucchini, and 2 teaspoons oil in a bowl. Sprinkle with salt and pepper. Arrange squash, cut sides down, in a single layer on a jelly-roll pan. Bake at 475° for 15 minutes or until squash is tender and lightly browned, stirring after 7 minutes. Sprinkle gremolata over squash. Serve immediately.

Serves 8 (serving size: about ¾ cup).

CALORIES 43; FAT 2.4g (sat 0.3g, mono 1.7g, poly 0.3g); PROTEIN 1.5g; CARB 4.7g; FIBER 1.5g; CHOL 0mg; IRON 0.2mg; SODIUM 92mg; CALC 5mg

9
SIDES

GLOBAL FLAVORS

Capers: Capers, which meld the pungent salinity of olives with the tartness of lemons, are immature flower buds that are sun-dried and cured in vinegar, wine, salt, or brine. The salt and brine methods can make capers high in sodium; to reduce it (and mellow the flavor), drain capers in a colander, then rinse under running water. You can also buy capers in salt; these have a more vivid flavor but definitely need lots of soaking. Use capers to infuse a savory sauce, salad, pizza, pasta, or dressing with their intense, herbal flavor.

Rosemary Mashed Sweet
Potatoes and Shallots

Rosemary Mashed Sweet Potatoes and Shallots 🌿

Jilt the traditional super-sugary sweet potato casserole for this more streamlined, fresher, and certainly healthier version.

Sweet potatoes are already naturally sweet. Why lay on more sugar? Here caramelized shallots add a savory note. Olive oil provides richness and bypasses the saturated fat you'd get from butter. Hands-on time: 16 min. Total time: 39 min.

5½ teaspoons extra-virgin olive oil, divided

½ cup thinly sliced shallots (about 2 medium)

1½ teaspoons brown sugar

1⅓ pounds sweet potatoes, peeled and diced

2 teaspoons finely chopped fresh rosemary

¼ teaspoon coarse sea salt

¼ teaspoon freshly ground black pepper

1. Heat 4 teaspoons oil in a medium skillet over low heat. Add shallots to pan; cook 5 minutes, stirring occasionally. Sprinkle with sugar; cook 20 minutes or until shallots are golden, stirring occasionally.
2. Place potatoes in a medium saucepan; cover with water. Bring to a boil; cook 8 minutes or until tender. Drain. Place potatoes in a large bowl; beat with a mixer at medium speed until smooth.

Add rosemary, salt, and pepper; beat until blended. Spoon into a bowl. Top with shallots; drizzle with remaining 1½ teaspoons oil.

Serves 4 (serving size: about ½ cup).

CALORIES 202; FAT 6.3g (sat 0.9g, mono 4.5g, poly 0.9g); PROTEIN 2.9g; CARB 34.9g; FIBER 4.8g; CHOL 0mg; IRON 1.2mg; SODIUM 278mg; CALC 55mg

Steamed Sugar Snap Peas 🌿

Fresh, crunchy, and (as the name implies) remarkably sweet, these snap peas are a versatile spring side dish.

With mint, the flavors are bright; with tarragon, they go slightly earthy. Hands-on time: 4 min. Total time: 9 min.

3 cups fresh sugar snap peas

1 tablespoon chopped fresh mint or tarragon

1 tablespoon butter

⅛ teaspoon salt

⅛ teaspoon freshly ground black pepper

1. Steam peas 5 minutes or until crisp-tender; drain. Combine peas, mint or tarragon, butter, salt, and pepper; toss well.

Serves 4 (serving size: ¾ cup).

CALORIES 46; FAT 3g (sat 1.8g, mono 0.8g, poly 0.2g); PROTEIN 1.4g; CARB 3.7g; FIBER 1.3g; CHOL 8mg; IRON 1mg; SODIUM 96mg; CALC 22mg

9

SIDES

Garlic Fries 🌿

Reader comments about these oven fries include "Legendary!" "Sooo good," "Deelish," "Fantastic," and "Just ridiculous."

We first introduced this recipe in 2002, and it remains a favorite. Tossing crisp oven fries in a small amount of butter and garlic after cooking makes them unbelievably rich, yet still lower in fat than fast-food fries. Younger children may prefer the fries without the garlic mixture, or with less garlic.

Hands-on time: 14 min. Total time: 42 min.

1½	pounds baking potatoes, peeled and cut into ¼-inch-thick strips
2	teaspoons canola oil
½	teaspoon salt
1	tablespoon butter
8	garlic cloves, minced (about 5 teaspoons)
2	tablespoons finely chopped fresh parsley
2	tablespoons grated fresh Parmesan cheese

1. Preheat oven to 450°.

2. Combine potatoes and oil in a large zip-top plastic bag; seal bag, and toss well to coat.

3. Arrange potatoes in a single layer on a baking sheet lined with parchment paper. Sprinkle with salt. Bake at 450° for 25 minutes or until potatoes are tender and golden brown, turning after 20 minutes.

4. Heat a large nonstick skillet over low heat. Add butter and garlic to pan; cook 4 minutes, stirring constantly. Add potatoes and parsley to butter mixture; toss to coat. Sprinkle with cheese. Serve immediately.

Serves 6 (serving size: about ¾ cup).

CALORIES 140; FAT 4.4g (sat 1.7g, mono 1.5g, poly 0.6g); PROTEIN 3.1g; CARB 22.7g; FIBER 2g; CHOL 7mg; IRON 0.5mg; SODIUM 256mg; CALC 52mg

CHOICE INGREDIENT

Potato Pointers: Potatoes are good for you, and if you eat the skin, they're great for you. The flesh of a medium-sized baking potato contains about 17% of the potassium, a third of the vitamin C, and almost 11% of the niacin you need in a day, with only 145 calories and little fat. The skin adds vitamin C and about 3 grams of fiber. Of the thousands of varieties, there are really just five main types of potatoes.

Russets are the most popular starchy variety for French fries and baking. They have rough brown skin and white flesh, and are usually large and oblong.

Yellow-skinned potatoes, such as Yukon golds, have smooth skin and dense, buttery flesh that can range from light yellow to golden. These are a favorite for mashed potatoes.

White potatoes have tan skin and white flesh that can be waxy or starchy. They're good for soups and stews.

Red potatoes have white, yellow, or reddish flesh under the red skin. Their waxy flesh makes them a good choice for roasting and good for mashing, especially if you prefer chunky potatoes.

Blue and purple potatoes have skin and flesh that range from lavender to navy in color. They're ideal for mashed potatoes or potato salads.

Bacon and Cheddar Smashed Potatoes

All the flavors of a loaded baked potato made healthy, served in comforting, creamy mashed form.

To make mashed potatoes ethereally fluffy and smooth, use a food mill instead of a potato masher.
Hands-on time: 10 min. Total time: 40 min.

2½ pounds Yukon gold or Russet potatoes, coarsely chopped

½ cup fat-free milk

½ cup (2 ounces) shredded extra-sharp cheddar cheese

½ cup light sour cream

⅓ cup sliced green onions

2 applewood-smoked bacon slices, cooked and finely chopped

½ teaspoon freshly ground black pepper

¼ teaspoon kosher salt

1. Place potatoes in a saucepan; cover with cold water. Bring to a boil. Reduce heat; simmer 15 minutes or until tender. Drain; return potatoes to pan. Add milk; mash with a potato masher to desired consistency. Cook 2 minutes or until thoroughly heated, stirring constantly. Remove from heat. Add cheese to pan; stir until smooth. Stir in sour cream and remaining ingredients.

Serves 6 (serving size: 1 cup).

CALORIES 245; FAT 5.9g (sat 3.7g, mono 1.4g, poly 0.2g); PROTEIN 9.8g; CARB 36.4g; FIBER 2.5g; CHOL 13mg; IRON 1.8mg; SODIUM 239mg; CALC 99mg

Cilantro-Jalapeño Latkes with Chipotle Sour Cream

The traditional Jewish favorite gets a makeover with the lively flavors of lime, jalapeño, cilantro, and smoked chiles.

Seeded jalapeño makes for mild latkes, but the sauce still has some kick. If you want fire in both, leave the seeds in and garnish with additional slices. Always use starchy potatoes, such as baking potatoes, for latkes; they'll hold together best. Hands-on time: 30 min. Total time: 1 hr. 10 min.

6 tablespoons light sour cream

1 tablespoon chopped chipotle chile, canned in adobo sauce

¾ teaspoon grated lime rind

1 teaspoon fresh lime juice

6 cups shredded peeled baking potato (about 1½ pounds)

1 cup grated fresh onion

6 tablespoons all-purpose flour

½ cup chopped fresh cilantro

2 tablespoons finely chopped seeded jalapeño pepper

1 teaspoon ground cumin

½ teaspoon salt

1 large egg

¼ cup olive oil, divided

1. Combine first 4 ingredients in a small bowl, stirring well. Cover and chill until ready to serve.

2. Combine potato and onion in a colander. Drain 30 minutes, pressing occasionally with the back of a spoon until barely moist. Combine potato mixture, flour, and next 5 ingredients (through egg) in a large bowl; toss well.

3. Heat a large skillet over medium-high heat. Add 2 tablespoons oil to pan; swirl to coat. Spoon ¼ cup potato mixture loosely into a dry measuring cup. Pour mixture into pan; flatten slightly. Repeat procedure 5 times to form 6 latkes. Sauté 3½ minutes on each side or until golden brown. Remove latkes from pan; keep warm. Repeat procedure with remaining 2 tablespoons oil and potato mixture to yield 12 latkes. Serve with sour cream mixture.

Serves 6 (serving size: 2 latkes and about 1½ tablespoons sour cream mixture).

CALORIES 260; FAT 11g (sat 2.2g, mono 6.9g, poly 1.2g); PROTEIN 5.6g; CARB 35.3g; FIBER 3.8g; CHOL 35mg; IRON 2.1mg; SODIUM 268mg; CALC 36mg

Classic Potato Latkes variation:

Omit sour cream, chipotle chile, lime rind, lime juice, cilantro, jalapeño, and cumin. Increase grated onion to 1¼ cups; add 1 teaspoon chopped fresh thyme with the flour. Serve with ¾ cup unsweetened applesauce combined with a dash of ground cinnamon.

CALORIES 215; FAT 8.7g (sat 1.3g, mono 6.1g, poly 1g); PROTEIN 4.4g; CARB 31.6g; FIBER 2.6g; CHOL 30mg; IRON 1.6mg; SODIUM 173mg; CALC 30mg

9

SIDES

TECHNIQUE

Creating Crisp, Light Latkes: Latkes require a deft hand and a good eye for crispy-tender success.

1. Shredding ingredients causes them to release moisture—the enemy of starch, which helps hold the cakes together. So be sure to drain well.

2. Combine the drained shredded mixture with egg, flour, and any flavoring options you like: chopped chiles, fresh herbs, ginger, garlic, or spice blends like curry powder.

3. Portion and form the latkes by scooping the mixture with a dry measuring cup. Once in the pan, flatten the top of each slightly, and pan-fry until golden brown.

Truffled Roasted Potatoes 🌿
Convenient precut potatoes go dinner-party elegant with a finishing drizzle of truffle oil.

White truffle oil delivers a powerful punch of flavor. For more tips, see page 287. Hands-on time: 5 min. Total time: 45 min.

2　**(20-ounce) packages refrigerated red potato wedges**

2　**tablespoons olive oil**

1　**tablespoon minced garlic**

½　**teaspoon kosher salt**

½　**teaspoon freshly ground black pepper**

1　**tablespoon white truffle oil**

2　**teaspoons fresh thyme leaves**

1. Preheat oven to 450°.
2. Place potatoes on a jelly-roll pan lined with parchment paper. Drizzle with olive oil; sprinkle with garlic, salt, and pepper, tossing well to combine. Bake at 450° for 35 minutes or until potatoes are browned and tender. Remove from oven. Drizzle potatoes with truffle oil; sprinkle with thyme. Toss gently to combine.

Serves 8 (serving size: about ¾ cup).

CALORIES 134; FAT 5.1g (sat 0.7g, mono 3.7g, poly 0.5g); PROTEIN 3.6g; CARB 18g; FIBER 3.6g; CHOL 0mg; IRON 0.8mg; SODIUM 269mg; CALC 3mg

Honey and Herb–Roasted Root Vegetables 🌿

The flavors of fall in a bowl—sweet butternut and parsnips, with earthy turnip and bright fennel.

Serve with roast pork loin, chicken, beef, ham, or duck. Hands-on time: 17 min. Total time: 40 min.

1½ cups sliced fennel bulb (about 1 small bulb)

1½ cups (½-inch) cubed peeled butternut squash

1¼ cups (½-inch) cubed red potato

1 cup (½-inch) cubed peeled turnip

1 cup (½-inch-thick) slices parsnip

1 tablespoon olive oil

½ teaspoon salt

½ teaspoon chopped fresh thyme

¼ teaspoon freshly ground black pepper

6 garlic cloves, peeled

3 large shallots, peeled and halved

Cooking spray

1 tablespoon honey

1½ teaspoons cider vinegar

1. Preheat oven to 450°.
2. Combine first 11 ingredients in a large bowl; toss well. Arrange vegetable mixture in a single layer on a jelly-roll pan coated with cooking spray. Bake at 450° for 25 minutes or until vegetables are browned and tender. Place vegetable mixture in a large bowl. Add honey and cider vinegar to vegetables; toss well.

Serves 4 (serving size: about ⅔ cup).

CALORIES 181; FAT 3.8g (sat 0.5g, mono 2.5g, poly 0.5g); PROTEIN 3.6g; CARB 36.2g; FIBER 6.4g; CHOL 0mg; IRON 1.8mg; SODIUM 351mg; CALC 104mg

Potato Gratin 🌿

Cheesy, creamy, and starchy, like the classic French potatoes dauphinoise that inspired it, but with far fewer calories and less fat.

For dishes that call for thin potato slices, a mandoline makes it a snap. The sharp blade cuts uniformly thin slices (so they'll cook evenly) in a fraction of the time it would take with a knife. Hands-on time: 20 min. Total time: 1 hr. 19 min.

1 garlic clove, peeled and halved

1 tablespoon olive oil

2½ cups whole milk

2 tablespoons minced shallots

¾ teaspoon kosher salt

¼ teaspoon freshly ground black pepper

Dash of grated whole nutmeg

2 pounds Yukon gold potatoes, peeled and cut into ⅛-inch-thick slices

⅓ cup (about 1½ ounces) shredded Gruyère cheese

¼ cup (1 ounce) grated fresh Parmigiano-Reggiano cheese

1. Preheat oven to 375°.
2. Rub a broiler-safe 11 x 7-inch glass or ceramic baking dish with garlic; discard garlic. Coat dish with oil. Combine milk and next 5 ingredients (through potatoes) in a skillet; bring to a simmer. Cook 8 minutes or until potatoes are almost tender. Spoon potato mixture into prepared baking dish. Sprinkle with cheeses. Bake at 375° for 35 minutes.
3. Preheat broiler. Broil 3 minutes or until golden. Let stand 10 minutes.

Serves 8 (serving size: about ½ cup).

CALORIES 198; FAT 7.5g (sat 3.6g, mono 2.9g, poly 0.5g); PROTEIN 7.8g; CARB 25.4g; FIBER 1.9g; CHOL 18mg; IRON 0.4mg; SODIUM 300mg; CALC 212mg

Wild Rice Stuffing

Pecans, dried fruit, and whole-grain rice make a nutty, sweet side for roast beef, ham, or turkey.

Vary the flavor with your favorite dried fruits. Try raisins, currants, dried cranberries, or dried figs.
Hands-on time: 8 min. Total time: 1 hr. 26 min.

Cooking spray
1½ cups chopped celery
1 cup chopped onion
1 cup uncooked wild rice
2 garlic cloves, minced
4 cups fat-free, lower-sodium chicken broth
1½ tablespoons chopped fresh sage
1 cup uncooked long-grain brown rice
½ cup dried sweet cherries
½ cup chopped dried apricots
½ cup chopped pecans, toasted
½ teaspoon salt
½ teaspoon freshly ground black pepper

1. Heat a Dutch oven over medium-high heat. Coat pan with cooking spray. Add celery, onion, wild rice, and garlic to pan; sauté 3 minutes, stirring frequently. Stir in broth and sage; bring to a boil. Cover, reduce heat, and simmer 25 minutes. Stir in brown rice; bring to a boil. Cover, reduce heat, and cook 30 minutes or until liquid is absorbed. Remove from heat; cover and let stand 10 minutes. Stir in cherries and remaining ingredients.

Serves 12 (serving size: ½ cup).

CALORIES 192; FAT 4g (sat 0.4g, mono 2.1g, poly 1.3g); PROTEIN 5.1g; CARB 34.4g; FIBER 3.6g; CHOL 0mg; IRON 1.2mg; SODIUM 243mg; CALC 35mg

Multigrain Pilaf with Sunflower Seeds

This is about as healthy—and tasty—a side as we can cook up: whole-grain goodness plus sunflower seeds and dried fruit.

This recipe calls for long-cooking barley and brown rice (both whole grains), but if you're in a hurry, substitute instant brown rice and quick-cooking barley. Just be sure to adjust cooking times according to package directions. Hands-on time: 11 min. Total time: 1 hr. 7 min.

4 teaspoons canola oil, divided
⅓ cup sunflower seed kernels
½ teaspoon salt, divided
2 teaspoons butter
1 cup thinly sliced leek (about 1 large)
2½ cups water
1½ cups fat-free, lower-sodium chicken broth
½ cup uncooked pearl barley
½ cup brown rice blend or brown rice
½ cup dried currants
¼ cup uncooked bulgur
¼ cup chopped fresh parsley
¼ teaspoon freshly ground black pepper

1. Heat a Dutch oven over medium-high heat. Add 2 teaspoons oil, sunflower seeds, and ¼ teaspoon salt to pan; sauté 2 minutes or until lightly browned. Remove from pan; set aside.

2. Add remaining 2 teaspoons oil and butter to pan. Add leek; cook 4 minutes or until tender, stirring frequently. Add 2½ cups water and next 3 ingredients (through rice); bring to a boil. Cover, reduce heat, and simmer 35 minutes. Stir in currants and bulgur; cover and simmer 10 minutes or until grains are tender. Remove from heat; stir in remaining ¼ teaspoon salt, sunflower seeds, parsley, and pepper. Serve immediately.

Serves 8 (serving size: ½ cup).

CALORIES 198; FAT 6.6g (sat 1.1g, mono 2.2g, poly 2.6g); PROTEIN 5g; CARB 32.7g; FIBER 4.9g; CHOL 3mg; IRON 1.5mg; SODIUM 266mg; CALC 26mg

Quinoa with Roasted Garlic, Tomatoes, and Spinach

Half a head of roasted garlic lends sweet allium love to chewy, protein-rich, whole-grain quinoa.

Be sure to rinse quinoa before cooking, or it may have a bitter taste. Hands-on time: 22 min. Total time: 1 hr. 48 min.

1 whole garlic head
1 tablespoon olive oil
1 tablespoon finely chopped shallots
¼ teaspoon crushed red pepper
½ cup uncooked quinoa, rinsed and drained
1 tablespoon dry white wine
1 cup fat-free, lower-sodium chicken broth
½ cup baby spinach leaves
⅓ cup chopped seeded tomato (1 small)
1 tablespoon shaved fresh Parmesan cheese
¼ teaspoon salt

1. Preheat oven to 350°.
2. Remove papery skin from garlic head. Cut garlic head in half crosswise, breaking apart to separate whole cloves. Wrap half of head in foil; reserve remaining garlic for another use. Bake at 350° for 1 hour; cool 10 minutes. Separate cloves; squeeze to extract garlic pulp. Discard skins.
3. Heat a saucepan over medium heat. Add oil to pan; swirl to coat. Add shallots and red pepper to pan; cook 1 minute. Add quinoa to pan; cook 2 minutes, stirring constantly. Add wine; cook until liquid is absorbed, stirring constantly. Add broth; bring to a boil. Cover, reduce heat, and simmer 15 minutes or until liquid is absorbed. Remove from heat; stir in garlic pulp, spinach, tomato, cheese, and salt. Serve immediately.

Serves 4 (serving size: ½ cup).

CALORIES 130; FAT 5g (sat 0.7g, mono 3.1g, poly 1g); PROTEIN 4.1g; CARB 16.6g; FIBER 1.8g; CHOL 1mg; IRON 1.7mg; SODIUM 305mg; CALC 49mg

Three-Grain Pilaf

Three grains with three textures: fluffy basmati rice, chewy quinoa, and crunchy millet.

With just broth, salt, butter, and green onions, the grains' flavors shine through. Hands-on time: 5 min. Total time: 43 min.

1½ tablespoons unsalted butter
½ cup uncooked basmati rice
¼ cup uncooked quinoa
¼ cup uncooked millet
1¼ cups fat-free, lower-sodium chicken broth
¾ cup water
¼ teaspoon salt
½ cup finely chopped green onions

1. Melt butter in a large nonstick skillet over medium heat. Add rice, quinoa, and millet to pan; cook 3 minutes, stirring frequently. Stir in broth, ¾ cup water, and salt; bring to a boil. Cover, reduce heat, and simmer 25 minutes. Sprinkle with onions.

Serves 6 (serving size: ⅔ cup).

CALORIES 116; FAT 3.7g (sat 1.9g, mono 0.9g, poly 0.5g); PROTEIN 3.1g; CARB 17.5g; FIBER 1.6g; CHOL 8mg; IRON 0.8mg; SODIUM 242mg; CALC 12mg

White Beans with Prosciutto

The convenience of canned beans is a gift. In less than 20 minutes, you can have a meaty, herbed bean side.

For lower-sodium beans, buy organic or no-added-salt canned versions. Hands-on time: 8 min. Total time: 16 min.

2 teaspoons extra-virgin olive oil

¼ cup finely chopped red onion

2 teaspoons minced fresh garlic

½ teaspoon minced fresh rosemary

2 tablespoons dry white wine

3 tablespoons fat-free, lower-sodium chicken broth

¼ teaspoon black pepper

1 (15-ounce) can cannellini beans, rinsed and drained

2 tablespoons chopped fresh parsley

1 ounce thinly sliced prosciutto, chopped (about ¼ cup)

1. Heat a large skillet over medium heat. Add oil to pan; swirl to coat. Add onion to pan; sauté 2 minutes. Add garlic and rosemary; sauté 30 seconds. Add wine; cook until liquid evaporates. Add broth, pepper, and beans; cook 3 minutes or until beans are thoroughly heated. Stir in parsley and prosciutto.

Serves 4 (serving size: about ⅓ cup).

CALORIES 94; FAT 3.1g (sat 0.6g, mono 1.7g, poly 0.3g); PROTEIN 5.9g; CARB 10g; FIBER 2.9g; CHOL 6mg; IRON 1.1mg; SODIUM 356mg; CALC 35mg

Corn Bread, Chorizo, and Jalapeño Dressing

Dinner heads South by Southwest with this corn bread flecked with smoky chorizo and spicy jalapeño.

The combination of crunchy and moist—not gummy—textures depends on controlling the liquid: You want it moist before baking but not soupy. If your stuffing comes out too wet, pop it back in the oven, uncovered, at 400° for a few minutes until the top crisps up. Hands-on time: 40 min. Total time: 2 hr.

4½ ounces all-purpose flour (about 1 cup)

1¼ cups low-fat buttermilk

1 cup yellow cornmeal

2 tablespoons sugar

2 tablespoons unsalted butter, melted

1 tablespoon baking powder

2 large eggs, lightly beaten

¾ cup reduced-fat shredded sharp cheddar cheese

Cooking spray

1 jalapeño pepper, halved

1 teaspoon olive oil

3 ounces Mexican chorizo, casing removed and crumbled

1¼ cups diced red bell pepper (1 large)

1 cup thinly sliced green onions

2 cups (½-inch) cubed French bread baguette (crusts removed)

¼ cup chopped fresh cilantro

2 large egg whites, lightly beaten

1 (14.5-ounce) can fat-free, lower-sodium chicken broth

1 lime, cut into wedges

1. Preheat oven to 350°. Place a 10-inch cast-iron skillet in oven as it preheats.

2. Weigh or lightly spoon flour into a dry measuring cup; level with a knife. Combine flour and next 6 ingredients (through eggs) in a large bowl; fold in cheese.

3. Remove pan from oven. Coat pan with cooking spray. Pour batter into hot pan. Bake at 350° for 35 minutes or until edges are lightly browned and a wooden pick inserted in center comes out clean. Cool completely on a wire rack. Crumble corn bread into a large bowl.

4. Remove seeds and membrane from half of jalapeño. Coarsely chop both jalapeño halves. Heat a large skillet over medium-high heat. Add oil to pan; swirl to coat. Add chorizo; sauté 2 minutes. Add jalapeño, bell pepper, and onions; sauté 3 minutes. Remove from heat. Add chorizo mixture to corn bread mixture; stir in bread, cilantro, egg whites, and broth, stirring until bread is moist.

5. Spoon corn bread mixture into a 13 x 9–inch glass or ceramic baking dish coated with cooking spray. Bake at 350° for 45 minutes or until lightly browned. Serve with lime wedges.

Serves 12 (serving size: ¾ cup).

CALORIES 218; FAT 8.1g (sat 3.6g, mono 3g, poly 0.7g); PROTEIN 8.9g; CARB 27.7g; FIBER 1.9g; CHOL 53mg; IRON 1.9mg; SODIUM 374mg; CALC 232mg

Sausage and Sourdough Bread Stuffing

If you don't fall into the camp that likes a fruity stuffing, here's a tasty option with tangy sourdough bread, spicy sausage, and lots of herbs.

Like your stuffing soft and creamy, or crunchy? No need to choose with a simple two-step baking process—covered first to allow the stuffing to steam, then uncovered to make the top a toasted, crispy brown. Hands-on time: 20 min. Total time: 1 hr. 45 min.

10 cups (½-inch) cubed sourdough bread (about 1 pound)

3 tablespoons unsalted butter

2 cups finely chopped onion

1 cup finely chopped celery

15 ounces hot turkey Italian sausage, casings removed

3 tablespoons chopped fresh thyme

3 tablespoons chopped fresh sage

3 tablespoons chopped fresh flat-leaf parsley

½ teaspoon black pepper

2 cups fat-free, lower-sodium chicken broth

1 cup water

1 large egg, lightly beaten

Cooking spray

1. Preheat oven to 350°.
2. Arrange bread in single layers on 2 jelly-roll pans. Bake at 350° for 20 minutes or until golden, rotating pans after 10 minutes. Turn oven off; leave pans in oven 30 minutes or until bread is crisp.
3. Melt butter in a large skillet over medium heat. Add onion and celery; cook 11 minutes or until tender, stirring occasionally. Transfer vegetables to a large bowl. Add sausage to pan. Increase heat; sauté 8 minutes or until browned, stirring to crumble. Remove sausage from pan using a slotted spoon; add sausage to vegetable mixture. Stir in bread, herbs, and pepper; toss. Combine broth, 1 cup water, and egg, stirring well. Drizzle broth mixture over bread mixture; toss. Spoon mixture into a 13 x 9–inch glass or ceramic baking dish coated with cooking spray; cover with foil. Bake at 350° for 25 minutes. Uncover and cook 20 minutes or until browned.

Serves 14 (serving size: about ¾ cup).

CALORIES 149; FAT 6.3g (sat 2.8g, mono 1.7g, poly 1g); PROTEIN 7.2g; CARB 15.9g; FIBER 1.3g; CHOL 34mg; IRON 1.6mg; SODIUM 396mg; CALC 61mg

9

SIDES

Chapter Sandwich

10:
es

Herbed Chicken Salad Sandwiches, page 354

The tricky thing about sandwiches—surely, in the end, America's favorite food—is that a serving is anything you can fit between two slices of bread. Thus the mile-high deli meat-wich, the megaburger, and the bagel with thumb-thick layers of cream cheese. Unbounded, the innately healthy bread-and-filling sandwich becomes one of the great calorie bombs. Americans used to the Dagwood approach are shocked by the dainty 'wiches of Scandinavia and the pale cucumber squares of Old England. But the sandwich is ripe for repair and celebration as one of the great, fast, delicious, and nutritious dishes. Here, you'll find recipes that point to a much healthier way, with full sandwich satisfaction guaranteed.

Chicken Parmesan Burgers

The patties are drenched in marinara and topped with cheese.

Basil stands in for lettuce and is perfectly suited for the flavor combination. Adding marinara sauce to the chicken patties pumps up the flavor. Hands-on time: 10 min. Total time: 25 min.

- 2 (3-ounce) square ciabatta rolls
- 1 garlic clove, halved
- ½ pound ground chicken
- ½ cup plus 2 tablespoons lower-sodium marinara sauce, divided
- ½ teaspoon chopped fresh rosemary
- ½ teaspoon chopped fresh thyme
- ¼ teaspoon crushed red pepper
- ⅛ teaspoon kosher salt
- ⅛ teaspoon freshly ground black pepper
- Cooking spray
- ¼ cup shredded part-skim mozzarella cheese
- 8 basil leaves

1. Preheat broiler.
2. Cut rolls in half. Place rolls, cut sides up, on a baking sheet. Broil 3 minutes or until lightly browned. Remove rolls from pan. Rub each slice with cut sides of garlic. Discard garlic. Set rolls aside.
3. Preheat oven to 375°.
4. Combine chicken, ½ cup marinara, rosemary, and next 4 ingredients (through pepper) in a bowl. Divide into 2 portions, shaping each portion into a ¼-inch-thick patty. Heat an ovenproof skillet over medium-high heat. Coat pan with cooking spray. Add patties to pan; cook 3 minutes. Turn patties; place pan in oven. Bake at 375° for 8 minutes. Top each patty with 2 tablespoons cheese; bake 1 minute. Top each roll bottom with 2 basil leaves, 1 patty, 1 tablespoon marinara, 2 basil leaves, and roll top.

Serves 2 (serving size: 1 burger).

CALORIES 427; FAT 14.4g (sat 4.5g, mono 5.3g, poly 2.3g); PROTEIN 28.9g; CARB 55.4g; FIBER 1.2g; CHOL 83mg; IRON 2.9mg; SODIUM 742mg; CALC 112mg

Burgers with Blue Cheese Mayo and Sherry Vidalia Onions
Sharp cheese plays against sweet onions in a seriously delicious sandwich, made lighter with lean beef.

Lean sirloin has about the same amount of saturated fat as ground turkey. With blue cheese mayo and tangy-sweet onions, it makes a mighty juicy burger—if you're careful not to overcook.
Hands-on time: 45 min. Total time: 45 min.

½   cup (2 ounces) crumbled blue cheese

¼   cup canola mayonnaise

2   teaspoons chopped fresh thyme, divided

¼   teaspoon hot pepper sauce

1   pound ground sirloin

1   teaspoon freshly ground black pepper, divided

⅛   teaspoon kosher salt

½   teaspoon extra-virgin olive oil

4   (¼-inch-thick) slices Vidalia or other sweet onion

Cooking spray

2   teaspoons sherry vinegar

4   (1½-ounce) 100% whole-wheat hamburger buns with sesame seeds, toasted

4   (¼-inch-thick) slices tomato

2   cups loosely packed arugula

1. Preheat grill to medium-high heat.

2. Combine blue cheese, mayonnaise, 1 teaspoon thyme, and hot pepper sauce in a small bowl; stir well.

3. Divide beef into 4 equal portions, shaping each portion into a ½-inch-thick patty. Sprinkle beef evenly with ½ teaspoon black pepper and salt.

4. Brush oil evenly over both sides of onion slices; sprinkle with remaining ½ teaspoon black pepper. Place patties and onion on grill rack coated with cooking spray; cover and grill 3 minutes on each side. Set patties aside; keep warm. Place onion slices in a zip-top plastic bag; seal. Let stand 5 minutes; toss with remaining 1 teaspoon thyme and vinegar.

5. Spread cut sides of buns evenly with mayonnaise mixture. Place 1 tomato slice on bottom half of bun; top with ½ cup arugula, 1 patty, 1 onion slice, and top half of bun.

Serves 4 (serving size: 1 burger).

CALORIES 424; FAT 21.8g (sat 5.1g, mono 10.6g, poly 5.2g); PROTEIN 31.7g; CARB 27.5g; FIBER 4.4g; CHOL 76mg; IRON 3.3mg; SODIUM 624mg; CALC 151mg

Wine Pairing
Burgers call for red wine, but a big, tannic red can make the blue cheese taste metallic. Try a light Barbera or pinot noir, which plays nicely with both the cheese and the arugula.

TECHNIQUE
Creating Better Burgers: For a moist, evenly cooked burger, follow these tips: Start with cold meat, and wash your hands under cold water to make them cold. Don't overhandle meat when shaping the patties. Gently press a dimple into the center of each patty so they won't puff in the middle. Never press on patties when grilling, as it squeezes out juices and dries out the meat.

Quick Black Bean Burger 🌿

It's time for the veggie burger to quit chasing the beef-wannabe bandwagon and embrace life on the light side.

Done right—and this one sure is—veggie burgers are full of unexpected, delicious flavors and positively packed with nutrition, courtesy of lean vegetable protein and fiber. We pan-fry our black bean patties so they're wonderfully crisp on the outside and moist within. Hands-on time: 13 min. Total time: 25 min.

- 1 (2-ounce) 100% whole-wheat hamburger bun, torn into pieces
- 3 tablespoons olive oil, divided
- 2 teaspoons chopped garlic
- 1 (15.25-ounce) can organic black beans, rinsed and drained
- 1 teaspoon grated lime rind
- ¾ teaspoon chili powder
- ½ teaspoon chopped fresh oregano
- ¼ teaspoon salt
- 1 large egg, lightly beaten
- 1 large egg white, lightly beaten
- 1½ tablespoons canola mayonnaise
- 1½ tablespoons minced chipotle chile in adobo sauce
- 4 (2-ounce) 100% whole-wheat hamburger buns, split and toasted
- 4 (½-inch-thick) slices tomato
- 4 (¼-inch-thick) slices red onion
- 16 spinach leaves
- 1 ripe avocado, peeled and sliced (optional)

1. Place 1 bun in a food processor; pulse 4 times or until crumbs measure about 1 cup. Transfer to a medium bowl.

2. Place 1 tablespoon oil, garlic, and beans in processor; pulse 8 times or until mixture forms a thick paste. Add bean mixture to breadcrumbs. Stir in rind and next 5 ingredients (through egg white). With moistened hands, divide bean mixture into 4 equal portions (about ⅓ cup per portion), shaping each portion into a 3-inch patty.

3. Heat a large nonstick skillet over medium-high heat. Add remaining 2 tablespoons oil to pan; swirl to coat. Add patties to pan; reduce heat to medium, and cook 4 minutes or until bottom edges are browned. Carefully turn patties over; cook 3 minutes or until bottom edges are done.

4. Combine mayonnaise and chipotle chile in a small bowl. Spread mayonnaise mixture evenly over 1 half of each bun. Place 1 patty on bottom half of each bun; top each serving evenly with tomato, onion, spinach, and, if desired, avocado. Cover with top halves of buns.

Serves 4 (serving size: 1 burger).

CALORIES 443; FAT 19.2g (sat 2.8g, mono 11g, poly 4g); PROTEIN 14.9g; CARB 56.7g; FIBER 11g; CHOL 55mg; IRON 4.4mg; SODIUM 709mg; CALC 159mg

Salmon Burgers

We've come to absolutely love the salmon burger: It can be every bit as satisfying as beef.

The trick with an oily fish is texture. Ground beef will form a patty, but ground salmon alone can be soft and difficult to work with, and a breadcrumb or egg binder can blur the rich salmon flavor. We puree one-fourth of the salmon into a fine paste and use *it* to bind the rest of the roughly chopped salmon. For best results, choose salmon from the meaty center of the fish, and avoid portions nearer the tail. Tail-end flesh contains more connective tissue than center-cut fillets. Use black sesame seed buns, if available.

Hands-on time: 18 min. Total time: 24 min.

1 pound skinless center-cut salmon fillets, cut into 1-inch pieces, divided

2 tablespoons Dijon mustard, divided

2 teaspoons grated lemon rind

2 tablespoons minced fresh tarragon

1 tablespoon finely chopped shallots (about 1 small)

½ teaspoon kosher salt

¼ teaspoon freshly ground black pepper

1 tablespoon honey

1 cup arugula leaves

½ cup thinly sliced red onion

1 teaspoon fresh lemon juice

1 teaspoon extra-virgin olive oil

Cooking spray

4 (1½-ounce) hamburger buns, toasted

1. Place ¼ pound salmon, 1 tablespoon mustard, and rind in a food processor; process until smooth. Spoon puree into a large bowl. Place remaining ¾ pound salmon in food processor; pulse 6 times or until coarsely chopped. Fold chopped salmon, tarragon, shallots, salt, and pepper into puree. Divide mixture into 4 equal portions, gently shaping each portion into a ½-inch-thick patty. Cover and chill until ready to grill.

2. Preheat grill to medium heat.

3. Combine remaining 1 tablespoon mustard and honey in a small bowl; set aside.

4. Combine arugula, onion, juice, and oil in a medium bowl. Set aside.

5. Lightly coat both sides of patties with cooking spray. Place patties on grill rack; grill 2 minutes. Carefully turn patties; grill 1 minute or until desired degree of doneness. Place 1 patty on bottom half of each bun; top each serving with ¼ cup arugula mixture, 1½ teaspoons honey mixture, and top half of bun.

Serves 4 (serving size: 1 burger).

CALORIES 372; FAT 16g (sat 3.2g, mono 5.9g, poly 5.8g); PROTEIN 27.3g; CARB 28.2g; FIBER 1.5g; CHOL 67mg; IRON 2.1mg; SODIUM 569mg; CALC 92mg

Steak Baguettes with Pesto Mayo

Store-bought pesto is a great shortcut when it's mixed with mayonnaise for a creamy spread that marries perfectly with steak.

Grill the steak and toast the baguette over the same flame for a delicious charred effect. This sandwich holds up well, so you can pack it for lunch fully assembled. Also try it on a toasted Kaiser roll. Or pile high onto a toasted *boule* slice for an open-faced, knife-and-fork version. When heirloom tomatoes are in season, use a variety of colors instead of plum tomatoes for visual appeal and nuanced flavor.

Hands-on time: 20 min. Total time: 20 min.

1   (12-ounce) boneless beef sirloin steak (about 1 inch thick), trimmed

¼   teaspoon kosher salt

⅛   teaspoon freshly ground black pepper

2   tablespoons canola mayonnaise

2   tablespoons refrigerated pesto

1   (12-ounce) piece white or whole-grain baguette, cut in half horizontally

1   cup packed baby arugula (about 1 ounce)

3   (⅛-inch-thick) slices red onion

2   plum tomatoes, thinly sliced lengthwise

1. Heat a grill pan over medium-high heat. Sprinkle steak with salt and pepper. Add steak to pan; cook 2½ minutes on each side or until desired degree of doneness. Remove steak from pan; let stand 5 minutes. Cut steak across grain into thin slices.

2. Combine mayonnaise and pesto, stirring until well blended. Spread mayonnaise mixture evenly over cut sides of bread. Layer bottom half of bread with arugula, onion, steak, and tomato; cover with top half of bread. Cut sandwich diagonally into 4 equal pieces.

Serves 4 (serving size: 1 sandwich piece).

CALORIES 346; FAT 9.1g (sat 1.6g, mono 4.6g, poly 1.4g); PROTEIN 21g; CARB 41.4g; FIBER 2.3g; CHOL 26mg; IRON 3.3mg; SODIUM 701mg; CALC 41mg

Wine Pairing

Merlot, a soft, fruity red, brings out the meatiness in the steak while letting the pesto mayo shine.

10

SANDWICHES

NUTRITION MADE EASY

Canola Mayonnaise: When buying commercial mayo, opt for one made with canola oil. It has no saturated fat (compared to 1.5 grams per serving in regular mayo) and is a source of omega-3 polyunsaturated fats—one of the good fats.

Almost Meatless Sloppy Joe

A more-veg, less-beef version from Mark Bittman is just as sloppily good as the original.

Proves again that a little beef adds a lot of meaty flavor, without all the sat fat of a full serving. Beans stand in for the rest of the meat, and whole-wheat rolls bump up the healthy factor even more in these messy sandwiches. Hands-on time: 13 min. Total time: 33 min.

2	tablespoons olive oil
½	cup finely chopped white onion
1	tablespoon minced garlic
¼	teaspoon salt
¼	teaspoon freshly ground black pepper
6	ounces ground sirloin
½	cup grated carrot
2	teaspoons chili powder
1	teaspoon brown sugar
½	teaspoon dried oregano
¼	teaspoon ground red pepper
2	cups canned crushed tomatoes
1	(15.5-ounce) can lower-sodium red beans, rinsed, drained, and divided
4	(2-ounce) whole-wheat sandwich rolls, split and toasted
4	(¼-inch-thick) slices red onion, separated into rings

1. Heat a large skillet over medium-high heat. Add oil to pan; swirl to coat. Add onion, garlic, salt, black pepper, and beef to pan; cook 5 minutes or until meat is browned and vegetables are tender, stirring occasionally to crumble beef.

2. Add carrot, chili powder, sugar, oregano, and red pepper; cook 2 minutes, stirring occasionally. Stir in tomatoes; bring to a boil. Reduce heat to medium; cook 10 minutes or until thick and carrot is tender, stirring occasionally.

3. Partially mash 1 cup beans with a fork or potato masher. Add mashed beans and remaining whole beans to pan; cook 1 minute or until thoroughly heated. Spoon 1 cup bean mixture onto bottom half of each roll; top each serving with 1 red onion slice and top half of roll.

Serves 4 (serving size: 1 sandwich).

CALORIES 405; FAT 14.4g (sat 3.2g, mono 7.5g, poly 2.3g); PROTEIN 19.4g; CARB 53.3g; FIBER 10.4g; CHOL 28mg; IRON 5.1mg; SODIUM 633mg; CALC 148mg

Banh Mi

This is our version of a classic, a gorgeous collision of French and Southeast Asian flavors, crunchy with carrot and radish and brightened with fresh cilantro.

You can make the pork and the mayonnaise mixture (steps 3 and 4) up to a day ahead. Hands-on time: 20 min. Total time: 1 hr. 42 min.

½ cup shredded carrot

½ cup grated peeled daikon radish

1 tablespoon cider vinegar

2 teaspoons sugar

¼ teaspoon kosher salt

3 tablespoons chili garlic sauce

1½ teaspoons sugar

1 (1-pound) pork tenderloin, trimmed

Cooking spray

½ teaspoon salt

3 tablespoons fat-free mayonnaise

2 (20-inch) baguettes (about 8½ ounces each)

16 thin cucumber slices (about 1 cucumber)

16 cilantro sprigs

¼ cup thinly sliced green onions (about 2)

1 seeded and thinly sliced jalapeño pepper

1. Combine first 5 ingredients; cover and let stand 15 minutes to 1 hour. Drain.

2. Preheat oven to 400°.

3. Combine chili garlic sauce and 1½ teaspoons sugar; stir well. Place pork on the rack of a small roasting pan or broiler pan coated with cooking spray. Spread 2 tablespoons chili garlic mixture evenly over pork; sprinkle pork with ½ teaspoon salt. Bake at 400° for 17 minutes or until a thermometer registers 145°. Cool; cover pork, and refrigerate.

4. Combine mayonnaise and remaining chili garlic sauce mixture in a bowl; cover and refrigerate.

5. Cut each baguette horizontally, cutting to, but not through, other side, using a serrated knife. Spread mayonnaise mixture evenly on cut sides of baguettes. Thinly slice pork; divide pork evenly between baguettes. Top evenly with carrot mixture. Arrange 8 cucumber slices and 8 cilantro sprigs on each baguette. Top evenly with onions and jalapeño. Press top gently to close; cut each baguette into 4 equal servings.

Serves 8 (serving size: 1 sandwich).

CALORIES 343; FAT 8.3g (sat 1.8g, mono 2.7g, poly 3.2g); PROTEIN 17.5g; CARB 50.2g; FIBER 4.2g; CHOL 37mg; IRON 2.1mg; SODIUM 721mg; CALC 20mg

10

SANDWICHES

Philly Cheesesteaks

Meaty, gooey, and delightfully messy, this lighter version of Philadelphia's signature sandwich offers comforting flavors you'll crave.

Thinly sliced and modestly seasoned flank steak is a much leaner sub for traditional rib-eye. The meat gets further beefed up with portobellos and savory grilled peppers and onions, while a homemade lean white sauce—instead of the popular artificial cheese sauce—delivers full satisfaction with less sat fat and sodium.
Hands-on time: 35 min. Total time: 45 min.

1	(12-ounce) flank steak, trimmed
¼	teaspoon kosher salt
¼	teaspoon freshly ground black pepper
2	(5-inch) portobello mushroom caps
2	teaspoons extra-virgin olive oil, divided
1	cup thinly sliced onion
1½	cups thinly sliced green bell pepper
2	teaspoons minced garlic
½	teaspoon Worcestershire sauce
½	teaspoon lower-sodium soy sauce
2	teaspoons all-purpose flour
½	cup 1% low-fat milk
1	ounce provolone cheese, torn into small pieces
2	tablespoons grated Parmigiano-Reggiano cheese
¼	teaspoon dry mustard
4	(3-ounce) hoagie rolls, toasted

1. Place beef in freezer 15 minutes. Cut beef across grain into thin slices. Sprinkle beef with salt and black pepper. Remove brown gills from undersides of mushroom caps using a spoon; discard gills. Remove stems; discard. Thinly slice mushroom caps; cut slices in half crosswise.

2. Heat a large nonstick skillet over medium-high heat. Add 1 teaspoon oil to pan; swirl to coat. Add beef to pan; sauté 2 minutes or until beef loses its pink color, stirring constantly. Remove beef from pan. Add remaining 1 teaspoon oil to pan. Add onion; sauté 3 minutes. Add mushrooms, bell pepper, and garlic; sauté 6 minutes. Return beef to pan; sauté 1 minute or until thoroughly heated and vegetables are tender. Remove from heat. Stir in Worcestershire and soy sauces; keep warm.

3. Place flour in a small saucepan; gradually add milk, stirring with a whisk until blended. Bring to a simmer over medium heat; cook 1 minute or until slightly thick. Remove from heat. Add cheeses and mustard, stirring until smooth. Keep warm (mixture will thicken as it cools).

4. Hollow out top and bottom halves of bread, leaving a ½-inch-thick shell; reserve torn bread for another use. Divide beef mixture evenly among bottom halves of hoagies. Drizzle sauce evenly over beef mixture; replace top halves of hoagies.

Serves 4 (serving size: 1 sandwich).

CALORIES 397; FAT 12.4g (sat 4.9g, mono 4.7g, poly 1.6g); PROTEIN 30.8g; CARB 44.1g; FIBER 3.7g; CHOL 37mg; IRON 4.6mg; SODIUM 637mg; CALC 213mg

Mushroom and Provolone Patty Melts

Beer, rye bread, mushrooms, and onion make this a wonderfully full-flavored version of a classic sandwich.

Extra-lean ground beef is 95% lean and 5% fat. For kids, use beef broth instead of beer, and try mild wheat bread. Hands-on time: 10 min. Total time: 29 min.

1	pound extra-lean ground beef
5	teaspoons olive oil, divided
¼	cup thinly sliced yellow onion
⅛	teaspoon salt
⅛	teaspoon freshly ground black pepper
1	(8-ounce) package sliced cremini mushrooms
1½	teaspoons all-purpose flour
¼	cup dark beer (such as porter)
8	(1.1-ounce) slices rye bread

Cooking spray

4	(¾-ounce) slices reduced-fat provolone cheese

1. Heat a large nonstick skillet over medium-high heat. Shape beef into 4 (4-inch) patties. Add 2 teaspoons oil to pan; swirl to coat. Add patties to pan; cook 4 minutes on each side or until done.

2. Heat a medium skillet over medium-high heat. Add remaining 1 tablespoon oil to pan; swirl to coat. Add onion, salt, pepper, and mushrooms to pan; sauté 3 minutes. Sprinkle flour over mushroom mixture; cook 1 minute, stirring constantly. Stir in beer; cook 30 seconds or until thick. Remove from heat; keep warm.

3. When patties are done, remove from pan. Wipe pan clean; heat over medium-high heat. Coat 1 side of each bread slice with cooking spray. Place 4 bread slices, coated sides down, in pan. Top each with 1 patty, 1 cheese slice, and one-fourth of mushroom mixture. Top with remaining bread slices; coat with cooking spray. Cook 2 minutes on each side or until browned.

Serves 4 (serving size: 1 sandwich).

CALORIES 424; FAT 16.4g (sat 4.9g, mono 6.9g, poly 1.6g); PROTEIN 34.6g; CARB 34.3g; FIBER 4.1g; CHOL 71mg; IRON 3.9mg; SODIUM 711mg; CALC 226mg

10

SANDWICHES

Slow-Roasted Pulled Pork Sandwiches

Low and slow is the way to make this meat tender and falling apart; sit back and let the oven do all the work.

Pork shoulder roast, often labeled "Boston butt," is a large, inexpensive, well-marbled cut from the upper part of the shoulder. It becomes amazingly succulent after a long, slow roast. Hands-on time: 12 min. Total time: 9 hr. 48 min.

Pork:

- 2 tablespoons dark brown sugar
- 1 tablespoon smoked paprika
- 1 tablespoon chili powder
- 2 teaspoons ground cumin
- 1 teaspoon salt
- 1 teaspoon freshly ground black pepper
- ½ teaspoon dry mustard
- ½ teaspoon ground chipotle chile pepper
- 1 (5-pound) boneless pork shoulder (Boston butt), trimmed

 Cooking spray

- 2 cups water, divided
- ½ cup cider vinegar
- ⅓ cup ketchup

Sauce:

- ¾ cup cider vinegar
- ½ cup ketchup
- 3 tablespoons dark brown sugar
- 2 teaspoons smoked paprika
- 1 teaspoon chili powder

Remaining ingredients:

- 16 (1.5-ounce) whole-wheat hamburger buns
- 32 pickle chips

1. To prepare pork, combine first 8 ingredients in a small bowl. Rub sugar mixture evenly over pork. Let pork stand at room temperature 1 hour.

2. Preheat oven to 225°.

3. Place pork on the rack of a roasting pan coated with cooking spray. Pour 1 cup water in bottom of roasting pan. Place rack in pan. Bake at 225° for 1 hour.

4. Combine ½ cup vinegar and ⅓ cup ketchup in a medium bowl; brush pork with ketchup mixture (do not remove from oven). Bake an additional 3 hours, basting every hour with ketchup mixture.

5. Pour remaining 1 cup water in bottom of roasting pan. Cover pork and pan tightly with foil. Bake an additional 3 hours and 45 minutes or until a thermometer registers 190°. Remove from oven; cover and let stand 45 minutes.

6. To prepare sauce, combine ¾ cup vinegar and next 4 ingredients (through 1 teaspoon chili powder) in a small saucepan. Bring to a boil over medium-high heat, stirring occasionally with a whisk. Boil 5 minutes or until slightly thick. Shred pork with 2 forks. Spoon about 3 ounces pork on bottom half of each bun; drizzle with about 1 tablespoon sauce. Arrange 2 pickle slices over each sandwich; top each with top half of bun.

Serves 16 (serving size: 1 sandwich).

CALORIES 398; FAT 17.5g (sat 5.9g, mono 7.3g, poly 2.4g); PROTEIN 29.9g; CARB 30.2g; FIBER 3.8g; CHOL 90mg; IRON 3.1mg; SODIUM 727mg; CALC 91mg

CHOICE INGREDIENT

The Right Bread for the Sandwich: Good bread is the essential foundation here. If you're working with a saucy mix, you want sturdy bread that resists turning soggy. If fillings are subtle, avoid bread with too much flavor, such as rye.

Bagels: A real bagel is chewy, substantial, and flavorful. Look for modest-sized ones, not monsters. Plain is best for many sandwiches, but seedy varieties can add nice texture. Don't fill too high—contents squeeze out.

Baguette: The sturdy, crusty loaf counterpoints nicely with creamy or soft fillings, cheeses, or grilled vegetables.

Boule: The rounded loaf shape yields large, flat slices—ideal for open-faced sandwiches where you want more surface area.

Ciabatta: This Italian bread with a crispy-chewy exterior and moist, spongy, dense interior works nicely with salad-type fillings that turn weaker breads soggy.

Flatbreads: Beyond pita, blistered Indian naan and pliable tortilla-like wraps make for an interesting change. One large flatbread may equal two or three regular bread servings.

Focaccia: It often comes as large, flat rounds that you can cut into wedges for interesting shapes, then slice open for filling. Varieties flavored with herbs and olive oil pair well with Italian and Mediterranean ingredients.

Hamburger buns: Soft rolls like these are great for barbecue chicken, pulled pork, or classic deli meats. Toasting helps the bread hold up if the filling is moist.

Sandwich loaves: The difference between a flabby superwhite supermarket loaf and a substantial pullman loaf is staggering. Try 100% whole grains and multigrain when you want grainy flavors.

Prosciutto, Fresh Fig, and Manchego Sandwiches

The salty ham and sweet fruit sing a classic Italian aria. Along with the cheese and jam, the sweet-savory notes are irresistible.

Great ingredients make all the difference, so look for a fine loaf of artisan bread and Prosciutto di Parma, sliced wispy-thin. Use a sharp vegetable peeler to shave the Manchego, which is a tangy Spanish cheese similar to pecorino Romano (which you can substitute, though it's a bit less rich).

Hands-on time: 5 min. Total time: 5 min.

4 teaspoons Dijon mustard
8 (¾-ounce) slices Italian bread, toasted
1 cup baby arugula
2 ounces very thinly sliced prosciutto
2 ounces Manchego cheese, shaved
8 fresh figs, cut into thin slices
2 tablespoons fig jam

1. Spread mustard evenly over 4 bread slices. Divide arugula and prosciutto evenly over bread slices; top evenly with cheese and fig slices. Spread jam evenly over remaining 4 bread slices. Top each serving with 1 bread slice, jam side down.

Serves 4 (serving size: 1 sandwich).

CALORIES 295; FAT 5.3g (sat 2.6g, mono 2.1g, poly 0.6g); PROTEIN 11.5g; CARB 52.3g; FIBER 4.2g; CHOL 18mg; IRON 1.8mg; SODIUM 805mg; CALC 114mg

Tartines with Cheese, Peppers, and Chard

A tartine is a French open-faced sandwich, best served on the heartiest bread you can find—nothing wimpy.

Hands-on time: 13 min. Total time: 32 min.

1 large red bell pepper
1 tablespoon olive oil
3 cups chopped Swiss chard leaves (about 1 bunch)
¼ teaspoon salt
⅛ teaspoon crushed red pepper
¼ teaspoon black pepper, divided
2 garlic cloves, thinly sliced
4 (1.5-ounce) slices rustic 100% whole-grain bread
2 teaspoons chopped fresh chives
½ teaspoon chopped fresh thyme
2 ounces soft goat cheese

1. Preheat broiler.
2. Cut bell pepper in half lengthwise; discard seeds and membranes. Place pepper halves, skin sides up, on a foil-lined baking sheet; flatten with hand. Broil 10 minutes or until blackened. Place in a paper bag; fold to close tightly. Let stand 5 minutes. Peel and cut into strips.
3. Heat a large nonstick skillet over medium-high heat. Add oil to pan; swirl to coat. Add chard, salt, crushed red pepper, ⅛ teaspoon black pepper, and garlic to pan; sauté 1½ minutes or until chard wilts, stirring frequently.
4. Arrange bread in a single layer on a baking sheet; broil 3 minutes on each side. Combine chives, thyme, cheese, and remaining ⅛ teaspoon pepper in a small bowl; spread 2 teaspoons cheese mixture over 1 side of each bread slice. Arrange roasted pepper slices evenly over cheese; top with chard mixture.

Serves 2 (serving size: 2 tartines).

CALORIES 323; FAT 14.4g (sat 5.1g, mono 6.3g, poly 1g); PROTEIN 12.3g; CARB 43.4g; FIBER 15.2g; CHOL 13mg; IRON 4.2mg; SODIUM 718mg; CALC 330mg

Prosciutto, Fresh Fig,
and Manchego Sandwiches

Tuna Melts with Avocado

It's the avocado that takes your basic tuna melt to a new level.

See page 115 for guidance on sustainable tuna choices. Hands-on time: 11 min. Total time: 14 min.

2½ tablespoons olive oil

2 tablespoons thinly sliced shallots

1 tablespoon Dijon mustard

¼ teaspoon freshly ground black pepper

1 (6-ounce) can solid white tuna in water, drained and flaked

1½ tablespoons fresh lemon juice

1 ripe peeled avocado, chopped

1 cup cherry tomatoes, quartered

⅓ cup shredded Swiss cheese

2 (6-ounce) pieces French bread, halved lengthwise and toasted

1. Preheat broiler.
2. Combine first 5 ingredients in a medium bowl, stirring well to coat. Place juice in a small bowl. Add avocado to juice; toss gently. Add avocado mixture and tomatoes to tuna mixture; toss well to combine. Sprinkle cheese evenly over cut sides of bread; broil 3 minutes or until cheese is bubbly. Place 1 bread slice, cheese side up, on each of 4 plates; divide tuna mixture evenly among bread slices.

Serves 4.

CALORIES 455; FAT 19.7g (sat 3.9g, mono 11g, poly 2.5g); PROTEIN 20.1g; CARB 49.7g; FIBER 5.3g; CHOL 26mg; IRON 3mg; SODIUM 787mg; CALC 140mg

Spicy Chicken Shawarma

This dish is scrumptious Middle Eastern street food, streamlined for the home cook.

Traditionally made by alternately stacking strips of fat and pieces of seasoned meat on a stick, it's then roasted slowly as the spit rotates over or in front of a flame. Toppings include hummus, tahini, tomato, cucumber, onion, garlic sauce, and even French fries. Hands-on time: 20 min. Total time: 20 min.

2 tablespoons finely chopped fresh parsley

½ teaspoon salt

½ teaspoon crushed red pepper

¼ teaspoon ground ginger

¼ teaspoon ground cumin

⅛ teaspoon ground coriander

5 tablespoons plain 2% reduced-fat Greek yogurt, divided

2 tablespoons fresh lemon juice, divided

3 garlic cloves, minced and divided

1 pound skinless, boneless chicken breasts, thinly sliced

2 tablespoons extra-virgin olive oil

1 tablespoon tahini (roasted sesame seed paste)

4 (6-inch) pitas, cut in half

½ cup chopped cucumber

½ cup chopped plum tomato

¼ cup chopped red onion

1. Combine first 6 ingredients in a bowl; stir in 1 tablespoon yogurt, 1 tablespoon juice, and 2 garlic cloves. Add chicken; toss to coat.
2. Heat a large nonstick skillet over medium-high heat. Add oil to pan; swirl to coat. Add chicken mixture to pan; sauté 6 minutes or until chicken is browned and done, stirring frequently.
3. Combine remaining ¼ cup yogurt, remaining 1 tablespoon juice, remaining 1 garlic clove, and tahini, stirring well. Spread tahini mixture evenly among pita halves. Fill each pita half evenly with chicken mixture, 1 tablespoon cucumber, 1 tablespoon tomato, and 1½ teaspoons onion.

Serves 4 (serving size: 2 stuffed pita halves).

CALORIES 402; FAT 10.7g (sat 1.9g, mono 6g, poly 2g); PROTEIN 36.4g; CARB 40g; FIBER 2.1g; CHOL 67mg; IRON 4.1mg; SODIUM 541mg; CALC 93mg

Homemade Condiments

Your own ketchup, mayonnaise, and pickles are worth making and having on hand for the best sandwiches.

Heirloom Tomato Ketchup 🌿

Half the sodium of regular ketchup, all the concentrated goodness of summer tomatoes.

2	garlic cloves
½	teaspoon yellow mustard seeds
½	teaspoon celery seeds
¼	teaspoon whole allspice
¼	teaspoon black peppercorns
3	pounds heirloom tomatoes, cut into chunks (about 4½ cups)
2	cups chopped onion (1 medium)
1	cup chopped red bell pepper (1 small)
⅓	cup cider vinegar
1	tablespoon sugar
½	teaspoon salt

1. Chop garlic; let stand 10 minutes.
2. Place mustard seeds, celery seeds, allspice, and peppercorns on a double layer of cheesecloth. Gather edges of cheesecloth together; tie securely.
3. Combine cheesecloth bag, garlic, tomatoes, and next 3 ingredients (through vinegar) in a large Dutch oven; bring to a boil. Cover, reduce heat, and simmer 20 minutes. Remove cheesecloth bag; set aside.
4. Place half of tomato mixture in a blender. Remove center piece of blender lid (to allow steam to escape); secure blender lid on blender. Place a clean towel over opening in blender lid (to avoid splatters). Blend until smooth. Strain smooth mixture through a fine sieve back into pan; discard solids. Repeat procedure with remaining cooked tomato mixture. Add cheesecloth bag, sugar, and salt to pan; bring to a boil. Reduce heat, and simmer, uncovered, until reduced to 1 cup (about 45 minutes).

Serves 16 (serving size: 1 tablespoon).

CALORIES 23; FAT 0.2g (sat 0g, mono 0g, poly 0.1g); PROTEIN 0.9g; CARB 5g; FIBER 1.2g; CHOL 0mg; IRON 0.3mg; SODIUM 79mg; CALC 11mg

Bread-and-Butter Pickles 🌿

Makes lots of cucumber pickles to keep on hand for picnics or snacks. Thin-skinned pickling cucumbers are essential. You'll save on sodium, too, compared to most commercial varieties.

5½	cups thinly sliced pickling cucumbers (about 1½ pounds)
1½	tablespoons kosher salt
1	cup thinly sliced onion
1	cup sugar
1	cup white vinegar
½	cup cider vinegar
¼	cup packed brown sugar
1½	teaspoons mustard seeds
½	teaspoon celery seeds
⅛	teaspoon turmeric

1. Combine cucumbers and salt in a large bowl; cover and chill 1½ hours. Drain; rinse cucumbers under cold water. Drain; return cucumbers to bowl. Add onion to bowl.
2. Combine sugar and remaining ingredients in a medium saucepan; bring to a simmer over medium heat, stirring until sugar dissolves. Pour hot vinegar mixture over cucumber mixture; let stand at room temperature 1 hour. Cover and refrigerate 24 hours. Store in an airtight container in refrigerator up to 2 weeks.

Serves 16 (serving size: about ¼ cup drained pickles).

CALORIES 18; FAT 0.1g (sat 0g, mono 0g, poly 0g); PROTEIN 0.4g; CARB 4.4g; FIBER 0.5g; CHOL 0mg; IRON 0.1mg; SODIUM 168mg; CALC 8mg

Homemade Mayonnaise 🌿

Nothing beats the texture and flavor of real, homemade mayo. So as not to worry about salmonella, use a pasteurized egg. Refrigerate any leftover mayonnaise; it will be good for four to five days. Adding minced garlic and using olive oil will yield a superb aioli.

1	tablespoon fresh lemon juice
½	teaspoon Dijon mustard
⅛	teaspoon salt
1	large pasteurized egg
¾	cup canola oil

1. Place first 4 ingredients in a blender; process until smooth. With blender on, gradually pour in oil; process until smooth and completely blended.

Serves 12 (serving size: 1 tablespoon).

CALORIES 130; FAT 14.3g (sat 1.1g, mono 9g, poly 4g); PROTEIN 0.5g; CARB 0.2g; FIBER 0g; CHOL 15mg; IRON 0.1mg; SODIUM 32mg; CALC 2mg

10

SANDWICHES

Curry Chicken Wraps with Nectarine Chutney

Here's exactly what to do with the basic grilled-chicken wrap: Add a yogurt-curry marinade, and top with chutney, ginger, and fresh mint.

Indian spices pair well with tangy nectarines; you can also use peaches. Hands-on time: 30 min. Total time: 2 hr. 20 min.

1 cup plain fat-free yogurt

3 tablespoons curry powder

1 tablespoon fresh lime juice

4 (6-ounce) skinless, boneless chicken breast halves

10 cilantro sprigs

6 garlic cloves, crushed

½ teaspoon salt

Cooking spray

Nectarine Chutney

6 (1.9-ounce) harvest wheat flatbreads

24 (⅛-inch-thick) slices cucumber

1½ cups loosely packed baby arugula

1 cup vertically sliced red onion

1. Combine yogurt, curry powder, and lime juice in a large heavy-duty zip-top plastic bag; squeeze bag to mix. Cut 3 shallow slits in each chicken breast. Add chicken, cilantro sprigs, and garlic to bag, squeezing to coat chicken. Seal and marinate in refrigerator 2 hours, turning occasionally.

2. Preheat grill to medium-high heat.

3. Remove chicken from bag; discard marinade. Sprinkle chicken with salt; place chicken on grill rack coated with cooking spray. Cover and grill 4 minutes on each side or until chicken is done. Let stand 5 minutes. Cut chicken across grain into thin slices.

4. Place ⅓ cup Nectarine Chutney in center of each flatbread. Divide chicken evenly among flatbreads. Top each flatbread with 4 cucumber slices, ¼ cup arugula, and about 2½ tablespoons red onion; roll up. Cut each wrap in half diagonally.

Serves 6 (serving size: 1 wrap).

(Totals include Nectarine Chutney)
CALORIES 332; FAT 4.3g (sat 0.4g, mono 0.4g, poly 0.4g); PROTEIN 34.9g; CARB 42.5g; FIBER 8.3g; CHOL 66mg; IRON 3.1mg; SODIUM 712mg; CALC 66mg

10

SANDWICHES

NECTARINE CHUTNEY

2 cups chopped nectarines

¾ cup thinly sliced green onions

⅓ cup mango chutney

2 tablespoons chopped fresh cilantro

2 tablespoons chopped fresh mint

2 tablespoons fresh lime juice

1 tablespoon grated peeled fresh ginger

¼ teaspoon ground red pepper

1. Combine all ingredients in a bowl; toss gently.

Serves 6 (serving size: ⅓ cup).

CALORIES 64; FAT 0.2g (sat 0g, mono 0.1g, poly 0.1g); PROTEIN 0.6g; CARB 14.8g; FIBER 1.4g; CHOL 0mg; IRON 0.4mg; SODIUM 121mg; CALC 15mg

Open-Faced Chicken Club Sandwiches
Canola mayonnaise and avocado move a sandwich high in saturated fat to the lighter side.

Going open-faced lets you pile on the fillings without pushing the calories and sodium beyond happy lunch levels. Hands-on time: 23 min. Total time: 34 min.

1 tablespoon olive oil

4 (6-ounce) skinless, boneless chicken breast halves

¼ teaspoon kosher salt, divided

¼ teaspoon freshly ground black pepper

3 tablespoons canola mayonnaise

2 teaspoons fresh lemon juice

1 ripe peeled avocado, coarsely mashed

4 (1-ounce) slices sourdough bread, toasted

4 green leaf lettuce leaves

2 plum tomatoes, each cut into 6 slices

4 center-cut bacon slices, cooked and drained

1. Heat a large skillet over medium-high heat. Add oil to pan; swirl to coat. Sprinkle chicken evenly with ⅛ teaspoon salt and pepper. Add chicken to pan; cook 6 minutes on each side or until done. Remove from pan; let stand 5 minutes. Slice.

2. Combine remaining ⅛ teaspoon salt, mayonnaise, juice, and avocado in a small bowl; stir until well blended. Spread about 3 tablespoons avocado mixture over each bread slice. Top each sandwich with 1 lettuce leaf, 1 chicken breast half, 3 tomato slices, and 1 bacon slice.

Serves 4 (serving size: 1 sandwich).

CALORIES 400; FAT 18g (sat 3.3g, mono 9.2g, poly 3.4g); PROTEIN 36g; CARB 22.5g; FIBER 4.8g; CHOL 85mg; IRON 2.5mg; SODIUM 597mg; CALC 45mg

Herbed Chicken Salad Sandwiches
Basic chicken salad is boosted with a hint of sweet onion, tarragon, lemon, and tangy Greek yogurt.

Greens surround the chicken salad, giving it a delicate crunch and preventing the bread from getting soggy. Making the salad a day or so ahead allows the flavors to marry. For a chicken salad panini, spoon inside a split wedge of focaccia, and toast in a grill pan. Hands-on time: 14 min. Total time: 14 min.

1 tablespoon finely chopped fresh tarragon

3 tablespoons canola mayonnaise

3 tablespoons plain 2% reduced-fat Greek yogurt

1 tablespoon fresh lemon juice

⅛ teaspoon kosher salt

2 cups chopped skinless, boneless rotisserie chicken breast

¼ cup minced sweet onion

8 (1½-ounce) slices rye bread

4 red leaf lettuce leaves

1 cup microgreens or arugula

1. Combine first 5 ingredients in a large bowl. Stir in chicken and onion. Top each of 4 bread slices with 1 lettuce leaf, about ½ cup chicken salad, ¼ cup microgreens, and 1 bread slice.

Serves 4 (serving size: 1 sandwich).

CALORIES 382; FAT 9g (sat 1.4g, mono 3.9g, poly 2.4g); PROTEIN 30.2g; CARB 42.9g; FIBER 5.1g; CHOL 60mg; IRON 3.2mg; SODIUM 745mg; CALC 89mg

Herbed Chicken Salad
Sandwiches

Pan-Seared Shrimp Po' Boys

Yes, deep-fried shrimp are a boardwalk treat. But sweet, fresh shrimp seared in a hot pan are delicious, and the homemade tartar sauce nails it.

The same recipe works for a fish sandwich, too. Hands-on time: 16 min. Total time: 20 min.

1 pound peeled and deveined large shrimp

1½ teaspoons salt-free Cajun seasoning

2 teaspoons olive oil

½ cup shredded romaine lettuce

8 (⅛-inch-thick) slices tomato

4 (⅛-inch-thick) slices red onion

4 (2½-ounce) French bread baguette portions, cut in half horizontally

Tartar Sauce

1. Heat a large nonstick skillet over medium-high heat. Combine shrimp and Cajun seasoning in a bowl; toss well. Add oil to pan; swirl to coat. Add shrimp to pan; cook 2 minutes on each side or until done.

2. Arrange 2 tablespoons lettuce, 2 tomato slices, 1 onion slice, and one-fourth of shrimp on bottom half of each baguette portion. Spread top half of each baguette portion with about 1 tablespoon Tartar Sauce; place on top of sandwich.

Serves 4 (serving size: 1 sandwich).

(Totals include Tartar Sauce)
CALORIES 429; FAT 15.6g (sat 1.4g, mono 9.1g, poly 4.7g); PROTEIN 26.9g; CARB 44.5g; FIBER 2.4g; CHOL 173mg; IRON 5.5mg; SODIUM 809mg; CALC 73mg

TARTAR SAUCE

¼ cup canola mayonnaise

1½ tablespoons sweet pickle relish

2 teaspoons chopped shallots

¾ teaspoon capers, chopped

⅛ teaspoon hot pepper sauce

1. Combine all ingredients in a small bowl.

Serves 4 (serving size: about 1 tablespoon).

CALORIES 109; FAT 11g (sat 0.5g, mono 7g, poly 3.5g); PROTEIN 0.1g; CARB 2.3g; FIBER 0.1g; CHOL 5mg; IRON 0.1mg; SODIUM 153mg; CALC 1mg

Picnic-Perfect Lobster Rolls

A New England favorite is made even better with the addition of tarragon, green onions, mustard, and lemon.

This sandwich comes together in a snap if you purchase lobster tails and have them steamed at the fish counter. You'll need to buy five (6-ounce) lobster tails to get the amount needed for this recipe; you'll get about 1½ cups meat. Hands-on time: 12 min. Total time: 1 hr. 12 min.

⅓ cup finely chopped celery

2 tablespoons chopped green onions

1 tablespoon finely chopped fresh tarragon

3 tablespoons canola mayonnaise

½ teaspoon grated lemon rind

1½ tablespoons fresh lemon juice

½ teaspoon Dijon mustard

¼ teaspoon kosher salt

¼ teaspoon freshly ground black pepper

⅛ teaspoon ground red pepper

¾ pound lobster meat, steamed and chopped

4 (1½-ounce) New England–style hot dog buns, toasted

1. Combine first 11 ingredients in a large bowl; cover and chill at least 1 hour. Divide lobster mixture evenly among buns.

Serves 4 (serving size: 1 sandwich).

CALORIES 284; FAT 10.3g (sat 0.8g, mono 4.9g, poly 2.7g); PROTEIN 21.7g; CARB 22.4g; FIBER 0.3g; CHOL 65mg; IRON 1.5mg; SODIUM 731mg; CALC 61mg

Grilled Zucchini Caprese Sandwiches

This one you can stack tall. It's a vegetable-packed ode to garden and farm bounty.

You can also try it with grilled red or green tomato slices, bell pepper, or yellow squash. Hands-on time: 15 min. Total time: 15 min.

1	zucchini, trimmed and cut lengthwise into 6 slices
4	teaspoons extra-virgin olive oil, divided
1	garlic clove, minced
1½	teaspoons balsamic vinegar
⅛	teaspoon kosher salt
⅛	teaspoon black pepper
4	(2-ounce) ciabatta rolls, split and toasted
8	large fresh basil leaves
1	tomato, thinly sliced
6	ounces fresh mozzarella cheese, thinly sliced

1. Heat a large grill pan over medium-high heat. Place zucchini in a shallow dish. Add 2 teaspoons oil and garlic; toss to coat. Arrange zucchini in grill pan; cook 2 minutes on each side or until grill marks appear. Cut each zucchini piece in half crosswise. Return zucchini to shallow dish. Drizzle with vinegar. Sprinkle with salt and black pepper.

2. Brush bottom halves of rolls with remaining 2 teaspoons oil. Top evenly with zucchini, basil, tomato, and mozzarella.

3. Brush cut side of roll tops with remaining liquid from shallow dish, and place on sandwiches. Heat sandwiches in pan until warm.

Serves 4 (serving size: 1 sandwich).

CALORIES 343; FAT 16.8g (sat 6.6g, mono 8g, poly 1.3g); PROTEIN 15.4g; CARB 35.3g; FIBER 2g; CHOL 34mg; IRON 2.3mg; SODIUM 722mg; CALC 229mg

Tex-Mex Falafel with Avocado Spread ✿

A fun riff on the falafel concept, this speedy sandwich stuffs spiced pinto bean patties into pitas with a guacamole-like spread.

The beauty of this twist on the classic Middle Eastern sandwich is its simplicity and, of course, flavor. Baked tortilla chips are crushed to bind the patties. Serve the remaining chips with salsa for a side.
Hands-on time: 10 min. Total time: 20 min.

Patties:

- 1 (15-ounce) can pinto beans, rinsed and drained
- ½ cup (2 ounces) shredded Monterey Jack cheese
- ¼ cup finely crushed baked tortilla chips (about ¾ ounce)
- 2 tablespoons finely chopped green onions
- 1 tablespoon finely chopped cilantro
- ⅛ teaspoon ground cumin
- 1 large egg white
- 1½ teaspoons canola oil

Spread:

- ¼ cup mashed peeled avocado
- 2 tablespoons finely chopped tomato
- 1 tablespoon finely chopped red onion
- 2 tablespoons fat-free sour cream
- 1 teaspoon fresh lime juice
- ⅛ teaspoon salt

Remaining ingredients:

- 2 (6-inch) pitas, cut in half
- 4 (⅛-inch-thick) slices red onion, separated into rings
- ¼ cup microgreens

1. To prepare patties, place pinto beans in a medium bowl; partially mash with a fork. Add cheese and next 5 ingredients (through egg white); stir until well combined. Shape bean mixture into 4 (½-inch-thick) oval patties.
2. Heat a large nonstick skillet over medium-high heat. Add oil to pan; swirl to coat. Add patties to pan; cook 3 minutes on each side or until patties are browned and thoroughly heated.

3. To prepare spread, combine avocado and next 5 ingredients (through salt), stirring well. Place 1 patty in each pita half. Spread about 2 tablespoons avocado spread over each patty in each pita half; top evenly with onion and greens.

Serves 4 (serving size: 1 stuffed pita half).

CALORIES 281; FAT 9.5g (sat 3.4g, mono 3.9g, poly 1.5g); PROTEIN 12.2g; CARB 37.4g; FIBER 5.9g; CHOL 13mg; IRON 2.4mg; SODIUM 625mg; CALC 188mg

Beer Pairing
Tex-Mex–inspired food like this falafel bursts with flavors, colors, and textures, and a complicated brew is easily overwhelmed. Pair this meal with an ice-cold Mexican lager—a simple, light, crisp beer.

10

SANDWICHES

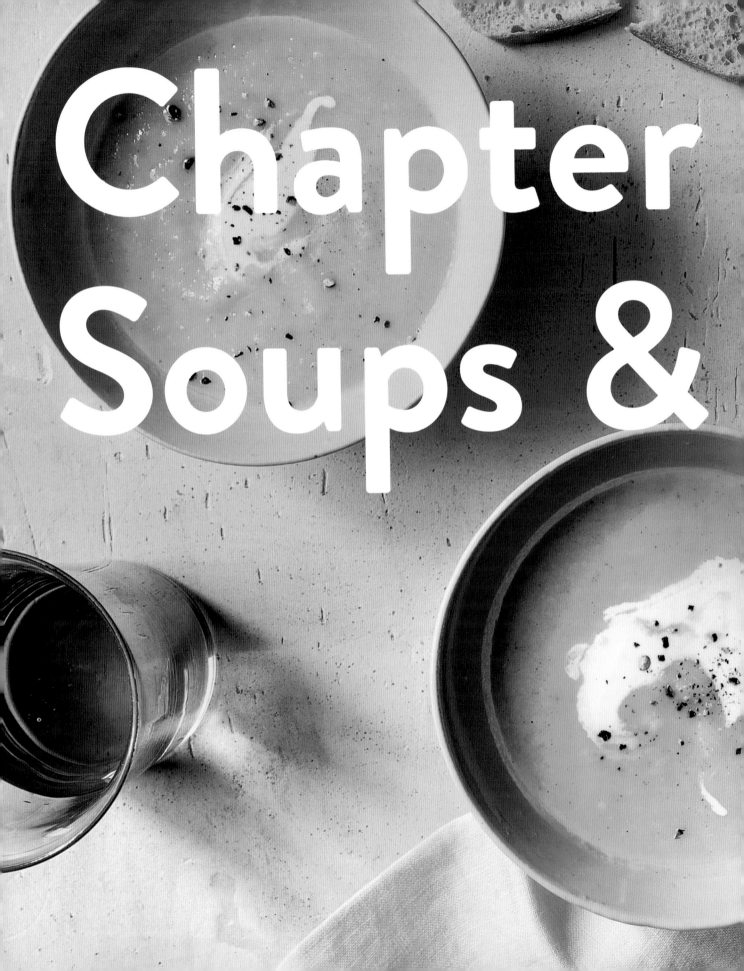

Chapter
Soups &

11:
Stews

Apple-Parsnip Soup, page 376

We love soups and stews not only for their hearty, warming qualities but also because they're much easier than many cooks think. Although we enjoy carefully made stocks as a base when we have time, for these recipes, we chose to use good lower-sodium store-bought broths and then deploy herbs, spices, and lots of grains, beans, vegetables, or seafood. This way, soups become a weeknight option and a good way to get more veggies and grains. We've included a few cold summer soups, too, highlighting the flavors of corn and tomatoes when they are just-picked and sweet.

Chilled Fresh Corn Soup with King Crab and Chives
This is like an ultralight cream soup: sweet, with a kiss of salt.

Crab shells are simmered with the freshest summer corn for clear, clean flavors. The shells come out, and the rest is pureed into a silky broth—an extremely bright-flavored, low-fat starter.
Hands-on time: 25 min. Total time: 2 hr. 45 min.

1	pound frozen cooked king crab legs (about 2), thawed
6	cups fresh corn kernels (about 11 ears)
4½	cups water
⅛	teaspoon ground red pepper
1	cup 2% reduced-fat milk
¼	cup chopped fresh chives
½	teaspoon freshly ground black pepper

1. Cut shell off crab with kitchen shears; reserve shells. Cut crabmeat into ½-inch pieces; cover and chill. Combine shells, corn, 4½ cups water, and red pepper in a large saucepan; bring to a boil over medium-high heat. Reduce heat; simmer 20 minutes or until corn is very tender. Discard shells.
2. Place half of corn mixture in blender. Remove center piece of blender lid (to allow steam to escape); secure blender lid on blender. Place a clean towel over opening in blender lid (to avoid splatters). Process until smooth. Press pureed corn mixture through a fine sieve over a bowl, reserving liquid; discard solids. Repeat procedure with remaining corn mixture. Stir in milk, chives, and

black pepper. Chill 2 hours or until cold. Top with reserved crabmeat.

Serves 8 (serving size: about ⅔ cup soup and about ¼ cup crabmeat).

CALORIES 115; FAT 2g (sat 0.6g, mono 0.5g, poly 0.6g); PROTEIN 10g; CARB 16.2g; FIBER 2.2g; CHOL 20mg; IRON 0.7mg; SODIUM 383mg; CALC 59mg

Wine Pairing
The fresh flavors of the corn and crab can be drawn out further with a slightly sweet wine. Try an off-dry sparkling wine from California, which is light like the soup and refreshing on the palate.

Melon Gazpacho with Frizzled Prosciutto

Mark Bittman reinvents the classic melon and prosciutto pairing as a refreshing soup.

Sherry vinegar, with rich notes of the oxidized wine from which it's made, adds tartness. Pair with prosecco or other sparkling wine for a lovely, light summer dinner. Serve half-size portions for a starter course.
Hands-on time: 27 min. Total time: 27 min.

5	cups cubed peeled cantaloupe (about 3½ pounds)
4	cups chopped ripe peaches (about 4 large)
½	cup water
2	tablespoons minced shallots
2	tablespoons fresh lemon juice
1	tablespoon sherry vinegar
⅜	teaspoon kosher salt
2	teaspoons olive oil
4	ounces thinly sliced prosciutto, cut into ribbons
4	teaspoons chopped fresh mint
¼	teaspoon freshly ground black pepper

1. Place first 7 ingredients in a blender; process until smooth (process in batches, if necessary). Place in freezer to chill while prosciutto cooks.

2. Heat a large skillet over medium heat. Add oil to pan; swirl to coat. Add prosciutto to pan; cook 10 minutes or until crisp, stirring occasionally. Drain on paper towels.

3. Spoon soup into bowls; top with prosciutto, mint, and pepper.

Serves 4 (serving size: about 1¾ cups soup, about 1 ounce prosciutto, 1 teaspoon mint, and a dash of pepper).

CALORIES 206; FAT 5.6g (sat 1.3g, mono 3g, poly 0.9g); PROTEIN 9.7g; CARB 32.7g; FIBER 4g; CHOL 16.7mg; IRON 1.3mg; SODIUM 638mg; CALC 34mg

Garden Minestrone
Bursting with the goodness of seven vegetables.

Make it vegetarian with vegetable or mushroom broth. Hands-on time: 22 min. Total time: 58 min.

2 teaspoons olive oil

1 cup chopped onion

2 teaspoons chopped fresh oregano

4 garlic cloves, minced

3 cups chopped yellow squash

3 cups chopped zucchini

1 cup chopped carrot

1 cup fresh corn kernels (about 2 ears)

4 cups chopped tomato, divided

3 (14-ounce) cans fat-free, lower-sodium chicken broth, divided

½ cup uncooked ditalini pasta (very short tube-shaped macaroni)

1 (15.5-ounce) can organic Great Northern beans, rinsed and drained

1 (6-ounce) package fresh baby spinach

¾ teaspoon salt

½ teaspoon freshly ground black pepper

1 cup (4 ounces) grated Asiago cheese

Coarsely ground black pepper (optional)

1. Heat a Dutch oven over medium-high heat. Add oil to pan; swirl to coat. Add onion to pan; sauté 3 minutes or until softened, stirring frequently. Add oregano and garlic; sauté 1 minute, stirring frequently. Stir in squash, zucchini, carrot, and corn; sauté 5 minutes or until vegetables are tender, stirring occasionally. Remove from heat.
2. Place 3 cups tomato and 1 can broth in a blender; process until smooth. Add tomato mixture to pan; return pan to heat. Stir in remaining 1 cup tomato and remaining 2 cans broth; bring mixture to a boil. Reduce heat; simmer 20 minutes.
3. Add pasta and beans to pan; cook 10 minutes or until pasta is tender, stirring occasionally. Remove from heat. Stir in spinach, salt, and ½ teaspoon pepper. Ladle soup into bowls; top with cheese. Garnish with coarsely ground black pepper, if desired.

Serves 8 (serving size: 1½ cups soup and 2 tablespoons cheese).

CALORIES 217; FAT 6.1g (sat 2.7g, mono 2g, poly 0.6g); PROTEIN 12.6g; CARB 30.5g; FIBER 7.9g; CHOL 12mg; IRON 2.7mg; SODIUM 664mg; CALC 206mg

Caramelized Onion and Shiitake Soup with Gruyère-Gorgonzola Toasts

Here's a buttery, rich onion soup, made even more complex by a mushroom broth. No need for old-fashioned cheese-dome overkill: A bit of Gorgonzola on the toasts gives a nice, pungent counterpoint.

For a main course option, pair with a salad that's lightly dressed so it doesn't overpower the soup.
Hands-on time: 23 min. Total time: 2 hr. 14 min.

Soup:
- 1 tablespoon olive oil
- 8 cups vertically sliced yellow onion (about 2 pounds)
- 5 cups sliced shiitake mushroom caps (about 10 ounces whole mushrooms)
- 4 garlic cloves, minced
- 2 thyme sprigs
- ½ cup dry white wine
- 1 (14-ounce) can fat-free, lower-sodium chicken broth
- 1 (14-ounce) can fat-free, lower-sodium beef broth
- ½ teaspoon freshly ground black pepper
- ¼ teaspoon salt

Toasts:
- 12 (½-inch-thick) slices French bread baguette (about 6 ounces), toasted
- ¼ cup (1 ounce) grated Gruyère cheese
- ¼ cup (1 ounce) crumbled Gorgonzola cheese
- ½ teaspoon finely chopped fresh thyme

1. To prepare soup, heat a large Dutch oven over medium-high heat. Add oil to pan; swirl to coat. Add onion to pan; sauté 15 minutes or until almost tender, stirring frequently. Reduce heat to medium-low; cook until deep golden brown (about 40 minutes), stirring occasionally.

2. Increase heat to medium. Add mushrooms to pan; cook 10 minutes or until mushrooms are tender, stirring frequently. Stir in garlic and thyme sprigs; cook 2 minutes, stirring frequently. Increase heat to medium-high. Add wine to pan; cook 2 minutes or until most of liquid evaporates. Add broths to pan; bring to a simmer. Reduce heat; simmer 45 minutes. Stir in pepper and salt. Discard thyme sprigs.

3. To prepare toasts, preheat broiler.

4. Arrange bread in a single layer on a baking sheet. Top each bread slice with 1 teaspoon Gruyère and 1 teaspoon Gorgonzola. Broil 2 minutes or until cheese melts. Sprinkle chopped thyme over cheese. Ladle about 1 cup soup into each of 6 bowls; top each serving with 2 toasts.

Serves 6.

CALORIES 208; FAT 5.4g (sat 2.3g, mono 2.2g, poly 0.4g); PROTEIN 8.9g; CARB 33.4g; FIBER 3.9g; CHOL 9mg; IRON 2.1mg; SODIUM 596mg; CALC 115mg

TECHNIQUE

Perfect Caramelized Onions: If you want true, sweet, melt-in-your-mouth caramelized onions for this soup or to top your burger or pizza, you need to cook them over medium-low to low heat for a long time, maybe up to an hour. We often use a high heat initially to soften the onions and allow them to release some liquid, but if you keep the heat cranked up to try to speed up the process, you'll get a different product—onions that may be crisp-tender and nicely browned but lack that characteristic translucence and meltingly tender quality you want. Bottom line: Know that caramelized onions take time, and plan to cook them when you can give them the time they need. The good news is that onions are not like garlic, and they will not burn in a heartbeat and ruin a dish. Just stir occasionally over low heat.

Vietnamese Beef-Noodle Soup with Asian Greens

Pho seduces with its fragrant broth, which is ladled over slippery rice noodles and tender steak.

The key is the mix of aromatic spices—cloves, cardamom, star anise. Traditional accompaniments of bean sprouts and chiles offer the soup's signature fresh crunch. Hands-on time: 17 min. Total time: 35 min.

1   (8-ounce) sirloin steak

4   ounces uncooked wide rice sticks (rice-flour noodles)

1½   cups thinly sliced yellow onion

3   whole cloves

2   cardamom pods

2   garlic cloves, halved

1   (3-inch) piece peeled fresh ginger, thinly sliced

1   star anise

3½   cups water

2½   cups fat-free, lower-sodium beef broth

1   tablespoon lower-sodium soy sauce

1   teaspoon brown sugar

2   teaspoons fish sauce

4   cups baby bok choy leaves

1   cup snow peas, trimmed

1   small fresh Thai chile, thinly sliced into rings

1   cup fresh bean sprouts

¼   cup fresh basil leaves

¼   cup fresh mint leaves

4   lime wedges

1. Freeze beef 10 minutes; cut across grain into ⅛-inch-thick slices.

2. Cook noodles according to package directions. Drain and rinse with cold water; drain.

3. Place onion and next 5 ingredients (through star anise) in a large saucepan; cook over medium-high heat 5 minutes, stirring frequently. Add 3½ cups water and broth; bring to a boil. Strain broth mixture though a fine sieve over a bowl; discard solids.

Return broth to pan. Add soy sauce, sugar, and fish sauce to pan; bring to a boil. Add bok choy and snow peas; simmer 4 minutes or until peas are crisp-tender and bok choy wilts.

4. Arrange ½ cup noodles in each of 4 large bowls. Divide raw beef and chile slices evenly among bowls. Ladle about 1⅔ cups hot soup over each serving (broth will cook beef). Top each serving with ¼ cup bean sprouts, 1 tablespoon basil, and 1 tablespoon mint. Serve with lime wedges.

Serves 4.

CALORIES 261; FAT 4.3g (sat 1.6g, mono 1.5g, poly 0.4g); PROTEIN 17.2g; CARB 37.7g; FIBER 3.8g; CHOL 28mg; IRON 3.9mg; SODIUM 722mg; CALC 131mg

Tortilla Meatball Soup
The flavors and crunch of a crispy beef taco, soup-ified, with corn and peppers.

When it's not fresh corn season, you can substitute 2 cups frozen corn kernels. Hands-on time: 43 min. Total time: 1 hr. 30 min.

2 jalapeño peppers

1 red bell pepper

2 ears corn on the cob

4 (6-inch) corn tortillas, cut into ½-inch-thick strips

Cooking spray

¾ teaspoon kosher salt, divided

6 garlic cloves, minced and divided

⅓ cup panko (Japanese breadcrumbs)

1 pound ground sirloin

1 large egg, lightly beaten

1 chipotle chile, canned in adobo sauce, minced

1 tablespoon olive oil

2 cups chopped onion

2 cups (¾-inch) cubed red potato

1 cup (½-inch-thick) slices carrot

3 cups fat-free, lower-sodium chicken broth

2 cups water

½ cup (2 ounces) shredded Monterey Jack cheese

¼ cup (1 ounce) shredded extra-sharp cheddar cheese

½ cup chopped fresh cilantro

1. Preheat broiler.

2. Cut jalapeños and bell pepper in half lengthwise; discard seeds and membranes. Place pepper halves, skin sides up, on a foil-lined baking sheet. Arrange corn on baking sheet with peppers. Broil 4 to 6 minutes or until blackened, turning corn once. Place peppers in a paper bag; fold to close tightly. Let stand 15 minutes; peel. Mince jalapeños; coarsely chop bell pepper. Cut corn kernels from cobs. Set aside.

3. Place tortilla strips in a single layer on a baking sheet; lightly coat with cooking spray. Broil 3 minutes or until golden brown, turning after 2 minutes. Set aside.

4. Combine ¼ teaspoon salt, 1 garlic clove, panko, and next 3 ingredients (through chipotle chile) in a large bowl; gently mix just until combined. Shape meat mixture into 24 meatballs with moist hands (about 2 tablespoons each).

5. Heat a Dutch oven over medium-high heat. Add oil to pan; swirl to coat. Add meatballs to pan; sauté 8 minutes, turning to brown on all sides. Remove from pan. Add onion, potato, and carrot to pan; sauté 5 minutes, stirring occasionally.

Add remaining 5 garlic cloves; cook 1 minute, stirring constantly. Add peppers, broth, and 2 cups water; bring to a boil. Reduce heat; simmer 20 minutes or until vegetables are almost tender, stirring occasionally. Return meatballs to pan. Add remaining ½ teaspoon salt and corn; return to a simmer. Cook 10 minutes or until meatballs are done. Ladle 1½ cups soup into each of 6 bowls; top each serving with 4 teaspoons Monterey Jack cheese, 2 teaspoons cheddar cheese, and 4 teaspoons cilantro. Top evenly with tortilla strips.

Serves 6.

CALORIES 380; FAT 16.3g (sat 6.5g, mono 6.1g, poly 1g); PROTEIN 25g; CARB 33.1g; FIBER 4.7g; CHOL 98mg; IRON 3mg; SODIUM 631mg; CALC 159mg

Beef-Barley Soup

Couldn't be simpler: a beefy, whole-grain soup that makes a one-dish meal.

If chuck roast is on sale, purchase a large one, and freeze the rest for later. If not, ask your butcher to cut off only the amount you need. Hands-on time: 10 min. Total time: 1 hr. 51 min.

Cooking spray

¾ pound boneless chuck roast, trimmed and cut into ½-inch pieces

1½ cups thinly sliced carrot

1½ cups thinly sliced celery

⅔ cup chopped onion

1 (8-ounce) package presliced mushrooms

4 cups fat-free, lower-sodium beef broth

⅔ cup uncooked whole-grain barley kernels

1 bay leaf

½ teaspoon freshly ground black pepper

¼ teaspoon salt

1. Heat a Dutch oven over medium-high heat. Coat pan with cooking spray. Add beef to pan; cook 4 minutes or until browned, stirring frequently. Remove beef from pan. Add carrot, celery, onion, and mushrooms to pan; cook 6 minutes or until liquid almost evaporates. Add beef, beef broth, barley, and bay leaf; bring to a simmer.

2. Cover, reduce heat, and simmer 1½ hours or until beef and barley are tender, stirring occasionally. Stir in pepper and salt. Discard bay leaf.

Serves 4 (serving size: about 2 cups).

CALORIES 308; FAT 9g (sat 2.9g, mono 3.3g, poly 0.9g); PROTEIN 24.7g; CARB 32.6g; FIBER 8.2g; CHOL 52mg; IRON 3.7mg; SODIUM 710mg; CALC 55mg

NUTRITION MADE EASY

Barley: Pearled barley boasts almost 8 grams of fiber in ¼ cup of uncooked, but it's not technically a whole grain. An intact bran (not fiber) is what determines if a grain falls into the whole-grain category. Hulled barley or whole-grain barley kernels have only the tough outer hull removed and are the least processed form of barley. Pearl barley is further polished to remove the bran leaving the inside "pearl." But it's a good choice, saving a significant amount of time and containing almost the same amount of fiber as whole-grain barley.

Quick Chicken Noodle Soup

An almost-homemade chicken noodle soup made faster with store-bought stock.

The broth mixture is heated in the microwave to jump-start the cooking. Meanwhile, sauté the aromatic ingredients in your soup pot to get this dish under way. Though we like the shape of strozzapreti, you can also make this soup with wide egg noodles, rotini, fusilli, or even orzo. Hands-on time: 20 min. Total time: 20 min.

2 cups water

1 (32-ounce) carton fat-free, lower-sodium chicken broth

1 tablespoon olive oil

½ cup chopped onion

½ cup chopped celery

½ teaspoon salt

½ teaspoon freshly ground black pepper

1 medium carrot, chopped

6 ounces strozzapreti pasta

2½ cups shredded skinless, boneless rotisserie chicken breast

2 tablespoons chopped fresh flat-leaf parsley

1. Combine 2 cups water and chicken broth in a microwave-safe dish; microwave at HIGH 5 minutes. **2.** Heat a large saucepan over medium-high heat. Add oil to pan; swirl to coat. Add onion, celery, salt, pepper, and carrot to pan; sauté 3 minutes or until almost tender, stirring frequently. Add hot broth mixture and pasta; bring to a boil. Cook 7 minutes or until pasta is almost al dente. Stir in chicken; cook 1 minute or until thoroughly heated. Stir in parsley.

Serves 6 (serving size: about 1 cup).

CALORIES 237; FAT 4.8g (sat 1g, mono 2.4g, poly 0.9g); PROTEIN 22.9g; CARB 23.9g; FIBER 1.7g; CHOL 50mg; IRON 1.8mg; SODIUM 589mg; CALC 28mg

Spicy Thai Coconut Chicken Soup

A lighter version of the soup served in Thai restaurants around the world. Light coconut milk smooths the edges of tart lime, salty fish sauce, and fiery chile paste.

Less fat, less salt than the original, and it's fast—perfect for a quick weeknight change-up when paired with something as simple as steamed rice and sautéed sugar snap peas.
Hands-on time: 25 min. Total time: 32 min.

2 teaspoons canola oil

1 cup sliced mushrooms

½ cup chopped red bell pepper

4 teaspoons minced peeled fresh ginger

4 garlic cloves, minced

1 (3-inch) stalk lemongrass, halved lengthwise

2 teaspoons sambal oelek (ground fresh chile paste)

3 cups fat-free, lower-sodium chicken broth

1¼ cups light coconut milk

4 teaspoons fish sauce

1 tablespoon sugar

2 cups shredded cooked chicken breast (about 8 ounces)

½ cup diagonally sliced green onions

3 tablespoons chopped fresh cilantro

2 tablespoons fresh lime juice

1. Heat a Dutch oven over medium heat. Add oil to pan; swirl to coat. Add mushrooms and next 4 ingredients (through lemongrass) to pan; cook 3 minutes, stirring occasionally. Add chile paste, and cook 1 minute. Add broth, milk, fish sauce, and sugar; bring to a simmer. Reduce heat to low; simmer 10 minutes. Add chicken to pan; cook 1 minute or until thoroughly heated. Discard lemongrass. Stir in onions, cilantro, and juice.

Serves 4 (serving size: about 1⅓ cups).

CALORIES 224; FAT 9g (sat 4.5g, mono 2.4g, poly 1.3g); PROTEIN 22.7g; CARB 15g; FIBER 1.1g; CHOL 58mg; IRON 1.1mg; SODIUM 463mg; CALC 35mg

Wine Pairing
A light, off-dry Washington riesling has the sweetness to tame the chile and a backbone of acidity to go head to head with the lime juice.

11

SOUPS & STEWS

CHOICE INGREDIENT

Store-bought Lower-Sodium Broths and Stocks: Broths and stocks seem simple, but ingredient labels reveal lots of sodium and frequent use of additives and flavorings. With various free-range, organic, and all-natural claims, it's tough to know which is best for your soup, stew, or risotto. We tasted a variety—some were too watery, and in others, one vegetable or another overpowered the base flavor. None of the beef broths thrilled us—we'll keep tasting—but two of our favorite chicken broths are Swanson's fat-free, lower-sodium chicken broth and Emeril's all-natural chicken stock. The same brands also provided our favorite vegetable broth: Swanson's organic vegetable broth and Emeril's all-natural vegetable stock.

Speedy Chicken Posole

The joy of posole is all about the hominy—dense, chewy, hearty, nutty essence of corn.

This fast version is lighter than the traditional, which is made with pork. Lime juice and tomatillos offer a tangy lift. Look for canned tomatillos in the Mexican foods section of your supermarket.

Hands-on time: 12 min. Total time: 20 min.

1	tablespoon olive oil
1	teaspoon dried oregano
¾	teaspoon ground cumin
½	teaspoon chili powder
2	garlic cloves, minced
1	(8-ounce) package prechopped onion and celery mix
4	canned tomatillos, drained and coarsely chopped
2	(14-ounce) cans fat-free, lower-sodium chicken broth
1	(15-ounce) can white hominy, rinsed and drained
2	cups chopped skinless, boneless rotisserie chicken breast
1	tablespoon fresh lime juice
¼	teaspoon salt
¼	teaspoon black pepper
4	radishes, thinly sliced
½	ripe peeled avocado, diced

Cilantro leaves (optional)

1. Heat a large saucepan over medium-high heat. Add oil to pan; swirl to coat. Add oregano and next 4 ingredients (through onion and celery mix) to pan; sauté 2 minutes. Stir in tomatillos; cook 1 minute. Add broth and hominy; cover. Bring to a boil. Uncover and cook 8 minutes. Stir in chicken; cook 1 minute or until heated. Remove from heat; stir in lime juice, salt, and pepper. Divide soup evenly among 4 bowls. Top with radishes and avocado. Garnish with cilantro, if desired.

Serves 4 (serving size: 1½ cups soup, 2 tablespoons avocado, and 1 radish).

CALORIES 290; FAT 11.2g (sat 2.2g, mono 5.9g, poly 2g); PROTEIN 28.2g; CARB 20.2g; FIBER 4.5g; CHOL 60mg; IRON 2.4mg; SODIUM 452mg; CALC 62mg

Escarole, Bean, and Sausage Soup with Parmesan Cheese

This tastes as if it's been bubbling away for hours in a rustic Italian kitchen, but it's ready in less than 30 minutes.

Escarole has a milder flavor than endive but still offers a slight bitterness that is balanced by the creamy beans and sausage. For a bit more heat, use hot turkey Italian sausage. Hands-on time: 13 min. Total time: 26 min.

2 teaspoons extra-virgin olive oil

1 cup chopped onion

½ cup thinly sliced fennel bulb

1 tablespoon minced garlic

3 (3.2-ounce) links sweet turkey Italian sausage, casings removed

2 cups fat-free, lower-sodium chicken broth

1 cup water

1 (15-ounce) can no-salt-added cannellini beans or other white beans, rinsed and drained

4 cups chopped escarole

2 tablespoons grated fresh Parmesan cheese

1. Heat a large saucepan over medium-high heat. Add olive oil to pan; swirl to coat. Add onion, fennel bulb, garlic, and sausage to pan; cook 7 minutes or until sausage is browned, stirring frequently to crumble. Add broth, 1 cup water, and beans; cover. Bring to a boil; cook 5 minutes, stirring occasionally. Stir in escarole; cook 4 minutes or until escarole wilts. Divide soup evenly among 4 bowls; sprinkle with Parmesan cheese.

Serves 4 (serving size: about 1¼ cups soup and 1½ teaspoons cheese).

CALORIES 230; FAT 4.6g (sat 2.6g, mono 1.7g, poly 0.3g); PROTEIN 17.9g; CARB 15.5g; FIBER 4.7g; CHOL 49mg; IRON 1.3mg; SODIUM 624mg; CALC 87mg

11

SOUPS & STEWS

Apple-Parsnip Soup

Here the lowly parsnip gets its due, adding earthy notes to apples and curry spices.

Pink Lady apples, great for applesauce, work well in this pureed appetizer soup. Sweet Fuji or all-purpose Spartan apples also work nicely. Hands-on time: 17 min. Total time: 56 min.

2 tablespoons olive oil

1 cup chopped onion

2½ cups chopped peeled Pink Lady apple (about 1 pound)

1 tablespoon curry powder

1½ teaspoons grated peeled fresh ginger

1 teaspoon ground cardamom

1 garlic clove, chopped

3½ cups chopped peeled parsnip (about 1½ pounds)

4 cups fat-free, lower-sodium chicken broth

1 cup apple cider

¼ teaspoon salt

⅛ teaspoon freshly ground black pepper

8 teaspoons crème fraîche

1. Heat a Dutch oven over medium heat. Add oil to pan; swirl to coat. Add onion to pan; cook 5 minutes or until tender, stirring frequently. Add apple and next 4 ingredients (through garlic); cook 1 minute, stirring constantly. Add parsnip, chicken broth, and apple cider; bring to a boil. Cover, reduce heat, and simmer 30 minutes or until parsnip is tender.

2. Place half of parsnip mixture in a blender. Remove center piece of blender lid (to allow steam to escape); secure blender lid on blender. Place a clean towel over opening in blender lid (to avoid splatters). Blend until smooth. Pour into a large bowl. Repeat procedure with remaining parsnip mixture. Stir in salt and pepper. Ladle about ¾ cup soup into each of 8 bowls; top each serving with 1 teaspoon crème fraîche.

Serves 8.

CALORIES 138; FAT 5.6g (sat 1.6g, mono 2.6g, poly 0.6g); PROTEIN 1.8g; CARB 21.6g; FIBER 4.2g; CHOL 5mg; IRON 0.7mg; SODIUM 307mg; CALC 31mg

Split Pea Soup

As the peas cook, they collapse into a thick puree that's reminiscent of the best mashed potatoes.

Canadian bacon offers salty pork notes and very little fat. Split peas are dried and halved along their natural seam and don't require presoaking. Hands-on time: 10 min. Total time: 1 hr. 57 min.

6½ cups water

3 cups organic vegetable broth

2 cups green split peas

¾ cup finely chopped yellow onion

5 ounces diced Canadian bacon (about ¾ cup)

1 cup finely chopped carrot

1 cup thinly sliced celery

½ teaspoon freshly ground black pepper

1 tablespoon fresh lemon juice

1. Combine first 5 ingredients in a large Dutch oven over medium-high heat; bring to a simmer. Cover, reduce heat, and simmer 1 hour, stirring occasionally.

2. Stir in carrot, celery, and pepper. Simmer, uncovered, 45 minutes or until peas are tender and soup thickens, stirring occasionally. Remove from heat; stir in juice. Serve immediately.

Serves 6 (serving size: 1¼ cups).

CALORIES 300; FAT 1.8g (sat 0.6g, mono 0.8g, poly 0.2g); PROTEIN 22.5g; CARB 49.3g; FIBER 1.2g; CHOL 12mg; IRON 2.6mg; SODIUM 650mg; CALC 28mg

Beer-Cheddar Soup

A heavy Wisconsin favorite made over with less cheese and no cream.

It gets big flavor, though, from extra-sharp cheddar, and onion and garlic boost its savory goodness. Use a pilsner or light ale. Serve the soup in a tureen with the toasted bread cubes and chives on the side, and let guests help themselves. Toast the bread cubes a day ahead, cool, and store at room temperature.

Hands-on time: 21 min. Total time: 1 hr. 22 min.

8   ounces sourdough bread, cut into 1-inch cubes

Cooking spray

2   cups chopped onion (about 2 medium)

2   garlic cloves, minced

1   (12-ounce) bottle beer

3   cups fat-free, lower-sodium chicken broth, divided

1   cup water

2.25   ounces all-purpose flour (about ½ cup)

2   cups fat-free milk, divided

1¼   cups (5 ounces) shredded extra-sharp cheddar cheese

¼   teaspoon freshly ground black pepper

¼   cup finely chopped fresh chives

1. Preheat oven to 450°.

2. Arrange bread cubes in a single layer on a jelly-roll pan; coat bread cubes with cooking spray. Bake at 450° for 10 minutes or until toasted. Set aside.

3. Heat a Dutch oven over medium-high heat. Coat pan with cooking spray. Add onion to pan; sauté 4 minutes, stirring frequently. Add garlic; sauté 1 minute, stirring frequently. Stir in beer; bring to a boil. Reduce heat; simmer 20 minutes or until onion is very tender.

4. Place beer mixture and 1 cup broth in a blender. Remove center piece of blender lid (to allow steam to escape); secure blender lid on blender. Place a clean towel over opening in blender lid (to avoid splatters). Blend until smooth.

Return pureed mixture to pan. Stir in remaining 2 cups broth and 1 cup water; bring to a boil. Reduce heat; simmer 10 minutes.

5. Weigh or lightly spoon flour into a dry measuring cup; level with a knife. Combine flour and 1 cup milk, stirring with a whisk until smooth. Add flour mixture and remaining 1 cup milk to pan; cook 12 minutes or until slightly thick. Remove pan from heat. Gradually add cheese, stirring until smooth. Stir in pepper. Serve with bread cubes and chives.

Serves 12 (serving size: about ⅔ cup soup, about 1 ounce bread cubes, and 1 teaspoon chives).

CALORIES 159; FAT 4.8g (sat 2.7g, mono 0.1g, poly 0.2g); PROTEIN 7.9g; CARB 20.7g; FIBER 1.1g; CHOL 13mg; IRON 1mg; SODIUM 362mg; CALC 154mg

NUTRITION MADE EASY

Cutting Cream: One way to reduce cream and still achieve creamy texture is to use a slurry. Whisk all-purpose flour into a small amount of cool water, broth, or milk, then gradually add the mixture to the hot soup while whisking diligently to prevent lumps.

Roasted Butternut Squash and Shallot Soup

Squash and shallots roast, brown, and soften, becoming a nutty-sweet base for this rich veggie-based soup.

Spicy fresh ginger complements the roasted veggies in this easy recipe. Serve with a grilled Gruyère cheese sandwich on multigrain bread for a wonderful supper. Hands-on time: 15 min. Total time: 1 hr. 19 min.

- 4 cups (1-inch) cubed peeled butternut squash (about 1½ pounds)
- 1 tablespoon olive oil
- ¼ teaspoon salt
- 4 large shallots, peeled and halved
- 1 (½-inch) piece peeled fresh ginger, thinly sliced
- 2½ cups fat-free, lower-sodium chicken broth
- 2 tablespoons (1-inch) slices fresh chives
  Cracked black pepper (optional)

1. Preheat oven to 375°.

2. Combine first 5 ingredients in a roasting pan or jelly-roll pan; toss well. Bake at 375° for 50 minutes or until tender, stirring occasionally. Cool 10 minutes.

3. Place half of squash mixture and half of broth in a blender. Remove center piece of blender lid (to allow steam to escape); secure blender lid on blender. Place a clean towel over opening in blender lid (to avoid splatters). Blend until smooth. Pour into a large saucepan. Repeat procedure with remaining squash mixture and broth. Cook over medium heat 5 minutes or until thoroughly heated. Top with chives and pepper, if desired.

Serves 6 (serving size: ⅔ cup soup and 1 teaspoon chives).

CALORIES 112; FAT 2.5g (sat 0.4g, mono 1.7g, poly 0.3g); PROTEIN 3.3g; CARB 22.4g; FIBER 3.6g; CHOL 0mg; IRON 1.6mg; SODIUM 266mg; CALC 84mg

NUTRITION MADE EASY

Vegetable Soups: If you're trying to work more vegetables into your diet, add veggie-heavy soups to your repertoire—a good way to get in at least one serving, possibly more. Bonus: Warm soups are filling and satisfying, and may help prevent overeating.

Tomato Soup with Roasted Chickpeas

Creamy, velvety tomato soup topped with a crunchy surprise of chickpeas and country ham.

Smoked paprika and roasted bell peppers give this soup added depth; chickpeas pack in fiber.
Hands-on time: 20 min. Total time: 1 hr. 8 min.

1	red bell pepper
3	tablespoons olive oil, divided
8	garlic cloves, divided
¼	cup heavy whipping cream
1	(28-ounce) can no-salt-added whole peeled tomatoes, undrained and crushed
½	teaspoon smoked paprika
⅜	teaspoon salt, divided
¼	teaspoon ground red pepper
2	ounces country ham, finely chopped
1	(15½-ounce) can organic chickpeas (garbanzo beans), rinsed and drained
¼	teaspoon ground cumin
¼	cup fresh flat-leaf parsley
2	tablespoons sliced almonds, toasted and chopped

1.. Preheat broiler.

2. Cut bell pepper in half lengthwise; discard seeds and membranes. Place halves, skin sides up, on a foil-lined baking sheet; flatten with hand. Broil 8 minutes or until blackened.

Place pepper halves in a paper bag; fold to close tightly. Let stand 10 minutes. Peel and discard skins.
3. Reduce oven temperature to 450°.
4. Heat a saucepan over medium heat. Add 1 tablespoon oil to pan; swirl to coat. Add 3 garlic cloves; cook 1 minute. Add cream and tomatoes; bring to a simmer. Add paprika, ¼ teaspoon salt, and ground red pepper; simmer 20 minutes, stirring occasionally. Cool 10 minutes. Combine tomato mixture and bell pepper in a blender; puree.

5. Combine remaining 5 garlic cloves, ham, and chickpeas in a roasting pan; drizzle with remaining 2 tablespoons oil, cumin, and remaining ⅛ teaspoon salt. Toss. Roast at 450° for 12 minutes, stirring once. Ladle ¾ cup soup into each of 4 bowls; top evenly with chickpea mixture, parsley, and almonds.

Serves 4.

CALORIES 340; FAT 19.5g (sat 5.4g, mono 10.5g, poly 1.9g); PROTEIN 12.6g; CARB 31g; FIBER 7.3g; CHOL 30mg; IRON 3.9mg; SODIUM 657mg; CALC 155mg

Loaded Potato Soup

All the appeal of a loaded baked potato, delivered in a hearty soup. It's about that simple.

If you aren't in a rush, you can chop the onions and cook the bacon in a skillet or baking sheet in the oven.
Hands-on time: 20 min. Total time: 20 min.

4 **(6-ounce) red potatoes**

2 **teaspoons olive oil**

½ **cup prechopped onion**

1¼ **cups fat-free, lower-sodium chicken broth**

3 **tablespoons all-purpose flour**

2 **cups 1% low-fat milk, divided**

¼ **cup reduced-fat sour cream**

½ **teaspoon salt**

¼ **teaspoon freshly ground black pepper**

3 **bacon slices, halved**

⅓ **cup shredded cheddar cheese**

4 **teaspoons thinly sliced green onions**

1. Pierce potatoes with a fork. Microwave at HIGH 13 minutes or until tender. Cut in half; cool slightly.

2. Heat a saucepan over medium-high heat. Add oil to pan; swirl to coat. Add onion to pan; sauté 3 minutes. Add broth. Combine flour and ½ cup milk; add to pan with remaining 1½ cups milk. Bring to a boil, stirring often. Cook 1 minute. Remove from heat; stir in sour cream, salt, and pepper.

3. Arrange bacon on a paper towel on a microwave-safe plate. Cover with a paper towel; microwave at HIGH 4 minutes. Crumble bacon.

4. Discard potato skins. Coarsely mash potatoes into soup. Top with cheese, green onions, and bacon.

Serves 4 (serving size: about 1¼ cups).

CALORIES 325; FAT 11.1g (sat 5.2g, mono 4.5g, poly 0.8g); PROTEIN 13.2g; CARB 43.8g; FIBER 3g; CHOL 27mg; IRON 1.3mg; SODIUM 670mg; CALC 261mg

Beer Pairing

Belgian ale is a classic pairing for a cheesy soup, accenting the sharp, tangy cheese and complementing the creamy base and savory bacon.

Crab Bisque

Starts with flour-thickened milk, finishes nicely with cream for that essential bisque richness.

You need to use a blender to achieve the smooth texture that defines this soup. But blenders are tricky with hot soups—they can erupt like a volcano. Puree in batches; be sure to remove the center part of the lid, and keep a firm hand and a kitchen towel over the lid. Hands-on time: 26 min. Total time: 32 min.

Cooking spray

1¼	cups thinly sliced shallots
1	celery stalk, finely chopped
4	garlic cloves, minced
3	tablespoons vermouth
¼	teaspoon black pepper
⅛	teaspoon kosher salt

Dash of ground red pepper

1	pound jumbo lump crabmeat, shell pieces removed and divided
3	cups fat-free milk
1	cup clam juice
1.5	ounces all-purpose flour (about ⅓ cup)
⅓	cup heavy whipping cream
2	tablespoons chopped fresh chives
1½	teaspoons fresh lemon juice

1. Heat a large Dutch oven over medium heat. Coat pan with cooking spray. Add shallots and celery to pan; cook 10 minutes or until softened, stirring occasionally. Add garlic; cook 1 minute. Stir in vermouth; cook 1 minute or until liquid evaporates. Add black pepper, salt, ground red pepper, and half of crabmeat.

2. Combine milk and clam juice in a bowl. Weigh or lightly spoon flour into a dry measuring cup; level with a knife. Whisk flour into milk mixture; add to pan. Bring to a boil, stirring constantly. Cook 1 minute or until slightly thick, stirring constantly.

3. Place half of milk mixture in blender. Remove center piece of blender lid (to allow steam to escape); secure blender lid on blender. Place a clean towel over opening in blender lid (to avoid splatters). Blend until smooth. Pour into a large bowl. Repeat procedure with remaining milk mixture. Return pureed mixture to pan. Stir in cream; cook 3 minutes or until thoroughly heated.

4. Combine remaining crabmeat, chives, and lemon juice in a medium bowl. Top soup with crabmeat mixture.

Serves 5 (serving size: 1 cup soup and about ⅓ cup crabmeat mixture).

CALORIES 270; FAT 8g (sat 4g, mono 2g, poly 0.9g); PROTEIN 26g; CARB 22.4g; FIBER 0.5g; CHOL 117mg; IRON 2mg; SODIUM 487mg; CALC 322mg

Clam Chowder

Purchase a bright, unoaked chardonnay, and sip while making and eating this satisfying soup.

Hands-on time: 37 min. Total time: 1 hr. 7 min.

1½	cups chopped onion, divided
½	cup unoaked chardonnay
3½	pounds littleneck clams
1	(8-ounce) bottle clam juice
1	bay leaf
1	tablespoon butter
1	slice bacon, chopped
3	cups diced red potato
½	cup chopped celery
⅛	teaspoon ground red pepper
3	tablespoons all-purpose flour
⅓	cup water
¾	cup half-and-half
¾	cup 2% reduced-fat milk
2	tablespoons chopped chives
1	teaspoon chopped thyme

1. Combine ½ cup onion, wine, and next 3 ingredients (through bay leaf) in a Dutch oven over medium-high heat; bring to a boil. Cover and cook 2 minutes or until clams open; discard any unopened shells. Strain through a cheesecloth-lined sieve over a bowl, reserving cooking liquid and clams. Remove meat from clams; chop. Discard shells.
2. Wipe pan clean. Melt butter in pan. Add bacon to pan; sauté 3 minutes. Stir in remaining 1 cup onion, potato, celery, and red pepper; sauté 4 minutes. Stir in flour; cook 1 minute. Stir in cooking liquid and ⅓ cup water; bring to a boil. Cover, reduce heat, and simmer 30 minutes, stirring occasionally. Stir in clams, half-and-half, and milk; cook 1 minute or until heated. Stir in herbs.

Serves 4 (serving size: 1¼ cups).

CALORIES 337; FAT 11.1g (sat 6.1g, mono 1.4g, poly 2.1g); PROTEIN 24.3g; CARB 34.9g; FIBER 3.1g; CHOL 78mg; IRON 20.6mg; SODIUM 310mg; CALC 204mg

11

SOUPS & STEWS

Avocado-Corn Chowder with Grilled Chicken

Avocado is brilliant in pureed soups—its natural, healthy unctuousness goes velvety smooth in the blender.

Fresh corn kernels and bell pepper offer crunchy contrast, while grilled chicken takes the soup into dinner territory. Grilled shrimp would also work. Hands-on time: 28 min. Total time: 28 min.

2 ripe avocados, divided

1½ cups water

½ cup fresh orange juice

1 teaspoon honey

1 teaspoon kosher salt, divided

½ teaspoon freshly ground black pepper, divided

¼ teaspoon ground red pepper (optional)

12 ounces skinless, boneless chicken breast

1 teaspoon olive oil

1 small garlic clove, cut in half

1½ cups fresh corn kernels (about 3 ears)

1 cup chopped red bell pepper

⅓ cup chopped green onions

¼ cup chopped fresh cilantro

4 lime wedges

1. Peel and coarsely chop 1 avocado, and place in a blender. Add 1½ cups water, orange juice, honey, ¾ teaspoon salt, ¼ teaspoon black pepper, and red pepper, if desired; blend until smooth. Place in freezer to chill while chicken cooks.
2. Heat a grill pan over medium-high heat. Brush chicken with oil; sprinkle with remaining ¼ teaspoon salt and remaining ¼ teaspoon black pepper. Place chicken in pan; cook 4 minutes on each side or until done. Remove chicken from pan; rub chicken with cut sides of garlic halves.

Let chicken stand 10 minutes; cut or shred into bite-sized pieces.
3. Peel and dice remaining avocado. Stir diced avocado, corn, bell pepper, and onions into chilled avocado puree. Spoon chowder into bowls; top with chicken and cilantro. Serve with lime wedges.

Serves 4 (serving size: 1¼ cups chowder, about 2 ounces chicken, 1 tablespoon cilantro, and 1 lime wedge).

CALORIES 359; FAT 17.9g (sat 2.7g, mono 11.2g, poly 2.6g); PROTEIN 24.5g; CARB 30g; FIBER 9.7g; CHOL 49mg; IRON 2mg; SODIUM 558mg; CALC 39mg

Three-Bean Vegetarian Chili 🌿

This meatless chili has so much going on—smoky cumin, sweet butternut squash, and a hefty dose of crushed red pepper.

Serve a hearty salad and corn bread or corn muffins on the side. Hands-on time: 33 min.
Total time: 1 hr. 45 min.

- 2 red bell peppers
- 3 tablespoons extra-virgin olive oil
- 1 cup chopped onion
- 2 teaspoons ground cumin
- 1 teaspoon crushed red pepper
- 1 teaspoon paprika
- ¼ teaspoon salt
- 4 garlic cloves, thinly sliced
- 2 cups organic vegetable broth
- 1½ cups (½-inch) cubed peeled butternut squash
- 1 (28-ounce) can no-salt-added tomatoes, undrained and chopped
- 1 (15-ounce) can organic pinto beans, rinsed and drained
- 1 (15-ounce) can organic cannellini beans, rinsed and drained
- 1 (15-ounce) can organic red kidney beans, rinsed and drained
- ½ cup thinly sliced green onions

1. Preheat broiler.
2. Cut bell peppers in half lengthwise. Remove and discard seeds and membranes. Place pepper halves, skin sides up, on a foil-lined baking sheet. Broil 15 minutes or until blackened. Place pepper halves in a paper bag; fold to close tightly. Let stand 15 minutes. Peel and chop peppers.
3. Heat a Dutch oven over medium-low heat. Add oil to pan; swirl to coat. Add onion to pan; cook 15 minutes, stirring occasionally. Stir in cumin and next 4 ingredients (through garlic); cook 2 minutes, stirring frequently. Add bell peppers, broth, squash, and tomatoes; bring to a simmer. Cook 20 minutes, stirring occasionally. Add beans; simmer 25 minutes or until slightly thick, stirring occasionally. Sprinkle with green onions.

Serves 6 (serving size: about 1½ cups).

CALORIES 264; FAT 8.3g (sat 1.2g, mono 5.2g, poly 1.3g); PROTEIN 9.5g; CARB 40.9g; FIBER 10.7g; CHOL 0mg; IRON 4.4mg; SODIUM 689mg; CALC 145mg

Poblano-Jalapeño Chili

Meaty, juicy, moderately spicy, very delicious.

Top with thinly sliced radishes for a bit of crunch. Hands-on time: 34 min. Total time: 1 hr. 4 min.

Cooking spray
1½ pounds ground sirloin
2 jalapeño peppers
1 tablespoon canola oil
3 cups chopped onion
1 cup chopped seeded poblano chiles
8 garlic cloves, minced
1 (12-ounce) bottle Mexican beer
1 tablespoon chili powder
1½ teaspoons ground cumin
¾ teaspoon kosher salt
2½ cups lower-sodium marinara sauce
1 cup fat-free, lower-sodium chicken broth
2 (15-ounce) cans no-salt-added kidney beans, rinsed and drained
1 (14.5-ounce) can diced fire-roasted tomatoes, undrained
¾ cup (3 ounces) shredded sharp cheddar cheese
½ cup light sour cream
¼ cup fresh cilantro leaves

1. Heat a Dutch oven over medium-high heat. Coat pan with cooking spray. Add beef; cook 10 minutes or until browned, stirring to crumble. Remove beef from pan; drain. Wipe pan clean with paper towels.
2. Remove and discard seeds and membranes from 1 jalapeño; finely chop both jalapeños. Heat pan over medium-high heat. Add oil to pan; swirl to coat. Add jalapeños, onion, poblanos, and garlic to pan; sauté 10 minutes or until onion is tender.

Add beer, scraping pan to loosen browned bits; cook 12 minutes or until about half of liquid evaporates. Add chili powder, cumin, and salt; cook 1 minute, stirring frequently. Stir in beef, marinara, broth, beans, and tomatoes; bring to a boil. Reduce heat; simmer, uncovered, 30 minutes or until slightly thick. Ladle about 1½ cups chili into each of 8 bowls; top each with 1½ tablespoons cheese, 1 tablespoon sour cream, and 1½ teaspoons cilantro.

Serves 8.

CALORIES 349; FAT 14.4g (sat 5.9g, mono 5.1g, poly 1g); PROTEIN 25.6g; CARB 44.9g; FIBER 6.5g; CHOL 71mg; IRON 3.2mg; SODIUM 625mg; CALC 142mg

Lamb Tagine

A splendid marriage: lamb, fragrant spices, sweet-tart apricots.

Serve over couscous, the traditional accompaniment. Hands-on time: 33 min. Total time: 1 hr. 38 min.

Cooking spray
1 (1-pound) boneless leg of lamb roast, trimmed and cut into ½-inch cubes
½ teaspoon kosher salt, divided
1½ cups chopped onion
1 teaspoon ground cumin
½ teaspoon ground cinnamon
½ teaspoon ground red pepper
6 garlic cloves, coarsely chopped
2 tablespoons honey
1 tablespoon tomato paste
½ cup dried apricots, quartered
1 (14-ounce) can fat-free, lower-sodium beef broth

1. Heat a Dutch oven over medium-high heat. Coat pan with cooking spray. Sprinkle lamb evenly with ¼ teaspoon salt. Add lamb to pan; cook 4 minutes, turning to brown on all sides. Remove from pan. Add onion; sauté 4 minutes, stirring frequently. Add remaining ¼ teaspoon salt, cumin, and next 3 ingredients (through garlic); sauté 1 minute, stirring constantly. Stir in honey and tomato paste, and cook 30 seconds, stirring frequently. Return lamb to pan. Add apricots and broth; bring to a boil. Cover, reduce heat, and simmer 1 hour or until lamb is tender, stirring occasionally.

Serves 4 (serving size: 1 cup).

CALORIES 386; FAT 12g (sat 4.8g, mono 4.8g, poly 0.7g); PROTEIN 41.6g; CARB 27.7g; FIBER 3.3g; CHOL 126mg; IRON 4.3mg; SODIUM 524mg; CALC 77mg

Poblano-Jalapeño Chili

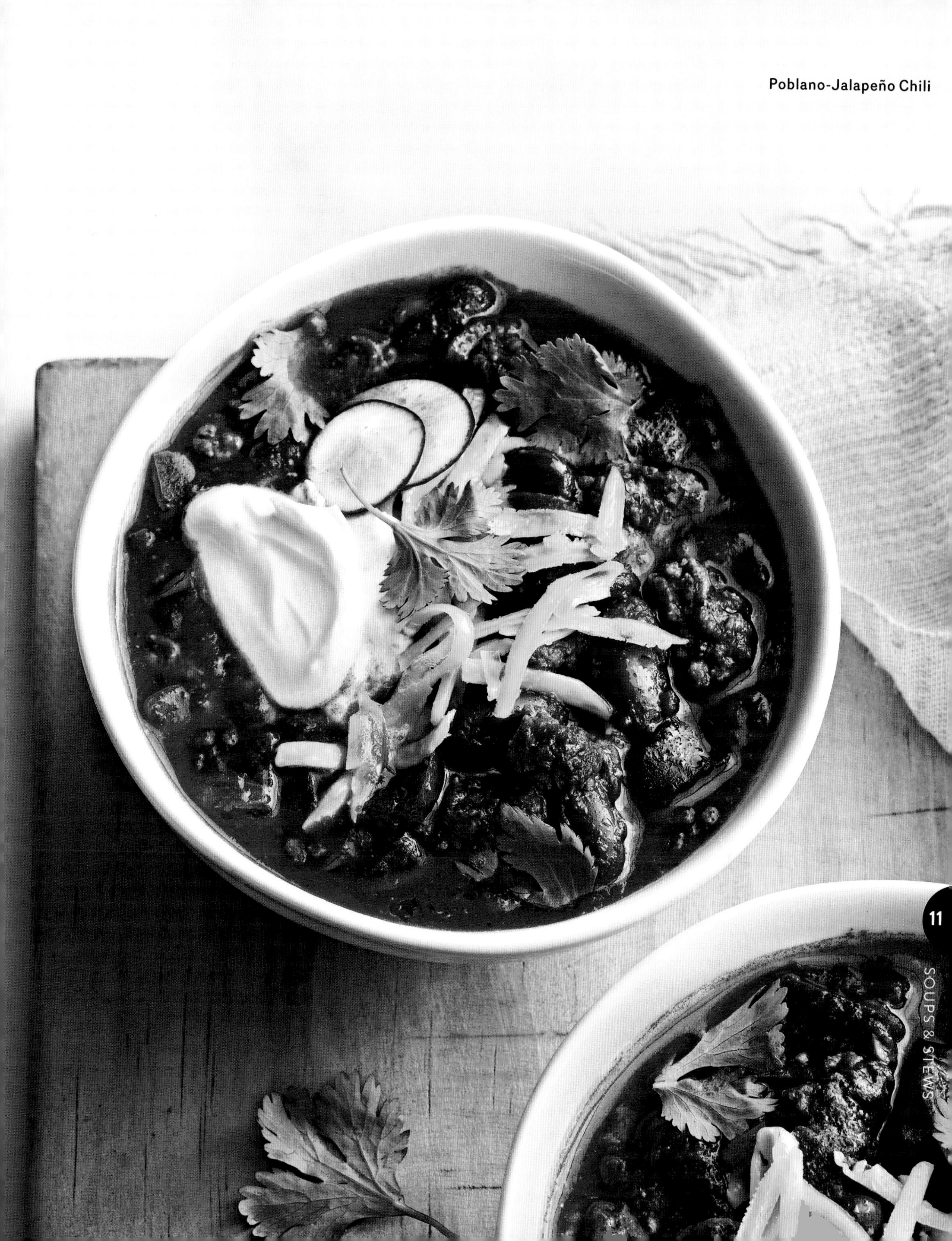

Seafood Cioppino

Use best-quality clams, scallops, and wild-caught shrimp, and cook gently for beautiful texture and sweetness.

Serve with warm sourdough bread. Hands-on time: 19 min. Total time: 45 min.

- 2 tablespoons olive oil, divided
- 2 cups vertically sliced onion
- 4 garlic cloves, sliced
- 1 cup dry white wine
- 1 cup organic vegetable broth
- 2 tablespoons chopped fresh basil
- 2 tablespoons chopped fresh oregano
- ½ teaspoon crushed red pepper
- 1 (35-ounce) can whole tomatoes with basil, rinsed, drained, and coarsely chopped
- 1 (10-ounce) yellowtail snapper fillet, cut into 8 (1-inch) cubes

- 4 sea scallops (about 6 ounces)
- ½ teaspoon freshly ground black pepper
- 12 littleneck clams, scrubbed
- 8 medium peeled and deveined shrimp (about 5 ounces)
- 2 tablespoons chopped flat-leaf parsley
- 1 tablespoon fresh lemon juice

1. Heat a large Dutch oven over medium-high heat. Add 1 tablespoon oil to pan; swirl to coat. Add onion to pan; sauté 1 minute. Add garlic; reduce heat to medium. Cover and cook 8 minutes, stirring occasionally. Add wine and next 5 ingredients (through tomatoes); cover. Bring to a boil.

Reduce heat; simmer, uncovered, 15 minutes.

2. Sprinkle snapper and scallops with black pepper. Heat a large skillet over high heat. Add remaining 1 tablespoon oil to pan; swirl to coat. Add snapper and scallops; cook 90 seconds on each side or until golden brown. Add snapper, scallops, clams, and shrimp to broth mixture. Cover and cook 4 minutes or until clams open; discard any unopened shells. Stir in parsley and lemon juice.

Serves 4 (serving size: about 1¾ cups).

CALORIES 319; FAT 8.8g (sat 1.3g, mono 5.2g, poly 1.4g); PROTEIN 33.4g; CARB 13.9g; FIBER 1.8g; CHOL 103mg; IRON 6.5mg; SODIUM 596mg; CALC 109mg

Shrimp Étouffée

A less fatty and salty version of the much-loved Cajun classic.

The key is the roux; be patient, and stir frequently. Hands-on time: 34 min. Total time: 58 min.

- 4 cups fat-free, lower-sodium chicken broth
- 1 teaspoon dried thyme
- 1 teaspoon dried basil
- 1 bay leaf
- ¼ cup canola oil
- 2.25 ounces all-purpose flour (about ½ cup)
- Cooking spray
- 1 tablespoon butter
- 1½ cups chopped onion
- ⅔ cup diced celery
- ½ cup chopped red bell pepper
- ½ cup chopped green bell pepper
- ¾ cup water
- ¼ cup tomato paste
- 1 tablespoon salt-free Cajun seasoning
- 1½ teaspoons minced garlic
- ¼ teaspoon salt
- ¼ teaspoon freshly ground black pepper
- ¼ teaspoon ground red pepper
- 1 teaspoon Worcestershire sauce
- ½ cup chopped green onions
- ¼ cup chopped fresh flat-leaf parsley
- 1 pound medium shrimp (about 30 shrimp), peeled and deveined
- 4 cups hot cooked long-grain rice

1. Combine first 4 ingredients in a saucepan over medium heat; bring to a simmer. Cover; remove from heat.

2. Heat a medium saucepan over medium heat. Add oil to pan; swirl to coat. Weigh or lightly spoon flour into a dry measuring cup; level with a knife. Add flour to pan; cook 8 minutes or until very brown, stirring constantly with a whisk. Remove from heat. Add 1 cup broth mixture to pan; stir with a whisk until smooth. Add remaining 3 cups broth mixture, stirring with a whisk until smooth; set aside.

3. Heat a large Dutch oven over medium-high heat; coat pan with cooking spray. Add 1 tablespoon butter to pan; swirl to melt. Add 1½ cups onion, celery, and bell peppers to pan; cook 10 minutes or until vegetables are tender and onion is golden brown, stirring occasionally. Stir in ¾ cup water, scraping pan to loosen browned bits. Add tomato paste and next 5 ingredients to onion mixture; cook 1 minute, stirring constantly. Add reserved broth-flour mixture and Worcestershire sauce to pan, stirring well to combine; bring to a simmer. Cook 10 minutes, stirring occasionally. Add green onions, parsley, and shrimp; cook 3 minutes or until shrimp are done. Discard bay leaf. Serve over rice.

Serves 6 (serving size: about 1¼ cups étouffée and ⅔ cup rice).

CALORIES 386; FAT 12.6g (sat 2.2g, mono 6.7g, poly 3.1g); PROTEIN 19.3g; CARB 48g; FIBER 3.4g; CHOL 117mg; IRON 4.7mg; SODIUM 656mg; CALC 76mg

TECHNIQUE

Rules of a Righteous Roux: Both a flavor agent and thickener, a perfect roux imparts a nutty taste and silken texture to soups and stews.

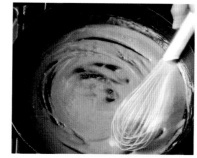

1. Slowly whisk the flour into the hot oil to form a thick paste. It will thin out and smooth as it cooks.

2. Frequent stirring keeps the flour from clumping and burning. The color will progress to blond.

3. Keep stirring as the color shifts from blond to brown. A deeper color yields a more flavorful roux.

Beef and Guinness Stew

The perfect cure for winter chills: a steamy bowl of fork-tender beef in caraway-scented beery broth with carrot, parsnip, and turnip.

Guinness Stout is key to the flavor—rich, heady, and slightly bitter. Serve rye or brown bread on the side.
Hands-on time: 48 min. Total time: 3 hr. 18 min.

3   tablespoons canola oil, divided

¼   cup all-purpose flour

2   pounds boneless chuck roast, trimmed and cut into 1-inch cubes

1   teaspoon salt, divided

5   cups chopped onion (about 3 onions)

1   tablespoon tomato paste

4   cups fat-free, lower-sodium beef broth

1   (11.2-ounce) bottle Guinness Stout

1   tablespoon raisins

1   teaspoon caraway seeds

½   teaspoon black pepper

1½   cups (½-inch-thick) slices diagonally cut carrot (about 8 ounces)

1½   cups (½-inch-thick) slices diagonally cut parsnip (about 8 ounces)

1   cup (½-inch) cubed peeled turnip (about 8 ounces)

2   tablespoons finely chopped fresh flat-leaf parsley

1. Heat a Dutch oven over medium-high heat. Add 1½ tablespoons oil to pan; swirl to coat. Place flour in a shallow dish. Sprinkle beef with ½ teaspoon salt; dredge beef in flour. Add half of beef to pan; cook 5 minutes, turning to brown on all sides. Remove beef from pan with a slotted spoon. Repeat procedure with remaining 1½ tablespoons oil and beef.

2. Add onion to pan; cook 5 minutes or until tender, stirring occasionally. Stir in tomato paste; cook 1 minute, stirring frequently. Stir in broth and beer, scraping pan to loosen browned bits. Return meat to pan. Stir in remaining ½ teaspoon salt, raisins, caraway seeds, and pepper; bring to a boil. Cover, reduce heat, and simmer 1 hour, stirring occasionally. Uncover and bring to a boil. Cook 50 minutes, stirring occasionally. Add carrot, parsnip, and turnip to pan. Cover, reduce heat to low, and simmer 30 minutes, stirring occasionally. Uncover and bring to a boil; cook 10 minutes or until vegetables are tender. Sprinkle with parsley.

Serves 8 (serving size: about 1 cup).

CALORIES 365; FAT 19.4g (sat 5.7g, mono 9.6g, poly 1.7g); PROTEIN 25.3g; CARB 18.8g; FIBER 3.6g; CHOL 62mg; IRON 2.6mg; SODIUM 454mg; CALC 52mg

Dijon Chicken Stew with Potatoes and Kale

A chicken dish that's just as hearty and comforting as any beef stew, with sweet-earthy kale and tender potato chunks.

For the best flavor, use a high-quality, feisty Dijon mustard, like Maille. You can substitute Swiss chard or mustard greens for kale. Hands-on time: 30 min. Total time: 1 hr. 49 min.

- 4 teaspoons olive oil, divided
- 2 cups sliced leek
- 4 garlic cloves, minced
- ⅓ cup all-purpose flour
- 1 pound skinless, boneless chicken thighs, cut into bite-sized pieces
- ½ pound skinless, boneless chicken breast, cut into bite-sized pieces
- ½ teaspoon salt, divided
- ½ teaspoon freshly ground black pepper, divided
- 1 cup dry white wine
- 3 cups fat-free, lower-sodium chicken broth, divided
- 1 tablespoon all-purpose flour
- 1½ cups water
- 2 tablespoons Dijon mustard
- 2 cups (½-inch) cubed peeled white potato (about 1 pound)
- 8 cups loosely packed torn kale (about 5 ounces)
- Crushed red pepper (optional)

1. Heat a Dutch oven over medium-high heat. Add 1 teaspoon oil to pan; swirl to coat. Add leek to pan; sauté 6 minutes or until tender and golden brown, stirring frequently. Add garlic; sauté 1 minute. Spoon leek mixture into a large bowl.

2. Place ⅓ cup flour in a shallow bowl or pie plate. Dredge chicken in flour, shaking off excess. Heat remaining 1 tablespoon oil in pan. Add half of chicken mixture to pan; sprinkle with ⅛ teaspoon salt and ⅛ teaspoon black pepper. Cook 6 minutes, browning on all sides. Add browned chicken to leek mixture. Repeat procedure with remaining chicken mixture, ⅛ teaspoon salt, and ⅛ teaspoon black pepper.

3. Add wine to pan, scraping pan to loosen browned bits. Combine 1 cup broth and 1 tablespoon flour, stirring with a whisk until smooth. Add broth mixture, remaining 2 cups broth, 1½ cups water, and mustard to pan; bring to a boil. Stir in chicken mixture, remaining ¼ teaspoon salt, and remaining ¼ teaspoon black pepper; cover. Reduce heat; simmer 30 minutes.

4. Stir in potato. Cover and simmer 30 minutes or until potato is tender. Stir in kale; cover and simmer 10 minutes. Garnish with crushed red pepper, if desired.

Serves 6 (serving size: 1½ cups).

CALORIES 324; FAT 7.9g (sat 1.5g, mono 3.5g, poly 1.7g); PROTEIN 30.9g; CARB 33.7g; FIBER 5g; CHOL 85mg; IRON 4.6mg; SODIUM 659mg; CALC 180mg

Chapter

Quick B

Yeast Br

12: reads & eads

Peanut Butter–Banana Bread, page 403

The big category of flour-plus-leavening baked goods includes everything from America's beloved biscuits and banana breads to the homemade yeast loaves that once seemed in danger of extinction but have bloomed again in the artisanal movement. A baker's dozen of quick breads should be in every cook's repertoire because they're among the easiest, most comforting treats for breakfast, snacks, and dinner. As for the yeast breads, it's silly to pretend they don't take time and practice to do well, but being a good yeast-bread baker provides the same deep satisfaction that any worthy craft does. It becomes something one does by touch and instinct. Instructions for handling batters and doughs are precise in our recipes—with less fat, you have less room for error in seeking the perfect crumb. There are many tips, as well, on the tricks of lower-fat baking.

TEST KITCHEN SECRETS

Five Tips for Perfect Muffins:

1. Leave a few small lumps. Overstirring toughens a muffin.

2. Spray the liners with cooking spray before adding batter.

3. Check for doneness early (about 5 minutes before specified time) since ovens can vary.

4. Cool in pan 5 minutes, and then eat warm or remove to a rack so muffins don't get soggy.

5. Store correctly so muffins stay fresh: Keep in an airtight container for a day or two. Or wrap individually in plastic wrap, place in a zip-top plastic bag, and freeze for up to a month. Thaw at room temperature, or microwave for 10 to 30 seconds.

Chocolate–Chocolate Chip Muffins

Cocoa batter encases chocolate minichips, which also melt atop for chocolaty goodness. Did we mention chocolate?

Canola oil keeps muffins moist and low in saturated fat. Vinegar in the batter amplifies flavor, similar to the way buttermilk would. Hands-on time: 12 min. Total time: 27 min.

7.9 ounces all-purpose flour (about 1¾ cups)

½ cup packed brown sugar

¼ cup unsweetened cocoa

1 teaspoon baking powder

1 teaspoon baking soda

¼ teaspoon salt

1 cup warm water

¼ cup canola oil

1 tablespoon red wine vinegar

1 teaspoon vanilla extract

1 large egg, lightly beaten

½ cup semisweet chocolate minichips, divided

Cooking spray

1. Preheat oven to 400°.

2. Weigh or lightly spoon flour into dry measuring cups; level with a knife. Combine flour and next 5 ingredients (through salt) in a large bowl, stirring with a whisk. Make a well in center of mixture. Combine 1 cup water and next 4 ingredients (through egg) in a bowl, stirring well with a whisk. Stir in ¼ cup minichips. Add oil mixture to flour mixture, stirring just until moist.

3. Place 12 muffin cup liners in muffin cups; coat liners with cooking spray. Divide batter evenly among prepared muffin cups. Sprinkle remaining ¼ cup minichips evenly over batter. Bake at 400° for 15 minutes or until a wooden pick inserted in center comes out clean. Cool 5 minutes in pan on a wire rack.

Serves 12 (serving size: 1 muffin).

CALORIES 191; FAT 7.6g (sat 1.9g, mono 3.9g, poly 1.5g); PROTEIN 3.1g; CARB 29g; FIBER 1.5g; CHOL 15mg; IRON 1.5mg; SODIUM 197mg; CALC 37mg

QUICK BREADS & YEAST BREADS

12

Pumpkin-Cranberry Muffins 🍃

It's amazing how moist these muffins are with a scant two tablespoons of oil in the batter.

The secret is the canned pumpkin. If you'd like a jolt of puckery tartness, use fresh cranberries in place of dried. Make a double batch to keep on hand; follow the freezing and reheating instructions on page 394.

Hands-on time: 15 min. Total time: 40 min.

6.75 ounces all-purpose flour (about 1½ cups)

1 teaspoon baking soda

¾ teaspoon ground ginger

½ teaspoon baking powder

½ teaspoon ground cinnamon

¼ teaspoon salt

⅛ teaspoon ground cloves

1 cup granulated sugar

1 cup canned pumpkin

½ cup low-fat buttermilk

¼ cup packed light brown sugar

2 tablespoons canola oil

1 large egg

⅔ cup sweetened dried cranberries, chopped

Cooking spray

1. Preheat oven to 375°.
2. Weigh or lightly spoon flour into dry measuring cups; level with a knife. Combine flour and next 6 ingredients (through cloves); stir well with a whisk. Combine granulated sugar and next 5 ingredients (through egg) in a large bowl; beat with a mixer at medium speed until well blended (about 3 minutes). Add flour mixture to sugar mixture; beat at low speed just until combined.

Fold in cranberries.
3. Place 12 muffin cup liners in muffin cups; coat liners with cooking spray. Divide batter evenly among prepared cups. Bake at 375° for 25 minutes or until muffins spring back when touched lightly in center. Remove muffins from pan immediately; place on a wire rack.

Serves 12 (serving size: 1 muffin).

CALORIES 199; FAT 3.2g (sat 0.4g, mono 1.6g, poly 0.9g); PROTEIN 2.8g; CARB 41.1g; FIBER 1.5g; CHOL 18mg; IRON 1.3mg; SODIUM 195mg; CALC 38mg

Whole-Wheat Buttermilk Pancakes 🍃🌾

These fluffy flapjacks will be your go-to Saturday breakfast.

Don't be tempted to thin the batter; it should be quite thick. Hands-on time: 12 min. Total time: 21 min.

3.5 ounces all-purpose flour (about ¾ cup)

3.6 ounces whole-wheat flour (about ¾ cup)

3 tablespoons sugar

1½ teaspoons baking powder

½ teaspoon baking soda

½ teaspoon salt

1½ cups low-fat buttermilk

4 teaspoons canola oil, divided

1 large egg

1 large egg white

¾ cup maple syrup

3 tablespoons butter

1. Weigh or lightly spoon flours into dry measuring cups; level with a knife. Combine flours, sugar, baking powder, baking soda, and salt in a large bowl, stirring with a whisk. Combine buttermilk, 1 tablespoon oil, egg, and egg white, stirring with a whisk; add to flour mixture, stirring just until moist.
2. Heat a nonstick griddle or nonstick skillet over medium heat. Add remaining 1 teaspoon oil;

swirl to coat. Spoon about ¼ cup batter per pancake onto griddle. Turn pancakes over when tops are covered with bubbles and edges look cooked. Serve with syrup and butter.

Serves 6 (serving size: 2 pancakes, 2 tablespoons syrup, and 1½ teaspoons butter).

CALORIES 354; FAT 10.8g (sat 4.6g, mono 4g, poly 1.5g); PROTEIN 7.4g; CARB 59g; FIBER 2.3g; CHOL 53mg; IRON 2mg; SODIUM 532mg; CALC 172mg

Whole-Wheat, Oatmeal, and Fruit Muffins 🍃 🌾

About as healthy and delicious as a muffin can get, with whole grains, healthy fats, and three kinds of dried fruit.

The fruit trio allows you to get a variety of antioxidants and fiber, and wheat germ is a good source of vitamin E. Look for untoasted wheat germ in the organic food section of the supermarket. Adding boiling water to the batter and allowing it to sit for 15 minutes before baking allows the hearty oats, wheat germ, and bran to soak up the liquid and soften for a more tender muffin. Hands-on time: 15 min. Total time: 1 hr.

4.75 ounces whole-wheat flour (about 1 cup)
¼ cup granulated sugar
¼ cup packed brown sugar
2 tablespoons untoasted wheat germ
2 tablespoons wheat bran
1½ teaspoons baking soda
1 teaspoon ground cinnamon
½ teaspoon salt
1½ cups quick-cooking oats
⅓ cup chopped pitted dates
⅓ cup raisins
⅓ cup dried cranberries
1 cup low-fat buttermilk
¼ cup canola oil
1 teaspoon vanilla extract
1 large egg, lightly beaten
½ cup boiling water
Cooking spray

1. Weigh or lightly spoon flour into a dry measuring cup; level with a knife. Combine flour and next 7 ingredients (through salt) in a large bowl, stirring with a whisk. Stir in oats, dates, raisins, and cranberries. Make a well in center of mixture.
2. Combine buttermilk, oil, vanilla, and egg; add to flour mixture, stirring just until moist. Stir in ½ cup boiling water. Let batter stand 15 minutes.
3. Preheat oven to 375°.
4. Place 12 muffin-cup liners in muffin cups; coat liners with cooking spray. Divide batter evenly among prepared muffin cups. Bake at 375° for 20 minutes or until muffins spring back when touched lightly in center. Remove muffins from pans immediately; place on a wire rack.

Serves 12 (serving size: 1 muffin).

CALORIES 204; FAT 6.4g (sat 0.8g, mono 3.2g, poly 1.8g); PROTEIN 4.6g; CARB 34.7g; FIBER 3.4g; CHOL 19mg; IRON 1.4mg; SODIUM 288mg; CALC 43mg

QUICK BREADS & YEAST BREADS

12

Toasted Almond and Cherry Scones 🌿 🌾

Nice nut-and-fruit counterpoint, and healthy: These scones have two types of whole grains and the same amount of fiber as a bowl of instant oatmeal.

Substitute an equal amount of chopped pistachios or walnuts for the almonds; use mixed dried berries, if you prefer. Hands-on time: 20 min. Total time: 44 min.

4.5   ounces all-purpose flour (about 1 cup)

3.3   ounces whole-wheat pastry flour (about ¾ cup)

½   cup old-fashioned rolled oats

¼   cup packed brown sugar

2   teaspoons baking powder

½   teaspoon baking soda

½   teaspoon salt

½   teaspoon ground cinnamon

¼   teaspoon ground allspice

5   tablespoons chilled butter, cut into small pieces

1   cup fat-free sour cream

1   teaspoon vanilla extract

⅓   cup chopped dried cherries

⅓   cup chopped almonds, toasted

Cooking spray

½   cup powdered sugar

4   teaspoons 2% reduced-fat milk

1. Preheat oven to 400°.

2. Weigh or lightly spoon flours into dry measuring cups; level with a knife. Place oats in a food processor; process until finely ground. Add flours, brown sugar, and next 5 ingredients (through allspice) to processor; pulse 3 times. Add butter; pulse 5 times or until mixture resembles coarse meal. Add sour cream and vanilla; pulse 3 times or just until combined (do not overmix). Add cherries and nuts; pulse 2 times.

3. Turn dough out onto a lightly floured surface; knead lightly 3 times. Pat dough to a ½-inch thickness; cut with a 2½-inch biscuit cutter to form 10 rounds. Place rounds 1 inch apart on a baking sheet lightly coated with cooking spray. Bake at 400° for 14 minutes or until golden brown. Remove from baking sheet; cool on a wire rack.

4. Combine powdered sugar and 4 teaspoons milk, stirring with a whisk. Drizzle glaze over scones.

Serves 10 (serving size: 1 scone).

CALORIES 258; FAT 8.7g (sat 3.9g, mono 3.1g, poly 0.9g); PROTEIN 5.7g; CARB 39.3g; FIBER 3.1g; CHOL 19mg; IRON 1.6mg; SODIUM 363mg; CALC 140mg

Ciabatta French Toast with Warm Apple Maple Syrup 🍃

The savory notes of shallots and Gruyère pair fantastically with apples and maple for a toast twist that's not too sweet.

Ciabatta's springy texture is perfect for French toast. Use a vegetable peeler to slice the cheese thinly. Rome or Fuji apples would also work. Hands-on time: 35 min. Total time: 35 min.

¼ cup apple cider

1 teaspoon cornstarch

6 teaspoons butter, divided

2 tablespoons finely chopped shallots

2 cups sliced McIntosh apples

¼ cup maple syrup

6 (2-ounce) slices ciabatta bread

3 ounces Gruyère cheese, cut into thin slices

½ cup fat-free milk

⅓ cup low-fat buttermilk

¼ teaspoon salt

⅛ teaspoon ground nutmeg

⅛ teaspoon freshly ground black pepper

1 large egg

1 large egg white

3 tablespoons chopped pecans, toasted

1. Combine cider and cornstarch in a small bowl, stirring with a whisk. Melt 2 teaspoons butter in a large nonstick skillet over medium heat. Add shallots to pan; cook 1 minute, stirring frequently. Add cider mixture, apples, and syrup to pan; bring to a boil, stirring frequently. Reduce heat to low; cook 3 minutes or until apples begin to soften, stirring occasionally. Set aside, and keep warm.

2. Cut a horizontal slit through bottom crust of each bread slice to form a pocket; stuff ½ ounce cheese into each pocket. Combine fat-free milk, buttermilk, and next 5 ingredients (through egg white) in a shallow dish, stirring well with a whisk. Working with 1 stuffed bread slice at a time, place bread slice into milk mixture, turning gently to coat both sides.

3. Heat a large nonstick skillet over medium-high heat. Melt 2 teaspoons butter in pan. Add 3 coated bread slices to pan; cook 2 minutes on each side or until lightly browned. Repeat procedure with remaining 2 teaspoons butter and remaining 3 coated bread slices.

4. Place 1 French toast slice onto each of 6 plates; top each serving with about 3 tablespoons sauce and 1½ teaspoons pecans.

Serves 6.

CALORIES 373; FAT 14.3g (sat 5.9g, mono 6.1g, poly 1.5g); PROTEIN 12.8g; CARB 51.3g; FIBER 2.4g; CHOL 57mg; IRON 2.4mg; SODIUM 607mg; CALC 205mg

Flaky Buttermilk Biscuits 🌿

Buttermilk richness and pull-apart flaky layers, with a kiss of honey sweetness and at least 50% less saturated fat than traditional recipes.

Start with the classic biscuit flavor, and then try the fragrant pumpkin or savory Parmesan variations. The technique of folding the dough creates distinct layers and helps prevent overworking, which will toughen these delicate creations. Gather dough scraps after cutting, and gently pat or reroll to a ¾-inch thickness to get more. Hands-on time: 30 min. Total time: 44 min.

9	ounces all-purpose flour (about 2 cups)
2½	teaspoons baking powder
½	teaspoon salt
5	tablespoons chilled butter, cut into small pieces
¾	cup nonfat buttermilk
3	tablespoons honey

1. Preheat oven to 400°.

2. Weigh or lightly spoon flour into dry measuring cups; level with a knife. Combine flour, baking powder, and salt in a large bowl; cut in butter with a pastry blender or 2 knives until mixture resembles coarse meal. Chill 10 minutes.

3. Combine buttermilk and honey, stirring with a whisk until well blended. Add buttermilk mixture to flour mixture; stir just until moist.

4. Turn dough out onto a lightly floured surface; knead lightly 4 times. Pat dough into a (½-inch-thick) 9 x 5-inch rectangle; dust top of dough with flour. Fold dough crosswise into thirds (as if folding a piece of paper to fit into an envelope). Roll dough into a (½-inch-thick) 9 x 5-inch rectangle; dust top of dough with flour. Fold dough crosswise into thirds; gently roll or pat to a ¾-inch thickness. Cut dough with a 1¾-inch biscuit cutter to form 14 dough rounds. Place dough rounds, 1 inch apart, on a baking sheet lined with parchment paper. Bake at 400° for 12 minutes or until golden. Remove from pan; cool 2 minutes on wire racks. Serve warm.

Serves 14 (serving size: 1 biscuit).

CALORIES 121; FAT 4.2g (sat 2.6g, mono 1.1g, poly 0.2g); PROTEIN 2.4g; CARB 18.4g; FIBER 0.5g; CHOL 11mg; IRON 0.9mg; SODIUM 198mg; CALC 63mg

Spiced Pumpkin Biscuit variation: 🌿

Add 1¼ teaspoons pumpkin pie spice to flour mixture. Decrease buttermilk to ⅓ cup; add ¾ cup canned pumpkin to buttermilk mixture. Bake at 400° for 14 minutes.

Serves 14 (serving size: 1 biscuit).

CALORIES 122; FAT 4.3g (sat 2.6g, mono 1.1g, poly 0.2g); PROTEIN 2.3g; CARB 18.9g; FIBER 0.9g; CHOL 11mg; IRON 1.1mg; SODIUM 192mg; CALC 59mg

Parmesan-Pepper Biscuit variation: 🌿

Add 1 teaspoon freshly ground black pepper to flour mixture. Decrease butter to ¼ cup. Add ½ cup (2 ounces) grated fresh Parmesan cheese to buttermilk mixture. Bake at 400° for 13 minutes.

Serves 14 (serving size: 1 biscuit).

CALORIES 131; FAT 4.7g (sat 2.9g, mono 0.9g, poly 0.2g); PROTEIN 4.2g; CARB 18.5g; FIBER 0.5g; CHOL 13mg; IRON 0.9mg; SODIUM 239mg; CALC 98mg

Sour Cream, Cheddar, and Green Onion Drop Biscuits

Break open the crisp-bumpy crust to discover the moist, flavor-packed interior. It's the yin-yang of textures that's so irresistible.

Plus, this is one of the easiest and most flavorful breads you can make—just stir together and plop mounds of dough onto a pan to bake (instead of rolling and cutting out dough). They're perfect with a bowl of chili or soup. Though best warm from the oven, leftovers can be stored in an airtight container for up to two days. To warm them, wrap loosely in aluminum foil, and place in a 300° oven for 5 to 10 minutes.

Hands-on time: 20 min. Total time: 35 min.

9   ounces all-purpose flour (about 2 cups)
1   tablespoon sugar
2   teaspoons baking powder
¾   teaspoon salt
¼   teaspoon baking soda
3   tablespoons chilled unsalted butter, cut into small pieces
½   cup (2 ounces) reduced-fat shredded sharp cheddar cheese
¼   cup finely chopped green onions
1   cup nonfat buttermilk
½   cup fat-free sour cream
Cooking spray

1. Preheat oven to 450°.
2. Weigh or lightly spoon flour into dry measuring cups; level with a knife. Combine flour and next 4 ingredients (through baking soda) in a large bowl, stirring with a whisk. Cut in butter with a pastry blender or 2 knives until mixture resembles coarse meal. Add cheese and onions; toss well. Add buttermilk and sour cream; stir just until moist.

3. Drop dough by ¼ cupfuls onto a baking sheet coated with cooking spray. Bake at 450° for 15 minutes or until edges are brown. Serve immediately.

Serves 12 (serving size: 1 biscuit).

CALORIES 137; FAT 4.2g (sat 2.5g, mono 0.8g, poly 0.2g); PROTEIN 4.4g; CARB 20.1g; FIBER 0.7g; CHOL 12mg; IRON 1mg; SODIUM 318mg; CALC 118mg

QUICK BREADS & YEAST BREADS

12

TEST KITCHEN SECRET

Working with Lower-Fat Dough: The recipes in this chapter reflect a lot of work and hard lessons concerning the handling of lower-fat batters and doughs. Recipes with lots of butter are more likely to stay moist and tender because of the fat, even if the dough is overmixed or overkneaded. With less fat to work with, you absolutely must use a light hand. That's why many of our biscuit and scone recipes instruct the cook to knead the dough lightly or pat it out (instead of rolling), and our cookie or piecrust recipes say to mix just until flour is incorporated. To be safe, stop machine mixing early and finish by hand. Vigorous mixing encourages gluten development, which creates a chewy or tough texture—great in a baguette but not in a biscuit or scone.

Peanut Butter–Banana Bread 🌿

This easy bread, with far less of the drenching saturated fat than most recipes, is one of the tastier treats to come out of our Test Kitchen.

Peanut butter is whipped into the basic recipe for a moist bread with a hint of nutty flavor. A small amount of chopped roasted peanuts offers crunch and more nutty goodness. Hands-on time: 18 min. Total time: 1 hr. 33 min.

Bread:

1½	cups mashed ripe banana
⅓	cup plain fat-free yogurt
⅓	cup creamy peanut butter
3	tablespoons butter, melted
2	large eggs
½	cup granulated sugar
½	cup packed brown sugar
6.75	ounces all-purpose flour (about 1½ cups)
¼	cup ground flaxseed
¾	teaspoon baking soda
½	teaspoon salt
½	teaspoon ground cinnamon
⅛	teaspoon ground allspice
2	tablespoons chopped dry-roasted peanuts

Cooking spray

Glaze:

⅓	cup powdered sugar
1	tablespoon 1% low-fat milk
1	tablespoon creamy peanut butter

1. Preheat oven to 350°.

2. To prepare bread, combine first 5 ingredients in a large bowl; beat with a mixer at medium speed. Add granulated and brown sugars; beat until blended.

3. Weigh or lightly spoon flour into dry measuring cups; level with a knife. Combine flour and next 5 ingredients (through allspice) in a small bowl. Add flour mixture to banana mixture; beat just until blended. Stir in nuts. Pour batter into a 9 x 5–inch loaf pan coated with cooking spray. Bake at 350° for 1 hour and 5 minutes or until a wooden pick inserted in center comes out clean. Remove from oven; cool 10 minutes in pan on a wire rack. Remove bread from pan; cool.

4. To prepare glaze, combine powdered sugar, milk, and 1 tablespoon peanut butter in a small bowl, stirring with a whisk. Drizzle glaze over bread.

Serves 16 (serving size: 1 slice).

CALORIES 198; FAT 7.4g (sat 2.3g, mono 2.7g, poly 1.8g); PROTEIN 4.7g; CARB 29.7g; FIBER 1.9g; CHOL 28mg; IRON 1.1mg; SODIUM 200mg; CALC 27mg

TECHNIQUE

Making the Best Banana Bread: Despite the rich flavor, our recipe doesn't call for a cup of oil or butter, as traditional recipes usually do; we use less than half that without sacrificing the moist texture that makes banana bread a treat.

1. Combine the wet ingredients, and beat with a mixer.

2. A mix of granulated and brown sugars adds sweetness and caramel notes. Beat to incorporate air into the batter.

3. Add dry ingredients, and stir into the sugar mixture. Weigh the flour, if you can. It's the most accurate way to measure.

4. Besides the bananas, you can add chopped nuts, chocolate chips, spices, and dried fruit.

Bananas Foster Bread 🌿

A slightly boozy variation on the classic quick bread.

This adult interpretation cooks the mashed bananas with butter and cognac. It's so delicious it qualifies as a dessert. Hands-on time: 22 min. Total time: 1 hr. 34 min.

1½ cups mashed ripe banana

1 cup packed brown sugar, divided

6 tablespoons butter, melted and divided

¼ cup cognac or dark rum, divided

⅓ cup plain fat-free yogurt

2 large eggs

6.75 ounces all-purpose flour (about 1½ cups)

¼ cup ground flaxseed

¾ teaspoon baking soda

½ teaspoon salt

½ teaspoon ground cinnamon

⅛ teaspoon ground allspice

Cooking spray

⅓ cup powdered sugar

1. Preheat oven to 350°.

2. Combine banana, ½ cup brown sugar, 5 tablespoons butter, and 3 tablespoons cognac in a nonstick skillet. Cook over medium heat until mixture begins to bubble. Remove from heat; cool. Place banana mixture in a large bowl. Add yogurt, remaining ½ cup brown sugar, and eggs. Beat with a mixer at medium speed.

3. Weigh or lightly spoon flour into dry measuring cups; level with a knife. Combine flour and next 5 ingredients (through allspice) in a small bowl. Add flour mixture to banana mixture; beat just until blended. Pour batter into a 9 x 5–inch loaf pan coated with cooking spray. Bake at 350° for 1 hour or until a wooden pick inserted in center comes out clean. Remove from oven; cool 10 minutes in pan on a wire rack. Remove bread from pan; place on wire rack.

4. Combine remaining 1 tablespoon butter, remaining 1 tablespoon cognac, and powdered sugar in a small bowl; stir until well blended. Drizzle over warm bread.

Serves 16 (serving size: 1 slice).

CALORIES 194; FAT 5.8g (sat 3g, mono 1.5g, poly 0.9g); PROTEIN 2.9g; CARB 31.1g; FIBER 1.5g; CHOL 34mg; IRON 1.1mg; SODIUM 181mg; CALC 32mg

Easy French Toast Casserole

Custard-soaked bread bakes atop caramel, then gets the upside-down treatment so the gooey sauce is the star.

It's an easy way to do French toast for a small crowd; prep and assemble the night before, and pop in the oven the next morning. French bread with a soft crust works best because it's easier to cut. You can omit the liqueur in the whipped topping. Hands-on time: 15 min. Total time: 12 hr. 44 min.

⅔ cup packed dark brown sugar

2 tablespoons butter

2 tablespoons dark corn syrup

Cooking spray

1½ cups 1% low-fat milk

½ cup egg substitute

1 teaspoon vanilla extract

¼ teaspoon salt

⅛ teaspoon grated orange rind

2 large eggs

6 (1½-inch-thick) slices French bread

6 tablespoons frozen fat-free whipped topping, thawed

1 to 2 teaspoons Grand Marnier (orange-flavored liqueur)

2 tablespoons finely chopped pecans, toasted

1. Combine first 3 ingredients in a small heavy saucepan over medium heat. Cook 5 minutes or until bubbly and sugar dissolves, stirring constantly. Pour sugar mixture into bottom of a 13 x 9–inch glass or ceramic baking dish coated with cooking spray. Spread mixture evenly over bottom of pan. Set aside; cool completely.

2. Combine milk and next 5 ingredients (through eggs) in a large shallow bowl; stir with a whisk. Dip 1 bread slice in milk mixture; arrange bread slice over sugar mixture in dish. Repeat procedure with remaining 5 bread slices. Pour any remaining egg mixture over bread slices. Cover and refrigerate overnight.

3. Preheat oven to 350°.

4. Bake at 350° for 30 minutes or until lightly browned.

5. While casserole bakes, combine whipped topping and Grand Marnier. Place 1 bread slice, caramel side up, on each of 6 plates; top each serving with 1 tablespoon topping and 1 teaspoon pecans.

Serves 6.

CALORIES 352; FAT 8.8g (sat 3.5g, mono 2.8g, poly 0.9g); PROTEIN 11.1g; CARB 58.1g; FIBER 1.2g; CHOL 83mg; IRON 2.6mg; SODIUM 466mg; CALC 191mg

Basic Beer-Cheese Bread 🌿

Here's a savory quick bread, a light variation on traditional Irish beer bread with a few flavor riffs.

The basic bread pairs well with soup and is ideal for an open house or casual get-together. We use just a bit of butter, and all of it goes on top of the loaf to create a buttery crust with an immediate flavor impact. The Manchego-Jalapeño is delicious with chili. Hands-on time: 11 min. Total time: 1 hr. 23 min.

1	tablespoon olive oil
½	cup finely chopped yellow onion
¼	teaspoon freshly ground black pepper
1	garlic clove, minced
13.5	ounces all-purpose flour (about 3 cups)
3	tablespoons sugar
2	teaspoons baking powder
1	teaspoon salt
1	cup (4 ounces) shredded Monterey Jack cheese
1	(12-ounce) bottle lager-style beer
	Cooking spray
2	tablespoons melted butter, divided

1. Preheat oven to 375°.
2. Heat oil in a small skillet over medium-low heat. Add onion to pan; cook 10 minutes or until browned, stirring occasionally. Stir in pepper and garlic; cook 1 minute.
3. Weigh or lightly spoon flour into dry measuring cups; level with a knife. Combine flour, sugar, baking powder, and salt in a large bowl, stirring with a whisk; make a well in center of mixture. Add onion mixture, cheese, and beer to flour mixture, stirring just until moist.

4. Spoon batter into a 9 x 5-inch loaf pan coated with cooking spray. Drizzle 1 tablespoon butter over batter. Bake at 375° for 35 minutes. Drizzle remaining 1 tablespoon butter over batter. Bake an additional 25 minutes or until deep golden brown and a wooden pick inserted in center comes out clean. Cool in pan 5 minutes on a wire rack; remove from pan. Cool completely on wire rack.

Serves 16 (serving size: 1 slice).

CALORIES 144; FAT 4.4g (sat 2.4g, mono 1.6g, poly 0.2g); PROTEIN 4.3g; CARB 20.6g; FIBER 0.7g; CHOL 10mg; IRON 1.3mg; SODIUM 257mg; CALC 89mg

Apple-Cheddar Beer Bread variation: 🌿

Substitute ½ cup minced shallots for onion. Place ½ cup shredded peeled Gala apple in paper towels; squeeze until barely moist. Cook shallots and apple in oil over medium heat for 7 minutes. Substitute 1 cup shredded extra-sharp white cheddar cheese for Monterey Jack. Substitute 1 (12-ounce) bottle hard cider for lager.

Serves 16 (serving size: 1 slice).

CALORIES 151; FAT 4.6g (sat 2.5g, mono 1.6g, poly 0.3g); PROTEIN 4.4g; CARB 21.9g; FIBER 0.8g; CHOL 11mg; IRON 1.3mg; SODIUM 265mg; CALC 87mg

Manchego-Jalapeño Beer Bread variation: 🌿

Substitute ¼ cup thinly sliced green onions and ¼ cup finely chopped jalapeño pepper for onion; cook over medium heat 3 minutes. Substitute 1 cup (4 ounces) shredded Manchego cheese for Monterey Jack cheese. Substitute 1 (12-ounce) bottle Mexican beer for lager-style beer.

Serves 16 (serving size: 1 slice).

CALORIES 148; FAT 4.6g (sat 2.4g, mono 1.7g, poly 0.3g); PROTEIN 4.7g; CARB 20.6g; FIBER 0.7g; CHOL 12mg; IRON 1.3mg; SODIUM 244mg; CALC 108mg

Sopressata-Asiago Beer Bread variation:

Substitute ½ cup minced shallots and 2 tablespoons chopped green onions for onion. Substitute ¾ cup (3 ounces) shredded Asiago cheese for Monterey Jack cheese. Substitute 1 (12-ounce) bottle Italian lager beer for lager-style beer. Stir 2 ounces finely chopped Sopressata salami into batter.

Serves 16 (serving size: 1 slice).

CALORIES 154; FAT 5g (sat 2.4g, mono 2g, poly 0.3g); PROTEIN 5g; CARB 21.2g; FIBER 0.7g; CHOL 11mg; IRON 1.4mg; SODIUM 301mg; CALC 89mg

Spicy Jalapeño Corn Bread 🌿 🌾

Zing goes the chile, pop goes the fresh, sweet corn, for those who like their corn bread busy.

When cutting corn from the cob, corral the kernels in a bowl so they don't fly all over your counter. You'll likely have leftovers; seal extra portions in plastic wrap, and store at room temperature for up to one day.

Hands-on time: 9 min. Total time: 53 min.

Cooking spray

1¼	cups stone-ground cornmeal
1	cup fresh corn kernels (about 2 ears)
¾	teaspoon kosher salt
½	teaspoon baking soda
1	cup nonfat buttermilk
½	cup (2 ounces) reduced-fat shredded cheddar cheese
2	tablespoons minced pickled jalapeño peppers
1½	tablespoons butter, melted
1½	tablespoons honey
1	tablespoon canola oil
2	large eggs, lightly beaten

1. Preheat oven to 375°.
2. Place a 9-inch cast-iron skillet coated with cooking spray in oven 5 minutes or until heated.
3. Combine cornmeal, corn, salt, and baking soda in a large bowl, stirring with a whisk; make a well in center of mixture. Combine buttermilk and next 6 ingredients (through eggs) in a small bowl; add to cornmeal mixture. Stir just until combined. Spoon mixture into preheated pan. Bake at 375° for 30 minutes or until a wooden pick inserted in center comes out clean. Cool in pan 10 minutes on a wire rack.

Serves 12 (serving size: 1 wedge).

CALORIES 138; FAT 5.1g (sat 1.9g, mono 1.4g, poly 0.6g); PROTEIN 4.7g; CARB 19.5g; FIBER 2.9g; CHOL 43mg; IRON 0.8mg; SODIUM 263mg; CALC 68mg

Blueberry-Lemon Coffee Cake 🌿
Almond paste makes this sweet and nutty.

Each slice has 300 fewer calories than a typical coffee cake. Hands-on time: 11 min. Total time: 46 min.

6.75 ounces all-purpose flour (about 1½ cups)
2 teaspoons baking powder
¼ teaspoon baking soda
½ teaspoon salt
½ cup sugar
⅓ cup almond paste
2 tablespoons chilled butter, cut into small pieces
1 tablespoon fresh lemon juice
1 large egg
¾ cup fat-free milk
1½ cups blueberries
2 teaspoons grated lemon rind
Cooking spray
¼ cup sugar

3 tablespoons sliced almonds, chopped
1½ tablespoons butter, melted
½ teaspoon ground cinnamon

1. Preheat oven to 350°.
2. Weigh or lightly spoon flour into dry measuring cups; level with a knife. Combine flour, baking powder, baking soda, and salt in a small bowl, stirring with a whisk.
3. Place ½ cup sugar, almond paste, and 2 tablespoons butter in a large bowl; beat with a mixer at medium speed until well blended. Add lemon juice and egg, beating well. Add flour mixture and milk alternately to sugar mixture, beginning and ending with flour mixture. Fold in blueberries and rind. Spoon batter into a 9-inch square metal baking pan coated with cooking spray.
4. Combine ¼ cup sugar and next 3 ingredients (through cinnamon) in a small bowl, tossing with a fork until moist. Sprinkle topping evenly over batter. Bake at 350° for 35 minutes or until a wooden pick inserted in center comes out clean. Cool in pan on a wire rack.

Serves 12 (serving size: 1 piece).

CALORIES 196; FAT 6.5g (sat 2.1g, mono 3.2g, poly 0.8g); PROTEIN 3.8g; CARB 31.6g; FIBER 1.4g; CHOL 27mg; IRON 1.2mg; SODIUM 243mg; CALC 82mg

Herbed Passover Rolls 🌿
We created a tender roll for the Seder table using the classic French technique used to make cream puffs and éclairs.

You can make these ahead, and freeze for up to a month. Hands-on time: 10 min. Total time: 1 hr. 20 min.

1¼ cups water
⅓ cup canola oil
1 tablespoon sugar
1 teaspoon kosher salt
2 cups matzo meal
4 large eggs
1 tablespoon chopped fresh chives
2 teaspoons finely chopped fresh thyme

1. Preheat oven to 375°.
2. Cover a large heavy baking sheet with parchment paper.
3. Combine first 4 ingredients in a medium saucepan over medium-high heat; bring to a boil. Reduce heat to low; add matzo meal, stirring well with a wooden spoon until mixture pulls away from sides of pan (about 30 seconds). Remove from heat; place dough in bowl of a stand mixer. Cool slightly. Add eggs, 1 at a time, beating at low speed with paddle attachment until well combined and scraping sides and bottom of bowl after each egg. Stir in chives and thyme.
4. With moistened fingers, shape about ¼ cupfuls of dough into 12 mounds; place 2 inches apart onto prepared pan. Bake at 375° for 55 minutes or until browned and crisp. Cool on a wire rack.

Serves 12 (serving size: 1 roll).

CALORIES 134; FAT 8g (sat 1g, mono 4.3g, poly 2.1g); PROTEIN 3.8g; CARB 12.5g; FIBER 0.6g; CHOL 71mg; IRON 1mg; SODIUM 181mg; CALC 13mg

No-Knead Overnight Parmesan and Thyme Rolls

A must-try if you want yeasty goodness without the knead.

The dough is more like a thick batter; don't add additional flour or the rolls will turn out dry.
Hands-on time: 23 min. Total time: 13 hr. 38 min.

½ teaspoon dry yeast

2 tablespoons warm water (100° to 110°)

2 tablespoons extra-virgin olive oil, divided

1 teaspoon dried thyme

⅓ cup 2% reduced-fat milk

½ cup (2 ounces) grated Parmigiano-Reggiano cheese, divided

1 tablespoon sugar

½ teaspoon kosher salt

1 large egg, lightly beaten

1.1 ounces whole-wheat white flour (about ¼ cup)

5.6 ounces all-purpose flour (about 1¼ cups), divided

Cooking spray

½ teaspoon cracked black pepper

1. Dissolve yeast in 2 tablespoons warm water in a large bowl; let stand 5 minutes or until bubbly.

2. Heat a small saucepan over medium heat. Add 1 tablespoon oil to pan; swirl to coat. Add thyme to pan; cook 1 minute or until bubbly and fragrant. Add thyme mixture and milk to yeast mixture, stirring with a whisk. Add ¼ cup cheese, sugar, salt, and egg, stirring well.

3. Weigh or lightly spoon whole-wheat white flour into a dry measuring cup; level with a knife. Using a wooden spoon, stir whole-wheat white flour into yeast mixture. Weigh or lightly spoon 4.5 ounces all-purpose flour (about 1 cup) into a dry measuring cup; level with a knife. Add all-purpose flour to yeast mixture, stirring well. Add enough of remaining 1.1 ounces all-purpose flour (about ¼ cup), 1 tablespoon at a time, to form a smooth but very sticky dough. Place dough in a large bowl coated with cooking spray, turning to coat top. Cover and refrigerate overnight. (Dough will not double in size.)

4. Remove dough from refrigerator. Do not punch dough down. Turn dough out onto a floured surface; sprinkle dough lightly with flour. Roll dough into a 12 x 7-inch rectangle. Brush dough with remaining 1 tablespoon oil. Sprinkle remaining ¼ cup cheese evenly over dough; sprinkle with pepper. Beginning with a long side, roll up dough, jelly-roll fashion. Pinch seam to seal (do not seal ends of roll). Cut roll into 8 (1½-inch) slices. Place slices, cut sides up, on a baking sheet covered with parchment paper. Cover and let rise in a warm place (85°), free from drafts, 1 hour or until rolls have risen slightly.

5. Preheat oven to 400°.

6. Place pan in oven, and immediately reduce heat to 375°. Bake rolls at 375° for 12 minutes or until golden brown. Serve warm.

Serves 8 (serving size: 1 roll).

CALORIES 161; FAT 6.3g (sat 2g, mono 3.3g, poly 0.6g); PROTEIN 6.3g; CARB 19.7g; FIBER 1.3g; CHOL 32mg; IRON 1.4mg; SODIUM 246mg; CALC 112mg

TECHNIQUE

Making No-Knead Rolls: Stir the dough together quickly before shaping and baking.

1. Brush dough with oil to help sprinkled ingredients adhere.

2. Roll up the dough. You don't need to roll it too tightly.

3. Slice the dough log using a thin, sharp knife or floss.

Brioche Rolls

Toasty, buttery, bakery flavor, with 80% less saturated fat.

A stand mixer streamlines prep, muffin tins keep portions in check, and an overnight rise in the fridge builds flavor and develops texture. Start a day ahead, as the overnight rise is essential for best results.
Hands-on time: 29 min. Total time: 12 hr. 2 min.

1	**package dry yeast (about 2¼ teaspoons)**
⅓	**cup warm 1% low-fat milk (100° to 110°)**
15.75	**ounces all-purpose flour (about 3½ cups)**
⅓	**cup sugar**
½	**teaspoon salt**
4	**large eggs, lightly beaten**
8½	**tablespoons unsalted butter, softened and divided**
	Cooking spray
1	**tablespoon water**
1	**large egg white**

1. Dissolve yeast in warm milk in bowl of a stand mixer fitted with paddle attachment; let stand 5 minutes.
2. Weigh or lightly spoon flour into dry measuring cups; level with a knife. Add flour, sugar, salt, and eggs to milk mixture; beat with a stand mixer at low speed until smooth, scraping down sides of bowl with spatula, as needed.

Remove paddle attachment; insert dough hook. Mix dough at low speed 5 minutes or until soft and elastic, and dough just begins to pull away from sides of bowl. Cut 6½ tablespoons butter into large cubes; add half of butter to dough, mixing at medium speed until blended. Add remaining half of butter to dough; mix at medium speed until incorporated. Mix dough at medium speed 4 minutes or until smooth and elastic. Place dough in a large bowl coated with cooking spray, turning to coat top. Cover and let rise in a warm place (85°), free from drafts, 1 hour or until doubled in size. (Gently press two fingers into dough. If indentation remains, dough has risen enough.) Punch dough down; form into a ball. Return dough to bowl; cover with plastic wrap, and refrigerate 8 hours or overnight.
3. Uncover dough; let stand 90 minutes or until dough is at room temperature. Divide dough into 4 equal portions. Working

with 1 portion at a time (cover remaining dough to prevent drying), cut dough into 6 equal pieces. Roll each piece into a 1½-inch ball. Repeat procedure with remaining 3 dough portions to make 24 rolls. Place rolls in muffin cups coated with cooking spray. Cover and let rise 45 minutes or until almost doubled in size.
4. Preheat oven to 350°.
5. Combine 1 tablespoon water and egg white; stir with a whisk. Gently brush rolls with egg mixture. Bake at 350° for 14 minutes or until golden. Place pans on wire racks. Place remaining 2 tablespoons butter in a microwave-safe bowl; microwave at HIGH 20 seconds or until butter melts. Brush butter onto rolls.

Serves 24 (serving size: 1 roll).

CALORIES 128; FAT 4.9g (sat 2.8g, mono 1.4g, poly 0.4g); PROTEIN 3.4g; CARB 17.2g; FIBER 0.6g; CHOL 41mg; IRON 1.1mg; SODIUM 94mg; CALC 13mg

Oatmeal Knots 🌿

Honey-sweetened rolls cook up beautifully when topped with oats and seeds.

If you can't find flaxseed meal, grind flaxseed in a coffee or spice grinder. Hands-on time: 38 min. Total time: 2 hr. 31 min.

1 cup old-fashioned rolled oats

½ cup honey

2 tablespoons butter

1½ teaspoons salt

2 cups boiling water

1 package dry yeast (about 2¼ teaspoons)

⅓ cup warm water (100° to 110°)

¼ cup flaxseed meal

14.5 ounces whole-wheat flour (about 3 cups)

6.75 ounces all-purpose flour (about 1½ cups), divided

Cooking spray

1 teaspoon water

1 large egg

1 tablespoon old-fashioned rolled oats

1 tablespoon poppy seeds

1 tablespoon sesame seeds

1. Combine first 4 ingredients in a large bowl; add 2 cups boiling water, stirring until well blended. Cool to room temperature.

2. Dissolve yeast in ⅓ cup warm water in a small bowl; let stand 5 minutes. Add yeast mixture to oat mixture; stir well. Stir in flaxseed meal.

3. Weigh or lightly spoon flours into dry measuring cups; level with a knife. Gradually add whole-wheat flour and 4.5 ounces all-purpose flour (about 1 cup) to oat mixture; stir until a soft dough forms. Turn dough out onto a lightly floured surface. Knead until smooth and elastic (about 8 minutes); add enough of remaining 2.25 ounces all-purpose flour (about ½ cup), 1 tablespoon at a time, to prevent dough from sticking to hands (dough will feel sticky).

4. Place dough in a large bowl coated with cooking spray, turning to coat top. Cover and let rise in a warm place (85°), free from drafts, 1 hour or until doubled in size. (Gently press two fingers into dough. If indentation remains, dough has risen enough.) Punch dough down; let rest 5 minutes.

5. Divide dough in half; cut each half into 12 equal portions. Working with 1 portion at a time (cover remaining dough to prevent drying), shape each portion into an 8-inch rope. Tie each rope into a single knot; tuck top end of rope under bottom edge of roll. Place rolls on a baking sheet coated with cooking spray. Cover with plastic wrap coated with cooking spray; let rise in a warm place (85°), free from drafts, 30 minutes or until doubled in size.

6. Preheat oven to 400°.

7. Combine 1 teaspoon water and egg in a small bowl; brush egg mixture over rolls. Combine 1 tablespoon oats, poppy seeds, and sesame seeds in a bowl; sprinkle evenly over rolls. Bake at 400° for 15 minutes or until golden. Cool on wire racks.

Serves 24 (serving size: 1 roll).

CALORIES 138; FAT 2.7g (sat 0.9g, mono 0.7g, poly 0.9g); PROTEIN 4.3g; CARB 25.6g; FIBER 2.9g; CHOL 13mg; IRON 1.4mg; SODIUM 160mg; CALC 22mg

QUICK BREADS & YEAST BREADS

12

CHOICE INGREDIENT

Active Dry Yeast: Yeast is the living substance that eats sugar and gives off carbon dioxide and ethyl alcohol to expand within pockets of gluten-strengthened dough, causing the bread to rise. Active dry yeast comes in jars or small foil-lined envelopes that equal about 2¼ teaspoons. When making bread from scratch, start by activating the yeast. Combine it with warm water or milk—when the mixture begins to bubble, you'll know the yeast is alive and growing. Water that's too hot will kill the yeast, and water that's too cold won't activate it. Store yeast in the refrigerator or freezer to prolong its life, but allow it to come to room temperature before you use it.

Raisin-Walnut Rye Bread
Rye is a delicious partner for dried fruit and nuts.

Because rye flour, whole-wheat flour, and cornmeal don't produce much gluten, we added high-gluten bread flour to ensure a lighter loaf with delicious texture. Hands-on time: 34 min. Total time: 2 hr. 38 min.

1	tablespoon sugar
1	package dry yeast (about 2¼ teaspoons)
1½	cups warm water (100° to 110°)
1	teaspoon olive oil
11.1	ounces bread flour (about 2⅓ cups), divided
4.75	ounces whole-wheat flour (about 1 cup)
2	ounces stone-ground rye flour (about ½ cup)
⅓	cup nonfat dry milk
¼	cup yellow cornmeal
1	teaspoon salt
¾	teaspoon coarsely ground black pepper
1	cup raisins
½	cup chopped walnuts
	Cooking spray

1. Dissolve sugar and yeast in 1½ cups warm water in a large bowl; let stand 5 minutes. Stir in oil. Weigh or lightly spoon flours into dry measuring cups; level with a knife. Combine 9.5 ounces bread flour (about 2 cups), whole-wheat flour, and next 5 ingredients (through pepper) in a bowl. Add flour mixture to yeast mixture. Turn dough out onto a lightly floured surface. Knead until smooth and elastic (about 10 minutes); add enough of remaining 1.6 ounces bread flour (about ⅓ cup), 1 tablespoon at a time, to prevent dough from sticking to hands. Knead in raisins and walnuts.
2. Place dough in a large bowl coated with cooking spray, turning to coat top. Cover and let rise in a warm place (85°), free from drafts, 45 minutes or until doubled in size.

(Gently press two fingers into dough. If indentation remains, dough has risen enough.) Punch dough down; cover and let rest 10 minutes. Shape dough into a ball; place in a 9-inch pie plate coated with cooking spray. Cover and let rise 30 minutes or until doubled in size.
3. Preheat oven to 400°.
4. Uncover dough. Score top of loaf in an X pattern using a sharp knife. Bake at 400° for 40 minutes or until loaf sounds hollow when tapped. Remove from pan; cool on a wire rack.

Serves 20 (serving size: 1 slice).

CALORIES 145; FAT 2.7g (sat 0.2g, mono 0.7g, poly 1.3g); PROTEIN 4.8g; CARB 26.5g; FIBER 2.7g; CHOL 0mg; IRON 1.5mg; SODIUM 127mg; CALC 28mg

Whole-Wheat Cinnamon Rolls

Everything you crave in a cinnamon roll, in a vastly lighter version: melt-in-your-mouth tenderness, warm spices, and that sweet glaze that oozes into the crevices.

All that, and it's a whole-grain choice. Hands-on time: 30 min. Total time: 2 hr. 56 min.

Dough:

1½	packages dry yeast (about 3¼ teaspoons)
¾	cup warm fat-free milk (100° to 110°)
¼	cup warm water (100° to 110°)
¼	cup butter, softened
¼	cup honey
½	teaspoon salt
1½	teaspoons fresh lemon juice
1	large egg
1	large egg white
11.25	ounces all-purpose flour (about 2½ cups), divided
7	ounces whole-wheat flour (about 1½ cups)
	Cooking spray

Filling:

¼	cup packed brown sugar
1½	tablespoons ground cinnamon
⅛	teaspoon ground nutmeg
⅓	cup raisins

Glaze:

¾	cup powdered sugar, sifted
¾	teaspoon vanilla extract
5	teaspoons fat-free milk

1. To prepare dough, dissolve yeast in warm milk and ¼ cup warm water in a large bowl; let stand 5 minutes or until foamy. Add butter and next 5 ingredients (through egg white); stir well. Weigh or lightly spoon flours into dry measuring cups; level with a knife. Add 9 ounces all-purpose flour (about 2 cups) and whole-wheat flour to yeast mixture, stirring until a soft dough forms.

2. Turn dough out onto a floured surface. Knead until smooth and elastic (about 8 minutes); add enough of remaining 2.25 ounces all-purpose flour (about ½ cup), 1 tablespoon at a time, to prevent dough from sticking to hands (dough will feel sticky). Place dough in a large bowl coated with cooking spray, turning to coat top. Cover and let rise in a warm place (85°), free from drafts, 1 hour or until doubled in size. (Gently press two fingers into dough. If indentation remains, dough has risen enough.) Punch dough down; roll into a 16 x 12-inch rectangle on a floured surface. Coat surface of dough with cooking spray.

3. To prepare filling, combine brown sugar, cinnamon, and nutmeg; sprinkle over dough, leaving a ½-inch border. Sprinkle raisins over dough, pressing gently into dough. Roll up rectangle tightly, starting with a long edge, pressing firmly to eliminate air pockets; pinch seam to seal. Cut dough into 16 rolls. Place rolls, cut sides up, in a 13 x 9-inch metal baking pan coated with cooking spray. Cover and let rise 45 minutes or until doubled in size.

4. Preheat oven to 375°.

5. Uncover rolls. Bake at 375° for 22 minutes or until lightly browned. Cool in pan on a wire rack.

6. To prepare glaze, place powdered sugar and vanilla in a small bowl. Add 5 teaspoons milk, 1 teaspoon at a time, stirring to form a thick glaze. Drizzle glaze evenly over rolls.

Serves 16 (serving size: 1 roll).

CALORIES 209; FAT 3.7g (sat 2g, mono 0.9g, poly 0.3g); PROTEIN 5.1g; CARB 40.4g; FIBER 2.6g; CHOL 21mg; IRON 2mg; SODIUM 111mg; CALC 39mg

QUICK BREADS & YEAST BREADS

12

Hot Cross Buns 🌿

These rich, tender, sweet yeast rolls are traditionally served on Good Friday. With 70% less saturated fat than full-fat versions, they don't have to be a once-a-year treat.

If currants are not available, you can double the raisins or add different small dried berries. These can be served at room temperature but are delicious warm. Hands-on time: 40 min. Total time: 3 hr. 15 min.

Rolls:

- ½ cup golden raisins
- ½ cup dried currants
- ¼ cup warm orange juice (120° to 130°)
- 19 ounces all-purpose flour (about 4¼ cups), divided
- 4.5 ounces whole-grain pastry flour (about 1 cup)
- 1 teaspoon salt
- 1 teaspoon grated lemon rind
- 1 teaspoon grated orange rind
- ½ teaspoon ground cinnamon
- ¼ teaspoon grated whole nutmeg
- 1 package quick-rise yeast (about 2¼ teaspoons)
- 1 cup warm fat-free milk (120° to 130°)
- ¼ cup honey
- ¼ cup unsalted butter, melted
- 2 large eggs, lightly beaten
- Cooking spray
- 1 tablespoon water
- 1 large egg white

Glaze:

- 1 cup powdered sugar
- 1 tablespoon 2% reduced-fat milk
- 1 teaspoon fresh lemon juice

1. To prepare rolls, combine first 3 ingredients in a small bowl; let stand 10 minutes. Drain fruit in a colander over a bowl, reserving fruit and juice.

2. Weigh or lightly spoon 18.5 ounces (about 4 cups plus 2 tablespoons) all-purpose flour and pastry flour into dry measuring cups; level with a knife. Combine flours and next 6 ingredients (through yeast) in bowl of a stand mixer with dough hook attached; mix until combined. Combine reserved orange juice, fat-free milk, honey, butter, and 2 eggs in a bowl, stirring with a whisk. With mixer on, slowly add milk mixture to flour mixture; mix at medium-low speed 7 minutes. Turn dough out onto a lightly floured surface. Add reserved fruit. Knead 2 minutes or until smooth and elastic; add enough of remaining 2 tablespoons all-purpose flour, 1 tablespoon at a time, to prevent dough from sticking. Place dough in a large bowl coated with cooking spray, turning to coat top. Cover and let rise in a warm, dry place (85°), free from drafts, 1 hour or until doubled in size. (Gently press two fingers into dough. If indentation remains, dough has risen enough.) Punch dough down;

cover and let rest 5 minutes. Divide dough into 24 equal portions; roll each portion into a ball. Place rolls in muffin cups coated with cooking spray. Cover and let rise 1 hour or until almost doubled in size.

3. Preheat oven to 350°.

4. Combine 1 tablespoon water and egg white; stir with a whisk. Gently brush rolls with egg white mixture. Bake at 350° for 20 minutes or until golden, rotating pans once during baking. Remove from pans; cool 10 minutes on a wire rack.

5. To prepare glaze, combine powdered sugar, 1 tablespoon milk, and 1 teaspoon juice in a bowl, stirring with a whisk. Microwave at HIGH 20 seconds or until warm. Spoon glaze into a zip-top plastic bag. Seal bag; snip a tiny hole in 1 corner of bag. Pipe a cross on top of each warm roll.

Serves 24 (serving size: 1 roll).

CALORIES 179; FAT 2.8g (sat 1.4g, mono 0.7g, poly 0.2g); PROTEIN 4.5g; CARB 34.8g; FIBER 1.6g; CHOL 23mg; IRON 1.4mg; SODIUM 111mg; CALC 29mg

Christmas Stollen 🌿

Jewel-like brandy-soaked fruit in an enriched dough—this bread is a joyous celebration of the season.

It's also a mighty fine gift that's a big step beyond fruitcake. You may need to order candied citron online, or omit it and add extra dried apricots and increase lemon rind to 1 tablespoon. Hands-on time: 32 min. Total time: 3 hr. 21 min.

16.9 ounces all-purpose flour (about 3¾ cups), divided

½ teaspoon salt

½ teaspoon freshly grated nutmeg

¼ cup fresh orange juice

2 tablespoons brandy

½ cup dried cherries

⅓ cup golden raisins

⅓ cup chopped dried apricots

½ cup warm 2% reduced-fat milk (100° to 110°)

¼ cup granulated sugar

1 package dry yeast (about 2¼ teaspoons)

6 tablespoons butter, melted

2 large eggs, lightly beaten

½ cup diced candied citron

½ cup sliced almonds, toasted

1½ teaspoons grated lemon rind

Cooking spray

2 tablespoons 2% reduced-fat milk, divided

1 large egg

½ cup powdered sugar

1. Weigh or lightly spoon flour into dry measuring cups; level with a knife. Combine 15.8 ounces flour (about 3½ cups), salt, and nutmeg in a large bowl. Combine orange juice and brandy in a microwave-safe bowl; microwave at HIGH 45 seconds. Add cherries, raisins, and apricots to orange juice mixture; let stand 20 minutes.

2. Combine warm milk, granulated sugar, and yeast in a bowl; let stand 5 minutes. Stir butter and 2 eggs into yeast mixture. Stir in juice mixture, ½ cup citron, almonds, and rind. Add flour mixture to yeast mixture, stirring until a soft dough forms. Turn dough out onto a lightly floured surface. Knead 5 minutes or until dough is smooth and elastic, adding remaining 1.1 ounces flour (about ¼ cup), 1 tablespoon at a time, to prevent dough from sticking to hands (dough will feel sticky).

3. Place dough in a large bowl coated with cooking spray, turning to coat top. Cover and let rise in a warm place (85°), free from drafts, 1 hour or until doubled in size. Punch dough down. Divide dough into 2 equal portions; roll each into an 11 x 8-inch oval. Fold 1 short end toward center; fold other short end toward center until it overlaps first end. Place loaves, seam sides down, on a baking sheet lined with parchment paper. Cover and let rise 1 hour or until doubled in size.

4. Preheat oven to 350°.

5. Combine 1 tablespoon milk and 1 egg. Uncover dough; brush gently with milk mixture. Bake at 350° for 32 minutes or until golden. Cool on wire racks. Combine remaining 1 tablespoon milk and powdered sugar, stirring until smooth; drizzle over loaves.

Serves 24 (serving size: 1 slice).

CALORIES 168; FAT 4.8g (sat 2.2g, mono 1.7g, poly 0.5g); PROTEIN 3.8g; CARB 26.5g; FIBER 1.4g; CHOL 34mg; IRON 1.4mg; SODIUM 83mg; CALC 26mg

Classic Walnut Boule 🌿

A double hit of walnuts—chopped nuts and oil—offers that distinctive toasty-bitter flavor, plus healthy omega-3 fatty acids.

Boule, the French word for ball, often refers to round loaves of crusty bread. You can use any leftovers to make sandwiches for lunch, or simply toast a slice, slather it with jam and a bit of butter, and enjoy it for breakfast or a snack. Hands-on time: 22 min. Total time: 2 hr. 55 min.

3   **tablespoons sugar**

1   **package dry yeast (about 2¼ teaspoons)**

1   **cup warm water (100° to 110°)**

1   **tablespoon toasted walnut oil**

10.7   **ounces bread flour (about 2¼ cups), divided**

4.75   **ounces whole-wheat flour (about 1 cup)**

1½   **teaspoons salt**

   Cooking spray

½   **cup coarsely chopped walnuts, toasted**

2   **tablespoons yellow cornmeal**

1   **tablespoon fat-free milk**

1   **large egg white**

1. Dissolve sugar and yeast in 1 cup warm water in a large bowl; let stand 5 minutes. Stir in oil. Weigh or lightly spoon flours into dry measuring cups; level with a knife. Add 9.5 ounces bread flour (about 2 cups), whole-wheat flour, and salt to yeast mixture; stir until a soft dough forms. Turn dough out onto a lightly floured surface. Knead until smooth and elastic (about 5 minutes); add enough of remaining 1.2 ounces bread flour (about ¼ cup), 1 tablespoon at a time, to prevent dough from sticking to hands (dough will feel sticky).

2. Place dough in a large bowl coated with cooking spray, turning to coat top. Cover and let rise in a warm place (85°), free from drafts, 1 hour or until doubled in size. (Gently press two fingers into dough. If indentation remains, dough has risen enough.)

Punch dough down; knead in walnuts. Shape dough into a 9-inch round on a lightly floured surface. Place dough on a large baking sheet sprinkled with cornmeal. Cover and let rise 1 hour or until doubled in size.

3. Preheat oven to 350°.

4. Uncover dough. Combine milk and egg white in a bowl; brush over dough. Score dough by making two diagonal slits with a sharp knife; make two diagonal slits in opposite direction to create a crosshatch pattern. Bake at 350° for 30 minutes or until bread is browned on bottom and sounds hollow when tapped. Cool on a wire rack.

Serves 16 (serving size: 1 slice).

CALORIES 122; FAT 3.4g (sat 0.3g, mono 0.6g, poly 2.3g); PROTEIN 4.1g; CARB 20.3g; FIBER 1.7g; CHOL 0mg; IRON 1.2mg; SODIUM 226mg; CALC 8mg

Garlic-Thyme Focaccia 🌿
The crunch of coarse salt is the crowning glory here; it's what makes this bread so memorable.

For a spicy variation, infuse the oil by adding ½ teaspoon crushed red pepper along with the garlic; strain through a sieve before brushing the flavored oil onto the dough. Hands-on time: 30 min. Total time: 1 hr. 52 min.

1 teaspoon sugar
1 package dry yeast (about 2¼ teaspoons)
1 cup warm water (100° to 110°)
½ teaspoon fine sea salt
11.1 ounces all-purpose flour (about 2⅓ cups plus 2 tablespoons), divided
Cooking spray
1 tablespoon olive oil
2 garlic cloves, thinly sliced
1 tablespoon chopped fresh thyme
¾ teaspoon coarse sea salt

1. Dissolve sugar and yeast in 1 cup warm water in a large bowl; let stand 5 minutes. Stir in fine sea salt. Weigh or lightly spoon flour into dry measuring cups and spoons; level with a knife. Add 9.6 ounces flour (about 2 cups plus 2 tablespoons) to yeast mixture, stirring to form a soft dough. Turn dough out onto a floured surface; knead until smooth and elastic (about 8 minutes). Add enough of remaining 1.5 ounces flour (about ⅓ cup), 1 tablespoon at a time, to prevent dough from sticking to hands (dough will feel sticky).
2. Place dough in a large bowl coated with cooking spray, turning to coat top. Cover and let rise in a warm place (85°), free from drafts, 45 minutes or until doubled in size. (Gently press two fingers into dough. If indentation remains, dough has risen enough.)
3. Heat a small skillet over medium-low heat. Add oil to pan; swirl to coat. Add garlic to pan; cook 5 minutes or until fragrant. Remove garlic from oil with a slotted spoon; discard garlic. Remove pan from heat.
4. Place dough on a baking sheet coated with cooking spray; pat into a 12 x 8-inch rectangle. Brush garlic oil over dough; sprinkle with thyme. Cover and let rise 25 minutes or until doubled in size.
5. Preheat oven to 425°.
6. Make indentations in top of dough using handle of a wooden spoon or your fingertips; sprinkle dough evenly with coarse sea salt. Bake at 425° for 14 minutes or until lightly browned. Remove from pan; cool on a wire rack.

Serves 10 (serving size: 1 piece).

CALORIES 128; FAT 1.7g (sat 0.2g, mono 1g, poly 0.3g); PROTEIN 3.5g; CARB 24.2g; FIBER 1.1g; CHOL 0mg; IRON 1.6mg; SODIUM 289mg; CALC 7mg

QUICK BREADS & YEAST BREADS

12

Cheese and Chive Challah 🌿

The traditional Jewish egg bread is enriched even more with the savory addition of fontina cheese and chives.

This makes two loaves, so you can be generous and give one away without missing out. We love the flavor of fontina, but Gruyère or another Swiss cheese would also work. Hands-on time: 37 min. Total time: 2 hr. 52 min.

1 cup warm 2% reduced-fat milk (100° to 110°)

1 teaspoon sugar

1 package dry yeast (about 2¼ teaspoons)

3 tablespoons butter, melted

1½ teaspoons salt

5 large egg yolks

3 large eggs

¾ cup (3 ounces) shredded aged fontina cheese

½ cup finely chopped fresh chives

10.7 ounces bread flour (about 2¼ cups)

13.5 ounces all-purpose flour (about 3 cups), divided

Cooking spray

1 large egg

2 tablespoons water

2 tablespoons grated fresh Parmigiano-Reggiano cheese

1. Combine first 3 ingredients in a large bowl; let stand 5 minutes or until bubbly. Stir in butter and next 3 ingredients (through 3 eggs). Stir in fontina and chives. Weigh or lightly spoon flours into dry measuring cups; level with a knife. Add bread flour and 12.4 ounces all-purpose flour (about 2¾ cups) to yeast mixture, stirring until a soft dough forms (dough will be sticky).

2. Turn dough out onto a lightly floured surface. Knead until smooth and elastic, adding remaining 1.1 ounces all-purpose flour (about ¼ cup), 1 tablespoon at a time, to prevent dough from sticking to hands. Place dough in a large bowl coated with cooking spray, turning to coat top. Cover with plastic wrap; let rise in a warm place (85°), free from drafts, 45 minutes or until doubled in size. Punch down dough; cover and let rise 50 minutes or until doubled in size. (Gently press two fingers into dough. If indentation remains, dough has risen enough.)

3. Divide dough into 6 equal portions. Roll each portion into a ball. Roll each ball into a rope about 15 inches long. Place 3 ropes parallel to one another; braid ropes. Pinch ends together; tuck under loaf. Repeat procedure with remaining 3 ropes. Place loaves on a baking sheet lined with parchment paper; coat with cooking spray. Cover and let rise 30 minutes or until doubled in size.

4. Preheat oven to 375°.

5. Combine 1 egg and 2 tablespoons water in a bowl, stirring well with a whisk. Brush loaves gently with egg mixture. Sprinkle loaves evenly with Parmigiano-Reggiano. Bake at 375° for 25 minutes or until golden. Remove from baking sheet; cool on a wire rack.

Serves 24 (serving size: 1 slice).

CALORIES 160; FAT 4.7g (sat 2.3g, mono 1.5g, poly 0.5g); PROTEIN 6.2g; CARB 22.5g; FIBER 0.8g; CHOL 78mg; IRON 1.6mg; SODIUM 210mg; CALC 51mg

QUICK BREADS & YEAST BREADS

Wheat Berry Bread

A toasted slab of this whole-grain bread with a small smear of butter or jam is a heavenly breakfast.

It's a hearty, high-fiber sandwich loaf speckled with chewy wheat berries. Whole-wheat and amaranth flours up the whole-grain quotient. Wheat bran gives the surface a nice rustic finish. The recipe makes two loaves, so you can freeze one for later. Hands-on time: 30 min. Total time: 4 hr. 31 min.

3	cups water
¾	cup uncooked wheat berries
1	package dry yeast (about 2¼ teaspoons)
1	cup 2% reduced-fat milk
2	tablespoons dark honey (such as buckwheat)
2½	teaspoons salt
14.3	ounces bread flour (about 3 cups), divided
9.5	ounces whole-wheat flour (about 2 cups)
3.8	ounces amaranth flour (about 1 cup)
	Cooking spray
2	tablespoons bread flour
2	tablespoons wheat bran

1. Combine 3 cups water and wheat berries in a saucepan; bring to a boil. Cover, reduce heat, and simmer 1 hour or until tender. Drain wheat in a colander over a bowl, reserving 1 cup cooking liquid; set wheat berries aside.

2. Let reserved cooking liquid stand until warm (100° to 110°). Stir yeast into cooking liquid.

3. Combine milk, honey, and salt in a small heavy saucepan, stirring with a whisk until honey and salt dissolve. Heat milk mixture over medium heat until warm (100° to 110°). Add milk mixture to yeast mixture, stirring with a whisk; let stand 5 minutes.

4. Weigh or lightly spoon flours into dry measuring cups; level with a knife. Stir 11.9 ounces bread flour (about 2½ cups), whole-wheat flour, and amaranth flour into yeast mixture.

5. Turn dough out onto a floured surface. Knead until smooth and elastic (about 10 minutes); add up to 2.4 ounces bread flour (about ½ cup), 1 tablespoon at a time, to prevent dough from sticking to hands (dough will feel sticky).

6. Place dough in a large bowl coated with cooking spray, turning to coat top. Cover and let rise in a warm place (85°), free from drafts, 1 hour or until doubled in size. (Press two fingers into dough. If indentation remains, dough has risen enough.) Punch dough down; cover and let rest 5 minutes. Coat two 9 x 5-inch loaf pans with cooking spray; dust each with 1 tablespoon bread flour.

7. Divide dough in half. Working with 1 portion at a time (cover remaining dough to prevent drying), knead half of wheat berries into dough; place dough in prepared pan. Sprinkle dough with 1 tablespoon wheat bran. Repeat procedure with remaining dough, wheat berries, and wheat bran. Cover and let rise 45 minutes or until doubled in size.

8. Preheat oven to 375°.

9. Bake at 375° for 45 minutes or until golden. Cool loaves in pans 10 minutes on a wire rack; remove from pans. Cool completely on wire rack.

Serves 18 (serving size: 1 slice).

CALORIES 198; FAT 1.4g (sat 0.3g, mono 0.2g, poly 0.4g); PROTEIN 7.2g; CARB 39.8g; FIBER 3.9g; CHOL 1mg; IRON 3.6mg; SODIUM 334mg; CALC 37mg

Partners for Beautiful Breads

Because any biscuit, slice of whole-grain toast, or scone perks up with the addition of a sweet topping, we offer these delicious jams and spreads.

Strawberry Cordial Jam 🌿

Adding liqueur to this jam provides flavor that's reminiscent of an old-fashioned cordial. If you prefer, substitute 2 tablespoons black currant syrup plus 1 tablespoon fresh lemon juice for the liqueur. Keep jam refrigerated for up to a month.

6	cups chopped strawberries (about 1½ pounds)
1	cup sugar
3	tablespoons crème de cassis (black currant-flavored liqueur)
1	tablespoon water
⅛	teaspoon ground cinnamon
⅛	teaspoon ground cardamom

1. Combine all ingredients in a saucepan over medium-high heat; bring to a boil. Reduce heat; simmer until reduced to 2 cups (about 1 hour and 10 minutes), stirring occasionally. Cool completely; cover and chill 8 hours.

Serves 16 (serving size: 2 tablespoons).

CALORIES 73; FAT 0.2g (sat 0g, mono 0g, poly 0.1g); PROTEIN 0.3g; CARB 16.8g; FIBER 0.2g; CHOL 0mg; IRON 0.2mg; SODIUM 1mg; CALC 6mg

Cherry-Berry Jam 🌿

Minimal sugar is added to this recipe, so the flavor of the fruit shines. It should stay fresh for up to three weeks in the refrigerator.

2	cups pitted fresh cherries (about 12 ounces)
1½	cups blackberries
1½	cups raspberries
¾	cup sugar
1½	teaspoons fresh lemon juice

1. Combine all ingredients in a medium, heavy saucepan over medium-high heat; bring to a boil. Reduce heat; simmer until reduced to 2 cups (about 1½ hours), stirring occasionally. Spoon into a bowl. Cover and chill.

Serves 24 (serving size: 2 tablespoons).

CALORIES 41; FAT 0.2g (sat 0g, mono 0g, poly 0.1g); PROTEIN 0.4g; CARB 10.1g; FIBER 1.2g; CHOL 0mg; IRON 0.2mg; SODIUM 0mg; CALC 6mg

Pomegranate and Pear Jam 🌿

Use a food mill to get fresh pomegranate juice from the seeds, leaving seeds in the mill. Or pulse seeds in a blender and strain through a fine sieve.

2	cups sugar
2	cups chopped peeled Seckel or other pear
⅔	cup strained fresh pomegranate juice (about 2 pomegranates)
¼	cup rosé wine
¼	cup pomegranate seeds
½	teaspoon butter
2	tablespoons fruit pectin for less- or no-sugar recipes
1	tablespoon grated lemon rind
1	teaspoon minced fresh rosemary

1. Combine first 4 ingredients in a large saucepan over medium heat; stir until sugar melts. Bring to a simmer; cook 25 minutes or until pear is tender. Remove from heat; mash with a potato masher. Add pomegranate seeds and butter to pan; bring to a boil. Stir in fruit pectin. Return mixture to a boil; cook 1 minute, stirring constantly. Remove from heat; stir in lemon rind and rosemary. Cool to room temperature. Cover and chill overnight.

Serves 32 (serving size: 1 tablespoon).

CALORIES 67; FAT 0.2g (sat 0.1g, mono 0g, poly 0g); PROTEIN 0.2g; CARB 16.9g; FIBER 0.5g; CHOL 0mg; IRON 0mg; SODIUM 9mg; CALC 14mg

Overnight Apple Butter 🌿

A combination of apple varieties, rather than just one type, will produce apple butter with rich, complex flavor. Good choices include Granny Smith, Jonathan, Northern Spy, Rome, Stayman, Winesap, and York.

1	cup packed brown sugar
½	cup honey
¼	cup apple cider
1	tablespoon ground cinnamon
¼	teaspoon ground cloves
⅛	teaspoon ground mace
10	medium apples (about 2½ pounds), peeled, cored, and cut into large chunks

1. Combine all ingredients in a 5-quart electric slow cooker. Cover and cook on LOW 10 hours or until apples are very tender.
2. Place a large fine-mesh sieve over a bowl; spoon one-third of apple mixture into sieve. Press mixture through sieve using the back of a spoon or ladle. Discard pulp. Repeat procedure with remaining apple mixture. Return apple mixture to slow cooker. Cook, uncovered, on HIGH 1½ hours or until mixture is thick, stirring occasionally. Spoon into a bowl; cover and chill up to a week.

Serves 16 (serving size: ¼ cup).

CALORIES 132; FAT 0g; PROTEIN 0.1g; CARB 35.3g; FIBER 3.1g; CHOL 0mg; IRON 0.7mg; SODIUM 6mg; CALC 18mg

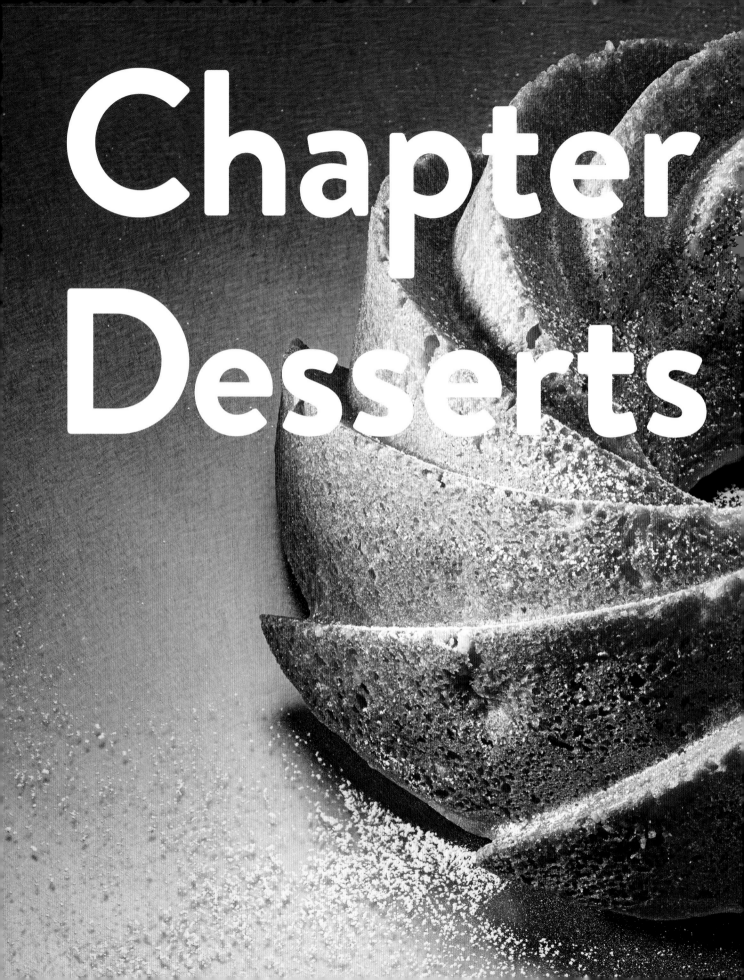

Chapter
Desserts

13:

13

Apple-Cinnamon Bundt Cake, page 464

Our philosophy on dessert is: Yes, please. We admit to having a fair number of sweet tooths on our kitchen staff. And while it's true that a bit of plain fruit is wonderful, it's all the more so when quickly cooked in something boozy, topped with something crunchy, or matched with something creamy, like mascarpone. About half the recipes in this chapter begin with a fruity base that is then syruped, sauced, glazed, or parfait-ed. But then we move on to do some baking. Healthy baking employs some graduate-level techniques, but we've worked out solid approaches in the Test Kitchen. We don't settle for gummy approximations; we test until we get the crunch, crumb, and true flavors that will deliver a sweet, perfect end to a healthy meal.

Bourbon-Glazed Peaches with Yogurt

It just makes sense to partner peaches with bourbon, as any sensible Southerner would tell you.

A peach is just a peach until July and August roll around, and then, as the fruit hangs on the trees soaking up sunshine during summer's hottest days, all the magic happens: Crisp flesh softens, and sugar levels rise to balance the tart acidity. The pristine fruits need little embellishment to make their flavors sing.

Hands-on time: 10 min. Total time: 1 hr. 30 min.

1 (2-inch) piece vanilla bean, split lengthwise

1 cup plain 2% reduced-fat Greek yogurt

5½ tablespoons dark brown sugar, divided

⅛ teaspoon fine sea salt, divided

3 tablespoons bourbon

½ teaspoon vanilla extract

4 firm ripe peaches, halved and pitted

1. Scrape seeds from vanilla bean into a medium bowl. Combine seeds, bean, yogurt, 1½ tablespoons sugar, and a dash of salt. Let stand 1 hour; discard bean.

2. Preheat oven to 350°.

3. Combine remaining ¼ cup sugar, remaining dash of salt, bourbon, and vanilla extract in a large bowl, stirring with a whisk. Add peaches; toss gently. Arrange peaches, cut sides down, on a parchment-lined baking sheet. Reserve sugar mixture. Bake peaches at 350° for 10 minutes. Turn peach halves over; drizzle cavities with reserved sugar mixture. Bake an additional 10 minutes or just until tender. Serve with yogurt and juices.

Serves 4 (serving size: 2 peach halves and about ¼ cup yogurt).

CALORIES 201; FAT 1.8g (sat 1g, mono 0g, poly 0g); PROTEIN 6.7g; CARB 36.4g; FIBER 2g; CHOL 3mg; IRON 0.5mg; SODIUM 87mg; CALC 76mg

Tropical Fruits with Limoncello and Mint

Lots of zing here, from pineapple and kiwi drenched in Limoncello, which is both sweet and lemon-peel fragrant.

The citrus dressing would also be delicious on a mixture of strawberries, raspberries, blueberries, and blackberries. Hands-on time: 11 min. Total time: 15 min.

3 tablespoons sugar

3 tablespoons Limoncello (lemon-flavored liqueur)

1 teaspoon grated lemon rind

2 cups (1-inch) cubed fresh pineapple

2 kiwifruit, peeled, halved lengthwise, and sliced

1 large mango, peeled and sliced

1 tablespoon chopped fresh mint

1. Combine first 3 ingredients in a large bowl. Add pineapple, kiwi, and mango; toss to coat. Let stand 5 minutes, stirring occasionally. Stir in mint.

Serves 4 (serving size: about 1 cup).

CALORIES 174; FAT 0.4g (sat 0.1g, mono 0.1g, poly 0.2g); PROTEIN 1.2g; CARB 38.9g; FIBER 3.3g; CHOL 0mg; IRON 0.5mg; SODIUM 3mg; CALC 31mg

Sparkling Blueberry-Sauced Fruit

Blueberries are whirred in a blender with a little sugar and then strained—delicious to mix with bubbly and drape over fruit.

Superfine sugar is sugar that has been ground very fine and dissolves almost instantly. To make your own, put white sugar into the food processor; whir for 1 to 2 minutes or until powdery. Hands-on time: 15 min. Total time: 15 min.

1 cup seedless red or green grapes

½ cup orange sections (about 2 oranges)

2 kiwifruit, peeled, halved lengthwise, and sliced

1 mango, peeled and chopped

1 cup fresh or frozen blueberries, thawed

3 tablespoons superfine sugar

1 cup chilled prosecco or other sparkling wine

1 tablespoon chopped fresh mint

1. Combine first 4 ingredients in a large bowl.

2. Place blueberries and sugar in a food processor or blender; process until smooth. Press blueberry mixture through a fine sieve over fruit mixture; discard solids. Add wine to fruit mixture; stir gently. Sprinkle with mint.

Serves 4 (serving size: about ¾ cup).

CALORIES 216; FAT 0.8g (sat 0.1g, mono 0.1g, poly 0.4g); PROTEIN 1.8g; CARB 45.2g; FIBER 5g; CHOL 0mg; IRON 0.5mg; SODIUM 4mg; CALC 56mg

NUTRITION MADE EASY

Frozen Berries: If you aren't finding locally grown berries, then the frozen ones may be sweeter and more nutritious than what you do find in the produce section of the supermarket. Right after being picked, fruit begins to lose nutrients and phytochemicals. Freezing preserves these nutrients, so fruits frozen shortly after picking retain more of their natural goodness than fresh ones that have traveled long distances.

Pear Tarte Tatin

A new twist on the classic upside-down tart—here made with paper-thin phyllo dough instead of piecrust.

Saving fat in the crust means you can have a dollop of rich crème fraîche on each slice. A cast-iron skillet helps caramelize fruit in a small amount of butter and sugar—a defining characteristic in this lightened tart. Combining canola oil and melted butter to brush on the phyllo keeps the yummy buttery richness without adding too much saturated fat. The classic blunder with phyllo is forgetting to move the frozen dough to the fridge so it can thaw overnight or for 24 hours before handling. The thaw can't be rushed. Hands-on time: 18 min. Total time: 59 min.

2 tablespoons butter, divided

½ cup sugar, divided

4 peeled ripe Anjou pears, cored and halved lengthwise

1 tablespoon canola oil

5 (14 x 9-inch) sheets frozen phyllo dough, thawed

3 tablespoons crème fraîche

1. Preheat oven to 400°.

2. Coat a 10-inch cast-iron skillet with 1½ tablespoons butter. Sprinkle 6 tablespoons sugar into pan. Arrange 7 pear halves, cut sides up, in a circle in pan, and place remaining pear half in center. Cover pan, and place over medium-low heat. Cook, without stirring, 15 minutes or until sugar mixture is bubbly and caramelized. Place pan in oven. Bake at 400° for 5 minutes.

3. Place remaining 1½ teaspoons butter and oil in a microwave-safe bowl. Microwave at HIGH 30 seconds or until butter melts. Lay 1 phyllo sheet lengthwise on a flat work surface; brush lightly with butter mixture. Sprinkle 2 teaspoons sugar evenly over phyllo. Place next phyllo sheet crosswise on top of first. Repeat procedure twice with remaining butter mixture, sugar, and phyllo, ending with phyllo. Fold edges to form a 9-inch circle.

4. Place phyllo circle in pan over pears, pressing gently. Bake at 400° for 16 minutes or until filling is bubbly and crust is browned. Remove from oven; let stand 5 minutes. Place a plate upside-down on top of pan; invert tart onto plate. Cut tart into 6 wedges. Top each wedge with 1½ teaspoons crème fraîche.

Serves 6.

CALORIES 258; FAT 10.3g (sat 4.4g, mono 2.9g, poly 1g); PROTEIN 2g; CARB 41.7g; FIBER 3g; CHOL 17mg; IRON 0.5mg; SODIUM 79mg; CALC 70mg

Oranges with Caramel and Cardamom Syrup
Enticingly fragrant from orange-flower water and cardamom.

Chilling overnight is crucial for imbuing the oranges with flavor. When adding the cardamom water to the caramel, pour down the side of the pan to prevent the caramel from sputtering too much. Whole-milk Greek yogurt adds tang and richness. Hands-on time: 14 min. Total time: 12 hr. 44 min.

½ cup water

2 cardamom pods, crushed

6 tablespoons sugar

5 medium navel oranges (about 2¼ pounds)

1 cup whole-milk Greek yogurt

2 tablespoons honey

⅛ teaspoon orange-flower water

Mint sprigs (optional)

1. Combine ½ cup water and cardamom in a small heavy saucepan; bring to a boil. Remove from heat; cover and let stand 20 minutes. Strain through a fine sieve over a small bowl; discard solids.

2. Combine 1 tablespoon cardamom water and sugar in pan over medium heat; cook 9 minutes or until sugar melts and is barely golden (do not stir). Increase heat to medium-high; cook 1 minute or until mixture darkens to a deep amber. Remove from heat; carefully pour remaining cardamom water down side of pan. Return pan to medium-high heat; stir until well blended. Remove pan from heat.

3. Peel oranges. Cut each orange crosswise into 6 slices. Arrange orange slices on a rimmed platter; pour hot syrup over oranges. Cover and chill overnight.

4. Combine yogurt, honey, and orange-flower water in a small bowl. Dollop yogurt mixture over oranges. Garnish with mint sprigs, if desired.

Serves 6 (serving size: 5 orange slices and 3 tablespoons yogurt mixture).

CALORIES 170; FAT 3.9g (sat 3g, mono 0.6g, poly 0g); PROTEIN 3.7g; CARB 32.3g; FIBER 2.6g; CHOL 7mg; IRON 0.1mg; SODIUM 12mg; CALC 73mg

Slow-Roasted Grape and Yogurt Parfaits
It's absolutely worth the time to cook grapes for three hours. Low and slow heat concentrates the grape-y sweetness and turns fruit buttery-soft with almost no effort.

This is a restaurant-quality dessert, easily made. The yogurt holds the layers together. Chopped walnuts on top add crunch and a dose of healthy fat. Hands-on time: 10 min. Total time: 3 hr. 43 min.

Cooking spray

1⅓ cups seedless black grapes

1⅓ cups seedless red grapes

1⅓ cups seedless green grapes

3 tablespoons sugar

2 cups plain fat-free Greek yogurt, divided

¼ cup walnut halves, toasted and coarsely chopped, divided

8 teaspoons honey, divided

1. Preheat oven to 200°. Coat a jelly-roll pan with cooking spray.

2. Rinse grapes; drain well, leaving slightly moist. Combine grapes and sugar in a large bowl; toss to coat. Arrange grapes on prepared jelly-roll pan. Bake at 200° for 3 hours or until grapes soften but still hold their shape. Remove from oven; cool completely.

3. Spoon ¼ cup yogurt into each of 4 parfait glasses. Top each serving with about ⅓ cup grapes, 1½ teaspoons walnuts, and 1 teaspoon honey. Repeat layers with remaining ingredients.

Serves 4 (serving size: 1 parfait).

CALORIES 298; FAT 5g (sat 0.5g, mono 0.7g, poly 3.5g); PROTEIN 12.2g; CARB 55.5g; FIBER 2g; CHOL 0mg; IRON 0.9mg; SODIUM 46mg; CALC 100mg

13

Slow-Roasted Grape and
Yogurt Parfaits

Drunken Figs with Black Pepper Granola

This recipe, from San Francisco Chef Luis Villavelazquez, makes a gorgeous use of summer's sweetest figs.

Fernet Branca is an herby, crazy-bitter liqueur imported from Italy. A full bottle will probably last 10 years in your bar, so if you're not adventurous in this regard, substitute pastis or ouzo. Make the figs and granola ahead of time and assemble when ready for dessert. Hands-on time: 15 min. Total time: 12 hr. 33 min.

Figs:

- 1 cup water
- 1 cup honey
- ¼ cup Fernet Branca or anisette liqueur
- 2 teaspoons fresh lemon juice
- ¼ teaspoon salt
- 24 fresh figs, quartered

Granola:

- 2 tablespoons butter
- 3 tablespoons brown sugar
- 1¾ cups old-fashioned rolled oats
- ¼ cup pine nuts, toasted
- ½ teaspoon freshly ground black pepper

Dash of salt

Remaining ingredient:

- 3 tablespoons mascarpone cheese

1. To prepare figs, combine first 5 ingredients in a small saucepan; bring to a boil. Place figs in a shallow dish; add hot honey syrup to dish. Cool to room temperature; cover and chill overnight.

2. Preheat oven to 325°.

3. To prepare granola, melt butter in a large nonstick skillet over medium heat; stir in sugar. Increase heat to medium-high; cook 2 minutes or until sugar begins to brown. Add oats, nuts, pepper, and dash of salt; cook 2 minutes, stirring frequently to coat. Arrange oat mixture in a single layer on a baking sheet lined with parchment paper. Bake at 325° for 16 minutes or until toasted, stirring after 8 minutes. Cool completely.

4. Remove figs from liquid using a slotted spoon; discard liquid. Divide fig quarters evenly among 8 bowls; top each serving with ¼ cup granola. Spoon about 1 teaspoon mascarpone on each serving.

Serves 8.

CALORIES 321; FAT 13.8g (sat 5.8g, mono 3.9g, poly 2.4g); PROTEIN 5.6g; CARB 48.3g; FIBER 6.4g; CHOL 25mg; IRON 1.6mg; SODIUM 59mg; CALC 87mg

DESSERTS

13

NUTRITION MADE EASY

Oats: Oats and oat flour are almost always a whole-grain choice because it's rare for the bran and germ to be removed in processing. And quick-cooking oats are no less nutritious than the slow kind. In dessert toppings, basic old-fashioned rolled oats are a good choice. For more flavor at breakfast, try the steel-cut option: They take longer to cook but taste wonderful.

Fresh Cherry Galette

Spectacular and ridiculously easy—just pile fresh cherries over store-bought crust, and bake.

Rainier cherries have delicate, white flesh and yellowish-red skin—they're larger and taste sweeter than Bings. If you can't find them, add an extra tablespoon of sugar. Hands-on time: 26 min. Total time: 1 hr. 11 min.

½ (14.1-ounce) package refrigerated pie dough

3 tablespoons granulated sugar, divided

1½ teaspoons cornstarch

3½ cups pitted fresh Rainier cherries (about 1¼ pounds)

½ teaspoon grated lemon rind

2 teaspoons fresh lemon juice

1½ tablespoons buttermilk

1 tablespoon turbinado sugar

1. Preheat oven to 400°.
2. Line a baking sheet with parchment paper. Unroll dough onto parchment; roll to a 12½-inch circle. Combine 1 tablespoon granulated sugar and cornstarch, stirring with a whisk. Sprinkle cornstarch mixture over dough, leaving a 2-inch border. Combine cherries, remaining 2 tablespoons granulated sugar, rind, and juice; toss well to coat. Arrange cherry mixture over dough, leaving a 2-inch border. Fold dough border over cherries, pressing gently to seal (dough will only partially cover cherries). Brush edges of dough with buttermilk. Sprinkle turbinado sugar over cherries and edges of dough. Bake at 400° for 25 minutes or until dough is browned and juices are bubbly. Remove from oven; cool on pan at least 20 minutes before serving.

Serves 6 (serving size: 1 wedge).

CALORIES 227; FAT 8.9g (sat 3.8g, mono 3.2g, poly 0.6g); PROTEIN 2.3g; CARB 38g; FIBER 1.9g; CHOL 4mg; IRON 0.3mg; SODIUM 177mg; CALC 12mg

Rum-Spiked Grilled Pineapple with Toasted Coconut

Six ingredients make one delicious dessert in less than 20 minutes.

Toasting coconut gives it that caramelized nuttiness and a texture that is both crispy and chewy. Cook the coconut in a skillet over medium heat until golden brown, stirring frequently. Hands-on time: 6 min. Total time: 15 min.

¼ cup packed brown sugar

¼ cup dark spiced rum

1 pineapple (about 1½ pounds), peeled, cored, halved lengthwise, and sliced lengthwise into 12 wedges

1 tablespoon butter

2 tablespoons flaked sweetened coconut, toasted

3 cups vanilla low-fat ice cream

1. Combine sugar and rum in a microwave-safe bowl. Microwave at HIGH 1½ minutes or until sugar dissolves. Brush rum mixture evenly over pineapple wedges.
2. Melt butter in a grill pan over medium-high heat. Add pineapple to pan; grill 3 minutes on each side or until grill marks form and pineapple is thoroughly heated. Sprinkle with coconut. Serve with ice cream.

Serves 6 (serving size: 2 pineapple wedges, 1 teaspoon coconut, and ½ cup ice cream).

CALORIES 226; FAT 4g (sat 2.6g, mono 0.5g, poly 0.1g); PROTEIN 3.7g; CARB 43.1g; FIBER 4.7g; CHOL 10mg; IRON 0.5mg; SODIUM 78mg; CALC 123mg

Fresh Cherry Galette

Vanilla-Bourbon Pumpkin Tart

A fluffy, delightful hybrid—part classic spiced pumpkin pie, part creamy cheesecake.

Wrap foil around the springform pan to make sure water doesn't sneak in from the water bath.
Hands-on time: 24 min. Total time: 5 hr. 47 min.

Crust:

- ¾ cup graham cracker crumbs (about 5 cookie sheets)
- 1 tablespoon finely chopped pecans
- 1 teaspoon granulated sugar
- 1 tablespoon butter, melted

Cooking spray

Filling:

- 1 cup (8 ounces) ⅓-less-fat cream cheese, softened
- ½ cup granulated sugar
- ¼ cup packed light brown sugar
- 1 (15-ounce) can unsweetened pumpkin
- 2 large eggs
- 2 tablespoons bourbon
- 2 teaspoons vanilla extract
- ½ teaspoon salt
- ½ teaspoon ground cinnamon
- ¼ teaspoon ground nutmeg
- ⅛ teaspoon ground allspice

Remaining ingredient:

- ½ cup frozen fat-free whipped topping, thawed

1. Preheat oven to 350°.

2. To prepare crust, combine first 3 ingredients in a bowl. Drizzle butter over crumb mixture; stir with a fork. Firmly press into bottom and 1 inch up sides of a 9-inch springform pan coated with cooking spray. Bake at 350° for 8 minutes or until lightly browned; cool on a wire rack.

3. To prepare filling, place cream cheese, ½ cup granulated sugar, and brown sugar in a large bowl; beat with a mixer at medium speed until smooth. Add pumpkin and eggs; beat until combined, scraping sides of bowl as needed.

Add bourbon and next 5 ingredients (through allspice); beat 1 minute or until combined. Pour cream cheese mixture into prepared pan. Place pan in a large roasting pan; add hot water to pan to a depth of 1 inch. Bake at 350° for 35 minutes or until center barely moves when side of pan is tapped. Cool completely on a wire rack. Cover and refrigerate at least 4 hours or overnight. Serve with whipped topping.

Serves 8 (serving size: 1 wedge and about 1 tablespoon whipped topping).

CALORIES 252; FAT 10.5g (sat 5.5g, mono 1.5g, poly 0.7g); PROTEIN 5.2g; CARB 33.1g; FIBER 2.7g; CHOL 77mg; IRON 0.9mg; SODIUM 337mg; CALC 47mg

No-Bake Fresh Strawberry Pie

Glorious spring berries are the focus here—tons of them, piled atop a thin layer of creamy vanilla filling.

No baking required; the crust sets up when the melted chocolate cools. Hands-on time: 35 min. Total time: 1 hr. 15 min.

25 chocolate wafers

3 ounces bittersweet chocolate, finely chopped

2 teaspoons canola oil

Cooking spray

¾ cup (6 ounces) ⅓-less-fat cream cheese, softened

⅓ cup powdered sugar

¾ teaspoon vanilla extract

2 cups frozen fat-free whipped topping, thawed

2 tablespoons seedless strawberry fruit spread

1 tablespoon Chambord (raspberry-flavored liqueur)

½ teaspoon fresh lemon juice

1 pound small strawberries, hulled and cut in half

1. Place chocolate wafers in a food processor; process until finely ground. Place chopped chocolate in a small microwave-safe bowl. Microwave at HIGH 45 seconds or until chocolate melts, stirring every 15 seconds. Add melted chocolate and oil to processor; process until well combined. Gently press mixture into bottom and up sides of a 9-inch pie plate or removable-bottom tart pan coated with cooking spray. Place in freezer 15 minutes or until set.

2. Place cream cheese, sugar, and vanilla in a medium bowl; beat with a mixer at medium speed until smooth. Fold in whipped topping. Carefully spread over bottom of crust. Place fruit spread in a large microwave-safe bowl; microwave at HIGH 10 seconds or until softened. Add Chambord and juice; stir with a whisk until smooth. Add berry halves; toss to combine. Arrange berry halves over pie. Chill 30 minutes before serving.

Serves 8 (serving size: 1 wedge).

CALORIES 294; FAT 11.5g (sat 5.5g, mono 2.9g, poly 0.9g); PROTEIN 4.3g; CARB 41.5g; FIBER 1.8g; CHOL 19mg; IRON 0.9mg; SODIUM 225mg; CALC 34mg

Raspberry-Rhubarb Pie

Rhubarb's mouthwatering acidity is balanced by a good amount of sweet raspberries.

It's a pie piled high with juicy fruit. Cornstarch and tapioca ensure a velvety filling by thickening the juices. Hands-on time: 25 min. Total time: 1 hr. 50 min.

2 tablespoons uncooked quick-cooking tapioca

4½ cups fresh raspberries (about 24 ounces)

3½ cups chopped fresh rhubarb (about 6 stalks)

1 cup packed brown sugar

¼ cup cornstarch

2 tablespoons crème de cassis (black currant-flavored liqueur)

⅛ teaspoon salt

½ (14.1-ounce) package refrigerated pie dough

Cooking spray

6 tablespoons all-purpose flour

¼ cup sliced almonds

2 tablespoons brown sugar

2 tablespoons chilled butter, cut into small pieces

¼ teaspoon almond extract

⅛ teaspoon salt

1. Preheat oven to 350°.
2. Place tapioca in a spice or coffee grinder; process until finely ground. Combine tapioca, raspberries, and next 5 ingredients (through ⅛ teaspoon salt) in a bowl; toss well. Let raspberry mixture stand 10 minutes; stir to combine.
3. Roll dough into an 11-inch circle. Fit dough into a 9-inch pie plate coated with cooking spray, draping excess dough over edges. Spoon raspberry mixture and remaining liquid into dough. Fold edges under; flute. Bake at 350° for 40 minutes.

4. While pie bakes, place flour and next 5 ingredients (through ⅛ teaspoon salt) in a food processor; pulse 10 times or until mixture resembles coarse crumbs.
5. Increase oven temperature to 375°.
6. Sprinkle topping evenly over pie. Bake at 375° for 15 minutes or until topping is golden brown and filling is thick and bubbly. Cool completely on a wire rack.

Serves 12 (serving size: 1 wedge).

CALORIES 248; FAT 7.9g (sat 3g, mono 3.4g, poly 0.5g); PROTEIN 2g; CARB 43.3g; FIBER 4g; CHOL 7mg; IRON 1.1mg; SODIUM 146mg; CALC 65mg

DESSERTS

13

Boston Cream Pie

The state dessert of Massachusetts isn't a pie at all but is welcome anywhere that approves of vanilla pudding between cake layers, coated with chocolate glaze.

Our version boozes up the chocolate glaze with a bit of Cointreau, though that can be omitted.
Hands-on time: 52 min. Total time: 2 hr. 12 min.

Cake:

Cooking spray

2	teaspoons cake flour
5	ounces sifted cake flour (about 1¼ cups)
1½	teaspoons baking powder
¼	teaspoon salt
½	cup granulated sugar
¼	cup butter, softened
1	teaspoon vanilla extract
1	large egg
¾	cup 1% low-fat milk
2	large egg whites
3	tablespoons granulated sugar

Filling:

½	cup granulated sugar
3	tablespoons cornstarch
⅛	teaspoon salt
1	cup plus 2 tablespoons 1% low-fat milk
⅓	cup egg substitute
1	tablespoon butter
½	teaspoon vanilla extract

Glaze:

2	ounces dark chocolate
2	tablespoons 1% low-fat milk
⅓	cup powdered sugar
2	teaspoons Cointreau (orange-flavored liqueur)

1. Preheat oven to 350°.

2. To prepare cake, coat bottom of a 9-inch round cake pan with cooking spray. Dust with 2 teaspoons cake flour; set aside.

3. Weigh or lightly spoon 5 ounces flour (about 1¼ cups) into dry measuring cups; level with a knife. Combine flour, baking powder, and ¼ teaspoon salt in a small bowl, stirring with a whisk. Place ½ cup granulated sugar and ¼ cup butter in a large bowl; beat with a mixer at medium speed until light and fluffy (about 5 minutes). Add 1 teaspoon vanilla and egg to sugar mixture, beating until well blended. Add flour mixture to sugar mixture alternately with ¾ cup milk, beginning and ending with flour mixture.

4. Place egg whites in a medium bowl; beat with a mixer at high speed until foamy, using clean, dry beaters. Gradually add 3 tablespoons granulated sugar, beating until stiff peaks form. Gently fold egg white mixture into batter; pour into prepared pan. Bake at 350° for 35 minutes or until a wooden pick inserted in center comes out clean. Cool in pan 10 minutes; run a knife around outside edge. Remove from pan; cool completely on a wire rack.

5. To prepare filling, combine ½ cup granulated sugar, cornstarch, and ⅛ teaspoon salt in a medium saucepan. Gradually add 1 cup plus 2 tablespoons milk and egg substitute to pan, stirring with a whisk until well blended. Bring to a boil over medium heat, stirring constantly with a whisk until thick. Remove from heat; stir in 1 tablespoon butter and ½ teaspoon vanilla. Place pan in a large ice-filled bowl until custard cools to room temperature (about 15 minutes), stirring occasionally.

6. To prepare glaze, place chocolate and 2 tablespoons milk in a microwave-safe bowl. Microwave at HIGH 20 seconds or until chocolate melts. Add powdered sugar and liqueur, stirring with a whisk until smooth.

7. Split cake in half horizontally using a serrated knife; place bottom layer, cut side up, on a serving plate. Spread cooled filling evenly over bottom layer; top with remaining cake layer, cut side down. Spread glaze evenly over top cake layer.

Serves 10 (serving size: 1 slice).

CALORIES 281; FAT 8.7g (sat 5.2g, mono 1.9g, poly 0.4g); PROTEIN 5.1g; CARB 46.4g; FIBER 0.5g; CHOL 39mg; IRON 1.5mg; SODIUM 262mg; CALC 110mg

Key Lime Pie

Billowy meringue crowns a sunny citrus filling in a pie with about one-fourth the fat of classic versions.

Vastly lighter but with that crucial balance of lime and sweetness. Best enjoyed the day it's made.
Hands-on time: 36 min. Total time: 3 hr. 34 min.

- 1½ **cups graham cracker crumbs (about 10 cookie sheets)**
- 2 **tablespoons butter, melted**
- 4 **large egg whites, divided**
- 1 **tablespoon water**

Cooking spray

- 2 **large eggs**
- 2 **large egg yolks**
- ½ **cup fresh Key lime juice or fresh lime juice (about 6 Key limes)**
- 1 **(14-ounce) can fat-free sweetened condensed milk**
- 1 **teaspoon grated Key lime or lime rind**
- ½ **cup sugar**
- 2½ **tablespoons water**

1. Preheat oven to 350°.
2. Combine crumbs and melted butter in a bowl. Place 1 egg white in a small bowl; stir well with a whisk until foamy. Add 2 tablespoons egg white to graham cracker mixture, tossing well with a fork to combine. Discard remaining beaten egg white. Add 1 tablespoon water to graham cracker mixture; toss gently to coat. Press into bottom and up sides of a 9-inch pie plate coated with cooking spray. (Moisten fingers, if needed, to bring mixture together.) Bake at 350° for 8 minutes. Cool completely on a wire rack.
3. Place 2 eggs and 2 egg yolks in a bowl; beat with a mixer at medium speed until well blended. Add juice and condensed milk, beating until thick; stir in rind. Spoon mixture into prepared crust. Bake at 350° for 20 minutes or until edges are set (center will not be firm but will set as it chills). Cool completely on a wire rack. Cover loosely; chill at least 2 hours.
4. Place remaining 3 egg whites in a bowl; beat with a mixer at medium speed until foamy, using clean, dry beaters.
5. Combine sugar and 2½ tablespoons water in a small saucepan; bring to a boil. Cook, without stirring, until a candy thermometer registers 250°. Pour hot sugar syrup in a thin stream over egg whites, beating at high speed 2 minutes or until stiff peaks form. Spread meringue over chilled pie (completely cover pie with meringue).
6. Preheat broiler.
7. Broil pie 1 minute or until meringue is lightly browned.

Serves 8 (serving size: 1 slice).

CALORIES 320; FAT 6.8g (sat 2.8g, mono 2.3g, poly 1.1g); PROTEIN 9g; CARB 55.5g; FIBER 0.5g; CHOL 118mg; IRON 1mg; SODIUM 214mg; CALC 146mg

TEST KITCHEN SECRET

How to Handle Egg Whites: Properly beaten egg whites are voluminous, smooth, and glossy, but they require care. First, separate whites from yolks delicately by letting the whites slip through your fingers. The presence of yolk can prevent the whites from attaining full volume. Let the whites stand for a few minutes; they whip best closer to room temperature. Whip with clean, dry beaters at high speed just until stiff peaks form—that is, until the peaks created when you lift the beater out of the bowl stand upright. Overbeat, though, and the whites will turn grainy and dry, and may separate.

Coconut Cream Pie

We fluff this one up with real coconut and a creamy Italian meringue—it has half the calories, 65% less saturated fat, and better flavor than the original.

Steeping milk and half-and-half with real coconut and vanilla bean simply draws out richer flavor than you'd get from bottled extracts. The coconut is then strained out, along with most of its calories and saturated fat. Hands-on time: 34 min. Total time: 4 hr. 10 min.

½ (14.1-ounce) package refrigerated pie dough

Cooking spray

2 cups 1% low-fat milk

1 cup half-and-half

1½ cups flaked sweetened coconut

1 vanilla bean, split lengthwise

⅔ cup sugar

⅓ cup cornstarch

¼ teaspoon salt

4 large egg yolks

2 tablespoons butter

3 large egg whites, at room temperature

½ teaspoon cream of tartar

½ cup sugar

¼ cup water

3 tablespoons flaked sweetened coconut, toasted

1. Preheat oven to 425°.

2. Roll dough into an 11-inch circle. Fit dough into a 9-inch pie plate coated with cooking spray. Fold edges under; flute. Line dough with foil; arrange pie weights or dried beans on foil. Bake at 425° for 10 minutes. Remove weights and foil; bake an additional 10 minutes or until golden. Cool completely on a wire rack.

3. Combine milk and half-and-half in a medium saucepan over medium heat. Add 1½ cups coconut to pan. Scrape seeds from vanilla bean; stir seeds and pod into milk mixture. Bring milk mixture to a simmer; immediately remove from heat. Cover and let stand 15 minutes. Strain through a cheesecloth-lined sieve into a bowl. Gather edges of cheesecloth; squeeze over bowl to release moisture. Discard solids.

4. Combine ⅔ cup sugar, cornstarch, salt, and egg yolks in a large bowl, stirring with a whisk. Gradually add milk mixture to egg yolk mixture, stirring constantly. Return milk mixture to pan; bring to a boil, whisking constantly. Remove from heat. Add butter to pan; whisk until smooth. Place pan in a large ice-filled bowl 6 minutes, stirring to cool. Pour into prepared crust. Cover and chill at least 1 hour.

5. Place 3 egg whites and cream of tartar in a large bowl; beat with a mixer at high speed until soft peaks form. Combine ½ cup sugar and ¼ cup water in a saucepan; bring to a boil. Cook, without stirring, until candy thermometer registers 250°. Pour hot sugar syrup in a thin stream over egg whites, beating at high speed until thick. Spread meringue over pie. Cover and refrigerate at least 2 hours. Top with toasted coconut before serving.

Serves 12 (serving size: 1 wedge).

CALORIES 266; FAT 11.5g (sat 5.7g, mono 2g, poly 0.4g); PROTEIN 4.2g; CARB 36.4g; FIBER 0.3g; CHOL 79mg; IRON 0.4mg; SODIUM 189mg; CALC 79mg

Oatmeal Pecan Pie

We've baked a lot of pecan pies: This is a favorite. Hearty, whole-grain oats replace some of the nuts and bulk up the filling.

Make the pie up to a day ahead, but store it in the refrigerator if you do. Hands-on time: 11 min. Total time: 1 hr. 31 min.

½ (14.1-ounce) package refrigerated pie dough

Cooking spray

1 cup packed dark brown sugar

1 cup light corn syrup

⅔ cup old-fashioned rolled oats

½ cup chopped pecans

2 tablespoons butter, melted

1 teaspoon vanilla extract

¼ teaspoon salt

2 large eggs, lightly beaten

2 large egg whites, lightly beaten

1. Preheat oven to 325°.

2. Roll dough into an 11-inch circle. Fit into a 9-inch pie plate coated with cooking spray, draping excess dough over edges. Fold edges under; flute.

3. Combine brown sugar and next 8 ingredients (through egg whites) in a bowl, stirring well with a whisk.

Pour into prepared crust. Bake at 325° for 50 minutes or until center is set. Cool completely on a wire rack.

Serves 12 (serving size: 1 wedge).

CALORIES 311; FAT 11.3g (sat 3.5g, mono 5g, poly 2.6g); PROTEIN 3.2g; CARB 51.4g; FIBER 1g; CHOL 42mg; IRON 0.8mg; SODIUM 181mg; CALC 30mg

DESSERTS

13

NUTRITION MADE EASY

Piecrusts: The convenience of refrigerated piecrusts makes a rustic tart or dazzling holiday pie an easier endeavor. Since our lighter homemade crust saves just 10 calories and a fraction of sat fat compared to store-bought, we deem refrigerated crust a worthy shortcut. After tasting 12 national brands, we chose Pillsbury for its buttery flavor and flaky texture. Another important factor? It has about 4 grams of sat fat and 70 less calories per serving than a traditional heavy piecrust, so you are making a move in a healthier direction. When you need a shortbread-type crust or a nut crust, it's time to exercise your pastry skills.

Lattice-Topped Blackberry Cobbler

Bubbling fruit topped with flaky pastry—it's stunning and deliciously healthy, with more than 8 grams of fiber per serving.

Using whole almonds in the topping adds a little color from the skins, but sliced or slivered almonds will work, too. The level of natural sugar in most fruits is set when harvested, so sample the fruit before making your cobbler. If the fruit is underripe and tastes tart, you can add an extra couple of tablespoons of sugar to the fruit filling. This cobbler is tasty on its own, or you can serve it with low-fat ice cream (reduce the serving size to about ½ cup). Hands-on time: 33 min. Total time: 2 hr. 36 min.

1 cup granulated sugar, divided

6 tablespoons butter, softened

1 large egg yolk

½ teaspoon vanilla extract

¾ cup whole almonds, toasted

6 ounces all-purpose flour (about 1⅓ cups)

¼ teaspoon baking powder

¼ teaspoon salt

3 tablespoons ice water

10 cups fresh blackberries (about 5 [12-ounce] packages)

3 tablespoons cornstarch

1 tablespoon fresh lemon juice

Cooking spray

2 tablespoons turbinado sugar

1. Place ⅓ cup granulated sugar and butter in a large bowl; beat with a mixer until combined (about 1 minute). Add egg yolk, beating well. Stir in vanilla.

2. Place almonds in a food processor; pulse 10 times or until finely ground. Weigh or lightly spoon flour into dry measuring cups; level with a knife. Combine nuts, flour, baking powder, and salt, stirring well with a whisk. Gradually add nut mixture to butter mixture, beating at low speed just until a soft dough forms, adding 3 tablespoons ice water, as necessary. Turn dough out onto a lightly floured surface; knead lightly 6 times or until smooth. Divide dough into 2 equal portions; wrap each portion in plastic wrap. Chill 1 hour or until firm.

3. Preheat oven to 375°.

4. Combine remaining ⅔ cup granulated sugar, blackberries, cornstarch, and lemon juice in a bowl; toss gently. Arrange berry mixture in a 13 x 9–inch glass or ceramic baking dish coated with cooking spray.

5. Unwrap dough. Roll each dough portion into a 13 x 9–inch rectangle on a lightly floured surface. Cut 1 rectangle crosswise into 1-inch-wide strips. Cut remaining rectangle lengthwise into 1-inch-wide strips. Arrange strips in a lattice pattern over fruit mixture; sprinkle dough with turbinado sugar. Bake at 375° for 50 minutes or until golden. Let stand 10 minutes.

Serves 12 (serving size: about ⅔ cup).

CALORIES 301; FAT 11.5g (sat 4.1g, mono 4.6g, poly 1.8g); PROTEIN 5.7g; CARB 47g; FIBER 8.6g; CHOL 32mg; IRON 2mg; SODIUM 103mg; CALC 75mg

DESSERTS

13

Blueberry Crisp à la Mode

A crisp is cousin to the cobbler, featuring a streusel topping instead of pastry. But you get the same, juicy fruit-and-crunchy-topping interplay.

The topping may also be made in the food processor: Place ⅔ cup flour, ½ cup brown sugar, oats, and cinnamon in the machine, and pulse 2 times or until combined. Add butter; pulse 4 times or until mixture resembles coarse meal. Hands-on time: 17 min. Total time: 47 min.

6	cups blueberries
2	tablespoons brown sugar
1	tablespoon all-purpose flour
1	tablespoon fresh lemon juice
3	ounces all-purpose flour (about ⅔ cup)
½	cup packed brown sugar
½	cup old-fashioned rolled oats
¾	teaspoon ground cinnamon
4½	tablespoons chilled butter, cut into small pieces
2	cups vanilla low-fat frozen yogurt

1. Preheat oven to 375°.

2. Combine first 4 ingredients in a medium bowl; spoon into an 11 x 7-inch glass or ceramic baking dish. Weigh or lightly spoon 3 ounces flour (about ⅔ cup) into a dry measuring cup; level with a knife. Combine 3 ounces flour, ½ cup brown sugar, oats, and cinnamon in a bowl; cut in butter with a pastry blender or 2 knives until mixture resembles coarse meal. Sprinkle over blueberry mixture.

3. Bake at 375° for 30 minutes or until bubbly. Top each serving with ¼ cup frozen yogurt.

Serves 8.

CALORIES 288; FAT 8.3g (sat 4.8g, mono 2g, poly 0.9g); PROTEIN 4.2g; CARB 52g; FIBER 3.8g; CHOL 22mg; IRON 1.3mg; SODIUM 96mg; CALC 77mg

Double-Chocolate Ice Cream

Cocoa powder lays a deep chocolate foundation, and melted bittersweet chocolate keeps the ice cream rich and round.

If you're using a 1½-quart tabletop ice-cream maker, it'll be pretty full. Hands-on time: 35 min. Total time: 2 hr. 5 min.

1⅓	cups sugar
⅓	cup unsweetened cocoa
2½	cups 2% reduced-fat milk, divided
3	large egg yolks
⅓	cup heavy whipping cream
2½	ounces bittersweet chocolate, chopped

1. Combine sugar and cocoa in a medium, heavy saucepan over medium-low heat. Add ½ cup milk and egg yolks, stirring well. Stir in remaining 2 cups milk; cook 12 minutes or until a thermometer registers 160°, stirring constantly. Remove from heat.

2. Place cream in a medium microwave-safe dish; microwave at HIGH 1½ minutes or until cream boils. Add chocolate to cream; stir until smooth. Add cream mixture to pan; stir until smooth. Place pan in a large ice-filled bowl. Cool completely, stirring constantly.

3. Pour mixture into the freezer can of an ice-cream freezer; freeze according to manufacturer's instructions. Spoon ice cream into a freezer-safe container; cover and freeze 1 hour or until firm.

Serves 10 (serving size: about ½ cup).

CALORIES 226; FAT 8.9g (sat 4.6g, mono 1.5g, poly 0.3g); PROTEIN 4g; CARB 35.6g; FIBER 1g; CHOL 79mg; IRON 0.7mg; SODIUM 37mg; CALC 75mg

Double-Chocolate
Ice Cream

Margarita Ice-Cream Sandwiches

Fresh lime zest and coarse sea salt mimic the flavors of a margarita in a treat that's lickably good.

Two sugars and two salts serve their purpose; turbinado and coarse sea salt add texture to the tops of the cookies, while table salt and granulated sugar mix well into the cookie dough. Hands-on time: 27 min. Total time: 8 hr.

1 cup sugar

½ cup unsalted butter, softened

1 large egg

5 teaspoons grated lime rind, divided

2 tablespoons fresh lime juice

11.25 ounces all-purpose flour (about 2½ cups)

1½ teaspoons baking powder

⅛ teaspoon table salt

1 teaspoon turbinado sugar

½ teaspoon coarse sea salt

2 cups vanilla reduced-fat ice cream, softened

2 cups lime sherbet, softened

1. Place sugar and butter in a large bowl; beat with a mixer at medium speed 5 minutes or until light and fluffy. Add egg, 1 tablespoon lime rind, and lime juice; beat 2 minutes or until well combined.

2. Weigh or lightly spoon flour into dry measuring cups; level with a knife. Combine flour, baking powder, and ⅛ teaspoon table salt; stir with a whisk. Add flour mixture to butter mixture; beat just until combined.

3. Divide dough into 2 equal portions. Shape each portion into a 6-inch log. Wrap logs individually in plastic wrap; chill 3 hours or until firm.

4. Preheat oven to 350°.

5. Cut each log into 16 (about ⅓-inch-thick) slices; place 1 inch apart on baking sheets lined with parchment paper. Sprinkle cookies evenly with remaining 2 teaspoons lime rind, turbinado sugar, and sea salt. Bake at 350° for 10 minutes or until edges are lightly browned. Cool 2 minutes on pans on a wire rack. Remove from pans; cool completely on wire rack.

6. Place ice cream and sherbet in a medium bowl; lightly fold and swirl together. Scoop ¼ cup ice cream mixture onto bottom of 1 cookie; top with another cookie. Repeat procedure with remaining ice cream and cookies. Cover sandwiches with plastic wrap; freeze 4 hours or until firm.

Serves 16 (serving size: 1 ice-cream sandwich).

CALORIES 231; FAT 7.1g (sat 4.2g, mono 1.7g, poly 0.4g); PROTEIN 3.4g; CARB 38.6g; FIBER 1.1g; CHOL 28mg; IRON 1.1mg; SODIUM 138mg; CALC 74mg

DESSERTS

13

Sparkling Apricot Sorbet

A soft, creamy sorbet that's best described as tasting pretty.

To peel the apricots, place in a saucepan of gently boiling water. Remove pan from heat; let apricots stand in water 20 seconds. Using a slotted spoon, transfer apricots to a large bowl of ice water. Use fingers to gently rub off skins. Hands-on time: 13 min. Total time: 4 hr. 15 min.

1 cup sugar

2 cups sparkling wine

2 (2-inch) strips lemon peel

1½ pounds apricots, peeled, pitted, and halved

Dash of salt

1. Combine all ingredients in a medium, heavy saucepan over medium-high heat. Bring mixture to a boil. Reduce heat; simmer 10 minutes. Remove from heat; cool to room temperature. Discard lemon peel. Transfer mixture to a blender; process until smooth. Pour mixture through a sieve over a bowl; discard solids. Cover and chill 45 minutes or until cool.

2. Stir sorbet mixture. Pour mixture into the freezer can of an ice-cream freezer; freeze according to manufacturer's instructions. Scrape sorbet into a freezer-safe container; cover and freeze 2 hours or until firm.

Serves 8 (serving size: ½ cup).

CALORIES 178; FAT 0.3g (sat 0g, mono 0.1g, poly 0.1g); PROTEIN 1.1g; CARB 35g; FIBER 1.6g; CHOL 0mg; IRON 0.3mg; SODIUM 19mg; CALC 11mg

Basil Plum Granita

Black plums, with their complex, winey flavor and inky hue, taste and look spectacular in this refreshing granita.

You can use another plum variety if you'd like. Scraping the granita during the freezing process helps prevent big chunks of ice from forming. Garnish with additional fresh basil leaves. Hands-on time: 20 min. Total time: 5 hr. 20 min.

1 cup water

⅔ cup sugar

¼ teaspoon vanilla extract

⅛ teaspoon salt

5 whole allspice

1½ pounds black plums, quartered and pitted

2 tablespoons fresh lime juice

¾ cup basil leaves

1. Place first 6 ingredients in a large saucepan over medium-high heat; bring to a boil. Reduce heat; simmer 15 minutes or until plums begin to fall apart, stirring occasionally. Place pan in a large ice-filled bowl; cool completely, stirring occasionally. Discard allspice.

2. Place plum mixture, lime juice, and basil in a blender; process until well blended. Press plum mixture through a fine sieve over a bowl; discard solids. Pour mixture into an 8-inch square glass or ceramic baking dish. Cover and freeze until partially frozen (about 2 hours). Scrape with a fork, crushing any lumps. Freeze 3 hours, scraping with a fork every hour, or until completely frozen.

Serves 4 (serving size: about 1 cup).

CALORIES 215; FAT 0.1g (sat 0g, mono 0g, poly 0.1g); PROTEIN 1.4g; CARB 56.3g; FIBER 2.7g; CHOL 0mg; IRON 0.7mg; SODIUM 74mg; CALC 19mg

Basil Plum Granita

Roasted Banana Pudding

Roasting bananas makes our take on this Southern classic taste richer and more decadent than the heavier versions, yet it has 500 fewer calories and about 17 fewer grams of sat fat.

Roasting banana amplifies its natural sugars, intensifying the flavor and adding richness without extra fat or sugar. Leave the peel on when roasting; it turns black in the oven but keeps the flesh intact and helps lock in the flavor. Removing some of the bananas early provides contrasting textures in the pudding. Many folks say banana pudding is best the next day, after the flavors have blended overnight and the cookies have softened. We don't disagree, though we don't always have the patience. Hands-on time: 36 min. Total time: 2 hr. 26 min.

5 ripe unpeeled medium bananas (about 2 pounds)
2 cups 2% reduced-fat milk
⅔ cup sugar, divided
2 tablespoons cornstarch
¼ teaspoon salt
2 large eggs
1 tablespoon butter
2 teaspoons vanilla extract
1 (12-ounce) container frozen fat-free whipped topping, thawed and divided
45 vanilla wafers, divided

1. Preheat oven to 350°.
2. Place bananas on a jelly-roll pan covered with parchment paper. Bake at 350° for 20 minutes. Remove 3 bananas; cool completely. Peel and cut into ½-inch-thick slices. Bake remaining 2 bananas at 350° for an additional 20 minutes. Carefully peel and place 2 bananas in a small bowl; mash with a fork until smooth.
3. Combine milk and ⅓ cup sugar in a saucepan over medium-high heat. Bring to a simmer (do not boil).
4. Combine remaining ⅓ cup sugar, cornstarch, salt, and eggs in a medium bowl; stir well with a whisk. Gradually add hot milk mixture to sugar mixture, stirring constantly with a whisk. Return milk mixture to pan. Cook over medium heat until thick and bubbly (about 3 minutes), stirring constantly. Remove from heat. Add mashed bananas, butter, and vanilla to pan, stirring until butter melts. Place pan in a large ice-filled bowl 15 minutes or until mixture comes to room temperature, stirring occasionally. Fold half of whipped topping into pudding.
5. Spread 1 cup custard evenly over the bottom of an 11 x 7-inch glass or ceramic baking dish. Top with 20 vanilla wafers and half of banana slices. Spoon half of remaining custard over banana. Repeat procedure with 20 wafers, banana slices, and custard. Spread remaining half of whipped topping evenly over top. Crush remaining 5 wafers; sprinkle over top. Refrigerate 1 hour or until chilled.

Serves 10 (serving size: about ⅔ cup).

CALORIES 295; FAT 5.6g (sat 2.1g, mono 1.7g, poly 0.2g); PROTEIN 3.9g; CARB 56.6g; FIBER 2g; CHOL 46mg; IRON 1mg; SODIUM 165mg; CALC 73mg

Bread Pudding with Salted Caramel Sauce

With its crunchy top, creamy interior, and bourbon-spiked buttery sauce, this is a much lighter bread pudding that'll make you swoon.

Toasting maximizes bread's capacity to soak up the custard. Instead of cream, low-fat milk combines with the concentrated, slightly caramelized flavor of fat-free evaporated milk, while bourbon, cinnamon, and vanilla offer a smoky-spiced flavor punch—all while slashing a hefty 550 calories and 28 grams saturated fat per serving from a classic version of this dish. Hands-on time: 25 min. Total time: 1 hr. 50 min.

Bread pudding:

- 5 cups (½-inch) cubed French bread (about 8 ounces)
- 1 cup evaporated fat-free milk
- ¾ cup 1% low-fat milk
- ⅓ cup granulated sugar
- 2 tablespoons bourbon
- 1 tablespoon vanilla extract
- 1 teaspoon ground cinnamon
- ¼ teaspoon kosher salt
- 2 large eggs

Sauce:

- ¾ cup packed light brown sugar
- 3 tablespoons bourbon
- 1 tablespoon unsalted butter
- 6 tablespoons half-and-half, divided
- 1 teaspoon vanilla extract
- ⅛ teaspoon kosher salt

Cooking spray

1. Preheat oven to 350°.

2. To prepare bread pudding, arrange bread in a single layer on a baking sheet. Bake at 350° for 8 minutes or until lightly toasted.

3. Combine evaporated milk and next 7 ingredients (through eggs) in a large bowl; stir well with a whisk. Add toasted bread cubes. Let stand 20 minutes, occasionally pressing on bread to soak up milk.

4. To prepare sauce, combine brown sugar, 3 tablespoons bourbon, and butter in a small saucepan over medium-high heat; bring to a boil. Simmer 2 minutes or until sugar dissolves, stirring frequently. Stir in 5 tablespoons half-and-half; simmer 10 minutes or until reduced to about 1 cup. Remove pan from heat. Stir in remaining 1 tablespoon half-and-half, 1 teaspoon vanilla, and ⅛ teaspoon salt. Keep warm.

5. Spoon half of bread mixture into a 9 x 5-inch loaf pan coated with cooking spray. Drizzle 3 tablespoons sauce over bread mixture. Spoon remaining half of bread mixture over sauce. Bake at 350° for 45 minutes or until a knife inserted in center comes out clean. Serve warm sauce with bread pudding.

Serves 8 (serving size: 1 slice bread pudding and about 1½ tablespoons sauce).

CALORIES 300; FAT 4.8g (sat 2.4g, mono 1.4g, poly 0.5g); PROTEIN 8.5g; CARB 50.6g; FIBER 0.9g; CHOL 63mg; IRON 1.6mg; SODIUM 349mg; CALC 172mg

Maple-Gingerbread
Pots de Crème

Creamiest Chocolate Pudding
Deep chocolate goodness with less fat and lots of calcium.

Store, tightly covered, in the refrigerator up to five days. Hands-on time: 12 min. Total time: 4 hr. 17 min.

½ cup granulated sugar

3 tablespoons cornstarch

3 tablespoons unsweetened cocoa

¼ teaspoon salt

2½ cups 1% low-fat milk

½ cup evaporated fat-free milk

2 ounces bittersweet chocolate (60 to 70 percent cocoa), finely chopped (about ¼ cup)

1 teaspoon vanilla extract
Fresh mint sprigs (optional)

1. Combine first 4 ingredients in a medium, heavy saucepan; stir with a whisk. Gradually add low-fat milk and evaporated milk to pan, stirring with a whisk. Bring to a boil over medium-high heat, stirring constantly with a whisk. Reduce heat; simmer 1 minute or until thick. Remove from heat; add chocolate, stirring until melted and mixture is smooth. Stir in vanilla. Pour about ⅔ cup pudding into each of 6 (8-ounce) ramekins; cover surface of each serving with plastic wrap. Chill at least 4 hours. Remove plastic wrap. Garnish with fresh mint sprigs, if desired.

Serves 6 (serving size: 1 ramekin).

CALORIES 194; FAT 4.6g (sat 2.7g, mono 0.9g, poly 0.1g); PROTEIN 5.9g; CARB 35g; FIBER 1.4g; CHOL 6mg; IRON 0.9mg; SODIUM 175mg; CALC 191mg

Maple-Gingerbread Pots de Crème
The crackly counterpoint to the silky custard occurs when you sprinkle a thin layer of sugar on top and broil to melt. The caramel hardens as it cools to a glasslike sheet.

Use ½ teaspoon granulated sugar for each custard; broil 1 to 2 minutes or until sugar liquefies and then turns golden brown. Hands-on time: 20 min. Total time: 5 hr. 50 min.

½ cup maple syrup

2 tablespoons dark brown sugar

8 large egg yolks

1¾ cups half-and-half

½ teaspoon ground ginger

Dash of salt

Dash of ground nutmeg

Dash of ground cloves (optional)

2 (3-inch) cinnamon sticks

1 vanilla bean, split lengthwise

1. Preheat oven to 300°.
2. Combine first 3 ingredients in a large bowl, stirring with a whisk.

3. Combine half-and-half and next 6 ingredients (through vanilla bean) in a medium, heavy saucepan over medium-high heat; cook until mixture reaches 180° or until tiny bubbles form around edge (do not boil). Gradually add hot milk mixture to egg mixture, stirring constantly with a whisk. Return milk mixture to pan. Reduce temperature to medium; cook until mixture thickens slightly (about 2 minutes), stirring constantly with a whisk. Remove from heat. Strain mixture through a sieve into a bowl; discard solids. Divide mixture evenly among 8 (4-ounce) ramekins or custard cups. Place ramekins in a 13 x 9-inch metal baking pan; add hot water to pan to a depth of 1 inch. Bake at 300° for 1 hour or until center barely moves when ramekins are touched. Remove ramekins from pan; cool completely on a wire rack. Cover and chill 4 hours.

Serves 8 (serving size: 1 cup).

CALORIES 192; FAT 10.6g (sat 5.4g, mono 3.8g, poly 1g); PROTEIN 4.3g; CARB 21.1g; FIBER 1g; CHOL 229mg; IRON 4.3mg; SODIUM 51mg; CALC 96mg

DESSERTS

13

Classic Crème Caramel

Faintly bitter caramel coats delicate baked custard that's made extra-rich with a bit of whipping cream.

This recipe calls for the caramel to be cooked until golden, but for adult palates, you can continue a little longer for a deep amber color and more bitter notes. The custards chill overnight, so they're a great make-ahead option for a dinner party. Baking at a low temperature means there's no need for a water bath. Because the seeds are not scraped from the vanilla bean, you can dry the bean out and use it another time.

Hands-on time: 22 min. Total time: 10 hr. 34 min.

4 cups 2% reduced-fat milk
1 vanilla bean, split lengthwise
Cooking spray
1⅔ cups sugar, divided
¼ cup water
¼ teaspoon kosher salt
6 large eggs
3 tablespoons heavy whipping cream

1. Preheat oven to 225°.
2. Place milk and vanilla bean in a medium, heavy saucepan over medium-high heat; cook until mixture reaches 180° or until tiny bubbles form around edge (do not boil); remove pan from heat. Cover and set aside.

3. Coat 10 (6-ounce) custard cups with cooking spray; arrange cups on a jelly-roll pan.
4. Combine 1 cup sugar and ¼ cup water in a small heavy saucepan; cook over medium-high heat until sugar dissolves, stirring frequently. Continue cooking 7 minutes or until golden (do not stir). Immediately pour into prepared custard cups, tipping quickly to coat bottoms of cups.
5. Combine remaining ⅔ cup sugar, salt, and eggs in a large bowl, stirring with a whisk. Remove vanilla bean from milk mixture; reserve bean for another use. Gradually pour warm milk mixture into egg mixture, stirring constantly with a whisk; stir in cream. Strain egg mixture through

a sieve into a large bowl; pour about ½ cup egg mixture over caramelized sugar in each custard cup. Bake at 225° for 2 hours or until custards are just set. Remove from oven; cool to room temperature. Place plastic wrap on surface of custards; chill overnight.
6. Loosen edges of custards with a knife or rubber spatula. Place a dessert plate upside down on top of each cup; invert onto plate. Drizzle any remaining caramelized syrup over custards.

Serves 10 (serving size: 1 custard).

CALORIES 236; FAT 6.5g (sat 3.1g, mono 2.2g, poly 0.5g); PROTEIN 7.1g; CARB 38.4g; FIBER 0g; CHOL 140mg; IRON 0.6mg; SODIUM 139mg; CALC 138mg

TECHNIQUE

Creating a Crème Caramel: There are a few tricks to getting the custard creamy and the caramel nutty.

1. Cook the sugar and water over medium-high heat until it's a deep golden brown.

2. Immediately pour just enough caramel to cover the bottom of a ramekin or custard cup coated with cooking spray.

3. Tilt the cup. Cover the bottom completely with caramel. Repeat with the remaining cups.

4. Fill each cup with the custard mixture. Cook until custards are just set. Cool custards to room temperature.

5. Place plastic wrap directly on surface of custards; chill overnight. Run a thin knife along the edge to loosen, and invert.

Red Velvet Cupcakes

There's that fun moment of discovery with any red velvet cake when you first bite in and uncover that shocking crimson-hued interior.

Real butter and real cream cheese make a frosting that takes this cupcake recipe from great to fantastic. Yes, red food coloring is added, but the reaction of cocoa powder with acidic buttermilk also reveals the reddish-brown anthocyanin in the cocoa. Hands-on time: 34 min. Total time: 1 hr. 3 min.

Cupcakes:

Cooking spray

10 ounces cake flour (about 2½ cups)

3 tablespoons unsweetened cocoa

1 teaspoon baking soda

1 teaspoon baking powder

1 teaspoon kosher salt

1½ cups granulated sugar

6 tablespoons unsalted butter, softened

2 large eggs

1¼ cups nonfat buttermilk

1½ teaspoons white vinegar

1½ teaspoons vanilla extract

2 tablespoons red food coloring (about 1 ounce)

Frosting:

5 tablespoons butter, softened

4 teaspoons nonfat buttermilk

1 (8-ounce) block cream cheese, softened

3½ cups powdered sugar (about 1 pound)

1¼ teaspoons vanilla extract

1. Preheat oven to 350°.
2. To prepare cupcakes, place 30 paper muffin cup liners in muffin cups; coat with cooking spray.
3. Weigh or lightly spoon flour into dry measuring cups; level with a knife. Combine flour and next 4 ingredients (through salt) in a medium bowl; stir with a whisk. Place granulated sugar and 6 tablespoons butter in a large bowl; beat with a mixer at medium speed until well blended (about 3 minutes). Add eggs, 1 at a time, beating well after each addition. Add flour mixture to sugar mixture alternately with 1¼ cups buttermilk, beginning and ending with flour mixture. Add vinegar, 1½ teaspoons vanilla, and food coloring; beat well.
4. Spoon batter into prepared muffin cups. Bake at 350° for 20 minutes or until a wooden pick inserted in center comes out clean. Cool in pan 10 minutes on wire racks; remove from pan. Cool completely on wire racks.
5. To prepare frosting, beat 5 tablespoons butter, 4 teaspoons buttermilk, and cream cheese with a mixer at high speed until fluffy. Gradually add powdered sugar; beat until smooth. Add 1¼ teaspoons vanilla; beat well. Spread frosting evenly over cupcakes.

Serves 30 (serving size: 1 cupcake).

CALORIES 205; FAT 7.3g (sat 4.5g, mono 2g, poly 0.3g); PROTEIN 2.3g; CARB 33.5g; FIBER 0.3g; CHOL 34mg; IRON 0.9mg; SODIUM 168mg; CALC 35mg

DESSERTS

13

Cranberry Swirl Cheesecake

We wanted that thick, almost show-stopping texture, plus lots of tang, like a New York cheesecake. The garnet swirl of fruit makes it very elegant.

If the cranberry mixture gets too thick, add a tablespoon of water and whirl it around in the food processor. You can also make this in an 8-inch springform pan; it'll be very full, so you should cook over a foil-lined baking sheet. The cook time will be the same. Hands-on time: 38 min. Total time: 10 hr. 53 min.

Cooking spray

- 4 ounces chocolate graham crackers
- 3 tablespoons canola oil
- 1½ cups fresh cranberries
- ½ cup sugar
- ¼ cup Chambord (raspberry-flavored liqueur)
- 3 tablespoons water
- 1 cup sugar
- 2 (8-ounce) blocks ⅓-less-fat cream cheese, softened
- ½ cup (4 ounces) block-style fat-free cream cheese, softened
- 1 cup plain fat-free Greek yogurt
- 2 teaspoons vanilla extract
- ⅛ teaspoon salt
- 3 large eggs
- 2 large egg whites

1. Preheat oven to 375°.

2. Wrap outside and bottom of a 9-inch springform pan tightly with a double layer of heavy-duty foil. Coat pan with cooking spray.

3. Place crackers in a food processor; process until finely ground. Drizzle with oil; pulse until combined. Press mixture into bottom and ½ inch up sides of prepared pan. Bake at 375° for 8 minutes; cool on a wire rack.

4. Reduce oven temperature to 325°.

5. Place cranberries, sugar, liqueur, and 3 tablespoons water in a saucepan; bring to a boil. Cook 8 minutes or until cranberries pop and mixture is syrupy. Cool 20 minutes. Place mixture in a food processor; process 1 minute or until smooth.

6. Combine 1 cup sugar and cheeses in a large bowl; beat with a mixer at medium speed until smooth. Beat in yogurt, vanilla, and salt. Add 3 eggs, 1 at a time, beating well after each addition.

7. Place 2 egg whites in a medium bowl; beat with a mixer at high speed until soft peaks form, using clean, dry beaters. Fold beaten egg whites into cream cheese mixture. Pour filling over crust. Spoon cranberry mixture over filling; swirl together using the tip of a knife. Place springform pan in a 13 x 9-inch metal baking pan. Add hot water to pan to a depth of 2 inches. Bake at 325° for 50 minutes or until center of cheesecake barely moves when pan is touched.

8. Turn oven off. Cool cheesecake in closed oven 30 minutes. Remove cheesecake from oven. Run a knife around outside edge. Cool on a wire rack. Cover and chill 8 hours.

Serves 12 (serving size: 1 wedge).

CALORIES 321; FAT 14.1g (sat 6.1g, mono 5g, poly 1.5g); PROTEIN 10g; CARB 37.8g; FIBER 0.9g; CHOL 81mg; IRON 0.5mg; SODIUM 333mg; CALC 81mg

Triple-Chocolate Cake
Chocolate splendor: Thick ganache-like glaze glides across a rich but light chocolate cake with a fluffy mousse filling.

The three chocolate layers of cake, filling, and glaze bring together unsweetened cocoa, bittersweet chocolate, and milk chocolate. Hands-on time: 25 min. Total time: 1 hr. 25 min.

Cake:

- 1 cup boiling water
- ½ cup plus 1 tablespoon unsweetened cocoa, divided
- 2 ounces bittersweet chocolate, finely chopped

Cooking spray

- 1¾ cups granulated sugar
- 6 tablespoons butter, softened
- 1 teaspoon vanilla extract
- 3 large egg whites
- ½ cup fat-free sour cream
- 8 ounces cake flour (about 2 cups)
- 1½ teaspoons baking powder
- ½ teaspoon baking soda
- ½ teaspoon salt

Filling:

- ⅓ cup fat-free milk
- 1 tablespoon granulated sugar
- 1 tablespoon cornstarch

Dash of salt

- 4 ounces milk chocolate, finely chopped
- ¾ cup frozen fat-free whipped topping, thawed

Glaze:

- ½ cup powdered sugar
- ¼ cup unsweetened cocoa
- 3 tablespoons fat-free milk
- 2 teaspoons butter
- ⅛ teaspoon instant espresso granules

Dash of salt

- 1 ounce bittersweet chocolate, finely chopped

1. Preheat oven to 350°.
2. To prepare cake, combine 1 cup boiling water and ½ cup cocoa. Add 2 ounces bittersweet chocolate; stir until smooth. Cool to room temperature. Coat 2 (8-inch) round cake pans with cooking spray; line bottoms of pans with wax paper. Coat wax paper with cooking spray; dust pans with remaining 1 tablespoon cocoa.
3. Place 1¾ cups granulated sugar, 6 tablespoons butter, and vanilla in a large bowl; beat with a mixer at medium speed 1 minute. Add egg whites, 1 at a time, beating well after each addition. Add sour cream; beat at medium speed 2 minutes. Weigh or lightly spoon flour into dry measuring cups; level with a knife. Combine flour, baking powder, baking soda, and ½ teaspoon salt in a bowl, stirring with a whisk. Add flour mixture to sugar mixture alternately with cocoa mixture, beginning and ending with flour mixture; beat just until combined.
4. Divide batter evenly between prepared pans. Bake at 350° for 30 minutes or until a wooden pick inserted in center comes out with moist crumbs clinging. Cool 10 minutes in pans on wire racks. Remove from pans; cool on wire racks. Discard wax paper.
5. To prepare filling, combine ⅓ cup milk and next 3 ingredients (through dash of salt) in a saucepan over medium-low heat; bring to a boil, stirring constantly. Cook 1 minute or until thick, stirring constantly. Remove from heat. Add milk chocolate, stirring until smooth. Pour into bowl. Cover and chill. Uncover; fold in whipped topping.
6. To prepare glaze, combine powdered sugar and next 6 ingredients (through 1 ounce chocolate) in a saucepan over low heat. Cook 2 minutes, stirring frequently. Place 1 cake layer on a plate. Spread filling over cake, leaving a ¼-inch border. Top with remaining layer. Drizzle glaze over top of cake, spreading it out over edges.

Serves 16 (serving size: 1 slice).

CALORIES 311; FAT 10.3g (sat 5.7g, mono 2.1g, poly 0.5g); PROTEIN 4.8g; CARB 50.6g; FIBER 1.8g; CHOL 49mg; IRON 2.2mg; SODIUM 224mg; CALC 66mg

Apple-Cinnamon Bundt Cake

A homey comfort classic made special with a dusting of sugar and a hidden filling of apple and nuts.

Hands-on time: 26 min. Total time: 2 hr. 16 min.

Filling:

1½ cups diced peeled Granny Smith or other tart apple

½ cup apple cider

1 tablespoon dark brown sugar

1 (3-inch) cinnamon stick

Streusel:

½ cup walnuts

2 tablespoons dark brown sugar

1 tablespoon all-purpose flour

½ teaspoon ground cinnamon

Cake:

Baking spray with flour

¾ cup granulated sugar

½ cup butter, softened

2 large eggs

1 large egg yolk

1 vanilla bean, split lengthwise

9 ounces all-purpose flour (about 2 cups)

2 teaspoons baking powder

1 teaspoon baking soda

¼ teaspoon salt

¾ cup plain 2% reduced-fat Greek yogurt

½ cup fat-free milk

Remaining Ingredient:

1 teaspoon powdered sugar

1. Preheat oven to 350°.

2. To prepare filling, combine first 4 ingredients in a saucepan over medium-high heat; bring to a boil. Reduce heat to medium; simmer 20 minutes or until liquid almost evaporates and apple is tender, stirring occasionally. Cool to room temperature. Discard cinnamon stick.

3. To prepare streusel, place walnuts and next 3 ingredients (through ground cinnamon) in a food processor; pulse until mixture resembles coarse meal.

4. To prepare cake, coat a 12-cup Bundt pan with baking spray. Place sugar and butter in a large bowl; beat with a mixer at medium speed until light and fluffy (about 3 minutes). Add eggs and egg yolk, 1 at a time, beating well after each addition. Scrape seeds from vanilla bean; add seeds to sugar mixture. Reserve bean for another use. Weigh or lightly spoon flour into dry measuring cups; level with a knife. Combine flour, baking powder, baking soda, and salt in a bowl, stirring well with a whisk. Combine yogurt and milk in a small bowl, stirring until smooth. Add flour mixture and milk mixture alternately to sugar mixture, beginning and ending with flour mixture; beat just until combined.

5. Spoon one-third of batter into prepared pan; sprinkle batter with half apple mixture and half walnut mixture. Repeat layers, ending with remaining third of batter; smooth with a spatula. Bake at 350° for 30 minutes or until a wooden pick inserted in center comes out with moist crumbs clinging. Cool on a wire rack 15 minutes; remove cake from pan. Cool on wire rack. Sprinkle with powdered sugar.

Serves 12 (serving size: 1 wedge).

CALORIES 279; FAT 11.7g (sat 5.5g, mono 2.9g, poly 2.5g); PROTEIN 5.9g; CARB 38.2g; FIBER 1.1g; CHOL 68mg; IRON 1.4mg; SODIUM 229mg; CALC 83mg

Canola Oil Pound Cake with Browned Butter Glaze

Heart-healthy canola oil helps lighten this classic dessert. And an ingenious technique deepens flavor and adds richness.

Warming a split vanilla bean in canola oil infuses the oil with deep vanilla essence as the seeds spill out and mingle in the liquid. This is a simple, quick step that is well worth the little bit of time and effort.

Hands-on time: 25 min. Total time: 1 hr. 50 min.

Cake:

- 6 tablespoons canola oil
- 1 vanilla bean, split lengthwise
- 1¾ cups sugar
- ½ cup unsalted butter, softened
- 2 large eggs
- 12 ounces cake flour (about 3 cups)
- 2 teaspoons baking powder
- ½ teaspoon salt
- 1 cup nonfat buttermilk

Baking spray with flour

Glaze:

- 1 tablespoon unsalted butter
- ¼ cup sugar
- 2 tablespoons 2% reduced-fat milk
- ½ teaspoon vanilla extract

1. Preheat oven to 350°.

2. To prepare cake, combine oil and vanilla bean in a small skillet over medium-high heat, and bring to a simmer. Remove from heat. Let stand 10 minutes or until mixture cools to room temperature. Scrape seeds from bean, and stir into oil; discard bean.

3. Combine oil mixture, 1¾ cups sugar, and ½ cup butter in a large bowl; beat with a mixer at medium speed until well blended (about 5 minutes). Add eggs, 1 at a time, beating well after each addition. Weigh or lightly spoon flour into dry measuring cups; level with a knife. Combine flour, baking powder, and salt, stirring well with a whisk. Add flour mixture and buttermilk alternately to sugar mixture, beginning and ending with flour mixture.

4. Spoon batter into a 10-inch tube pan coated with baking spray, and spread evenly. Bake at 350° for 1 hour or until a wooden pick inserted in center comes out clean. Cool in pan 10 minutes on a wire rack, and remove from pan.

5. To prepare glaze, melt 1 tablespoon butter in a small skillet over medium heat; cook 2 minutes or until lightly browned. Remove from heat. Add sugar, milk, and vanilla, stirring until smooth. Drizzle glaze over warm cake.

Serves 16 (serving size: 1 slice).

CALORIES 294; FAT 12.6g (sat 4.7g, mono 5.3g, poly 1.9g); PROTEIN 3.2g; CARB 42.8g; FIBER 0.4g; CHOL 44mg; IRON 1.7mg; SODIUM 149mg; CALC 60mg

Texas Sheet Cake

A big, flat classic. Toasty nuts and fudgy cake get topped with a thin, crackly glaze. It's easy, and it's been a reader favorite since it first appeared in the magazine in 2000.

You can also make this recipe in a 13 x 9–inch metal baking pan. Bake at 375° for 22 minutes.
Hands-on time: 17 min. Total time: 1 hr. 5 min.

Cake:

Cooking spray

2	teaspoons all-purpose flour
9	ounces all-purpose flour (about 2 cups)
2	cups granulated sugar
1	teaspoon baking soda
1	teaspoon ground cinnamon
¼	teaspoon salt
¾	cup water
½	cup butter
¼	cup unsweetened cocoa
½	cup low-fat buttermilk
1	teaspoon vanilla extract
2	large eggs

Icing:

6	tablespoons butter
⅓	cup fat-free milk
¼	cup unsweetened cocoa
3	cups powdered sugar
2	teaspoons vanilla extract
¼	cup chopped pecans, toasted

1. Preheat oven to 375°.

2. To prepare cake, coat a 15 x 10–inch jelly-roll pan with cooking spray; dust with 2 teaspoons flour. Set aside.

3. Weigh or lightly spoon 9 ounces flour (about 2 cups) into dry measuring cups; level with a knife. Combine 9 ounces flour and next 4 ingredients (through salt) in a large bowl, stirring well with a whisk. Combine ¾ cup water, ½ cup butter, and ¼ cup cocoa in a small saucepan; bring to a boil, stirring frequently. Remove from heat; pour into flour mixture. Beat with a mixer at medium speed until well blended. Add buttermilk, 1 teaspoon vanilla, and eggs to bowl; beat well. Pour batter into prepared pan. Bake at 375° for 17 minutes or until a wooden pick inserted in center comes out clean. Place on a wire rack.

4. To prepare icing, combine 6 tablespoons butter, fat-free milk, and ¼ cup cocoa in a saucepan; bring to a boil, stirring constantly. Remove from heat. Gradually stir in powdered sugar and 2 teaspoons vanilla. Stir in pecans. Spread over hot cake. Cool completely on wire rack.

Serves 20 (serving size: 1 piece).

CALORIES 298; FAT 10g (sat 5.5g, mono 3.2g, poly 0.7g); PROTEIN 3.1g; CARB 49.8g; FIBER 0.5g; CHOL 44mg; IRON 1.1mg; SODIUM 188mg; CALC 25mg

Carrot Cake

Carrot cake, soaked with oil, is usually a fat and calorie disaster, with some recipes delivering more than 1,400 calories and 28 grams of saturated fat per serving. This one boasts a thick cream cheese frosting and tender, lightly spiced cake. No disaster, just delicious.

Flaked coconut and crushed pineapple enhance the cake with chewy-tender-juicy bits.

Hands-on time: 24 min. Total time: 1 hr. 29 min.

Cake:

6.75 ounces all-purpose flour (about 1½ cups)

1⅓ cups granulated sugar

½ cup flaked sweetened coconut

⅓ cup chopped pecans

2 teaspoons baking soda

2 teaspoons ground cinnamon

1 teaspoon salt

3 tablespoons canola oil

2 large eggs

2 cups grated carrot

1½ cups canned crushed pineapple, drained

Cooking spray

Frosting:

2 tablespoons butter, softened

1 (8-ounce) block ⅓-less-fat cream cheese, softened

3 cups powdered sugar

2 teaspoons vanilla extract

1. Preheat oven to 350°.

2. To prepare cake, weigh or lightly spoon flour into dry measuring cups; level with a knife. Combine flour and next 6 ingredients (through salt) in a large bowl; stir well with a whisk. Combine oil and eggs; stir well. Stir egg mixture, grated carrot, and pineapple into flour mixture. Spoon batter into a 13 x 9–inch metal baking pan coated with cooking spray. Bake at 350° for 35 minutes or until a wooden pick inserted in center comes out clean. Cool completely on a wire rack.

3. To prepare frosting, combine butter and cream cheese in a large bowl. Beat with a mixer at medium speed until smooth. Beat in powdered sugar and vanilla just until smooth. Spread frosting over top of cake.

Serves 16 (serving size: 1 piece).

CALORIES 322; FAT 10.4g (sat 4.2g, mono 3.2g, poly 1.5g); PROTEIN 4.1g; CARB 54.4g; FIBER 1.4g; CHOL 40mg; IRON 1mg; SODIUM 403mg; CALC 29mg

DESSERTS

13

TEST KITCHEN SECRET

Avoid Underbaking Cakes and Breads: Overcooked baked goods disappoint, but we've found that less experienced bakers are more likely to undercook them, with a gummy result. You won't get that irresistible browning unless you have the confidence to fully cook the food. Really look at the baked treat: Even if the wooden pick comes out clean, if it's pale, it's not finished. Let it go another couple of minutes until it has an even golden-brownness. Once you've done this a few times and know exactly what you're looking for, it becomes second nature.

Cranberry-Oatmeal Bars

Somewhere between a soft granola bar, a blondie, and a jam cookie. Not too sweet, not too tart.

Be sure to zest the orange before you squeeze the juice. Hands-on time: 15 min. Total time: 1 hr. 15 min.

Crust:

4.5	ounces all-purpose flour (about 1 cup)
1	cup quick-cooking oats
½	cup packed brown sugar
¼	teaspoon salt
¼	teaspoon baking soda
¼	teaspoon ground cinnamon
6	tablespoons butter, melted
3	tablespoons orange juice

Cooking spray

Filling:

1⅓	cups dried cranberries (about 6 ounces)
¾	cup sour cream
½	cup granulated sugar
2	tablespoons all-purpose flour
1	teaspoon vanilla extract
½	teaspoon grated orange rind
1	large egg white, lightly beaten

1. Preheat oven to 325°.

2. To prepare crust, weigh or lightly spoon flour into a dry measuring cup; level with a knife. Combine flour and next 5 ingredients (through cinnamon) in a medium bowl, stirring well with a whisk. Drizzle butter and juice over flour mixture, stirring until moistened (mixture will be crumbly). Reserve ½ cup oat mixture. Press remaining oat mixture into the bottom of an 11 x 7–inch glass or ceramic baking dish coated with cooking spray.

3. To prepare filling, combine cranberries, sour cream, granulated sugar, and next 4 ingredients (through egg white) in a medium bowl, stirring well. Spread cranberry mixture over prepared crust; sprinkle reserved oat mixture evenly over filling. Bake at 325° for 40 minutes or until edges are golden. Cool completely in pan on a wire rack.

Serves 24 (serving size: 1 bar).

CALORIES 133; FAT 4.6g (sat 2.6g, mono 0.8g, poly 0.2g); PROTEIN 1.5g; CARB 21.9g; FIBER 0.9g; CHOL 13mg; IRON 0.6mg; SODIUM 67mg; CALC 20mg

Cherry-Oatmeal Bars variation:
Substitute dried cherries for the dried cranberries and lemon rind for the orange rind in the filling.

Serves 24 (serving size: 1 bar).

CALORIES 135; FAT 4.6g (sat 2.6g, mono 0.8g, poly 0.2g); PROTEIN 1.7g; CARB 21.5g; FIBER 1.3g; CHOL 13mg; IRON 0.7mg; SODIUM 68mg; CALC 27mg

Maple-Date-Oatmeal Bars variation:
Substitute chopped pitted dates for the dried cranberries. Omit granulated sugar from the filling, and add 2 tablespoons maple syrup and 2 tablespoons brown sugar.

Serves 24 (serving size: 1 bar).

CALORIES 124; FAT 4.6g (sat 2.6g, mono 0.8g, poly 0.2g); PROTEIN 1.7g; CARB 19.8g; FIBER 1.1g; CHOL 13mg; IRON 0.7mg; SODIUM 68mg; CALC 26mg

Peanut Butter Cup Blondies

If you're seduced by the chocolate–peanut butter proposition, you'll love these bars.

They seem wonderfully indulgent yet are low in calories. Substitute crunchy peanut butter to boost the texture with little nutty nuggets. Hands-on time: 20 min. Total time: 2 hr.

5.6 ounces all-purpose flour (about 1¼ cups)
1 cup granulated sugar
½ teaspoon baking powder
¼ teaspoon salt
⅓ cup creamy peanut butter
¼ cup butter, melted and cooled slightly
2 tablespoons 2% reduced-fat milk
1 teaspoon vanilla extract
2 large eggs, lightly beaten
¼ cup semisweet chocolate chips

Cooking spray
4 (0.75-ounce) peanut butter cups, coarsely chopped

1. Preheat oven to 350°.
2. Weigh or lightly spoon flour into dry measuring cups; level with a knife. Combine flour and next 3 ingredients (through salt), stirring well with a whisk. Combine peanut butter and next 4 ingredients (through eggs), stirring well. Add peanut butter mixture to flour mixture; stir until combined. Stir in chocolate chips.

3. Scrape batter into a 9-inch square metal baking pan lightly coated with cooking spray; arrange peanut butter cups over batter. Bake at 350° for 19 minutes or until a wooden pick inserted in center comes out with moist crumbs clinging. Cool in pan on a wire rack.

Serves 20 (serving size: 1 blondie).

CALORIES 153; FAT 7g (sat 2.9g, mono 2g, poly 0.8g); PROTEIN 3.2g; CARB 20.8g; FIBER 0.7g; CHOL 28mg; IRON 0.7mg; SODIUM 98mg; CALC 17mg

Snickerdoodles

Silly name, serious cookie.

Simply roll sugar-cookie dough in cinnamon sugar for the snickerdoodle effect—cookies that crack on the outside and are soft on the inside. Hands-on time: 20 min. Total time: 49 min.

¾ cup granulated sugar
⅔ cup light brown sugar
½ cup butter, softened
1 teaspoon vanilla extract
1 large egg
6.75 ounces all-purpose flour (about 1½ cups)
1 teaspoon baking powder
½ teaspoon ground cinnamon
¼ teaspoon salt
⅓ cup granulated sugar
1½ teaspoons ground cinnamon

Cooking spray

1. Preheat oven to 400°.
2. Combine ¾ cup granulated sugar, brown sugar, and butter in a medium bowl; beat with a mixer at medium speed until light and fluffy. Beat in vanilla and egg.
3. Weigh or lightly spoon flour into dry measuring cups; level with a knife. Combine flour, baking powder, ½ teaspoon cinnamon, and salt, stirring well with a whisk. Add flour mixture to butter mixture; beat just until combined. Shape dough into 30 balls.
4. Combine ⅓ cup granulated sugar and 1½ teaspoons cinnamon in a small shallow dish. Roll balls in sugar mixture; place 2 inches apart on baking sheets coated with cooking spray. Bake at 400° for 8 minutes or until tops crack. Cool in pans 1 minute. Remove from pans; cool on a wire rack.

Serves 30 (serving size: 1 cookie).

CALORIES 99; FAT 3.3g (sat 2g, mono 0.9g, poly 0.2g); PROTEIN 0.9g; CARB 16.9g; FIBER 0.3g; CHOL 15mg; IRON 0.5mg; SODIUM 59mg; CALC 17mg

Classic Fudge-Walnut Brownies

Crowned our best chocolate recipe ever when we did a 25-year look-back, these deliver that intense, back-of-the-throat chocolate satisfaction from the first bite.

Large chunks create big, luxurious pockets of melty chocolate in the brownies. The key to keeping regular brownies moist is usually loads of butter or other fat. There's less margin for error here: To ensure a nice fudgy texture, take care not to overbake. For taller brownies, bake them in an 8-inch square pan and add about 5 minutes to the cook time. Hands-on time: 15 min. Total time: 45 min.

3.38 ounces all-purpose flour (about ¾ cup)

1 cup granulated sugar

¾ cup unsweetened cocoa

½ cup packed brown sugar

½ teaspoon baking powder

¼ teaspoon salt

1 cup bittersweet chocolate chunks, divided

⅓ cup fat-free milk

6 tablespoons butter, melted

1 teaspoon vanilla extract

2 large eggs, lightly beaten

½ cup chopped walnuts, divided

Cooking spray

1. Preheat oven to 350°.

2. Weigh or lightly spoon flour into a dry measuring cup; level with a knife. Combine flour and next 5 ingredients (through salt) in a large bowl. Combine ½ cup chocolate and milk in a microwave-safe bowl; microwave at HIGH 1 minute, stirring after 30 seconds. Stir in butter, vanilla, and eggs. Add milk mixture, remaining ½ cup chocolate, and ¼ cup nuts to flour mixture; stir to combine.

3. Pour batter into a 9-inch square metal baking pan coated with cooking spray; sprinkle with remaining ¼ cup nuts. Bake at 350° for 19 minutes or until a wooden pick inserted in center comes out with moist crumbs clinging. Cool in pan on a wire rack. Cut into squares.

Serves 20 (serving size: 1 brownie).

CALORIES 186; FAT 9.1g (sat 4.2g, mono 2.2g, poly 1.7g); PROTEIN 2.8g; CARB 25.4g; FIBER 1.4g; CHOL 30mg; IRON 0.9mg; SODIUM 74mg; CALC 23mg

Chocolate-Cherry Oatmeal Cookies

Chewy texture and chocolate-packed flavor make these feel like a guilty pleasure. Whole-wheat flour, whole-grain oats, and dried cherries mean they're not.

Bittersweet chocolate has a deeper flavor that's fitting for hearty oats. Hands-on time: 18 min. Total time: 48 min.

1.5 ounces all-purpose flour (about ⅓ cup)

1.5 ounces whole-wheat flour (about ⅓ cup)

1½ cups old-fashioned rolled oats

1 teaspoon baking soda

½ teaspoon salt

6 tablespoons unsalted butter

¾ cup packed light brown sugar

1 cup dried cherries

1 teaspoon vanilla extract

1 large egg, lightly beaten

3 ounces bittersweet chocolate, coarsely chopped

Cooking spray

1. Preheat oven to 350°.
2. Weigh or lightly spoon flours into dry measuring cups; level with a knife. Combine flours and next 3 ingredients (through salt) in a large bowl; stir with a whisk.
3. Melt butter in a small saucepan over low heat. Remove from heat; add brown sugar, stirring until smooth. Add sugar mixture to flour mixture; beat with a mixer at medium speed until well blended. Add cherries, vanilla, and egg; beat until combined. Fold in chocolate. Drop dough by tablespoonfuls 2 inches apart onto baking sheets coated with cooking spray. Bake at 350° for 12 minutes. Cool on pans 3 minutes or until almost firm. Remove cookies from pans; cool on wire racks.

Serves 30 (serving size: 1 cookie).

CALORIES 94; FAT 3.2g (sat 1.6g, mono 0.6g, poly 0.2g); PROTEIN 1.5g; CARB 15.7g; FIBER 1.3g; CHOL 10mg; IRON 0.6mg; SODIUM 88mg; CALC 15mg

Chocolate Chip Cookies

We opt for fewer chocolate chips so you get more buttery–brown sugar cookie flavor—and enough chocolate to please.

Store up to a week in an airtight container, if they last that long. Hands-on time: 15 min. Total time: 37 min.

10.1 ounces all-purpose flour (about 2¼ cups)

1 teaspoon baking soda

¼ teaspoon salt

1 cup packed brown sugar

¾ cup granulated sugar

½ cup butter, softened

1 teaspoon vanilla extract

2 large egg whites

¾ cup semisweet chocolate chips

Cooking spray

1. Preheat oven to 350°.
2. Weigh or lightly spoon flour into dry measuring cups; level with a knife. Combine flour, baking soda, and salt in a bowl, stirring with a whisk.
3. Combine sugars and butter in a large bowl; beat with a mixer at medium speed until well blended. Add vanilla and egg whites; beat 1 minute. Add flour mixture and chips; beat until blended.

4. Drop dough by level tablespoons 2 inches apart onto baking sheets coated with cooking spray. Bake at 350° for 10 minutes or until lightly browned. Cool on pans 2 minutes. Remove from pans; cool completely on wire racks.

Serves 48 (serving size: 1 cookie).

CALORIES 88; FAT 3g (sat 1.8g, mono 0.5g, poly 0.1g); PROTEIN 1g; CARB 14.6g; FIBER 0.2g; CHOL 5mg; IRON 0.4mg; SODIUM 56mg; CALC 5mg

Chocolate Shortbread

Heart-healthy canola oil fills in for much of the butter here. The cookies keep their characteristic crisp texture, and plenty of buttery flavor remains.

Because the dough goes into the oven dark, it's hard to tell when the shortbread browns. Check the temperature using an oven thermometer, and bake just until the shortbread is set. This shortbread keeps for several days in an airtight container. Hands-on time: 16 min. Total time: 1 hr. 30 min.

4.5   ounces all-purpose flour (about 1 cup)

3   tablespoons unsweetened premium dark cocoa

¼   teaspoon salt

½   cup powdered sugar

5   tablespoons butter, softened

¼   cup canola oil

Cooking spray

1. Weigh or lightly spoon flour into a dry measuring cup; level with a knife. Combine flour, cocoa, and salt in a small bowl; stir with a whisk.

2. Place sugar, butter, and oil in a medium bowl; mix with hands until combined. Add flour mixture; mix with hands until combined. Wrap in plastic wrap. Refrigerate 30 minutes.

3. Preheat oven to 325°.

4. Place dough on a baking sheet coated with cooking spray; press dough into an 8 x 5-inch (about ⅜-inch-thick) rectangle. Pierce entire surface liberally with a fork.

Bake at 325° for 30 minutes or just until set. Cut shortbread into 24 pieces. Cool completely.

Serves 24 (serving size: 1 cookie).

CALORIES 72; FAT 4.8g (sat 1.7g, mono 2.1g, poly 0.8g); PROTEIN 0.7g; CARB 7g; FIBER 0.3g; CHOL 6mg; IRON 0.3mg; SODIUM 42mg; CALC 2mg

Lemon Shortbread variation:
A little bit of cornstarch ensures a short texture in the cookies. Substitute 3 tablespoons cornstarch for the unsweetened cocoa. Add ½ teaspoon grated lemon rind to flour mixture. Knead dough lightly 4 times or just until smooth before chilling. Bake 30 minutes or just until set and edges are golden. You can also use grated orange rind in place of lemon.

Serves 24 (serving size: 1 cookie).

CALORIES 74; FAT 4.8g (sat 1.7g, mono 2g, poly 0.8g); PROTEIN 0.6g; CARB 7.5g; FIBER 0.2g; CHOL 6mg; IRON 0.3mg; SODIUM 42mg; CALC 2mg

Brown Sugar Shortbread variation:
Using light brown sugar yields sweet treats with caramel notes. These double easily; just bake each batch separately for the best results. Use a total of 5.5 ounces all-purpose flour (about 1¼ cups), and substitute 3 tablespoons cornstarch for the cocoa. Omit powdered sugar and oil, and use ½ cup packed light brown sugar and 7 tablespoons butter (total), softened. Sprinkle dough with 1½ teaspoons ice water; knead dough lightly 4 times or just until smooth. Bake 25 minutes or just until set and edges are golden.

Serves 24 (serving size: 1 cookie).

CALORIES 74; FAT 3.4g (sat 2.1g, mono 0.9g, poly 0.2g); PROTEIN 0.7g; CARB 10.4g; FIBER 0.2g; CHOL 9mg; IRON 0.4mg; SODIUM 50mg; CALC 6mg

Chocolate-Hazelnut Meringues

Crisp, airy meringue cookies are sweet little kisses that melt away. They're basically fat-free, too, so we dipped them in chocolate and coated them with hazelnuts.

Make up to two days ahead, and store in an airtight container at room temperature.
Hands-on time: 20 min. Total time: 2 hr. 21 min.

5	large egg whites
½	teaspoon cream of tartar
⅛	teaspoon salt
½	cup granulated sugar
½	cup packed brown sugar
1	teaspoon vanilla extract
3	ounces semisweet chocolate
⅓	cup blanched whole hazelnuts, toasted and finely chopped

1. Preheat oven to 250°.

2. Place egg whites in a large bowl; beat with a mixer at high speed until foamy. Add cream of tartar and salt, beating until soft peaks form. Gradually add sugars, 1 tablespoon at a time, beating until stiff peaks form. Add vanilla; beat 1 minute.

3. Cover 2 baking sheets with parchment paper. Spoon 24 (2-inch-round) mounds of dough onto prepared baking sheets. Place in oven; bake at 250° for 1 hour or until dry to the touch, rotating pans halfway through cooking. (Meringues are done when surface is dry and meringues can be removed from paper without sticking to fingers.) Turn oven off. Cool meringues in oven 1 hour. Remove from oven; carefully remove meringues from paper.

4. Place chocolate in a medium glass bowl. Microwave at HIGH 1 minute or until almost melted, stirring until smooth. Dip side of each meringue in melted chocolate and chopped hazelnuts.

Serves 12 (serving size: 2 meringues).

CALORIES 135; FAT 4.3g (sat 1.4g, mono 1.7g, poly 0.3g); PROTEIN 2.6g; CARB 22.7g; FIBER 0.4g; CHOL 0mg; IRON 0.6mg; SODIUM 51mg; CALC 13mg

CHOICE INGREDIENT

Cream of Tartar: A by-product of winemaking, cream of tartar is found in stores near the baking powder and baking soda. A small amount added to egg whites keeps them stable and adds volume when beaten to make a meringue. It can prevent sugar from crystallizing, too, so it's sometimes used to create smooth icings, syrups, and caramels.

Chocolate Baklava

This is a simply amazing recipe—layers of crisp phyllo interspersed with mixed nuts and hazelnut-chocolate spread, with just enough butter to enhance the flavor yet keep the sat fat low.

Lightly spiced honey syrup gives the gooey, sticky quality that makes baklava so heavenly.
Hands-on time: 25 min. Total time: 1 hr. 21 min.

¾ cup honey

½ cup water

1 (3-inch) cinnamon stick

1 cup hazelnut-chocolate spread

½ cup toasted hazelnuts, coarsely chopped

½ cup roasted pistachios, coarsely chopped

⅓ cup blanched toasted almonds, coarsely chopped

⅓ cup toasted walnuts, coarsely chopped

½ teaspoon ground cinnamon

⅛ teaspoon salt

Cooking spray

24 (14 x 9-inch) sheets frozen phyllo dough, thawed

½ cup butter, melted

1. Combine first 3 ingredients in a medium saucepan over low heat; stir until honey dissolves. Increase heat to medium; cook, without stirring, until a candy thermometer registers 230° (about 10 minutes). Remove from heat; keep warm. Discard cinnamon stick.

2. Preheat oven to 350°.

3. Place hazelnut-chocolate spread in a microwave-safe bowl; microwave at HIGH 30 seconds or until melted. Combine hazelnuts and next 5 ingredients (through salt). Lightly coat a 13 x 9-inch glass or ceramic baking dish with cooking spray. Working with 1 phyllo sheet at a time (cover remaining dough to prevent drying), place 1 phyllo sheet lengthwise in bottom of prepared pan, allowing ends of sheet to extend over edges of dish; lightly brush with butter. Repeat procedure with 5 phyllo sheets and butter. Drizzle about ⅓ cup melted hazelnut-chocolate spread over phyllo. Sprinkle evenly with one-third of nut mixture (about ½ cup). Repeat procedure twice with phyllo, butter, hazelnut-chocolate spread, and nut mixture. Top last layer of nut mixture with remaining 6 sheets phyllo, each lightly brushed with butter. Press gently into pan.

4. Make 3 lengthwise cuts and 5 crosswise cuts to form 24 portions using a sharp knife. Bake at 350° for 35 minutes or until phyllo is golden. Remove from oven. Drizzle honey mixture over baklava. Cool in pan on a wire rack. Cover; store at room temperature.

Serves 24 (serving size: 1 piece).

CALORIES 238; FAT 13.4g (sat 4.3g, mono 5.6g, poly 2g); PROTEIN 4g; CARB 27.8g; FIBER 1.6g; CHOL 10mg; IRON 1.3mg; SODIUM 148mg; CALC 29mg

DESSERTS

13

Bourbon-Caramel Truffles

Truffles typically have lots of cream and butter. Our bite-sized treats forgo those riches while maintaining the soft, creamy texture.

Chocolate tends to scorch, separate, or become grainy if not heated carefully, and all the more so without cream or butter to stabilize it. We add cane syrup and evaporated milk to solve that problem. Chopped bits of chocolate melt smoothly and quickly, also helping eke out the desired creamy texture.
Hands-on time: 20 min. Total time: 4 hr. 21 min.

3   tablespoons brown sugar

2   tablespoons evaporated whole milk

1   tablespoon golden cane syrup

Dash of salt

1   tablespoon bourbon

½   teaspoon vanilla extract

3.5   ounces bittersweet chocolate, finely chopped

1.75   ounces milk chocolate, finely chopped

2   tablespoons unsweetened cocoa

1. Combine brown sugar, milk, cane syrup, and salt in a saucepan over medium-high heat; bring to a boil. Cook 1 minute or until sugar dissolves. Remove from heat. Stir in bourbon and vanilla extract. Add bittersweet and milk chocolates; let stand 1 minute. Stir until smooth. Pour into a shallow dish; cover and chill 4 hours.

2. Heat a tablespoon measure with hot water; pat dry. Scoop chocolate mixture with spoon; dip in cocoa. Roll into balls. Cover and refrigerate until ready to serve.

Serves 19 (serving size: 1 truffle).

CALORIES 60; FAT 2.7g (sat 1.6g, mono 0.5g, poly 0g); PROTEIN 0.8g; CARB 8g; FIBER 0.7g; CHOL 1mg; IRON 0.2mg; SODIUM 14mg; CALC 12mg

Chapter
Strategie
Techniqu

14:
s &
es

The Flavor Principles of Healthy Cooking

There is no mystery about light cooking, but attention needs to be paid to flavor balance when you cut fat and salt. Through trial and error and 25 years of experimentation, our Test Kitchen has coaxed out solutions to these challenges. Here are a few things we've learned.

Keep the Flavor Ship Righted

A balanced dish is generally one that plays several flavor notes—salty, sour, bitter, sweet, or spicy—in harmony, without one flavor overpowering the others. In traditional recipes, fat is often the great enabler of harmony, smoothing out sharp edges and providing a rounded, balanced mouthfeel. Consider the beautiful way that the acidic notes of fresh lemon play off the unctuous, mouthfilling quality of a cream or butter sauce. Such contrast and balance is one of the central principles of much cooking. In light cooking, when you use less cream, you sometimes need to use less of the complementary ingredient, too—or you need to find a less fatty ingredient that stands in for the original.

These are factors we consider when developing recipes. For the home cook, it's important to taste as you go and use a light hand with acids and spices until you've tasted your work. If a dish tastes off, you can often right the ship with a contrasting flavor. If it's too sour, a pinch of sugar might bring it into balance. If too bitter, a dash of salt will help. If the dish doesn't seem salty-savory enough, yet you're limiting sodium, try a squeeze of lime, a dash of hot sauce, or a drizzle of a flavorful oil.

Embrace High-Fat Flavorings—in Small Amounts

We love the milky richness of butter, the smoky wallop of the best bacon, and the crunch of coarse salt, yet these are ingredients we use in reduced amounts. To get the most from them, we add them at the right time so they'll have the most impact. Typically, that means toward the end of cooking. Good sea salt sprinkled on top of food, for example, will hit your palate first and strike a louder note than it would if buried in the dish. It makes little sense to add salt to marinades (except brines), breading crumbs, or batter; much of that salt will be left in the bowl. Instead, reserve the salt and add it directly to the food. In pasta dishes and soups, we often get better results when we use no-salt-added canned tomatoes and then add a small amount of salt.

Another technique in this vein: With a pound cake that contains less butter and more heart-healthy oil, we might use a browned-butter glaze because browned butter packs big butter flavor. We also scatter crumbled bacon over clam chowder or toss a bit into vinaigrettes.

Know When to Skimp and When to Splurge

Where does the most pleasure in a food lie? In traditional lasagna, for instance, it's not necessarily in the buttery béchamel; it's in the cheese. So, in our Butternut Squash, Caramelized Onion, and Spinach Lasagna (page 269), we forgo the traditional butter-flour roux and deploy flour-thickened low-fat milk for the sauce, which allows for more creamy-gooey kick from fontina cheese.

Turn on the Flavor Boosters

Experiment with concentrated ingredients that are low in fat and salt—and look to other cultures. Some of our favorites include Asian staples such as Sriracha, sambal oelek (chile paste), and a growing range of curry pastes and Mexican pepper sauces. From the fresh aisle, herbs, garlic, and citrus rind and juice are essential. From the spice aisle, crushed red pepper flakes, smoked paprika, chipotle powder, cumin, and coriander are mainstays. Dried mushrooms can add deep flavor, particularly earthy dried porcini mushrooms, which can be reconstituted with hot water or ground into a super-mushroomy powder.

Remember: Texture Determines Flavor

All cooks seek to take food off the stove when the texture is perfect, but cooking with less fat often reduces the margin of error. Without fatty sauces to compensate or fatty cuts of meat that hold their moistness, a dish is a bit more naked. Food quickly dries or becomes sad and bland. Check for doneness early, and, in the case of meat, give it a rest after it comes off the heat. Yes, resting adds a few minutes, but rushing is a false economy. If meat doesn't rest (five minutes for a chicken breast, small steak, or chop; more for bigger cuts), it will spill its juices when carved: Sayonara, precious meaty flavor.

14

Equipping Your Healthy Kitchen

Great kitchen tools make for better food and more pleasurable cooking, and that, in turn, tends to make you want to cook more often—probably the best foundation for healthy eating. We're not big gadget users; we draw a sharp distinction between junk that clutters up the kitchen drawers and those specialized tools—mandolines, Microplane-style graters—that do their jobs superbly. Toss stuff you don't need and replace it with excellent tools that suit your own cooking habits.

Nonstick Skillets

Despite improvements in technology, cookware with a nonstick surface shows wear relatively quickly (as opposed to copper or stainless cookware, which can last a lifetime), so replace it after the surface shows nicks or scratches—as often as every year or two. We favor three sizes—8-, 10-, and 12-inch.

Cast-Iron Cookware

Some cooks don't like the seasoning and cleaning that cast-iron demands, but we find a 10-inch cast-iron skillet indispensable for searing scallops, crisping salmon skin, or making corn bread with little added fat. You can now find preseasoned pans that will save you that step. An enamel-coated cast-iron Dutch oven (a big pot with a tight-fitting lid) is a slow-cooking investment that's worth every penny. We find that Dutch ovens often yield better results than electric slow cookers.

Baking Pans and Dishes

In our recipes, "pan" means metal, usually for baking, and "dish" means glass or ceramic, typically for casseroles. You need thick, heavy baking sheets (cookie sheets) and jelly-roll pans (large, flat sheets with 1-inch sides). Also stock 8- and 9-inch square metal pans—great for brownies—as well as 8- and 9-inch round cake pans, a 9 x 5–inch loaf pan, and a 13x 9–inch pan. If you are using old or hand-me-down pans that have acquired a patina of gunk, invest in new, sturdy pans; it really affects results. We prefer heavy, nonshiny aluminum pans, not dark or nonstick surfaces. In the glass or ceramic category, buy 8-inch square, 11 x 7–inch, and 13 x 9–inch dishes.

Measuring Tools

A healthy kitchen is a precise kitchen. A scale can improve your cooking immediately. Measuring flour by weight produces lighter cakes, cookies, and muffins. A scale can also help with proper portioning; learn what a 4-ounce raw pork chop, a 6-ounce halibut fillet, or a 2-ounce serving of dry pasta looks like.

Measuring cups, both dry and liquid versions, are crucial. Liquid measuring cups usually have a handle and spout and are designed so that you can view the contents at eye level to see if you have the correct amount. It pays to have a few different ones: 1-cup, 2-cup, and 4-cup.

Dry measuring cups are flat on top so that you can mound in dry ingredients (flour, cocoa, couscous, rice) and level off to reach the intended measurement.

As for measuring spoons, it's handy to have two sets.

Boards and Knives

Having several cutting boards prevents cross-contamination—of bacteria from meats, poultry, and seafood to uncooked food, and of flavors—and also fosters a neat, orderly kitchen by keeping tasks separated. A big meal might put two or three cutting boards into action at the same time. Have a board for vegetables; another for

fruit; and another for meat, fish, and poultry (or, if you have the room and the inclination, one for each protein). Buy sturdy boards that have less chance of warping.

Great knives bring great joy and boost confidence by facilitating precision. They can be pricey but will last for many years if not abused. There is no rule about how many you need, after you get an excellent chef's knife. The most important thing is that they feel good in your hand. Professional sharpening is worth the trouble.

Other Cutting and Grating Tools

Mandolines make paper-thin slices for the most beautiful shaved-veggie salads and efficiently cut a pile of ⅛-inch-thick potato slices for your potato gratin. You can spend a lot of money on one of these, but we've had great success with lower-priced options. Just buy a sturdy model and use the safety guard. Microplane-style graters are also essential in the healthy kitchen for zesting citrus, grating ginger or garlic, and turning frozen bread into instant breadcrumbs.

Storage Systems

A move to more whole grains—most economically bought in bulk—requires orderly storage; plastic bags pile up and collapse into each other. Clear out the pantry, and then buy sturdy, clear, straight-sided stackable containers.

For the freezer, where we like to house that nugget of pancetta or extra cup of marinara sauce, zip-top freezer bags are fine. Label clearly with the date, and flatten for stacking.

The Watchful Cook: Time and Temperature

Many old cookbooks were thin on detailed instruction, perhaps because the cook was assumed to already know how to "bake the roast in a low oven until fork-tender" (there are at least 15 vague terms for various oven temperatures). We favor a bit more detail, not just because we're kitchen nerds, but also because we understand from painful experience that lower-fat brownies baked just two minutes too long have missed their shot at being truly fudgy, and that tender beef stew requires a gentle simmer, not a low boil. Less fat in the food calls for more vigilance from the cook. It's not difficult, but it is necessary. Here are a few pointers.

First, Know Your Oven

It seems reasonable to expect an oven set to 350° to heat to 350°. But many ovens—including new, expensive models—hit far from the mark, and many change as they age. That's why you should always keep an oven thermometer in the oven. Knowing that your oven heats 25° hotter than it's supposed to allows you to compensate.

Next, be aware of hot spots. You've probably seen the result of these mini thermal anomalies baked into a cake: Uneven, wavy tops signal a hot-spot problem. Try the bread test: Arrange bread slices in a single layer to cover the middle oven rack. Bake at 350° for a few minutes, and see if any slices get singed; if they do, you've found your oven's hot spot(s) and can avoid those areas or rotate pans accordingly.

Use Probe Thermometers and Timers

An oven thermometer is only the first defense. The second is an internal-temperature thermometer, useful for meats, candies, and even some breads. This is the most important tool for cooking lean meats, such as whole turkeys or beef tenderloins, which are very sensitive to overcooking. A digital version allows you to keep the thermometer inside the meat as it cooks, while a wire leads out of the oven to a display. An alarm goes off when the desired internal temperature is reached.

Timers are built into microwaves and ovens (and smart phones). Even if you're the sort of person who can wake up in the morning without an alarm, don't expect to transfer this skill to, say, monitoring the browning of delicate pine nuts while multitasking. One or two minutes can make all the difference.

Take Meats Out of the Fridge

Meats cook much more evenly if you allow them to stand at room temperature for 15 minutes to an hour (depending on the size of the cut) to take the chill off. A large roast that goes into the oven cold may end up overcooked on the outside while the core struggles to reach a safe temperature—the so-called bull's-eye effect. This is less of a problem with smaller cuts like boneless chicken breasts, but even those benefit from five or 10 minutes out of the fridge.

Check Early When Baking

Because ovens are vague and lower-fat cakes require precision, it's good to remember that you can always add more time, but you can't take time away. We check all baked goods at least five minutes before the recommended cook time.

Use Your Judgment

That said, keep your eye on the effect you want in the food. A sad, pale pan of corn bread will technically test as done—the toothpick comes out clean—but if you want a golden-brown crust, cook it a few minutes longer. The same holds true for that delicious "sugar crust" on a pound cake, or the golden-brown pastry atop a pie. We know cooks who consistently pull baked goods a few minutes too early, with pallid results.

Preheat Aggressively

It's easy, in a rush, to barely heat the skillet before adding oil and tossing in onions for a sauté. Next comes…nothing. No sizzle. A hot pan is essential for sautéing veggies or creating a great crust on scallops or steak. And it helps prevent food from sticking. The same rule applies for some oven applications. Cornmeal batter gains its classic crispy edges when it goes into a hot cast-iron skillet. Ideally, pizza should cook on a blazing-hot pizza stone; if raw dough hits a moderately heated (or cold) pan, it's harder to achieve a crisp, blistered-in-spots crust.

Know Low and Slow

When braising or stewing tough cuts of meat that break down through long, low-heat cooking, do not be tempted to rush things by raising the temperature. A braise requires simmering—heating the liquid to the point that a bubble breaks the surface every couple of seconds; more active gurgling means you're boiling. Meat will toughen up and then, even with prolonged cooking, never quite achieve the gorgeous texture you're looking for. The same low-and-slow principle applies to the delicate poaching of salmon.

With the exception of heavy cream, dairy products require careful simmering, too. Milk, buttermilk, sour cream, or yogurt is likely to "break"—to separate and curdle—if heated to the point of boiling.

It's possible to force chopped onions into a browned state using high heat, but this isn't real caramelization; onions that are translucent, creamy-silky, and buttery-soft require melting over medium-low to low heat for a long time, perhaps more than an hour. The best marinara or Bolognese sauce is simmered at length, with time in the pan yielding depth, richness, and complexity that simply doesn't come about if you hurry the cooking. If you don't have the time, go for a superfast pasta sauce of sautéed fresh tomatoes.

The bread test reveals hot spots in your oven.

Stovetop Cooking

The light cook needs to be especially adept at the stovetop because healthy cooking favors a lot of sautéing, stir-frying, pan-frying, and pan-grilling, using judicious amounts of healthy oils and, of course, flavor-enhancing bits of butter. Done properly, stovetop cooking caramelizes, crisps, and generally accentuates the natural flavors of food—pronto. But it's easy to make simple stovetop errors, detailed below, resulting in food that fails to sear or brown properly, or sucks up too much oil. A light touch at the stovetop involves developing confidence with ingredients, pans, and heat.

Sautéing

This means quickly cooking food in a small amount of fat over medium-high heat.

Equipment: A skillet or sauté pan is your wingman in the kitchen, so invest in a good one: dense-bottomed to distribute heat evenly, with nice heft and balance. Nonstick works well if you get a durable, highly rated pan and treat it properly on stove and in sink. Anodized aluminum and stainless steel also work well.

Ingredients: Time in the pan is brief, so the easiest approach is to start with naturally tender ingredients cut to even sizes. Go for pork tenderloin medallions, fish fillets, and boneless chicken. Sugar snap peas and sliced mushrooms will obviously sauté more easily than turnips—but tougher veggies, shaved thin or parboiled first, will cook up nicely on the stovetop, as will many tougher meat cuts if sliced very thinly and cooked with a light touch. Choose oil that holds its own over medium-high heat—

canola, peanut, or olive oil (not extra-virgin), or use a bit of butter mixed with oil.

Temperature: A classic error is to begin the sauté before the pan is ready. Heat it over medium-high heat for a few minutes. A drop of water in the pan should spit and sizzle.

Technique: After the pan is hot, add oil (or butter) and swirl to coat. Don't overcrowd the pan—a common error. Food releases

steam as it cooks, and crowded food overwhelms the pan's ability to brown. Suddenly, you're in the dreaded steaming mode, from which there is generally no return. Sautéing in batches is the solution. Or use a bigger pan.

When sautéing vegetables and bite-sized pieces of meat, stir frequently to promote even browning and cooking. But don't overdo it or the food won't have time to brown. Meat

(chicken breasts, steaks, or pork medallions) should only be turned once so there's enough time to form a nice crust, which will also prevent sticking.

Pan-Frying

It's similar to sautéing, but this method uses a bit more oil and sometimes lower heat: It gets some deep-frying action going without a full oil-bath immersion. The goal, again, is a nice crust on the food.

Equipment: We prefer nonstick skillets and sauté pans, so that breading will stick to the food, not the pan.

Ingredients: Here you want fish fillets, boneless chicken, or pork chops—fast-cooking, naturally tender pieces. Dense, less-juicy vegetables, like shredded potatoes (for latkes) or firm green tomato slices that have been dredged in flour or cornmeal, work well. Choose oil with a fairly mild flavor, like canola, peanut, or regular olive oil; boost flavor by mixing in a bit of butter.

Temperature: Some of our recipes call for medium-high heat to initiate browning, then, with a nice crust established, a temperature drop to allow the food (say, a thicker cut of fish) to finish cooking without overbrowning. Other dishes may work fine at one constant temperature.

Technique: Give the food room to party in the pan. Don't overcrowd. A sudden drop in pan temperature can cause breading to stick. And resist the temptation to peek or prematurely flip. The pan works its best magic during that initial kiss of food to hot surface; indeed, that first crust will be prettier and is the presentation side when you plate the dish.

Stir-Frying

This technique involves cooking small pieces of food quickly over very high heat.

Equipment: You can use a skillet in a pinch, but you won't get wok results, which come from food tossing about in a very hot pan that has a huge surface area. Look for the biggest rolled-carbon-steel or enamel-clad cast-iron wok that will sit over your burner. Flat-bottomed pans are needed for induction or electric elements. Nonstick is a nonstarter for serious practitioners of the art because it's not recommended for the kind of heat needed.

Ingredients: Because stir-frying is superfast, you need bite-sized pieces of meat that will stay tender and vegetables that will yield a gorgeous crunch after being cooked enough to lose their raw flavors.

Temperature: Hot, hotter, hottest—for true stir-fried yumminess (something the Cantonese call *wok hay*), you must cook briefly, at the highest temperature your stove can muster. Preheat the wok for several minutes; a drop of water flicked into the pan should dance across the surface and almost instantly evaporate (some wok cooks spit into the pan; we have seen this).

Technique: Once food goes in the pan, it needs to stay in constant motion. This means you must have all ingredients prepped and within reach. As with all stovetop cooking, don't overcrowd—everything should be dancing on the sizzling surface. You also need plenty of room in the wok to flip the food around.

Pan-Grilling

This is what you do when it's too cold or inconvenient to fire up the barbie. It yields appetizing grill marks and a moderate amount of grill flavor on the stovetop.

Equipment: A grill pan looks like a frying pan with raised ridges that impart grill marks while the rest of the food sits above the heat of the pan. Pans come in stainless steel, cast iron (these are very heavy, and need to be seasoned to prevent food from sticking, but they give the best sear), and various aluminums, with or without nonstick surfaces. Cleaning them can be a pain. If your pan is nonstick (and make sure you have one with a coating suitable for high heat, such as ceramic), it should wipe clean with little effort, but if it's not, it'll need a good scrubbing. Boiling water in it after cooking can help.

Ingredients: Foods that have flat surfaces (chops, burgers, fish steaks) do best because you want as much contact with those hot ridges as you can get. Vegetables cut into thick slices—onions, eggplant, zucchini—are ideal, too. We don't recommend glazes, which will run between the ridges and gunk up the pan.

Temperature: High is best. Turn the vent on, especially if there's a spice rub, which tends to smoke.

Technique: Preheat the pan until it's very hot—several minutes. It's best to oil the food (not the pan). It's usually best to turn food just once as it cooks; if you try to turn it too soon, before the grates have had a chance to sear completely, the food is destined to stick. If it's still not done but has dark grill marks, turn the heat down to medium and rotate the food 90 degrees so that you start new, crosshatched grill marks while the food continues to cook.

The Careful Baker

If cooking is an art, and baking a science, then light baking is a newer science, one that we have spent much energy studying in our Test Kitchen. The light baker faces two challenges—the fact that any ingredient substitution in a recipe will change how, say, a cake behaves in the oven, and the added complication that the goal of reducing fat can affect the moistness, intensity of flavor, perceived richness, and sometimes volume of your baked goods. A lot of the pleasures of these foods—crumb, crust, crunch, creaminess—are the result of the magical (i.e., chemical) interplay of fat—often butterfat—with sugars and proteins under the influence of heat. When we lighten up a brownie, a cookie, or a cake, we are not interested in trading away those pleasures.

The recipes in the dessert and bread chapters of this book are the product not of compromise but of innovation. We don't favor wholesale swaps—for example, substituting applesauce for butter, which usually produces a too-sticky muffin or cake—or zero-calorie sweeteners. Rather, we try to exploit the benefits of a high-fat star ingredient like mascarpone while surrounding it with a matrix of reduced-fat foods (such as excellent Greek yogurt) that, together, yield a delicious result.

The careful baker is simply one who understands that precision is a virtue. The light baker knows that even one tablespoon too much of flour can change the texture of a reduced-fat cake. Here are some fundamentals to keep in mind.

Measuring

Flour: We usually call for flour by weight and volume; buying a kitchen scale may be one of the best investments you can make as a baker. If a recipe calls for 4.5 ounces all-purpose flour (about 1 cup), "4.5 ounces" refers to the weight, and the "about 1 cup" measurement refers to the volume. To get the volume right, use a dry measuring cup, the kind with a flat top and no spout. It's best to stir flour in the canister before scooping it out, so it's not too compacted. Spoon it into the cup so that it mounds over the rim; don't tap the cup down, but simply level off the flour with the flat side of a knife.

Brown sugar: We don't give weight for brown sugar. Pack it into a dry measuring cup firmly enough that when you turn the cup over, the sugar holds its shape as it falls out.

Ingredients

Flours: The ratio of all-purpose, whole-wheat, or other flours in our recipes is precise; altering the ratios will affect the results, sometimes drastically.

Oils and solid fats: Liquid fats behave differently from solid fats. Methods and ratios for fats are carefully detailed, and substitutions can affect results. We use butter, not butter substitutes. If a recipe calls for softened butter, it should yield slightly to gentle pressure. If it's too soft, cookies may spread, or cakes may end up dense. Let butter soften at room temperature for about 30 minutes. Avoid using the microwave—it's too easy to get the butter more melted than soft.

Dairy products: We use a range of full-fat and reduced-fat dairy products in precise ratios. Substituting lower-fat products (or higher-fat, for that matter) will change the results. If a recipe calls for buttermilk, it's because of the useful acid and thickness; substitutions are asking for trouble.

Eggs: Large eggs are usually specified.

Dry versus liquid sugars: Dry sugars are important to the chemistry of baking when we call for them. Liquid sugars (honey, agave nectar) change the intensity of sweetness and the texture.

Salt: We use it judiciously. Leaving it out could produce bland, flat flavors.

Techniques

Combining dry ingredients: We usually don't sift flour with other dry ingredients, but instead use a whisk to combine; it's quicker, with much the same effect.

Aerating: Beating butter and sugar to get air into batter is one of the most critical steps in cake-making. Do it for the amount of time described, until the mixture is well blended and fluffy.

Folding: This is a careful combining of, say, beaten egg whites with a batter—gentle enough not to deflate the mixture, thorough enough not to result in streaky separation of the two elements.

Equipment

Pans: Use the pan size the recipe calls for. If you use 9-inch pans for a recipe that specifies 8-inch, you'll end up with flat layers. Also, choose aluminum pans with a dull finish since they absorb and conduct heat evenly. Avoid shiny pans, which deflect heat, and dark metal pans (including nonstick), which cause cakes to brown too quickly on the outside before they're done in the middle. Glass conducts heat differently, too. If you must use dark pans or glass, decrease the baking temperature by 25 degrees, and check for doneness early.

Oven thermometer: Use one to determine if your oven is baking too hot or cool. Correct timing depends on correct temperature.

Cooling racks: Buy some. Leaving cakes too long in pans steams them and makes them gummy on the bottom.

Parchment paper: Best not to omit if the recipe calls for it. Stock some in the pantry.

Baking sheets: It's worth investing in thick, heavy baking sheets—thin ones make cookies burn more easily.

Whisk: We love a good sturdy whisk with an easy-to-grasp handle.

Time

Inevitably it's somewhat approximate, whatever the recipe says. Use a timer and start checking for doneness about five minutes earlier than the recipe says, to account for variations in your oven or other factors. Once a cake has gone too far, there's no pulling it back. Recipes give cues for judging doneness. Though you should turn a cake out onto a rack to cool, you shouldn't do this immediately after it comes out of the oven—it may not be strong enough to hold together.

Temperature

In addition to using an oven thermometer, check your oven for hot spots (see page 486), which can cause food to be overcooked in one area, undercooked in another. If you are baking at high altitude, we don't supply directions with each recipe, but there is plenty of information online about the art of baking in thin air.

Strategies of the Fast, Healthy Cook

Cooking more often is the best strategy for healthy eating. The cook is the gatekeeper for what goes into his or her food, and all the more so if he or she does most of the household shopping. Lack of time is a universal affliction of modern life, though, and is a deal-breaker for many cooks on many days—but it doesn't have to be.

For one thing—and people who struggle with cooking don't believe this—cooking can be a stress reliever and a healthy transition between work time (whether work is at home or at the office) and nighttime. For another, the ideas in these cooking-strategy pages, when brought to bear on good recipes, make efficient, delicious cooking a realistic goal.

We've loaded this book with many fast weeknight options. (We've also added plenty of longer recipes for leisure cooking on downtime days.) Every recipe includes start-to-finish time, as well as how much of that time is hands-on. Total time may not be your enemy; it's hands-on time that counts most. You can multitask during down moments, while a pot bubbles on the stove.

Stock the Pantry

A pantry filled with quick-meal essentials is the best assurance of healthy eating during the week. If the cupboard contains little more than flavored vinegars, dried mushrooms, and spices, cooking up a fast meal becomes nearly impossible (unless you have the ingenuity of a TV chef-testant). But if you have couscous, dried apricots, and chicken broth, you're well on your way to a simple Moroccan-style tagine. Make a long list of must-have staples, and be sure to keep them on hand. These form the backbone of every weeknight meal; you'll just need to supplement with fresh meat or produce.

Keep in mind, though, that packaged foods are often loaded with sodium and sometimes too much fat, too. Check labels. A few products we love: canned organic beans (lower in sodium than conventional); boil-in-bag brown rice; precooked whole grains like farro or brown rice; lower-sodium marinara sauce (we like McCutcheon's and Amy's); lower-sodium chicken broth; canned diced tomatoes; and quick-cooking pasta. Shop the global-food aisle for more go-tos, such as canned light coconut milk, curry paste, and rice noodles. And consider your freezer a pantry extension: Stash bags of frozen peas, corn, edamame, and blueberries, all of which can offer peak-seasonal nutrition during the off-season. (And keep prewashed salad greens in the fridge while you're at it.)

Organize Your Kitchen

Clear clutter from countertops: If you don't use something daily or at least several times a week, stash it away for more counter space. Organize drawers and get rid of useless gadgets. Keep knives sharpened and within reach. A garbage bowl on the countertop is a good idea; make cleanup even faster by lining it with a plastic grocery bag. As you start on dinner, get out all the ingredients you'll need and have them on the counter. There's less chance that you'll forget an essential component or find yourself scrambling during a critical process.

Love Your Microwave

The microwave is a godsend in the kitchen, helpful for so much more than heating leftovers. You can speed up a soup by bringing broth to a simmer in the microwave while you sauté veggies in the pot. Pop fresh pizza dough in for 30 or 45 seconds at 50% power, and you shave off the 30 minutes you'd normally have to spend resting the dough. Fast-track beets by wrapping individually in parchment paper and microwaving three to five minutes—this can save you more than an hour. We've even learned how to make a miraculous homemade ricotta cheese in the microwave in about 10 minutes (see recipe on page 258).

Get Ahead Whenever Possible

Do some weekend-warrior cooking and prep. Chop vegetables to tuck away in the fridge. Parboil parsnips, butternut squash, or carrots—they'll take just a few minutes to cook when you're ready. Precook broccoli, cauliflower, or green beans by boiling until crisp-tender, then shocking with cold water to stop the cooking; stash them in the fridge and reheat by quickly sautéing in a little oil or butter with a sprinkling of fresh herbs. Cook dishes that keep well (soups, stews, casseroles), and refrigerate or freeze; you can reheat during the week for superspeedy meals. Boil some whole grains or beans on the weekend, and keep in the fridge or freezer. Remember that those grains can also be used for savory breakfast dishes.

Go Simple

When you have a great fast entrée, make the rest of the meal radically simple: a bag of microwave-ready haricots verts or sugar snap peas for the vegetable, and a whole-grain roll with a smidge of honey butter for the starch. Or, if you'd rather have a side dish as the meal's star, cook something easy for the entrée: seared scallops, sautéed shrimp, or pan-grilled chicken. Finally, remember the egg: the ultimate fast-cooking food.

Portion Control

Cooking healthy is one thing; eating the right amount of what you cook is another. The cooking part is probably the easier part of the equation. Portioning happens mostly at table, when the cooking is done and the habit takes over. When we serve ourselves and others at the table, when we reach for generous seconds, when we give in to the happy pleasures of the table without thinking of portions—we risk defeating the purposes of cooking light. Psychologists attack the problem by prescribing mindful eating: the slowed-down appreciation of every bite, in contrast to mindless eating habits that might have been learned during devil-may-care youth. Savor your food, they say; don't gobble it.

There are some practical steps you can take to get portions under control.

Weigh Your Meats

A piece is not the same as a serving. The industrial-farmed chicken breast, for example, has doubled over the years (a serving is six ounces raw, four ounces cooked). A kitchen scale keeps things honest with chicken, chops, steaks, and such. Also, do you know what a cup of cooked pasta or rice looks like on a plate? When we researched in the field, we found that many people had no idea.

Divide the Plate

Follow the USDA's MyPlate model and divvy your plate this way: Fill half with vegetables and/or fruit, and the other half with equal parts protein and starch (preferably whole-grain). This is an easy way to see what a balanced meal looks like, and it keeps portions in check. Steak and potatoes, or spaghetti and meatballs, are only half a meal—incomplete without fruits and vegetables on the other half of the plate. A common pitfall is to shrink the meat portion but boost starch or whole grains, resulting in too many calories. Generally, it's vegetables and fruits that we need more of.

Shrink Your Plates and Bowls

On an 8- or 10-inch plate, a healthy portion of lasagna looks ample. On a 12-inch plate, it looks like a side dish. Use smaller bowls for ice cream and cereal, and opt for tall, slender glasses over squat, wide ones. The same idea applies to edible vessels, like tortillas: The bigger the container, the more filling you'll put into it.

Practice Plating

Until you have repeatedly measured out and plated one cup of cooked pasta or poured yourself five ounces of wine, you won't be able to eyeball it. Measuring portions may make you feel like you're back in home-ec class, but as you practice you'll be able to better estimate what a true serving is.

Favor "Free" Foods

The nutrition numbers on our recipes show that some dishes are so low-calorie that you can basically have as much of them as you want. These will typically be

salads and nonstarchy vegetable sides. Serve these foods family-style at the dinner table—but leave the higher-calorie foods in the kitchen. If you feel unsatisfied after finishing your plate, help yourself to more veggies.

Become a Label Reader

Pay close attention to the number of servings for packaged foods. Many snack packs and drink containers contain two or more servings.

Pre-Portion Treats

High-calorie foods, even healthy ones, can move from snack to entrée size in a hurry. If you buy nuts in bulk, don't eat in bulk—make your own little snack packs by scooping one-ounce portions into zip-top bags or small containers.

Mind the Out-of-Sight Rule

Studies show that many people are much more likely to reach for food, often absentmindedly, if it's out in the open. Store cookies in ceramic instead of glass cookie jars; stash individual servings of brownies in the freezer. What *should* be kept in view is fresh produce for snacking.

Nutrition Numbers and Kitchen Measurements

···

Nutrition Analysis: What the Numbers Mean For You

To interpret the nutritional analysis in *The New Way to Cook Light*, use the figures below as a daily reference guide. One size doesn't fit all, so take lifestyle, age, and circumstances into consideration. For example, pregnant or breast-feeding women need more protein, calories, and calcium. Go to choosemyplate.gov for your own individualized plan.

	Women ages 25 to 50	Women over 50	Men ages 25 to 50	Men over 50
Calories	2,000	2,000*	2,700	2,500
Protein	50 g	50 g	63 g	60 g
Fat	65 g*	65 g*	88 g*	83 g*
Saturated Fat	20 g*	20 g*	27 g*	25 g*
Carbohydrates	304 g	304 g	410 g	375 g
Fiber	25g to 35 g	25 g to 35 g	25 g to 35 g	25 g to 35 g
Cholesterol	300 mg*	300 mg*	300 mg*	300 mg*
Iron	18 mg	8 mg	8 mg	8 mg
Sodium	2,300 mg*	1,500 mg*	2,300 mg*	1,500 mg*
Calcium	1,000 mg	1,200 mg	1,000 mg	1,000 mg

*Or less, for optimum health

Nutritional values used in our calculations either come from the food processor, version 10.4 (ESHA research), or are provided by food manufacturers.

···

Nutritional Analysis Abbreviations

SAT	saturated fat	**CARB**	carbohydrates	**g**	gram
MONO	monounsaturated fat	**CHOL**	cholesterol	**mg**	milligram
POLY	polyunsaturated fat	**CALC**	calcium		

Metric Equivalents

The information in the following charts is provided to help cooks outside the United States successfully use the recipes in this book. All equivalents are approximate.

Cooking/Oven Temperatures

	Fahrenheit	Celsius	Gas Mark
Freeze Water	32° F	0° C	
Room Temp.	68° F	20° C	
Boil Water	212° F	100° C	
Bake	325° F	160° C	3
	350° F	180° C	4
	375° F	190° C	5
	400° F	200° C	6
	425° F	220° C	7
	450° F	230° C	8
Broil			Grill

Liquid Ingredients by Volume

¼ tsp	=	1 ml					
½ tsp	=	2 ml					
1 tsp	=	5 ml					
3 tsp	=	1 Tbsp.	=	½ fl oz	=	15 ml	
2 Tbsp.	=	⅛ cup	=	1 fl oz	=	30 ml	
4 Tbsp.	=	¼ cup	=	2 fl oz	=	60 ml	
5⅓ Tbsp.	=	⅓ cup	=	3 fl oz	=	80 ml	
8 Tbsp.	=	½ cup	=	4 fl oz	=	120 ml	
10⅔ Tbsp.	=	⅔ cup	=	5 fl oz	=	160 ml	
12 Tbsp.	=	¾ cup	=	6 fl oz	=	180 ml	
16 Tbsp.	=	1 cup	=	8 fl oz	=	240 ml	
1 pt	=	2 cups	=	16 fl oz	=	480 ml	
1 qt	=	4 cups	=	32 fl oz	=	960 ml	
				33 fl oz	=	1000 ml	= 1l

Equivalents for Different Types of Ingredients

Standard Cup	Fine Powder (ex. flour)	Grain (ex. rice)	Granular (ex. sugar)	Liquid Solids (ex. butter)	Liquid (ex. milk)
1	140 g	150 g	190 g	200 g	240 ml
¾	105 g	113 g	143 g	150 g	180 ml
⅔	93 g	100 g	125 g	133 g	160 ml
½	70 g	75 g	95 g	100 g	120 ml
⅓	47 g	50 g	63 g	67 g	80 ml
¼	35 g	38 g	48 g	50 g	60 ml
⅛	18 g	19 g	24 g	25 g	30 ml

Length

(To convert inches to centimeters, multiply the number of inches by 2.5.)

1 in	=				2.5 cm		
6 in	=	½ ft		=	15 cm		
12 in	=	1 ft		=	30 cm		
36 in	=	3 ft	=	1 yd	=	90 cm	
40 in	=				100 cm	=	1 m

Dry Ingredients by Weight

(To convert ounces to grams, multiply the number of ounces by 30.)

1 oz	=	¹⁄₁₆ lb	=	30 g
4 oz	=	¼ lb	=	120 g
8 oz	=	½ lb	=	240 g
12 oz	=	¾ lb	=	360 g
16 oz	=	1 lb	=	480 g

Seasonal Produce Guide

When you use fresh fruits, vegetables, and herbs, you don't have to do much to make them taste great. Although many fruits, vegetables, and herbs are available year-round, you'll get better flavor and prices when you buy what's in season. This guide helps you choose the best produce so you can create tasty meals all year long.

....

Spring

Fruits
- Bananas
- Blood oranges
- Coconuts
- Grapefruit
- Kiwifruit
- Lemons
- Limes
- Mangoes
- Navel oranges
- Papayas
- Passion fruit
- Pineapples
- Strawberries
- Tangerines
- Valencia oranges

Vegetables
- Artichokes
- Arugula
- Asparagus
- Avocados
- Baby leeks
- Beets
- Belgian endive
- Broccoli
- Cauliflower
- Dandelion greens
- Fava beans
- Green onions
- Green peas
- Kale
- Lettuce
- Mushrooms
- Radishes
- Red potatoes
- Rhubarb
- Snap beans
- Snow peas
- Spinach
- Sugar snap peas
- Sweet onions
- Swiss chard

Herbs
- Chives
- Dill
- Garlic chives
- Lemongrass
- Mint
- Parsley
- Thyme

Summer

Fruits

Apricots
Blackberries
Blueberries
Boysenberries
Cantaloupes
Casaba melons
Cherries
Crenshaw melons
Figs
Grapes
Guava
Honeydew melons
Mangoes
Nectarines
Papayas
Peaches
Plums
Raspberries
Strawberries
Watermelons

Vegetables

Avocados
Beans: snap, pole,
  and shell
Beets
Bell peppers
Cabbage
Carrots
Celery
Chile peppers
Collards
Corn
Cucumbers
Eggplant
Green beans
Jicama
Lima beans
Okra
Pattypan squash
Peas
Radicchio
Radishes
Summer squash
Tomatoes

Herbs

Basil
Bay leaves
Borage
Chives
Cilantro
Dill
Lavender
Lemon balm
Marjoram
Mint
Oregano
Rosemary
Sage
Summer savory
Tarragon
Thyme

Fall

Fruits

Apples
Cranberries
Figs
Grapes
Pears
Persimmons
Pomegranates
Quinces

Vegetables

Belgian endive
Bell peppers
Broccoli
Brussels sprouts
Cabbage
Cauliflower
Eggplant
Escarole
Fennel
Frisée
Leeks
Mushrooms
Parsnips
Pumpkins
Red potatoes
Rutabagas
Shallots
Sweet potatoes
Winter squash
Yukon gold potatoes

Herbs

Basil
Bay leaves
Parsley
Rosemary
Sage
Tarragon
Thyme

Winter

Fruits

Apples
Blood oranges
Cranberries
Grapefruit
Kiwifruit
Kumquats
Lemons
Limes
Mandarin oranges
Navel oranges
Pears
Persimmons
Pomegranates
Pomelos
Tangelos
Tangerines
Quinces

Vegetables

Baby turnips
Beets
Belgian endive
Brussels sprouts
Celery root
Escarole
Fennel
Frisée
Jerusalem artichokes
Kale
Leeks
Mushrooms
Parsnips
Potatoes
Rutabagas
Sweet potatoes
Turnips
Watercress
Winter squash

Index

K

L

M

N

O

T

V

W

Y

Z